Meandering Scribbles
of an
Old Fart

Joe Barfield

DEDICATION

To those who still believe there is hope for America.
Time is running out...

And to Ruth Graham who said:
"If God doesn't punish America for her immorality, then he will need
to apologize to Sodom and Gomorrah."

MEANDERIN MEANDERING SCRIBBLES
OF AN OLD FART
TABLE OF CONTENTS

Joe Barfield

ACKNOWLEDGMENTS

To all the military living and dead who served the United States of America, with honor and sacrifice for freedom and their country, may the actions of our Presidents and Congress not make their dedication to God and country be in vain.

WARNING!
This is for mature audiences so if you're a Democrat or Republican who always voted the same ticket, this is not for you, because it means you are incapable of thinking on your own, so I'd rather you **not** buy it. If you are a **frustrated American** upset with the current administrations then you may find these scribbles quit enjoyable. **Another WARNING; these are notes and thoughts scribbled down quickly and all unedited.**

Should I Forget
A simple reminder, since I might forget. These are scribbles of an Old Fart and you may find repetitions. This is due to "Oldheimers."

DISCLAIMER
Any resemblance to political persons in office is purely intentional.

FOR PETA'S SAKE!
For your peace of mind let it be known that NO animals were injured during the making of these meandering scribbles.

GIVE ME A BREAK!
I'm not a racist, and I'm not a terrorist, I'm just trying to be funny and open your eyes to other solutions. If you have better ideas then you write a book.

FINAL WARNING!
Before you read this I must remind you that you have three choices. You can only pick one so be careful. You are a Democrat, a Republican or an American. If you picked one of the first two then don't get this book and if you do then don't complain. Americans tell the truth, the other two don't.
Offended yet? You will be; unless you're an American.

FOR OBAMA I'M AMERICA'S BIGGEST THREAT
I'm a white, Christian, heterosexual, and I believe in traditional marriage.
I am America's Biggest Threat.
Get Over It!

1
FAMOUS QUOTES

The quotes below show the brilliance of men throughout history. A few of the quotes show their ignorance. I hope you enjoy them as much as I do.

I see in the near future a crisis approaching that unnerves me and causes me to tremble for the safety of my country. Corporations have been enthroned and an era of corruption in high places will follow, and the money power of the country will endeavor to prolong its reign by working upon the prejudices of people until all wealth is aggregated in a few hands and the Republic is destroyed. --Abraham Lincoln, 1864

"I tremble for my country when I reflect that God is just." - Thomas Jefferson

Throughout history every great empire has collapsed. There have been no exceptions." - Joe Barfield

"America will never be destroyed from the outside. If we falter and lose our freedoms, it will be because we destroyed ourselves." - Abraham Lincoln

Throughout history every great empire has collapsed. There have been no exceptions." - Joe Barfield

"We has seen the enemy and they is us." - Pogo

Tolerance is the last virtue of a dying society - Aristotle

"The closer you are to death, the more alive you feel." – James Hunt, Champion Formula 1 driver

"Something more powerful than the fear of death is the will to win!" – James Hunt, Champion Formula 1 driver

"There is a lie all drivers tell themselves. Death is something that happens to other drivers." -- James Hunt, Champion Formula 1 driver

Give me liberty or give me death -– Patrick Henry

I have not yet begun to fight – John Paul Jones

I only regret that I have but one life to give for my country. – Nathan Hale

Battle not with monsters, lest ye become a monster. And if you gaze long into the abyss, the abyss gazes into you. - *Friedrich Nietzche*

These are the times that try men's souls. - Thomas Paine

"If God doesn't punish America for her immorality, then he will need to apologize to Sodom and Gomorrah." - Ruth Graham just before she died

"The Constitution is not an instrument for the government to restrain the people, it is an instrument for the people to restrain the government - lest it come to dominate our lives and interests." - Patrick Henry

Suppose you were an idiot. And suppose you were a member of Congress. Oh, but I repeat myself. - Mark Twain

Obama giving his inauguration speech on MLK Day is like listening to a porn star give a church sermon about abstinence.

Ignorance is the single greatest tool of oppression.

Patriotism is supporting your country all the time and your government when it deserves it. – Mark Twain

Never forget that everything Hitler did in Germany was LEGAL. – Martin Luther King Jr.

"If the American people ever allow private banks to control the issue of their currency, first by inflation, then by deflation, the banks and the corporations which grow up around them will deprive the people of all property until their children wake up homeless on the continent their fathers conquered." - Ben Franklin

There are only two problems with the Federal Government—Democrats and Republicans. - Joe Barfield

Don't steal…Congress hates the competition. - Unknown

I'm taking my true representatives to Congress—Smith and Wesson! - Joe Barfield

Friend, you cannot legislate the poor into freedom by legislating the wealthy out of freedom.

What one person receives without working for, another person must work for without receiving.

The government can't give to anybody anything that the government does not first take from somebody.

When half of the people get the idea they don't have to work because the other half's going to take care of them, and when the other half get the idea it does no good to work because somebody's going to get what I work for. That, dear friend, is about the end of any nation."- Dr. Rogers

"We the people are the rightful masters of both Congress & the courts, not to overthrow the Constitution, but overthrow the men who pervert the Constitution." - Abraham Lincoln

You cannot multiply wealth by dividing it. - Unknown

When it comes to a diet you need to remember only one thing: If it tastes good then it's bad for you. – Joe Barfield

The historical cycle seems to be: From bondage to spiritual faith; from spiritual faith to courage; from courage to liberty; from liberty to abundance; from abundance to selfishness; from selfishness to apathy; from apathy to dependency; and from dependency back to bondage once more. – Alexander Tyler

"The budget should be balanced, the Treasury should be refilled, public debt should be reduced, the arrogance of officialdom should be tempered and controlled, and the assistance to foreign lands should be curtailed lest Rome become bankrupt. People must again learn to work, instead of living on public assistance." --Cicero - 55 BC

America will never be destroyed from the outside. If we falter and lose our freedoms, it will be because we destroyed ourselves." - Abraham Lincoln

I don't make jokes. I just watch the government and report the facts. - Will Rogers

"Ask not what your country can do for you, but rather why does your country keep doing it to you." - Joe Barfield

"Courage is being scared to death - and saddling up anyway." - John Wayne

"The two enemies of the people are criminals and government. So let us tie the second down with the chains of the Constitution so that the second will not become the legal version of the first." - Thomas Jefferson

I contend that for a nation to try to tax itself into prosperity is like a man standing in a bucket and trying to lift himself up by the handle. - Winston Churchill

A government which robs Peter to pay Paul can always depend on the support of Paul. - George Bernard Shaw

There are only two kinds of liars in Congress; Democrats and Republicans. --Joe Barfield

A liberal is someone who feels a great debt to his fellow man, which debt he proposes to pay off with your money. - G. Gordon Liddy

Democracy must be something more than two wolves and a sheep voting on what to have for dinner. - James Bovard, Civil Libertarian (1994)

Foreign aid might be defined as a transfer from poor people in rich countries to rich people in poor countries. - Douglas Casey, Classmate of W. J. Clinton

Giving money and power to government is like giving whiskey and car keys to teenage boys. - P. J. O'Rourke, Civil Libertarian

Government is the great fiction, through which everybody endeavors to live at the expense of everybody else. - Frederic Bastiat, French Economist (1801-1850)

"The only thing necessary for the triumph of evil, is for good men to do nothing." - Edmund Burke 1729 - 1797

Government's view of the economy could be summed up in a few short phrases: If it moves, tax it. If it keeps moving, regulate it. And if it stops moving, subsidize it. - Ronald Reagan (1986)

Money is not Democracy - Unknown

If you think health care is expensive now, wait until you see what it costs when it's free. - P. J. O'Rourke

If you want government to intervene domestically, you're a liberal.
If you want government to intervene overseas, you're a conservative.
If you want government to intervene everywhere, you're a moderate.
If you don't want government to intervene anywhere, you're an extremist.
- Joseph Sobran, Editor of the National Review (1995)

In general, the art of government consists in taking as much money as possible from one party of the citizens to give to the other. - Voltaire (1764)

Just because you do not take an interest in politics doesn't mean politics won't take an interest in you. - Pericles (430 B. C.)

No man's life, liberty, or property is safe while the legislature is in session.
-- Mark Twain (1866)

Talk is cheap- except when Congress does it. - (Unknown)

The government is like a baby's alimentary canal, with a happy appetite at one end and no responsibility at the other. - Ronald Reagan

Fathom the odd hypocrisy that Obama wants every citizen to prove they are insured, but people don't have to prove they are citizens. ~ Ben Stein

The inherent vice of capitalism is the unequal sharing of the blessings. The inherent blessing of socialism is the equal sharing of misery. - Winston Churchill

The only difference between a taxman and a taxidermist is that the taxidermist leaves the skin. - Mark Twain

The ultimate result of shielding men from the effects of folly is to fill the world with fools. - Herbert Spencer, English Philosopher (1820-1903)

There is no distinctly native American criminal class, save Congress. - Mark Twain

What this country needs are more unemployed politicians.
-- Edward Langley, Artist (1928 - 1995)

Give me liberty or give me death -- Patrick Henry

 I have not yet begun to fight – John Paul Jones

I only regret that I have but one life to give for my country. – Nathan Hale

Battle not with monsters, lest ye become a monster. And if you gaze long into the abyss, the abyss gazes into you. - *Friedrich Nietzche*

"America will never be destroyed from the outside. If we falter and lose our freedoms, it will be because we destroyed ourselves." - Abraham Lincoln

These are the times that try men's souls. - Thomas Paine

"In accordance with the principles of double-think it does not matter if the war is not real. For when it is, victory is not possible. The war is not meant to be won, but it is meant to be continuous." - George Orwell, *1984*;

"The difference between Genius and Stupidity - Genius has its limits." - A. Einstein

The problems we face will not be solved by the minds that created them! - Unknown

Ayn Rand in *Atlas Shrugged*: 'Watch money,' she said. 'Money is the barometer of a society's virtue. When you see that trading is done not by consent, but by compulsion – when you see that in order to produce, you need to obtain permission from men who produce nothing – when you see that money is flowing to those who deal not in goods, but in favors – when you see that men get rich more easily by graft than by work, and your laws no longer protect you against them, but protect them against you – when you see corruption being rewarded and honesty becoming a self-sacrifice – you may know that your society is doomed. '

Doug Casey: The people will never get it. . .
"When I was on the Phil Donahue Show, the day before the national elections in 1980… I explained how they, the taxpayers, would have to pay for all the goodies—like Social Security and unemployment compensation—that they wanted. A middle-aged guy in the audience asked: "Well, why can't the government pay for these things?" And the rest of the audience roared approval. It was then that I first realized that resistance was futile and the situation was basically hopeless. And that someone who can seem perfectly sensible when he's discussing sports, or the weather, or the state of the roads, was likely to be a moron when it came to economics."

In my many years I have come to a conclusion that one useless man is a shame, two is a law firm and three or more is a congress. - John Adams

If you don't read the newspaper you are uninformed, if you do read the newspaper you are misinformed. - Mark Twain

A liberal is someone who feels a great debt to his fellow man, which debt he proposes to pay off with your money. - G. Gordon Liddy

A nation can survive its fools, and even the ambitious. But it cannot survive treason from within. An enemy at the gates is less formidable, for he is known and he carries his banners openly. But the traitor moves among those within the gate freely, his sly whispers rustling through all the galleys, heard in the very hall of government itself. For the traitor appears not a traitor – he speaks in the accents familiar to his victims, and wears their face and their garment, and he appeals to the baseness that lies deep in the hearts of all men. He rots the soul of a nation – he works secretly and unknown in the night to undermine the pillars of a city – he infects the body politic so that it can no longer resist. A murderer is less to be feared." - Cicero, 42 B. C.

A government big enough to give you everything you want, is strong enough to take everything you have. - Thomas Jefferson

Margaret Thatcher: "The trouble with Socialism is, sooner or later you run out of other peoples' money."

"When you subsidize poverty and failure, you get more of both." - James Dale Davidson, National Taxpayers Union

"The more corrupt the state, the more it legislates." - Tacitus

"A Liberal is a person who will give away everything he doesn't own." – Unknown

"Democracy is two wolves deciding what to eat for dinner.
Liberty is a well- armed lamb contesting the vote." -Thomas Jefferson-

Fathom the hypocrisy of a Government that requires every citizen to prove they are insured but not everyone must prove they are a citizen.

Back when I studied the Holocaust in high school, I remember thinking, "How did Hitler get over six million people to follow along blindly and not fight back?" Then I realized I'm watching my fellow Americans take the same path. – Porcupine Missiles

Remember: Criminals don't register guns.

"No matter where you go, there you are." - Buckaroo Banzai

We need more gun laws because we don't have time or manpower to enforce the ones we have. – Joe Biden

I am absolutely convinced the best formula for giving us peace and preserving the American way of life is freedom, limited government, and minding our own business overseas. - Ron Paul

This is a frightening statistic. More people vote in 'American Idol' than in any US election. - Rush Limbaugh

The American Republic will endure until the day Congress discovers that it can bribe the public with the public's money. - Alexis de Tocqueville

We must reject the idea that every time a law's broken, society is guilty rather than the lawbreaker. It is time to restore the American precept that each individual is accountable for his actions. - Ronald Reagan

President Obama is the greatest hoax ever perpetrated on the American people. - Clint Eastwood

GREAT QUOTES BY THOMAS SOWELL
When you want to help people, you tell them the truth. When you want to help yourself, you tell them what they want to hear.

If you have been voting for politicians who promise to give you goodies at someone else's expense, then you have no right to complain when they take your money and give it to someone else, including themselves

One of the consequences of such notions as entitlements is that people who have contributed nothing to society feel that society owes them something, apparently just for being nice enough to grace us with their presence.

The assumption that spending more of the taxpayer's money will make things better has survived all kinds of evidence that it has made things worse. The black family- which survived slavery, discrimination, poverty, wars and depressions-

began to come apart as the federal government moved in with its well-financed programs to "help."

It is amazing that people who think we cannot afford to pay for doctors, hospitals, and medication somehow think that we can afford to pay for doctors, hospitals, medication and a government bureaucracy to administer it.

If you have always believed that everyone should play by the same rules and be judged by the same standards, that would have gotten you labeled a radical 60 years ago, a liberal 30 years ago and a racist today.

T think this man (Obama) really does believe he can change the world & people like that are infinitely more dangerous than mere crooked politicians."

Socialism in general has a record of failure so blatant that only an intellectual could ignore or evade it.

"I have never understood why it is greed to want to keep the money you have earned but not greed to want to take somebody else's money."

"It is hard to imagine a more stupid or more dangerous way of making decisions than by putting those decisions in the hands of people who pay no price for being wrong."

"Much of the social history of the Western world, over the past three decades, has been a history of replacing what worked with what sounded good."

I think it's important to understand that you can't have 100 percent security and then have 100 percent privacy and zero inconvenience. We're going to have to make some choices as a society. – Barack Obama

Any society that would give up a little liberty to gain a little security will deserve neither and lose both. - Benjamin Franklin

Famous Presidential Quotes

Nixon I am not a crook.

Clinton I did not have sex with that woman.

Bush,Sr. Read my lips

Bush,Jr. Go ahead bring it on!

Obama:

I will have the most transparent administration.

I have Shovel ready jobs.

The IRS is not targeting anyone.

It was about a movie.

If I had a son.

I will put an end to the type of politics that "breeds division, conflict and cynicism".

You didn't build that.

I will restore trust in Government.

The cops acted stupidly.

I am not after your guns.

The Public Will Have 5 Days To Look At Every Bill That Lands On My Desk.

It's not my red line it is the world's red line.

Whistle blowers will be protected.

"We got back Every Dime we Used to Rescue the Banks, with interest.

I will close Gitmo.

I am not spying on American citizens.

ObamaCare will be good for America.

You can keep your family doctor.

Premiums will be lowered by $2500.

You can keep your current healthcare plan.

I, Barrack Hussain Obama pledge to preserve, protect and defend the Constitution of the United States of America.

STUPID OBAMA QUOTES

Washington is broken. My whole campaign has been premised from the start on the idea that we have to fundamentally change how Washington works. Obama Sept. 11, 2008

Guantanamo will be closed no later than one year from now. Obama on his third day in office (first term)

I think that health care, over time, is going to become more popular. - Obama – Not really. Health care usually deals with severe health problems and/or death.

I favor legalizing same-sex marriages, and would fight efforts to prohibit such marriages. - Obama 1996– and the day freedom of speech and religion died.

I fought with you in the Senate for comprehensive immigration reform. And I will make it a top priority in my first year as President. - Obama 2008. Two weeks ago he told Univision the Republicans were responsible for it not happening.

And I will do everything that I can as long as I am President of the United States to remind the American people that we are one nation under God, and we may call that God different names but we remain one nation.

But let me perfectly clear, because I know you'll hear the same old claims that rolling back these tax breaks means a massive tax increase on the American people: if your family earns less than $250,000 a year, you will not see your taxes increased a single dime. I repeat: not one single dime.

We're no longer a Christian nation.

America has been arrogant.

After 9/11, America didn't always live up to her ideals.

You might say that America is a Muslim nation.- President Barack Obama, Egypt 2009

I think what you're seeing is a profound recognition on the part of the American people that gays and lesbians and transgender persons are our brothers, our sisters, our children, our cousins, our friends, our co-workers, and that they've got to be treated like every other American. And I think that principle will win out.

AND EVEN DUMBER QUOTES FROM HILLARY CLINTON

The American people are tired of liars and people who pretend to be something they're not.

Well, human security is a concept that I am very committed to enshrining in American foreign policy.

"What difference does it make how these men died?

REMEMBER BENGHAZI - Hillary plans on running for president in 2016…that is if America as we know it still exists.

DUMBEST QUOTE: "My friends, we live in the greatest nation in the history of the world. I hope you'll join with me, as we try to change it." --Barack Obama

CORRECT RESPONSE: "Life's tough, pilgrim, and it's even tougher if you're stupid." - John Wayne

2
SOME OF MY PERSONAL QUOTES AND THOUGHTS

Throughout history every great empire has collapsed. There have been no exceptions.

When Obama is gone and nothing but dust,
America will return to "In God We Trust."

Work keeps interfering with my life.

Politicians are the reason guns were invented.

Christians believe in the cross. Liberals believe in the Double cross.

There are only two problems with the Federal Government—Democrats and Republicans.

I'm taking my true representatives to Congress—Smith and Wesson!

Ask not what your country can do for you, but rather why does your country keep doing it to you.

Save America; nuke Washington DC

It's okay to be a liberal or a conservative, but neither of the two exist in Washington D. C.

If Thomas Jefferson and George Washington were alive today they would overthrow this government.

Today is the TIME for a SERIOUS Boston Tea Party.

Axis of Evil? The Senate, House of Representatives, and the President.

The real American Evil is the 535

Save America – Remove the 535

Help! I know where 535 terrorists reside.

(NOTE: For those that don't know there are 435 Representatives and 100 Senators from the 50 states. YOU would be surprised how many Americans don't know that fact so there it is)

Cheney said the troops are safer in Iraq than Washington D. C. If that's true shouldn't the troops be back in America protecting the people?

The other Axis of Evil – Obama, Pelosi, Reid

HELL IS COMING! And it's Congress

Congress has a problem for every solution

Global Warming? Not really. All the hot air is in Washington D. C. Get rid of them and the earth might experience an Ice Age.

Did you know that the Sahara Desert was once a lush tropical jungle? Hey, Al Gore, how many SUV's did it take to turn that jungle into a desert.

Hey, I believe in green and the environment. We should turn Congress into Soylent Green.

My doctor said "second hand smoking" is worse than smoking. So I took up smoking to be safer.

Obama, Reid and Pelosi are living proof God no longer favors America.

Confusion divided by chaos equals Congress

Can you tell me why we're in Afghanistan?

In God we Trust has nothing to do with Congress or the President

If at first you don't succeed, well then you must be a Congressman.

What would you say if someone killed a Congressman? Only 534 to go.

Give me Liberty or Give me Death, but don't give me any more Democrats or Republicans.

Two million American jobs lost but 23 new staff jobs for Michelle Obama

What's the difference between Citicorp, Bank of America, and a Loan Shark? The Loan Shark is honest.

A. I. G. – American Institute of Greed

A. I. G. - Al Qaeda In our Government

Does anyone speak English anymore?

We are so busy protecting each individual's rights that we no longer have any rights.

The Greatest Ponzi scheme in History? Social Security. If Madhoff is in prison then shouldn't Congress be there too?

CEO—Chief Embezzlement Officer.

Help me. Congress stole my Social Security to pay AIG their bonus.

How did Madoff learn to do a Ponzi scheme? Social Security

Get our troops out of the Middle East, the enemy combatants are in Washington DC

Tuff times are coming – better buy some gun cleaner.

Congress – Does your medical plan cover lead poisoning?

If we could convince Congress to take a 365 day vacation every year we would need to worry only one day every four years.
Democrats and Republicans are not the solution. They ARE the problem.

Have you seen the Manchurian Candidate? There's 535 of them in Congress.

Remember the truth will set you free…. or get you hung.

Congressmen aren't worthless---they can still be used as "Soylent Green."

Know how to pay off the Debt? Issue hunting permits for CEO's and Politicians.

What's more valuable than gold and silver? Lead—it'll get you all the gold and silver you need.

Bush and Paulson – Socialism
Obama and Pelosi – Communism

The American Dream has Become a Nightmare!

Mission Accomplished: Why I'm a Military hero: A short talk by President Bush.

If a Congressman was killed by an angry American what would it be called? Assassination – killing someone important. Murder – killing an average person. Execution – punishment for the treason they committed. You decide.

You have three choices but you can only be one. Democrat, Republican or American.

If money is the root of all evil, then why do the churches keep begging for it?

Our Government lacks only three qualities; honor, integrity and honesty.

What is the difference between Al Qaeda, Enemy Combatants and Congress? Not much.

THE DREAM TEAM—How about we get Ted Kennedy drunk and have him give the President a ride over the Chappaquiddick

Name me one thing George Bush has done for the American people!

Name me one thing Barrack Obama has done for the American people!

Democrats and Republicans should try something different – like representing the people

America, love it or leave it! Halliburton did.

WMD – A Bush fairy tale.

Only in America do the poor pay taxes for the welfare of the wealthy.

If Congress says there is no money for Social Security, then how come they came up with a trillion dollars to bailout their wealthy buddies on Wall Street in less than a week?

Forty-five million Welfare recipients can't all be wrong.

God is with us…..well maybe not. It seems like when we were told by American ministers to pray against Obama they forgot to tell us to vote.

The bright side is that now Obama can finish his destruction of America. This will come fast; two years max.

His government is as transparent as mud. We are at 16 trillion and mark my words it will 20 trillion in two years. That is the point of no return. I see a hundred year lease on San Diego to China.

If you think you're paying too much in taxes now, wait until next year.

I wonder who he will blame for the last four years?

And welcome to the Muslim Brotherhood. Allah Akbar. You could lose your head over it.

I understand the phones at companies are being changed to, "Para Ingles, presar dos." For those that don't know, you will need to press two.

From Congress let us say, "Tienes buen dia."

For free college education please say, "No hablo Ingles."

The American political system is sick. What America needs is a huge enema!

"Do unto others before they do it unto me."

As far as help from your FBI is concerned, remember this: In a chicken shed the chicken ladder is covered with chicken shit from top to bottom . . . you find bad even in high places where you trust."

Why are we chasing terrorists in Iraq? We have 535 of them in Washington D. C.

Amnesty is something all politicians understand. Most of them are hoping for it when they get out of office.

We bring you **change**" A new word for more taxes.

We could save Somali if they had OIL.

When Obama promised "change" he meant that would be all that was left of a dollar when he finished.

For every Victory there is also a Defeat. For every dollar spent it is a dollar that must be paid back.

Einstein said it best, "For every action, there is an opposite and equal reaction." If that is true, then Congress had better start gearing up for the "reaction."

Wake up America before we have no rights and no power.

Washington D. C. is our countries crime capital. Also the home of Congress. Seems fitting.

Yes we need to punish those responsible for New York…and Oklahoma City, but you don't see us flying down Interstate 10 with F-14's taking out Ryder trucks.

What do you call George H Bush and George W Bush? A double Bush-whacking of America.

The quickest way to pay off the National Debt would be to charge a large hunting fee and make it open season on politicians. I'd buy a license for that.

What Obama says about not losing in Afghanistan is the same thing Napoleon said just before Waterloo.

Senator Edwards; The Family Values Man

Looks like Arnolds got a kid in every closet

Arnold wasn't kidding when he told the maid, "I'll be back."

Arnold's new movie? "The Impregnator."

What is the difference between Howdy Doody and Bush? Bush is the puppet and Howdy Doody is the one with the brains.

The three people who helped Al-Qaeda destroy the United States? Obama, Pelosi and Reid.

Let's invite Obama, Reid and Pelosi to a real "Tea Party" and fit them with concrete shoes.

What's the difference between a loan shark and MasterCard? The loan shark is honest.

The more technologically advanced we become, the farther behind we get.

What's the difference between the Lottery and Las Vegas? You have a chance of winning in Las Vegas.

I'm not a racist and I'm not a terrorist; I'm just trying to be funny.

Congress has a problem for every solution

There is only one thing Congressmen don't do. That is to represent the people who elected them.

Drug tests for welfare—AND for Congress!!!

I'm a successful failure.

Mondays are a terrible way to end the weekend.

I'm going to make money the old-fashioned way. I'm going to print it.

Forget Obama's birth certificate. That is not the certificate you want to see.

After all my losses in the stock market I had to refigure my retirement and finally came up with a date. I can retire two years after I die.

I'm going nowhere fast and I've already arrived.

The next time I hear a Republican say he believes in "family values," I'm gonna puke.

The most dangerous job in the country? The boys choir in a Catholic church

"The Truth" - a very short story by the members of Congress

USA if I need to tell you what that means you aren't an American. New Name: USSA – United Socialist States of America. Read it and weep...

Washington D. C. (CNN) – In response to criticism about broadcasting inaccurate news, CNN had this to say. Our latest survey shows that three out of four people make up at least 75% of the population, plus or minus a few.

Smith and Wesson, the permanent solution to our problems in Washington D. C.

The Truth is out there. . . somewhere. . . just not in Congress.

Hitler did it, why can't Obama?

Where Christians believe in the cross, Liberals believe in the Double cross

You're only as good as your word, which means there are no good men in Congress.

Isn't it ironic that the most immoral people in the world, Congress, make laws of morality for Americans to follow.

When Government fails to listen; rebellion in inevitable.

Congress should be tied to the loss of our Social Security

I think my mother said it best when she tried to describe Congress, "You can't make chicken salad out of chicken shit."

The Battling Boys of Benghazi
(Author Unknown)

The Battling Boys of Benghazi

We're the Battling Boys of Benghazi,
no fame, no glory, no paparazzi.
Just a fiery death in a blazing hell,
defending the country we loved so well.

It wasn't our job, but we answered the call,
fought to the consulate, and scaled the wall.
We pulled twenty countrymen from the jaws of fate,
led them to safety, and stood at the gate.

Just the two of us, and foes by the score,
but we stood fast to bar the door.
Three calls for reinforcement, but all were denied,
so we fought and we fought, and we fought till we died.

We gave our all for our Uncle Sam,
but Barack Obama didn't give a damn.
Just two dead SEALs, who carried the load,
no thanks to us -- we were just "bumps in the road."

3
What Would George Washington Say?

George Washington Addresses Today's Congress

Through a miracle of science too difficult to explain, scientists brought George Washington in full body and spirit to current day America. President Washington was limited to a one-week stay before he returned to his own time. Politicians quickly moved in and together with representatives from big business they suggested showing him some of the miracles of present day America. When he requested to see his home, the White House, and Congress instead, the leaders gave in and reluctantly drove him around to those places, all the time deluging him with tales of their modern accomplishments. After two days he grew weary of their boasting and told them he wanted to talk to fellow Americans. The politicians and business leaders became angry and demanded even more of his time. Washington refused, stating that he wanted to spend time in a library and learn what had happened to the United States in the span of over 200 years. During the following days he read and studied, with very little sleep.

With only one day of the former president's stay remaining, Congress demanded Washington give them his complete attention. To their surprise, he requested a chance to address Congress. The event was set up immediately and the next morning Washington proudly stood before Congress and addressed them with these words:

Inventions like the automobile and computers are utterly remarkable. And men have walked on the moon--beyond comprehension and belief. Such tremendous advances in technology and medicine. Only in America, and still there is more. Men are equal and I understand now that we should have eliminated slavery sooner. I'm glad you have achieved that and also equal rights for women. All these dreams accomplished by my fellow Americans. I would not believe it, if I had not seen these things with my own eyes. *Congressional members were already patting themselves on the back.* But for all your advances you have made larger missteps. The Constitution and the Bill of Rights were written for a reason. Laws you passed have been misguided, and you have been extravagant with the number of new laws you've passed over the years. You have diluted the important and substantial laws until they have become so confusing nobody understands them. When we originally drew up the Constitution, we knew there should have been no income tax. That tax and the program you devised to collect those taxes were your biggest mistake. Your income tax law should be abolished. Your social security was good in theory, but why has the government failed in its promise to save those monies and instead spent them?

I hear talk in Congress there is not enough money to pay social security benefits to those who have put their hard-earned dollars into the program all their lives. If indeed there is not enough money, then this government has more serious problems than I thought. Now you want to give that same social security to what they call illegal aliens. If they are illegal, they deserve nothing. They paid nothing; they should get nothing. Immigrants are welcome, for they are the backbone of this country.

But these illegal aliens provide another problem that could sound the death knell to our country. We speak English in America. Those that want to be citizens should be required to speak English. There are great opportunities here for those who speak the nation's language. But a divided language is a divided country. United we stand, divided we fall. If we must provide care for illegal aliens, then their own countries should be billed and forced to pay, or a tariff should be put on their exports until the debt is paid in full. Congress has no other choice.

Also, I see Americans who get government subsidies for doing nothing. I asked one able male why he didn't work. He told me the government gave him more money than he could earn at a real job. This government is breeding welfare. Even I must admit, if I was given more money for doing nothing than I could make with my crops, I surely must take the money. That is not, and should not be, the American way. Everyone must work. In our day it was simple. If you didn't work; you didn't eat.

Discipline and hard work are the only solution. And discipline should be firm and swift. I saw a little boy yell at his mother. I told the woman to slap the rude child. Someone told me that if you slapped a child you could be arrested. I have heard people say, "Spare the rod, spoil the child." That does not work. I say, use the rod and save the child. Discipline is important.

All political contributions to individual candidates should be eliminated. When a politician accepts money from business or wealthy individuals, he or she longer represents the people. To take money from business so as to be elected is no better than corruption. Monies should be collected in a general fund and distributed equally among all candidates, including those that are not Democrat or Republican. After seeing decisions made by both parties in Congress, I see no difference in either party. The current two-party system gives the people no choice and no representation. Both parties represent big business and have failed the people. The Constitution was never written to represent business.

Today America fights a war to give freedom to a country called Iraq. Our president asks for Americans to sacrifice. The same should be demanded of companies that make a fortune off that war and the sacrifice of brave American soldiers. Now those same companies move to foreign countries, that one day, could very well be our enemies. We force freedom on a country that fight and kill each other. They do not believe in freedom of religion. A country, that does this, will never be free.

And on the matter of business, any business sending jobs to foreign countries should be treated the same way we did the tea tax in Boston. They should be dumped overboard. Business in America has shown it cares nothing about the American people. This must change.

In my day we knew math well. We borrowed money and we paid it back with interest. Today the numbers are still one through ten and the math is the same, but Congress must have forgotten. Our government's debt is out of control. If you do not stop it now it will be too late. I have read about our former presidents. This country had a great leader in Abraham Lincoln. Pay heed to his words, "America will never be destroyed from the outside. If we falter and lose our freedoms, it will be because we destroyed ourselves." This is the one thing I see that Congress is close to accomplishing.

You have the opportunity to change history, but your current path will doom the United States of America to failure. We fought for a dream; you squabble over greed. Your technological advances amaze me, but I'm ashamed at what you have done to the people you represent. If the members of the Continental Congress and those that signed the Declaration of Independence were alive today, I'm sure they would agree with me when I tell you we would overthrow this government and install freedom once more.

I have seen two parties but neither represents the people. One party wastes money and valuable tax dollars by giving money to those who have nothing and do nothing, while the other party does the same with the money but gives it to those who have everything. Both have become elitist and have forgotten the simple document we wrote over two centuries ago. It was created of the people, by the people, and for the people.

Every congressman and woman here today is supposed to serve this country. Instead you give yourselves entitlements you do not deserve. You were elected to represent the people of America; they do not serve you.

Even today as I speak, Congress passes bills to give money away to help the economy. When a man drinks poison do you treat him by giving him more poison? No. The American economy is in trouble because Congress has spent too much money. The cure is not by spending more but by spending less. Giving money away will not save the country or buy you the votes you want. In 1776 the Continental Congress gave you the right path. Can you find it again?

My final words to you are these. Remember throughout history every great empire has collapsed. There have been no exceptions. Sadly, this seems to be the path Congress is taking. Today the enemy of the United States resides in Congress. You have the opportunity to change history or watch as history repeats. May God guide your decisions as he guided us. And if you believe in God, whatever he may be, may he have mercy on your souls.

4

WGA Strike

I received the following in an e-mail. It might affect you because there are rules writers must follow even if you're not a member of the WGA.

The WGA Strike
Many writers are concerned about the WGA strike and if they are allowed to market their screenplays during this time. After reading through the WGA strike rules and speaking with the WGA, the below is what we have learned:
Writers who are not members of the WGA are allowed to market their screenplays to production companies who are not struck or signatory companies. Many independent, non-signatory producers and production companies are not affected by the strike and can still look at material.
It behooves all writers to not market to struck companies during the strike. This can lead to future complications with entry into the WGA. You can find a list of all the struck companies on the WGA website:
We encourage all writers to read the WGA rules listed on their site.

The above implies that the WGA will not allow me to become a member if I submit to companies they strike. That possibility made me wonder and start thinking. I want my script to be the next movie. A strike that will help writers is what we all want. With that in mind, I decided to join the WGA and back their strike. But first I needed some answers. Why did the members of the WGA strike? What is so great about membership to the WGA? Why must I abide by their rules when I'm not a member? What if I joined? I decided to see for myself and this is what I learned. It seems the writers want a percentage of the DVD sales. That doesn't seem like much. A producer invests millions in the hope their movie will make money. The writers get paid for the script even if the investor loses money. If a writer wants to share in the profit, should they also be willing to share in the loss? Are the WGA writers willing to sacrifice to get more? Writing is not the only thing that makes a movie.

We all want our scripts made into movies or else we wouldn't write them. Same for those that write novels. You want somebody to change your novel into a script and have it made into a movie, and that's why something like the WGA is important. Or is it?

I decided to join the WGA, but first I wanted to see what happened when I submitted my scripts to production companies. What I learned was interesting.

After submitting a query, I followed up with one company. They were a little rude when they asked, "Who are you? What have you done?" When I told them I had sent them a script they laughed. Basically, they said I hadn't done anything and that I was a "nobody." They finished by telling me they couldn't look at my scripts unless I was a member of the WGA.

There was still one more company I wanted to talk with. This one was for a television series. I made the contact and told them I had a script already written. They said they were sorry, but they only took scripts from within their group. I reminded them that a few weeks earlier the show had been written by Stephen King. They said, "But that was Stephen King." Uh-oh, I could see the "nobody" syndrome coming. I got irritated and let them know.

The guy felt sorry for me, so he told me that if I knew somebody I could get it submitted. He laughed and said, "But you probably don't know anybody."

I laughed right back and said, "So the scripts for your shows are like incest. You only do it within the family." That didn't help me but I felt better. Hmmm, nepotism at its finest.

Wow! Two contacts and I quickly found out I was a nobody that didn't know anybody.

Still I wasn't discouraged. Alright maybe a little. I kept calling and asking and I finally ended up with a perfect score. The companies I contacted would not take my work or look at it unless I was a member of the WGA.

There are a few companies that will look at non-WGA members but you will need to be a friend of a friend or know somebody, so that they will look at your work. Well, that let me out. I don't need to remind you, I'm a nobody that doesn't know anybody.

I may be dumb but I'm not stupid...or was that stupid but not dumb? Anyway, this was the easiest thing in the world to figure out. I was going to join the WGA. A few days ago I contacted them. Guess what happened when I tried to join? They told me I can't join the WGA unless I have sold a script or have one under contract. Uh, oh. Wait a minute. If nobody will look at my script unless I'm a member of the WGA and the WGA will not let me join until I sell a script, then if I'm not mistaken, this is a real problem. I think it's called a Catch-22.

I argued with the person at the WGA and tried to explain the contradiction. He didn't understand what I was trying to say. I think he was about to go on his striker's picket or coffee break. He did add an interesting comment. "Companies come to the WGA because of the quality of material we provide."

I quickly quipped, "Have you been to a lot of movies lately or seen some of the movies of the week?" No response. "Some of that is not quality material. And, if you're not willing to screen and take new members into your "exclusive club" how will you ever know what quality material is?"

He responded with, "I'm sorry there's nothing we can do for you."

Now that was the truth. There is nothing the WGA can do for writers unless you're already in their "club." A strike by these people suddenly seems ludicrous.

The whole thing reminded me of the NBA players' strike. I remember watching a high profile player whining. He said, "People don't understand how hard this is on us when we're used to making two million a year." I haven't watched a basketball game since. The basketball strike was uncalled for. Greedy players wanting more. When hourly workers strike it is for a few dollars more and a better way of life. Something else troubled me. Members of the writers union or WGA, sold scripts quickly before the strike. An estimated ten million dollars were spent buying scripts weeks, even days, prior to the strike. Like little squirrels they stored their nuts. I never heard of a union where the workers could do that. The really sad thing about this is that the striking writers want the people who are paid hourly not to cross their picket lines. Those people didn't get millions to sit out a strike. They need their hourly jobs to survive. If the writers want others to sacrifice, they should show they are willing to do the same. Getting the money up front is not a sacrifice. Whose side are you on, the ones that stored the nuts and want a percentage of the profits without worrying about a loss or the workers trying to make it day to day?

What I've learned is that to make it in this business, you must know somebody, or be related, or already be a member.

I'll support the strikers as long as the WGA makes sure that at least five percent of all scripts sold are from non-members. Make it like Fan Story, where the writer members are to read a minimum number of scripts per month written and submitted by those who have never sold a script, and then have the top ten posted on the webpage of the WGA.

The WGA requires all writers to conform to their rules under threat of banishment, even though they have no intention of allowing non-members to join.

I think every writer on Fan Story should call the WGA (323-782-4500) and ask if you can join. Just because someone sold something to their uncle or brother, this doesn't make it quality material. Common sense says if we can't show our material unless we are members, then the WGA should do something about it. We should be able to be associate members and have them promote our material. If the WGA thinks they have quality material then they need to take a look at the work produced by some of their members.

Don't get me wrong; there is a lot of fine material in the WGA, but great material is being overlooked and that material is not on the WGA. They need fresh material and a way to let producers see it. I've seen good material on Fan Story: *Project Greenlight* (Matt Damon and Ben Affleck) and *Triggersteet* (Kevin Spacey). And the WGA is preventing other writers and their scripts from being seen by other companies.

Does this strike help writers or just the WGA? Is it justified? You decide.

Maybe we, the writers of America, need to strike the striking WGA members.

The thing to do is open our own service to counter the WGA. Give the production companies an option. This will be for script writers, but we will allow anyone to join. It will be a counter option to the WGA that we will call American Script Services or ASS for short. Who wants to join me?

I don't mind failure; just give me the opportunity to fail.

5
Worried About Retirement?

Worried About Retirement? Not me; it's too late.

Yesterday five of us were cussing and discussing retirement. Then somebody asked me, "When are you going to retire?"

I chuckled, "When? How about; what with?"

Another said, "I was counting on retiring with the stocks I have but they are still going down and I can't retire for some time."

"I know all about stock," I said, trying to act like I knew what I was talking about. "If you want to retire take a careful look at my stock portfolio. You can use it as a go-by for your future investments. After a careful analysis of my investments you will come to the conclusion that you don't want to buy anything I've bought. But I can give you a helpful hint on how to invest in a stock. Check it out carefully. See how the stock has performed. Then you need to see if the company has a CEO; if they do then don't buy the stock."

They laughed but one of my friends called me out. "They all have CEOs."

"Bingo. See, you have it all figured out too."

He rolled his eyes.

"Look, I know that retirement home of mine is now gonna need to be a secondhand travel trailer but I think I might have a solution," I said. With a smirk I continued, "All kidding aside, I know how you can live like a king, but it will take a little work on your part."

"What is that?" someone asked.

"First you need to study Spanish and when you become proficient you need to cross the border into Mexico. Next you will need to swim back across the Rio Grande, into the United States. When you get caught you will need to cry. Go to your knees in a praying position and say, "Dios Mio! Me ayudas, por favor. Yo no hablo Ingles." (My God! Please help me. I don't speak English.)

"After that the government will give you all the medical aid, housing, food, and social security you need. You will now be able to live like a king."

My friends laughed at my ramblings and then I was asked the same question. "Really, when are you going to retire?"

I thought about it and after careful consideration I told him, "Well, I've done the math and I will be able to retire two years after I die."

Hasta la vista,

Mis Amigos

6
THE ROMAN EMPIRE

Our American military marches to victory not much differently than did the British troops in their bright red uniforms more than two hundred years ago. At that time the British were unbeatable, but they lost. Now America is unbeatable but has exposed its Achilles' heel. There is still time to correct it before it's too late. Not unlike the British Empire, George W. Bush and his American Empire are headed for the same fate.

You say, "Impossible! You are wrong!" I hope so. After all, *Moon Shadow* is only a work of fiction, but it is said truth is stranger than fiction. And don't forget what we were taught when we were in school: History repeats itself.

I have always believed history repeats. Man is an intelligent animal but he refuses to learn from his mistakes. What truly terrifies me are not the terrorists but the political and business leaders of our country. They have lost their honor and integrity.

Two and two is four, always has been and always will be. But that is not true for the politicians that run our country. You can pay them to make two and two equal something else. Our congressmen can look us in the face and swear two and two is five and we'll believe them, while at the same time another congressman will tell us two and two is three, and we'll believe him. Because of this, unless our leaders change their ways, our country is doomed. I believe we are now looking at a president that is capable of destroying our country.

Abraham Lincoln could see this and summed it up best when he said, "America will never be destroyed from the outside. If we falter and lose our freedoms, it will be because we destroyed ourselves."

Today we see our leaders at a point in time where they can learn from their mistakes and change history, but instead they continue to repeat the same mistakes. Has anything really changed?

From the beginning of time every empire has collapsed. There have been no exceptions.

In many ways we are like the Roman Empire.

REASONS FOR THE COLLAPSE OF THE ROMAN EMPIRE

Military – the military was spread so thin around the known world that the Empire could not defend its own borders. Military forces expanded and so did the pay. The Empire conquered distant but wealthy provinces but were unable to continue holding the territories. The burden to support the military became so great that the financial collapse from within began. Slowly the Empire pulled the military away from conquered and controlled territories. Gradually other countries took over these territories.

Taxes - the emperors were forced to raise taxes to pay for the huge military spending.

Values and Morals – declined as leaders wasted money on lavish extravagances to please themselves and the people.

Health and the Environment – these declined as the wealthy kept the money and the government lacked the money to help the people. Alcohol was abused.

Corruption – the corruption of political and business leaders became rampant as they rewarded themselves and their followers.

Unemployment - increased as the small farmer virtually vanished when they were bought up and run by a few of the wealthy who lowered pay and expected more.

Inflation – lack of work hurt the poor as the wealthy horded most of the gold coins forcing the people to barter or steal for their needs.

Language – numerous dialects and languages were allowed. Communications became increasingly difficult. Eventually the various languages prevailed, ending communications with the Empire.

Urban Decay – became more prevalent as the poor were unable to afford rent, forcing many to crime for survival.

Technology – arrogant about their own abilities leaders let the technology lag behind other countries.

Chemicals – lead in pipes made the Romans sick and many died.

Islam - some even point to the rise of Islam as a reason

Where does the United States stand today?

Referenced from **Killeen Harker Heights Connections**

7
VOTE FOR ME, I'M A CHRISTIAN

Although I consider myself a Christian, I'm having trouble with our elected officials and candidates running for President of the United States. I also think many of the churches have gone too far. After all, when I hear both parties talking about each other, it's like having the KKK go to Jeremiah Wright's Trinity United Church of Christ and talking about brotherhood. They just don't go together.

While doing some research on Democrats and Republicans I found the term "doomed conformist," which means "a member of a large group of people who blindly follow one another on a course of action that will lead to destruction for all of them."

When Bush touted being a Christian and won, it started an avalanche of Christianity. From that point forward every candidate's platform was, "I'm a Christian, vote for me."

Christians in politics is not a good idea. Most people are not looking at the candidate but whether or not that person is a Christian. A dangerous precedent. Don't get me wrong, a Christian is not the problem, but people claiming to be Christian are the danger. Bush continues to say, "I'm a Christian." That's great but Christians are supposed to try to be fiscally responsible and not tout revenge and war. You know, love your enemy. I guess that means we need to love Congress. Sorry.

To win an election today you need to claim to be a Christian. Some may believe this country was formed on Christian values, but the truth is it was formed on freedom of religion. Even our forefathers wanted freedom of religion and a separation of church and state.

Something that has always bothered me is how some ministers say to stay away from non-Christians. And yet they tell you to go out among the non-Christians, show the love of God, and convert them. You can't do both. It may come as a surprise to some of those ministers, but there are a lot of non-Christians in America. Not bad people, just non-Christians.

Recently, someone told me, "We must vote for a Christian."

I asked him, "Do you believe in Armageddon?"

He said he did and I asked him how he would know it was near.

"The Antichrist will be present in the world, and before him there will be false prophets, who will claim to be Christian but they won't be Christian."

I tried to look amazed, and stupid, when I asked, "You mean like President Bush?"

The look on his face was priceless. He gasped and asked, "You don't really think Bush is the Antichrist?"

I shrugged. "I didn't say that. You did." His mouth dropped open. "It's okay, Bush is not the Antichrist." I laughed and said, "It's Cheney."

29

The noise his head made sounded like his stomach trying to digest food. I swear he was having indigestion in his brain. He looked sick. His brain kept churning. In apparent shock he managed to say, "But they all claim to be Christian."

I tried to look terrified. "Oh, my God. We're too late."

As his mind tried to digest his thoughts I walked away.

It is important in the coming election that we elect the best person to run the country. Maybe, just maybe that person will be a Christian. To be president you must have been born in this country or born of American parents. Nowhere in the Constitution does it say you must be a Christian.

I had an argument with Bob, Larry, and Steve, three members of my church, over this same issue. They all firmly believed the United States is obligated to elect a Christian. All believed we needed a good Christian, like Bush, to protect us and save us the way he did after 911.

It was hard for them to understand that what Bush did was for revenge and not anything based on Christian values. They just couldn't understand. They believed what he did was justice for the Twin Towers of New York.

"War is never the answer," I told them. "Besides, fifteen of the nineteen terrorists were from Saudi Arabia."

Steve said, "Saddam got what he deserved. He was evil and a terrorist."

"There are a lot of bad leaders but we can't remove them all. If what you say is true, then shouldn't we be going down the freeways looking for suspicious Ryder trucks that might be carrying bombs and blow them off the road?"

Larry interjected, "That's different!"

"Actually, it isn't different. A terrorist is a terrorist, and Timothy McVeigh was just that, but we don't hunt down and kill the militia."

"You don't understand," said Bob. "Non-Christian's will destroy our country."

"Oh, I understand. You mean like Bush? Wait, isn't he a Christian? Where are his Christian values?"

Steve was angry. "God is on our side."

I chuckled and irritated my Christian friends. "Okay, let's say God is on our side. Are Methodists, Protestants, Baptists, Catholics, and Episcopalians all Christian religions?"

They all nodded.

"A good Christian minister or priest will pray for God to watch over the members of our church as they go into battle, right?"

Again they nodded.

"Now let's say a Protestant is going into battle and the minister asks God to protect him in battle, and a Catholic priest does the same for the men in his church. Then both of these good Irish men meet on the field of battle, aim and then shoot at each other. My question to you is who does God pick?"

They didn't respond.

With a shake of my head I finished, "That's what I thought too."

Every side truly believes they are righteous but do they act righteously?

The point is this; some people will blindly follow a leader that says he is a true Christian. Before doing this please try to learn the truth. Vote for who you believe will best represent the people of our country. And if you are a Christian, remember that the best person for the office might not be the same religion as you.

Note:

I hate to see religion involved in politics. The United States is a mixture of many religions. Vote for somebody to run the country not somebody based on religion. If we push to far to the right the old saying, "What goes around comes around," could come back to haunt us. Research what you read on the Internet. Most of what is sent to you are lies or are very misleading. Please don't make a judgment based on lies.

And to all our Democrat and Republican leaders; may you all, very soon, be voted out of office.

8

NATIONAL DEBT, THE DEFICIT AND SPENDING

(Originally written in 2005, current debt has been added)

"The budget should be balanced; the treasury should be refilled; public debt should be reduced; and the arrogance of public officials should be controlled." **-Cicero.106-43 B. C.**

For my novel *Moon Shadow* to be credible, I had to come up with a reasonable way the United States could be invaded. I looked at Russia, Mexico, and other countries that had collapsed previously. All had gone bankrupt. I wondered if the same thing could happen to the United States.

Let me clarify the National Debt and the deficit. The National Debt is the total amount of money owed by the government. The federal budget deficit is the yearly amount by which spending exceeds revenue. When you add up all the deficits and surpluses (of which there are very few) for the past 200 years, you will come up with the current National Debt. Our politicians love to brag about how "The deficit is down!" like it's a great accomplishment. Don't let them fool you. Here is an example: Let's say the amount of taxes collected is 2.3 trillion but the budget is 2.8 trillion, which will give us a 500 billion deficit already figured into the budget for the year. Suppose they only spend 2.7 trillion. Now they can brag about how they cut the deficit by 100 billion dollars when in reality they still added 400 billion to the debt. All smoking guns. Surely you will remember how under Clinton they continually bragged about the large surplus. Not true. Every year the National Debt increased under Clinton, but by using the example above they tell us we had a surplus. At the bottom of this article are the yearly increases in National Debt since 1978. Not since 1960 did the government spend less than the money it took in, which is something it should try to do every year.

The National Debt is huge and climbing at the rate of around $75 million an hour, but as long as the economy is strong there is no fear. The government and almost all politicians assume it will stay strong, hence the National Debt continues to rise—at an alarming rate. The best comparison is you as an individual. You make enough money to pay all of your debts and there is really no problem. In thirty years the house is paid and most of your bills are gone. But suppose you were laid off or injured and out of work for six months without any other source of income. What happens? You go bankrupt. Here is another scenario which is happening to our own government. Currently our government is spending thirty percent more than it takes in each year. Suppose you did the same. As an example if you made $100,000 per year and added thirty percent to your debt each year along with interest it would take fifteen years to reach a point where you owed one million dollars. At this point the interest you owed would exceed what you make. You

32

would be bankrupt.

Our government is not immune to the same problem. In 2003 the interest on the National Debt exceeded $322 billion. Only two departments in the government exceed that spending: the military is one of them.

During 2004 the Federal Government took in 2.5 trillion dollars but spent approximately 3.1 trillion for a 600 billion dollar deficit. Here are some other interesting figures. Currently the National Debt stands at $8,003,104,666,539.23. To pay this amount off, each and every American would need to come up with $25,000 today. From 1980, when Reagan took office, until 1992 when Bush left office, the debt went from less than one trillion dollars to over four trillion dollars. From 2000 to 2004 the National Debt under our current President Bush has increased more than two trillion dollars to its current level. At this rate when President Bush's second term is finished we will have a debt of nearly ten trillion dollars. The interest on that debt at five percent interest will be $500 billion. But suppose inflation hits. At ten percent the interest is one trillion dollars. At fifteen percent the interest would be a staggering 1.5 trillion dollars. Think of those numbers. The interest alone would be more than the money required to run the government.

I know that sounds like heavy inflation and more like a depression which surely won't happen. They probably thought the same thing in 1929. Still, interest did hit double digits as recently as the 1990s. It can and will happen again. But when? How safe are we?

Another sad note is that Social Security is treated like any other tax and has already been spent. Social Security is part of the deficit and really doesn't exist anymore. Social Security is not part of the Federal Budget Fund. It is supposed to be a separate account with its own source of income and its own separate trust fund. Social Security payments do not go into the general fund, and should NOT be counted as general revenue. The trust fund is supposed to be used to pay benefits. But Congress ordered the Treasury Department to use the money in the Social Security Trust Fund as though it were general revenue, promising to pay it back. Now that promise is part of the National Debt. In reality Social Security is just another very large tax collection tool.

The Social Security Trust Fund is simply a meaningless record of taxes that have been collected for future needs, spent for current desires, and then recorded and counted as an asset. Fraud is a better description.

If something severe ever occurred in the next eight years like a combination of double digit inflation along with double digit unemployment, then the United States of America could possibly reach its darkest hour. The possibility exists for the United States to be bankrupt before the year 2012.

What you will see in the next few years is loss of government benefits to the people, not government employees, and a severe rise in the taxes.

That is exactly what happens in my novel *Moon Shadow*.

If you are interested in the National Debt go to these websites:
www. brillig. com/debt_clock/
www. toptips. com/debtclock. html
www. publicdebt. treas. gov/opd/opdpenny. htm

I went to the "toptips" site and found the National Debt increased approximately $20,000 a second. In four seconds the National Debt increases enough to pay my salary for a year. Only four seconds! On November 19, 2004 our Congress had to pass a last minute bill that enabled our government to borrow 8.18 trillion dollars. On average the National Debt is increasing more than 1.6 billion dollars a day

Sometime on October 18, 2005, our National Debt surpassed $8,000,000,000,000.00 (that is eight trillion). Go to the websites above and see how much the National Debt has increased since this was written.

I'm neither for nor against our presidents. I'm against the debt and the potential problems such a huge debt will bring our country. Did you ever wonder if our representatives have ever told us the truth? They never actually told us a lie but what they said could be classified as lies by omission. Note the years under Clinton and the supposed "surplus." There never was a surplus. The last year Clinton was in office the National Debt only increased 18 billion dollars. Not bad, but definitely no surplus. Under Bush's administration the National Debt has accelerated at an alarming rate. From November, 2004 to November, 2005 the National Debt increased in eleven of those months. Of particular interest are nine of those months. The debt in "each" of those nine months exceeded the total added to the National Debt during Clinton's last year as President. Even more shocking is that on October 5, 2005, the next 24 hours found the National Debt increasing almost as much as the last year of Clinton's administration. During the month of October, 2005 the National Debt increased almost 100 billion dollars.

On Sunday, October 16, 2005 at approximately 7:58:03 PM, Central Standard Time, the National Debt exceeded 8 trillion dollars for the first time ever.

Below are the years and the National Debt back to 1959.

09/15/2011 $14,696,963,596,782.73
09/30/2010 $13,668,825,497,341.36
09/30/2009 $11,893,091,028,361.01
09/30/2008 $10,530,893,033,778.21
09/30/2007 $9,058,380,277,039.94
09/30/2006 $8,506,973,899,215.23
09/30/2005 $7,932,709,661,723.50
09/30/2004 $7,379,052,696,330.32
09/30/2003 $6,783,231,062,743.62
09/30/2002 $6,228,235,965,597.16
09/28/2001 $5,807,463,412,200.06
09/29/2000 $5,674,178,209,886.86
09/30/1999 $5,656,270,901,615.43
09/30/1998 $5,526,193,008,897.62
09/30/1997 $5,413,146,011,397.34
09/30/1996 $5,224,810,939,135.73
09/29/1995 $4,973,982,900,709.39
09/30/1994 $4,692,749,910,013.32
09/30/1993 $4,411,488,883,139.38

09/30/1992 $4,064,620,655,521.66
09/30/1991 $3,665,303,351,697.03
09/28/1990 $3,233,313,451,777.25
09/29/1989 $2,857,430,960,187.32
09/30/1988 $2,602,337,712,041.16
09/30/1987 $2,350,276,890,953.00
09/30/1986 $2,125,302,616,658.42
09/30/1985$1,945,941,616,459.88
09/30/1984$1,662,966,000,000.00
09/30/1983$1,410,702,000,000.00
09/30/1982$1,197,073,000,000.00
09/30/1981$1,028,729,000,000.00
09/30/1980$ 930,210,000,000.00
09/30/1979$ 845,116,000,000.00
09/30/1978$ 789,207,000,000.00
09/30/1977$ 718,943,000,000.00
09/30/1976$ 653,544,000,000.00
09/30/1975$ 576,649,000,000.00
09/30/1974$ 492,665,000,000.00
09/30/1973$ 469,898,039,554.70
09/30/1972$ 449,298,066,119.00
09/30/1971$ 424,130,961,959.95
09/30/1970$ 389,158,403,690.26
09/30/1969$ 368,225,581,254.41
09/30/1968$ 358,028,625,002.91
09/30/1967$ 344,663,009,745.18
09/30/1966$ 329,319,249,366.68
09/30/1965$ 320,904,110,042.04
09/30/1964$ 317,940,472,718.38
09/30/1963$ 309,346,845,059.17
09/30/1962$ 303,470,080,489.27
09/30/1961$ 296,168,761,214.92
09/30/1960$ 290,216,815,241.68 * (The last surplus)
09/30/1959$ 290,797,771,717.63

One final thought. Could the National Debt reach ten trillion dollars by 2008? If so, what will happen to the economy? Remember I said earlier that our government collects about 2.3 trillion dollars but needs 2.8 trillion to run the government? Let's say we reach a 10 trillion dollar debt in three more years and suppose interest is say ten percent, then the interest on the National Debt will be one trillion dollars leaving only 1.3 trillion to run a government that is spending close to 2.8 trillion per years. This simply won't work.

Unless they do something very soon our government will be unable to pay off the National Debt. Financially our government is rapidly reaching a "point of no return."

9

MY POEMS, SOME POLITICAL

These are a little on the far side so I hope you enjoy them.

American Nation
(Based on the song Cherokee Nation)

They took the whole American nation
Changed our laws for their satisfaction.
Took away our ways of life,
Our jobs and gave us strife
Took away our English tongue.
Forced their Spanish on our young.
And all things once made in our land,
Are now a days made in Pakistan.

American people, American pride
Once so proud to live, now so bound to die.

They took the whole American nation,
Rocked us with their condemnation.
The Book that gave us faith in our land,
Are now taught from the Koran.
For our deep rooted belief,
The atheist and Muslims gave us grief.
Though they wear a shirt and tie
I'm still the American deep inside.

American people, American pride
Once so proud to live, now so bound to die.

American's what a sad sight,
We're no longer willing to fight.
If changes don't come soon,
Our American life is doomed.

American people, American Nation
So proud to live, now an Obama-nation.

But maybe someday if we learn
Our American nation will return,
Will return, will return, will return.

The End
(From my novel "Live For Today")

For the End, nothing would be the same.
This was the last play of the game.

They needed four,
They had to score.

The quarterback said, "End, wide right.
Are you up for the fight?"

They came to the line,
For the very last time.

At the snap the End pushed hard,
And caught the defense off guard.

He ran with all his might,
His speed, such a sight.

He flew through the night,
To the flashes of light

Down the field spiraled the ball,
Too high, much too tall!

The End leaped for the sky.
His body so very, very high

Up, up even higher he did soar
As the frantic fans gave a thunderous roar.

The ball touched his fingertip.
He couldn't let it slip.

Another hand, it wasn't much.
Again, oh what a touch!

He gathered the ball in.
Touchdown--the End!

The Legend of Moon Shadow

Below is an excerpt from my novel, *Moon Shadow*.
With the Moon full, they set the wooden structures ablaze. All the time, they chanted and danced around the separate fires of each of their fallen comrades. The ritual was the legend of Moon Shadow. The Karankawa Indians believed a warrior's shadow had to be seen during the full moon, then disappear with the fire in order to set his spirit free. As the fires blazed, they would chant the words to the Legend of Moon Shadow:
If the ritual was not performed, and the fallen Indian's shadow remained after the first full moon, his haunted spirit would roam the island forever never finding peace.

When Moon Shadows fall,
Come footsteps in the sand
Where no one follows.
From brave warriors far away

In flames! The Spirits recall,
Memories by the sea.
They dance the land of Moon Shadows,
Eternal rest from the warrior's earthly stay!

America, Love It or Leave It?

Billons spent, then questions rose,
Soon Halliburton stuck up their nose.

"No more money? Time to say Goodbye."
We'll find more when we reach Dubai.
Money is our game,
And we want more of the same.

While soldiers die
And women cry,
Halliburton said, "Goodbye."

I Hear

Every night I hear
Your sighs, so very clear
Even though you're no longer here.

Water Brought Down Three Presidents

Caution: this will offend you if you're a Democrat or Republican.

Water Brought Down Nixon

A war Nixon did end
No more men would he send
To save America was a must,
On with his power lust.
When it came to sneaky,
Nixon tried to be tricky
He gave America a weak reason;
Democrats may have committed treason.
We will never forget his name,
Nixon, forced to resign in shame
Because, for him, it was too late,
Everyone knew about Watergate

Water Brought Down Clinton

Poor Bill played with Lewinsky
Now he was doomed to face Hillary
Be careful of Hillary, don't push her
Or you might end up like Foster
Bill quipped, "I like to shoot for par
But I'd rather play with my cigar."
Some say he will lie
While brave men die
He, and his future President wife,
Were cause for great American strife
The papers they did hide
Began the wild, Whitewater ride

Water Brought Down Bush

When Bush accused Saddam of WMD's
American companies charged large fees
They made money by the ton,
A company called Halliburton
"Listen, I'm an outstanding Christian,
I'll make Iraq my personal mission."
Bush screamed, "Operation Iraqi Liberation!"
"No," his men begged, those words will rile the nation
Those words spell OIL from the letters,

So use "Freedom," that's much better
The army rolled through Baghdad,
Sweet revenge for Bush's dad
"Mission Accomplished," the war was won,
Not so, it had just begun
He threatened, "Bring it on!"
They did, from dusk to dawn.
Firmly, he said, "Terror, we're going to attack!"
To Cheney he whispered, "What country is that?"
All the dead really looked bad
And this made Bush mad
Soon the war began to fizzle
He said, "Quick, shoot another missile."
Then he said, "Listen to me, I'm smarter.
By God, we'll win this with Blackwater."

So now everyone can see
They weren't as bright as can be

Blackwater, Whitewater or Watergate
All three waters sealed their fate.

Gone

I met a girl not long ago
I thought she would love me so.
She came like a gift from above,
And made me fall in love.
Now we're apart,
With her she took my heart.

Finding Love

I look at you and see
A dream, come true for me.
I looked for love
There was nothing I could do
Then one day
God sent me you.
So close, so far, no longer apart
For you I give all my heart.

Live For Today
(From my novel "Live For Today")

Come with me back in time,
When things were so fine.

It was a different scene,
As we listened to Jan and Dean,

With their music we hung ten in the surf.
We still played football on real turf.

It was a time to smile.
Remember the quarter mile?

That Chevy SS 396
Really gave us some kicks.

Oh, what a time,
When we cranked up the 409

But the car that was mine,
Was the Mustang 289

It was nasty, not really very nice,
When the NFL championship was played in snow and ice.

Neither team had any slackers,
As the Cowboys were beaten by the Packers.

The Cowboy fans shed many a tear,
But it was the same thing the following year.

Then came the military draft,
But none of us laughed

The Beatles said I feel fine,
Somehow we always found time.

With Friday night lights
We were up for the fight.

In California the Beach Boys were king
And surfing was the thing.

There was nothing so cool
As "Be Tue to Your School."

Joe Barfield

In Texas it was football
We all stood tall.

Your father said you were born,
To be a Texas longhorn.

We were rough and ready,
Tuff and steady.

But we listened to Rock and Roll, even Fever Tree
It was best of times, can't you see?

The Byrds, Turtles, and Doors
We played the music and still wanted more.

They called it the amazing race,
U. S. versus Russia; who'd be first in space?

Then there was talk that soon,
A man would walk on the moon.

The Grassroots sang "Live For Today."
That was it, there's nothing more to say.

It was like a little bit of heaven
Back in the year 1967.

Jack be Nimble, But Kennedy be Quick

Sometimes a man should stand firm
But from Kennedy, a lesson we can learn
Don't stay around,
Let them drown
Learn from the dark waters of Chappaquiddick
Always leave the scene quick!

Obama Nation

With Obama, Reid and Pelosi,
Our country is doomed, can't you see?

We voted for his hope and change
His lies covered a wide range.
He demanded, "I'm Obama the President,
Now everyone be subservient."

Be careful don't disagree
He'll knock us to our knees.
He said he'd bring us change
But most knew he was deranged.

Obama said, "Tax and spend."
Americans got it in the end.
Under Obama, America's vision
Quickly turned to Communism.

He looked to friends for suggestions,
That gave us all indigestion.
There was Jeremiah Wright the un-American priest,
And Bill Ayers the terrorist killer elite.

When he refused to salute the flag it was a sign.
Americans should have asked him to resign.
To Americans he shouted words of scorn
Because we ask where he was born.

To the Arabs he bowed down,
But he looked more like a clown.

He said, "If I must, I'll side with the Muslims."
Most of us thought that was puzzling.
Obama praised Hamas deeds,
While he ignored America's needs.

Obama promised a Mosque at ground zero
He believed he was America's new hero.
A place where Americans died
Obama continued his lies.

The Book that gave us faith in our land,
He wants taught from the Koran.
For our deep rooted belief,
Obama has given us grief.

Islam has sent us the Manchurian Candidate,
We need to remove him before it's too late.

Americans said things that weren't very nice.
Some thought he might be the Antichrist.

Obama's words made us scared,
When he said we'd die without Obama Health Care.

Medical care for less.
Came the lies from Obama and Congress.
He will pay in time
'Cause what he's done is a crime.
It's a very simple reason,
He's committed treason.

What Obama, has done will destroy us,
He wants, "all Americans to the back of the bus."
Our once proud American nation,
Has become an Obamanation.

Obama took our great nation
And changed our laws for his satisfaction.

He's taken away our ways of life,
Our jobs and given us strife

And our Bill of Rights,
He took away at night.

Illegal aliens with no papers we fear,
But for Obama we continue to cheer.
Give me a moment to comment
Where's that birth certificate document?
All of America should be in tears,
Obama is the one to fear.

Obama moved very quick
This President was very slick
He said, "I'll fix the American institution,
As soon as I get rid of the Constitution."
He put up a scary fight,
To take away our Bill of Rights.

The things Obama does are strange,
The man is obviously deranged,
His choices are beyond bizarre,

just look at his communist czars.

The lies from Holder
Only made Obama bolder

With the disaster of BP
It knocked business to it's knee.

Save the environment, no more wells
So American business and jobs went to hell.
But it was okay for Brazil to drill,
While Americans were forced to be still.

Americans began to shout and holler,
As Obama gave away American dollars,
To drill for Soros and Brazil,
And it made some Americans ill.

What about Brazil's environment?
But Obama made no comment.

Americans showed their temper,
But they turned away with a whimper.

Don't worry, as long as Obama can print money
Americans will believe every day is sunny.

Obama wanted his popularity to soar
So he took Libya to war.
And again all Americans saw
Obama break Constitutional Law.
Sternly, he said, "Save Libya,
Give it to Al Qaeda."

Then the men of Fox
Gave Obama hard knocks

Clinton said, "When your popularity is down
Hunt the enemy like a blood hound."

While Obama sipped his coffee
He said, "Quick kill Kaddafi."

"No time for slumber,
We need to jack up my numbers."

Give it to the Navy SEALS

To Finish up the deal.

So he killed Osama bin laden
But we still have Obama been Lying.
Come on SEALS, before it's too late,
We still have one more to eliminate.

Obama's words and security leaks
Are what really killed Seal Team six..
Again Obama went on a trip while he denied
He was the reason Seal Team Six died

In Libya Americans died
While Obama lied.

When Americans point at what he was doing
President Obama has a knack
For whining and saying
You say that because I'm black.

Damned be us
If we should discuss
And make light,
Of the fact he is also white.

When it came to bankruptcy for GM
Things looked pretty grim.
But Obama came to save the day
So the unions could continue to play.
He said, "I will save the unions, you will see."
But soon those jobs were sent to China, overseas.

When it comes to the militant Holder
For America he is dangerously bolder.
All of his audacious crimes,
Prove he is nothing but slime

Obama said, "Now hold on a minute!"
He was determined, even adamant
That he would save the environment.

He shut down America's mines of coal
To ruin America was his goal,
While he gave money to Brazil
To sweeten Banker's secret deal,
Because he was willing
to let Soros to do foreign drilling.

Trump offered millions, but not another dime
It's time to see his sealed collegiate crime
But he continues to delay
Proof, of his collegiate foreign aid.
Still Obama continues to deny
He has told any lies

"HELP!" they pleaded, but in the end
The rescue Obama refused to send,
So in Benghazi with help denied
Five brave Americans died.

When you ask Obama about Benghazi
He responds more like a Nazi.
Hillary spoke, but still the truth was never told
As she sneered, "The Seals were just a bump in the road."

Lies and promises of the 2008 election
Took us down a path of an un-American direction.

Holder said, "Don't check voter registration"
So he could continue the death of our nation.

It's not a gift, it's not a loan,
Vote for Obama and we'll give you a phone.

Although it was a lie
Obama said no more children will die.
It's time to get rid of guns,
I'm Obama, I said it; it's done.

But Holder was asked by the Mexican drug cartel,
"Will those guns also be for sale?"
And Al Qaeda who killed our soldiers
Went to Libya and were given weapons from Holder.

Goodbye Constitution and Bill of Rights,
Americans have forgotten how to fight.

Obama has pushed for politically correct,
And made America a wreck.

"The only way
Is to do as I say.
I'm Obama, all must obey."

Obama we bow down to you our King,
For you have promised us everything.

The truth Obama, you shout blasphemy
For all Americans you are the enemy.

When Obama is gone and nothing but dust,
Will America return to, "In God We Trust?"

American's what a sad sight,
We're no longer willing to fight.
If changes don't come soon,
Our American life is doomed.

Lonely

You can't stay, I know
You say you must go
I thought our love was so sweet
Now you say it was incomplete

Now I'll cry
'Cause I love you so
And inside I'll die
'Cause you must go.

The pain inside
Can't be denied.
Don't you know,
I still love you so?

My world is empty
Now that you've left me
Still, every night I hear
Your sighs, so very clear.
Like rain come my tears,
I can't stop these fears.
How can I go on,
Now that you are gone?

She said she wasn't mad
It made me feel really bad.
Now I'm so sad.

The Office Clown

On a day dark and dreary,
In a drafting room tired and weary.

We knew the time had come,
This would be the last day for some.

Then our Office Clown tried to be funny.
He told us we didn't need the money.

We knew it was trouble to stay,
But management promised a better way.

Workers gave up their money,
When promised milk and honey.

For sure our money they would pay,
But we would have to wait another day.

Then pleading, they begged us alas,
Take a pay cut to save our ass.

They said to Bob
You're lucky to have a job.

The management gave us assurance,
We need not worry about our insurance.

The next day our insurance was double,
Which caused many grief and trouble.

They promised our money was in the 401k,
That seemed to make a better day.

When we learned the money wasn't there,
It made for a day of despair.

They promised a better tomorrow,
Instead they gave us grief and sorrow.

Word came down about a layoff.
The drafting room became chaos.

Just when everyone was down,
We were saved by the drafting room clown.

Joe Barfield

American Terrorists, the 535

American laws passed by Congress,
Have destroyed America's progress.

Congress took our great nation
And changed our laws for their satisfaction.
They've taken away our ways of life,
Our jobs and given us strife

The Book that gave us faith in our land,
Are now taught from the Koran.
For our deep rooted belief,
The atheist and Muslims gave us grief.

Tax the poor and give to the wealthy?
Not an idea that is very healthy.
Welfare for the wealthy has failed,
It is time for Congress to be jailed
When it came to America's need,
Congress succumbed instead to their greed.

They say they work hard to strive,
They're to blame, the five-thirty-five.
And all things once made in our land,
Are now made in foreign lands.

Their greed and corruption doomed to failure.
We can blame it all on America's legislature.
With Congress in control, America's vision
Has quickly turned to socialism.

And our Bill of Rights,
They took away at night
Obama, Reid and Pelosi made us scared,
When they said we'd die without Obama Health Care.

Medical care for less.
Came the lies from Congress.
Congress will pay in time
'Cause what they've done is a crime.
It's a very simple reason,
They've committed treason.

With Boxer, Reid and Pelosi,
Our country is doomed, can't you see?

From our forefathers, Washington and Jefferson
We can learn a valuable lesson
When your leaders spread tyranny and lies,
You must be willing to fight and die.
It's time for all Americans to rise

No more words, enough said,
It's time for packing lead.

Let's go to Congress with Smith and Wesson,
And teach those un-American traitors a lesson.

American's are really a sad sight,
Don't give up, there's still time to fight.
But hurry, if changes don't come soon,
Our American life is doomed.

10

CRAZY THOUGHTS AND OTHER WORTHLESS MEANDERING SCRIBBLES

NOTE:

I put this together when I found something I had written about the President in 1991. I've lost many over time but here are those I could find over the last twenty years. Ironically they start with the dates 9/11 and end with 9/11 spanning the twenty years of frustration and anger with our government. I was also on a passenger jet during the attack of 911.

BUSH DADDY (1989-1992)

The Truth of a Man is in His Actions (Or Lack of It)
(09.11.91)

George Washington: I cannot tell a lie. The father of our country did not. He wanted to be free and when offered a position of King in the United States of America he refused. After serving as President he quit so others could have the opportunity.

Douglas MacArthur: I shall return! He did as he promised and in World War II he returned to the Philippines, rescuing them from the Japanese.

George Bush: Read my lips! We still are. Never has one man said so much and contradicted all he stood for.

The same man that said read my lips also said he believed in the right to bear arms, freedom of choice and no new taxes. Forget the issues and remember he compromised his stand on these issues.

At a time when the world is at peace he decides to "declare war" against drugs, savings and loan fraud and child abuse. How many times does he have to declare war before he goes into action and quits with the idle rhetoric.

Bush told the American public that he declared war against drugs. Then he said Americans needed to help give money to the fight. As if the taxes are not enough. As if the 200 billion for our fighting forces could not accomplish the war on drugs, he

needs more money. When is the war going to start?

In a war against drugs you set a carrier at Brownsville and one at San Diego. Fighters will continue to patrol the border with helicopters strategically placed along the length of the border. Since none of this was done I assume he intends to do nothing in

the battle against drugs. When he was on television he showed cocaine to the American public. He knows how to buy it but he can't stop it. Why? If he knows the source then he can stop it, which means he has no intention of stopping it. Why? I don't know.

I feel sorry for Russia because Bush condemns communism but he refuses to

help Gorbachov now that they are the brink of democracy. I don't mean monetary help. What I mean is American companies investing in the Russian economy. Bush refuses while
other companies jump on the band wagon. Again Bush fails.

This is a man that says he had no knowledge of the Iran-Contra affair. Take a moment and ponder this statement. This is a man that was the head of the C. I. A. and he says that the men that had been appointed by Reagan did it without the Presidents or his knowledge. There are only two scenarios. One he has no control over those that are appointed, which is a sad turn of events. Who is running the country? The only other
alternative is that he is a liar. What do you think? The thought of either one is unsettling.

Everything he has done is disturbing. Now he wants to set trade sanctions against the Japanese. Don't get me wrong, some of the sanctions are deserved. After all we have a 40 billion trade deficit with them. Suppose we get tuff. Do we eliminate their products? Of course. That's what the President would have you believe. We'll just throw out Nissan, Toyota, Mazda, Honda, Yamaha, Suzuki, Mitsubishi, Sony and countless others. Do we eliminate them all of randomly pick a few? How many American jobs will be eliminated? I bet Bush hasn't thought about that, nor have any of the Senators or Representatives. But don't worry they roar like a lion but are as dangerous as a mouse. Mark my words the President is screaming idle rhetoric, but intends to do nothing.

The Deficit is bad and it is inevitable that taxes will increase. But when taxes increase, watch closely. You will find that the deficit will continue to increase. Mark my words for every dollar they collect our government will spend a dollar fifty. This is called fiscal irresponsibility. We are told to watch what we do but they continue to spend. What our government needs to do is cut every program by 20 per cent. Will they? Of
course not. Our government officials are as responsible as the heads of our failed savings and loan institutions. These men are leading our country into bankruptcy.

Now to back up to the sanctions against Japan. Something needs to be done but not to Japan. I believe Japan will take care of the problem themselves. There is something more terrifying than Japan. Something that in ten years will destroy this country. The president needs to do something and do it now. This problem has almost brought our country to financial ruin. What is it? OPEC. I heard from American friends returning from Saudi Arabia, that it has been rumored that the Middle East can bring the U. S. to its knees without firing a shot. It's relatively simple. Send the prices up let American firms invest in exploration, then send the prices
plummeting. Leave them low and the institutions fail, Americans lose their jobs and fail to pay loans. Financial institutions fall and the American government auctions the repossessed property for pennies on the dollar. There is an answer, but the president
will do nothing. A failure to act can only mean he is an accomplice to the fact.

Bush is a man that is so worried about others yards that he fails to take care of his own.

Unity and Freedom are the Reasons for English
(03.14.92)

This is in reaction to Andy Hernandez article on May 26, 1992. Your article will only breed ignorance and eventually destroy the few remaining freedoms we have. I'm sure politicians love your view, then they can take a small group of people to present their ideas to those who don't know English and persuade them to vote their way. How many times have you heard two sides of a story, with both being so diverse and different? With knowledge of English, Hispanics can understand both sides. It gives them greater latitude to choose for themselves. Learning English gives those people the opportunity to contribute to their country instead of being a burden. Being in the Engineering field I have seen Hispanics killed because of their lack of understanding of the English language. Is that what you want?

Understanding is Freedom and sometimes life. There are no obstacles if they understand English. Ignorance is poverty, desperation and eventually welfare. Food and shelter programs that burden everyone.

And Mr. Hernandez, why is there such a burning desire to vote, when there is no desire to understand the language of the country they have adopted? If they had the initiative and determination to learn English, like they have the desire to vote, there would be no need to have bilingual ballots. If you like history then you know when a country is so diverse with languages they falter and very seldom enjoy the freedoms we have come to expect. So I ask all guard our freedom. Is it too much to ask to **understand** English?

The most depressing thing in your article are the racist undertones. You seem to want to stir the cauldron of racial conflict. If your article is read it will continue to leave your people in squalor and poverty. Their ignorance is your power.

The article is written by a man with blinders. Never once did your article mention Koreans, Filipinos, Japanese, Chinese and European nationalities. In reality they are the minority and Hispanics are the majority! Isn't that strange. When we do a bilingual ballot which language do we choose? All I have ever heard is give it to the minorities. Well which one?

What do you suggest? I say English. Pride in the United States.

I am sick and tired of hearing, I'm Hispanic, I'm Mexican-American, I'm Afro-American, I'm Chinese-American. It goes on and on and on, with on end. If everyone is in such an all fired hurry to get to the United States, then why do they want to stay close to their past?

I can trace my ancestry to French, English and German. That's nice--but what am I? Black, White, Brown or Yellow? I am called something I have not heard in almost twenty five years. Something you never used **once** in your article. Maybe you don't know the words either. Mr. Hernandez let me tell you what I am lest one day we all forget these words:

I'm an **American** and damn proud of it! Are you?

I wrote the article about English in reply to Andy Hernandez article. What do you do? I'm not a violent person; I've never been to jail. But I'm becoming more and angrier with each passing day. Thank God for my writing which enables me to relieve my anger. The anger is aimed at judges, politicians and attorneys. Those three groups have put the United States in a position where it is about to collapse. The judges are worried about the rights of criminals and not the victims. The attorneys want to be able to sue if you walk or breathe--and they are winning! And the only way to understand politicians is to find a lip reader. Since Nixon not a president has kept his word. The Graham-Rudman act was the solution but they cast it aside. And now I hear once more we will be offered no choice. The president will be either Republican or Democrat--which is no choice. Remember they call it the Republican or Democratic "Party." Turn out the lights the "Party" is almost over. It's time to get down to "business" like Perot offered. An alternative. You don't have to be Nostradamus to predict the collapse of the United States government. It's already broke. One day the American people will wake to that startling realization.

As I watched Barbara Jordan sit on the expensive podium built with taxpayers money and heard her say "We bring you **change**," I realized it was a new word for more government and more taxes.

This system is sick. What the Unites States political system needs is a huge enema!

Sheila Jackson Lee
(04.01.92)
Equality, Quota or Quality?

What price must we pay before we return to quality. I'm really amazed at the comments that I hear from Councilwoman Sheila Jackson Lee and Joan Raymond.

I'm not sure I agree with police Chief Watson but I would like to defend her. First she was promoted through the ranks and she should know best who she would want to serve her in the positions she chooses. I don't care if she chooses all black or all women. In her position of law enforcement she has the right to have those she feels she can most rely on.

What Lee wants is quota and quantity without regards to quality. All I hear is numbers. She may be right there might be a dozen blacks equally qualified. Did Watson pass on blacks "more" qualified? If Lee wants to complain why didn't she question mayor Whitmire's choice of Lee Brown? Did she not question the choice because Brown is black? What Lee doesn't know is that it was an affront to her intelligence and other blacks in Houston by picking Brown. Why? Because Whitmire in essence said that out of 2 million people in Houston not a single person was qualified
to run the police department including blacks. Look at Whitmire's choice HISD Superintendent Joan Raymond. Again another person not from Houston. Why weren't people promoted through HISD? Are they not qualified? What incentive is there for teachers in HISD knowing that no matter how hard they work no one is qualified to run HISD. Unless they come from out of town. As long as we're talking about quotas let's talk about Whitmire's choices. How many heterosexual white males has she chosen? You don't hear white men complaining. The choices are hers.

Here is something for Lee to think about. What if quotas become law. Suppose when she runs for office she is required to hire 60% white. Real bummer, huh? If quotas were law we would have to fire almost 70% of the NBA black players. Football would have to fire 60% of their blacks and baseball would have to release 30% of their blacks. In sports they only play with the best and I'll be the first to admit that blacks are the best athletes. When it comes to mentality there are none better than Chinese and Japanese. What I'm trying to get at is that I would like to see quality as a reference instead of people like Lee using numbers.

Lee's own words make her out to be a bigot and sounds like she discriminates against whites. But I'm sure I just misunderstood her good intentions.

I find it strange that most ethnic groups do not demand equality through quotas like many Afro-Americans and Mexican Americans. When equal rights were guaranteed by the civil rights laws of the seventies it did not say give away everything to
obtain equality.

Everyone has the opportunity to reach the top through the efforts of their labors. The old saying holds true today, "You can lead a horse to water but you can't make it drink."

To answer Lee's obvious question, yes I'm white, but I believe a person is what he or she makes themselves. I'm in the engineering field in Houston and have had the opportunity to have as bosses a white female, black female, Pakistani, Mexican
American, black male, Iranian and Vietnamese. The black female was a wonderful person but I found the black male to be extremely prejudice against whites. Now the Vietnamese was a very interesting person. He escaped on a boat at the end of the Viet
Nam war. When he came to America he learned English, went to night school and became an Engineer. The opportunity was here but he didn't expect anything to be given to him.

I don't like people being given things if they do not work for it. I also want to let Lee know that I was married to a Filipino, engaged to a girl from El Salvador, dated one from Puerto Rico and also dated a black woman. I have a friend, Ruben whom I suppose you would call Mexican-American. I think of him as a Texan or an American. Strange word, "American", it's a word I've not heard in almost twenty years. But as for Ruben I call him "best friend."

There are two reasons that I'm writing this. One is that anyone chosen to an appointed position should come from this area, regardless of the color. There are enough qualified people in Houston.

The second might have to do more with Joan Raymond. Ever wonder why she doesn't want the Chronicle to see the scholastic records of her employees? I think I know. It's because she has something to hide.

A teacher friend of mine said that there was an opening for two principals. There were four nominees each from ten schools. Two were white and they were eliminated on the first round of questioning. That should please Lee.

Here's the problem. The same teacher received his Masters degree at Prairie View A & M. He said if you showed for the classes you received your degree. He said two of the students were black and that they could barely read English.

If this is part of the quotas then our schools are in real trouble. Is this what Raymond is hiding?

Someone needs to check on some of the degrees that students are receiving. Not only the college I just mentioned but the other colleges.

I hope I'm wrong. God I hope I'm wrong.

11
CLINTON THE CIGAR MASTER (1993-2000)

A man who won the presidency with only 43 percent of the popular vote.

A Way for Congress to Save Money
(02.06.94)
I have come up with an idea to save the federal government a lot of money. It is said that the average Senator spends about seven million dollars a year on staff, expenses, jaunts around the country and foreign fact finding missions. I'm sure it is close to the same for the House of Representatives.

We all know that each representative represents approximately 500,000 people. Since they appear unable to balance the budget or do their job I propose an idea that at least will help the taxpayer. Since members of the House of Representatives don't seem to represent their constituents then I propose there be one representative for every 1,000,000 people. This will cut expenses in half. Since they don't represent the 500,000 people they can just as easily not represent 1,000,000.

A Deal with the Devil
(4.11.94)
To have National Health Care is to put another huge financial burden on every American, lose some of our last rights as Americans, and to make another deal with the Devil--the Executive and Legislative branch of the United States of America.

Before we look at National Health Care, let's look at some of the other "deals" Americans have made with our government so we can better understand what we can look forward to.

Never have I seen such a loss of personal freedoms as I have under the last three Presidents. The Bill of Rights has been discarded like an uninteresting piece of trash. Using political lies and tricks Congress has stripped us of the right to bear arms, religious freedom, installed double jeopardy in trials and with the new income tax law done away with the "ex post facto" guaranteed to us by the Constitution of the United States of America.

Since Income tax was first enacted we have slowly lost our freedoms. Not that a tax wasn't needed, but look at the broken promises along the way. When has the government kept a promise? Income Tax was originally meant to tax the rich and only 6% of their income. Now it has expanded, giving the IRS powers such as to rival the Nazi Gestapo. Someone who becomes financially incapable is suddenly strapped with interest and penalties that would make loan sharks drool with envy. There is no debtors prison, only the IRS standing over all of us like a vulture waiting to pick our bones. Income Tax was a deal we made with the Devil.

Look at government programs and political "Pork Barreling," none of which has really helped the American people. For example the Federal government spends millions to speak against smoking, and millions to support the smoking industry. This is how our government supports both sides of every issue, which shows it would be cheaper if the government stayed out of everything. The government has spent to a point where it will never recover, yet politicians cast the debt aside like it doesn't exist and tell the American people to have confidence and trust the very politicians who have created the quagmire from which there is no escape. Read the back of the dollar bill; "In God we Trust." There is no mention of trusting politicians.

Listen to the terms; "Government Control," and "Fiscal Responsibility." All oxymoron's if I ever heard any. There is no control and no responsibility. The worst "deal with the Devil" is Social Security. Wake up America--the money is gone and no longer exists. While Federal officials bask in the luxury of entitlements they steal from the people struggling to pay, and survive, the extra taxes heaped upon them, yet Government employees and officials pay no Social Security. With a 4 trillion dollar debt how can anyone really believe Social Security exists? Where is that money? Our government has borrowed against it and has no intention of paying it back. Recently Clinton said two things that horrify me and seems to have brought no response from the American populous. First he said the government has control of the situation and cut the deficit 40%. Not true! Congress estimated the cost of government would exceed the collected taxes by 295 billion dollars for the year. When Clinton cut the estimated figure to 180 billion dollars, he told the American people he had cut the deficit by 40%. The American people lapped it up like a happy puppy. In reality we have added 180 billion dollars to the more than 4 trillion National Debt that is already owed. We will exceed the 180 billion because Congress uses an accounting method that does not include entitlements. At the end of Clinton's administration we will owe more than 6 trillion dollars. At that time, half the taxes we pay will go to service only the interest on the National Debt--that is if inflation doesn't hit and interest doesn't go up, then it could be worse. But what are the odds of interest going up and an increase in inflation with a Democrat as President?

Clinton also said he could not cut government spending because it would stymie the American economy. But a retroactive Income tax won't hurt? Added taxes on every aspect of American life won't affect the American economy? Wake up America before it is too late and you have no rights or money. The new tax will not only slow the economy, it is illegal. When Congress and Clinton passed the retroactive income tax they broke the laws of the Constitution, in Article 1, Section 9, which specifically states, "No Bill of Attainder or *ex post facto* Law shall be passed." Still no one has done anything to confront Congress, which means Americans don't care or they never took the time to read or understand one of the greatest documents of all time created for free men. Take time, if you care, and read carefully the Constitution and the first ten amendments--your Bill of Rights.

Now let's think about health care again. When Hillary Clinton spoke of health care, and people spoke against the idea, she became angry. Not the anger of one with an ideal, but one who was about to lose a large commission. What do you think will happen with a National Health care plan? National Health care will be no different than Income Tax or Social Security. Have you noticed the one thing they have not explained, is how we will pay for this health care? First Congress wants to sneak it through, then Congress will suck us in by telling us it will only be 3 or 4 percent. Next they will demand matching funds from our employers, and then they will increase the percentage to 6, 7 then 8 percent, along with the employers matching funds. All the while government spending will increase and Income Tax will not even pay for the interest on the National Debt.

Watch Congress: they are going to accomplish something no country, no spy and no traitor have ever accomplished--Congress has almost destroyed this great country! Ironically we will be destroyed from within by guileless, deceitful, greedy, selfish men, we have elected. Rightfully so, the men in Congress will see the demise of this country they say they love and vow to protect. We would be better off with Benedict Arnold, at least he knew where he stood and he fought for what he believed in. This can't be said for Congress. Find where the dollar goes and you'll find where your Congressman is. There is no way to stop a meteor when it enters the earth's atmosphere and there is no way to stop the

Federal government.

History repeats itself and so will the United States as it trips over the same mistakes made by all previous empires. When I write a novel, I put in foreshadowing for my reader so they can anticipate coming events. Russia in a way is foreshadowing of things to come for the United States. We are further in debt than Russia, so what does our government expect?

There are three solutions; the government can cut spending, cut taxes and balance the budget. On these points you can trust the government to do nothing as proven by the Graham-Rudman Bill, which was voted out as soon as it was enacted. For the bill to take effect, politicians would have lost too many of their entitlements, so this solution will never work. The second solution is simple; Democrats blame the Republicans and the Republicans blame the Democrats. Both sides are right. The only way to change the shape of things to come is to vote for neither Republicans nor Democrats and vote everyone currently in--out! Send them a message and vote for anyone other than these two parties. . . show them the party is over!

The third solution Congress already suspects, which is why they have given so much power to the IRS and ATF. With those two agencies active in the United States no group can stand against Congress. Finally with gun laws and retroactive taxes, they will be able to shut down all Americans, even if they rise up against the system. Government will only listen if there is a violent upheaval against the system and that may be hard to accomplish until everything is taken from us.

Congress reminds me of myself when I was 7 years old(and they have the same mentality as a 7 year old). I went with my mother to the hardware store and was amazed when she bought some things and left the store without paying. I asked her how she did it and she smiled and told me she charged it. Well for the next month I went in to the same hardware store and proceeded to charge two or three models and toys a week. I'll never forget the house shaking to my father's thunderous roar when he received the bill. When he asked me what happened, I told him not to worry because it didn't cost any money--I charged it! Well I got a good ass kicking, and brother that's what is in store for Congress.

For the last sixty years Congress has been like a parasite living off its host. Now Congress has become a cancerous malignancy killing its host, which will inevitably be its own destruction.

Einstein said it best, "For every action, there is an opposite and equal reaction." If that is true, then Congress had better start worrying about the reaction to the

National Debt. Imagine an opposite and equal reaction to the National Debt! Double digit inflation? It's coming! What about a debt so large the taxes collected won't cover the interest? It's coming! Remember what happened to the peso?

If our forefathers were alive now, there would be a rebellion to take our rights back. But the American people will do nothing, because they are too apathetic, an apathy that will eventually destroy this country like all great empires throughout history.

Wake up America before we have no rights and no power.

A final passing note:

A few weeks ago Senator Dole and Foley were on television discussing Whitewater. Both were quoted as saying, "Clinton should be held accountable."

Amazing. I'm not a Clinton fan, in fact I will side with no Republican or Democrat (unless they intend to limit government control, cut entitlements, cut spending by at least 20% and immediately restore common sense to our government), but to me it seems like all Clinton is guilty of is a bad investment and bad association.

I challenge both Dole and Foley and say the American people hold both of them and the rest of their cronies, Congress, guilty of stealing American liberty, breaking the laws of our Constitution, that they have sworn to uphold, and responsible and "accountable" for the American deficit that will never be paid off.

Joe Barfield

Congress Wants to Check Business
(02.06.96)

Recently, I have read Congress wants to investigate the business practices of major oil producers, specifically in the pricing increases of gasoline. Now I'm not too favorable to some of their previous practices of major layoffs and not appearing to care about individuals. But lets take a look at what we received when gas was a dollar a gallon.

The oil companies would explore for oil and find it. Next they would drill, recover and ship the crude oil. After this came the refining process, then distribution delivery and retail sales. All of this for only $.60 a gallon. That's right only $.60. So what of the other $.40 of the dollar? Taxes. And what do they provide the consumer? Nothing. Who should really be investigated? Since we appear to receive nothing for the taxes then the solution is simple. Since government does nothing for $.40 then why don't they take off $.20 of taxes per gallon and do a lot less of nothing.

The Hearst Corporation Editorial Department
(11.11.96)

For the first time you told the truth in an editorial on Thursday, November 7, 1996 when you wrote:

We believe the passage of the referendum is a wise embrace to an opportunity to help taxpayers and the public in general. In fact, those who opposed the referendum on the basis of the effect it might have on their taxes (which should be minimal) would have seen upward pressure on taxes come sooner had the proposition failed.

Does this mean that everything you printed on the vote for the proposition were untruths(I wouldn't want to accuse the Houston Chronicle of lying). All I read about was how there would be no new taxes. You and I both know that is an untruth. There was a large tax increase just before the election. To say there would be a tax increase sooner had we not decided to take on a nearly billion dollar debt is ludicrous and poor, very poor news reporting by a newspaper that many(sadly) rely on for honest and truthful reporting.

These are the facts. First an analogy:

When has a politician ever told the truth? They said no taxes to pay off the new stadium.

Second I don't think the overburdened taxpayers should be expected to pay for rich millionaires follies. If you are poor think about this. If a new domed stadium would make money do you honestly(oops there is that word again) think those wealthy sports owners would actually let us invest in a stadium? Absolutely not! So what does that mean? You don't have to be a genius(or the editorial department of a newspaper) to understand that the stadiums are a losing proposition. Also realize that every team owner in the NFL receives more than 100 million dollars each for their television rights. But that money is very important. It pays spoiled millionaire players who will probably not be on your team next year. That is called reality! Now the fans will be even less likely to be able to attend. Actually every taxpayer in Houston deserves a free ticket to a pro game of their choice since the taxes will be so much.

Since The Chronicle prints things colored in their favor let me tell you what to watch for; your water, electrical and gas bills. They will increase again. If you don't think so then ask somebody outside of Houston for their water bill. We pay a lot. And watch the Bonds. Bonds are a cover for large taxes to pay for political officials follies. Bonds are coming. Of course your local politicians will tell you it takes more to run a large city. False. It shouldn't take more, after all it is just a proportion that goes up as do the people. The only reason it takes more is because of fiscal irresponsibility. If they are telling the truth then we shouldn't annex Kingwood or any other area. If we remain smaller so will our taxes. Maybe we should cut Houston into four areas and really lower our taxes. No, it makes too much sense so it will never happen. Logically, politicians should be made to operate within their tax base or be removed from office. Spock would never stand for this; it is too illogical. Remember the analogy when they come to defend themselves with double talk: When has a politician every told the truth? Is the Houston Chronicle a politician, or do they report the news without their own personal slant?

When Oil Companies Were Good
(6.02.96)

Recently, I have read Congress wants to investigate the business practices of major oil producers, specifically in the pricing increases of gasoline. Now I'm not too favorable to some of their previous practices of major layoffs and not appearing to care about individuals. But let's take a look at what we received when gas was a dollar a gallon.

The oil companies would explore for oil and find it. Next they would drill, recover and ship the crude oil. After this came the refining process, then distribution delivery and retail sales. All of this for only $.60 a gallon. That's right only $.60. So what of the other $.40 of the dollar? Taxes. And what do they provide the consumer? Nothing. Who should really be investigated? Since we appear to receive nothing for the taxes then the solution is simple. Since government does nothing for $.40 then why don't they take off $.20 of taxes per gallon and do a lot less of nothing.

A letter to Bud Adams
(02.20.98)

A lawsuit against the NFL and Houston Oilers on behalf of Houston and Houston fans.

The points of the lawsuit I want to address are, defamation of character against the city of Houston and Houston fans, and extortion and breach of verbal contract by Tagliabue for the NFL.

I want to leave Greenbay exempt from the lawsuit because it is owned by the city of Greenbay.

DEFAMATION OF CHARACTER:

A Houston Oiler preseason game was canceled because of a lump in the carpet of the Astrodome. I believe this was a ploy to embarrass and humiliate the city of Houston by the NFL on behalf of Bud Adams to enable Adams to obtain a new stadium or to make the move to Nashville easier.

Points:

1. When was the last NFL game canceled because of carpet? When was the last NFL game canceled?

2. To show this was with malicious intent I only have to point to numerous games played in San Francisco on wet fields with holes that looked like they had been dug with shovels. I also point to the frozen fields of Greenbay in playoff games against Dallas during the 60's where the field was frozen and players actually had frostbite. These games and many others were never canceled.

EXTORTION:

1. Bud Adams threatened to leave Houston unless changes were made to the Astrodome and even Tagliabue hung the carrot of a Superbowl if the city of Houston paid $53 million dollars to make the changes. Upon completion and removal of the famous fireworks sign, Bud Adams declared the Astrodome not good enough and even Tagliabue suddenly said the Astrodome was too old. Now they want more by issuing a threatening ultimatum to Denver that they will be like Houston if a new stadium is not built. I say let Houston be the first city to show the NFL what happens if they do not abide by their word.

BREACH OF VERBAL CONTRACT:

1. Representing the NFL, Tagliabue promised to bring a Superbowl to the city of Houston if the Astrodome was renovated. Now the NFL has backed down from its promise. I understand a Superbowl brings revenues of up to $200 million dollars to a city where the game is played. These are actual damages.

I propose a lawsuit on behalf of the city of Houston and Houston fans--by the fans. I don't believe a single fan can file a lawsuit so appeal to season ticket holders through the newspapers to get signatures of disgruntled fans and file a class action suit. I believe the damages are real and the $53 million could be collected in triple damages just as the breach of contract for $200 million.

To get the NFL's attention an injunction should be filed to freeze all monies paid by Fox, NBC, CBS and ABC until the lawsuit is settled using the point some teams may file bankruptcies to side step paying the lawsuit. We can freeze future assets paid by the networks. If this works we can definitely get the attention of the NFL owners.

We Will Buy a New Stadium
(02.20.98)

Why should we pay $250 million for a stadium that will only be used 8 times a year that is if we get a football team. Or 82 times a year if baseball stays. Contrary to popular belief a city can survive without pro teams. Lets build the arts and bring activities to Houston. Besides the lack of attendance at Houston Pro Games proves that people do have other things they do. Mayor Lanier is wrong when he says we will not have to pay for a stadium. We will pay and the heavy expenses of such a project will just be another burden on people who cannot afford it and are already unable to attend sports they cannot already afford. How come we do not build a new skyscraper or office complex for companies like Pennzoil, Exxon or Compaq? After all they do provide income and jobs in Houston 365 days a year.

If people like Roberto Alomar are considered role models we may have to change our priorities. Sadly Alomar is a direct reflection of most of baseball, football and basketball owners; disrespectful, arrogant, selfish, rude and greedy. They have no honor or character. There are no more Nolan Ryan's or Joe Montana's. The message Alomar and many others like him send to our children is loud and clear: If you are a pro-athlete and wealthy you can do anything you want and not get punished.

The Clinton Chronicles
(08.17.98)

Editor of the Houston Chronicle

I take exception to the article by Gore Vidal on Sunday. His article is a contradiction of statements all slanted in the direction of his opinion. He degrades many politicians and portions of the United States Government while praising the health issue by Mrs. Clinton. What I disliked most was the statement that 90 percent of those polled confessed to being habitual liars. The pole was obviously taken by members of a prison institution or the United States Congress. It's sad to think Mr. Vidal appears to agree with this survey. A little common sense if this is true will tell him his defense of the President is useless since he too obviously falls in the 90 percent category like Vidal himself.

Adultery appalls me but I want to say to President Clinton and other politicians that I along with most Americans are open minded enough to forgive the President for his indiscretion if it be true. If the accusations are true and he had come out and admitted his affair I could have accepted it and expected him to continue running the country unhindered.

That is not what happened. Even if the President is innocent I keep asking why he tried to side step every legal move by Starr. If he was innocent and confronted Starr head on this thing could have been over a year ago.

Some people say he is running the country fine so leave him alone and forget it. Hillary says she knows he is innocent and done nothing wrong. She said the same thing with Flowers. If the President is making advances with the women he meets and sleeping with the interns he bumps into, then I ask, "When does he have time to run the country?"

I have another problem with adultery. Those that commit adultery are sneaks, cheats and liars. I'm sure everybody knows that.

One more thing; I have found those I know that have committed adultery conduct themselves the same way on the job. If this is true then President Clinton is doing the same thing to the American people he is doing to his wife and most important Chelsea. In my eyes if the accusations are true he has also lost his honor and integrity.

Countries have come and gone but there have always been families. If you have no honor with your family and cannot be trusted by them then who can believe in you and trust you.

The Chronicle Editor,

The Chronicle's almost full front page article in Outlook by Gore Vidal upsets me immensely. If Vidal is correct is saying 90 percent of people are habitual liars then the only thing the Chronicle prints that is true are the comics and the sports page. It also means the President lied again. But wait that is false you can't lie if you don't say anything. Listen to his words again and you will understand. I think the movie Contact illustrates what I mean when Clinton talks in the movie and you realize he could be talking about anything and never says what he is talking about.

Another problem: Forget his indiscretion and go on. I agree with that--but how many indiscretions do you get? Flowers, Jones, Lewinsky. I don't see an indiscretion, I see a pattern.

I hear the President is doing a fine job. What has he done? I'm sure he could have done a better job if the Secret Service wasn't always protecting the door behind which President Clinton was doing his job with the intern. I find it hard to believe Monica is the only one.

Another thing--the money Starr spent in the investigation. It seems if Hillary had answered questions about the Whitewater affair to begin with instead of papers mysteriously disappearing and reappearing the investigation could have ended earlier. Remember that the Monica thing would never have surfaced if the Jones thing had never happened. Again Clinton should have answered the questions a year ago. Starr was not the problem.

Now to the Democrats and Republicans--you are becoming the laughing stock of the World. If nothing is done to Clinton than there is nothing sacred about the Presidency of the United States of America and the sooner people start voting you out the better. Show your moral character one way or the other.

I think it's so sad it's funny. You know we say Xerox when in reality it is copy and Kleenex when in reality it is tissue paper. Soon Republican will be associated with; sneak, cheat and liar. Democrat will be associated with adultery. Maybe that association has already been made.

There are only two problems with this country and they are not Clinton and Starr. They are Republicans and Democrats.

If Gore Vidal is correct, then the United States of America is truly facing its greatest crisis.

P. S. On the lighter side. If the President wants work after his term expires he should apply for a position on Melrose Place. On that show they all sleep with each other and never tell the truth.

Clinton Wags the Dog

(12.07.98)

Day before yesterday Saddam Hussein moved into check mate. It was the best thing for Congress and the president of the United States.

Congress can now smile and tell their constituents that they were about to do the right thing for the people in regards to Clinton. They won't say what it was they were going to do but the people being naive and apathetic will believe their representative was about to impeach or leave in office the president as they believe, when in actuality the words will be vague and misleading. Remember what they say will be misleading and false but not a lie.

It is against the Constitution of the United States to remove a President from office during war or a National Emergency.

Here are my predictions.

The president will declare a state of emergency that can last for a year. He will bomb Iraq at least one more time in the next three weeks. This will enable him to carry through for the year and tell the people it is a national emergency because he is afraid of retaliation and the U. S. must be prepared. Don't be surprised if there is a retaliation. Each time we bomb Iraq the sentiment for Hussein and against the U. S. grows. Contrary to what Americans think Hussein is a hero over there for standing against the U. S.

But here is a more terrifying thought. Here is my analogy.

In 1898 it was said the United States blew up the U. S. S. Maine to get national sympathy for the war against Spain. President Johnson orchestrated the Gulf of Tonkin incident to gain favor for him in the re-election against Goldwater. Both incidents worked. What I am afraid of is that something might be orchestrated in New York, Houston, or Los Angeles to gain sympathy for the president without regards to American lives or property. A terrible thought but keep that in mind when something happens over here in the next year.

Impeachment

((01.08.99)

First of all lets tell it like it is--the President will not be Impeached. You ask why? The answer is relatively simple but I think I should use an analogy everybody will understand. We will compare Clinton to the Gary Graham, the prisoner on death row. Graham keeps saying he is innocent even after all the witnesses continue to say to the contrary and one even remembers being shot by Graham when he did the killing. Now Graham is angry that they don't let him go and has promised violence and maybe even death to others to prove his point. Sounds like Clinton. In Graham's case he is now preaching what he practiced. Just like Clinton's assistants, Graham has Glover and others protecting him; people that don't know what happened, won't confront the victims and scream racism. They even say Graham may have done those things and maybe killed someone else but not the one he is going to the death chamber for. Same for Clinton who may have misled us and not told the truth--but he never lied. And like Graham screaming racism, Clinton screams Republicans. When I listen to him I realize that as long as there are Republicans and Democrats there will be racism.

Suppose they decided to give Graham a new trial. And suppose those on the jury were all of those on death row with Graham. Now what do you suppose the decision would be? With Congress voting what do you think the outcome will be this time?

This trial will be a lot about morality in America. The poles say 70 or 80 percent of the people say leave him alone. I'm not sure who takes the poles or where they are taken but for this countries sake I hope they are wrong. If Clinton had done these things at any company in America he would already have been removed. He said it is private and nobodies business. What he did was done on the job. I know of people that were removed from their jobs because of sex with employees after job hours. Aren't laws passed and enforced by Congress for the people and Congress, including the President.

Clinton knows so well the laws and how to use his words, but turns everything around when it points to him. The affair is not as critical as the perjury although I think the perjury is worse. I have a flaw because I love my country but my children and wife are first. I believe that is the way it should be. So if you will commit adultery and lie to your wife, what will you do to your country. Clinton's integrity and honor have been misplaced. I hear people say it was an incident. It was an incident during his presidency but after all of the women that have been paraded before us I call it, not an incident but a pattern.

I heard people say well Jefferson and Washington did it. At that time it was acceptable as were slaves and women denied the right to vote. Times have changed; slavery is not acceptable, discrimination against race and sex is unacceptable---and, I hope, adultery, is not to be condoned. I think adultery can be forgiven and put aside so people can move on. But how many affairs do you forgive before you say enough? But perjury? It can be neither tolerated nor forgiven.

If Clinton wanted to save the Democratic Party, if he had one bit of integrity and honor remaining, he would step down. I hear people laugh at the words "family values" when the Democratic Party is mentioned.

It is up to Congress, specifically the Senate, to speak out against adultery and perjury. Like Graham being tried by those on death row the President of the United States watches. Now Congress can show us the consistency of their honor, integrity and morality as they vote on Impeachment. The people are watching.

12
BUSH BRING IT ON, THEY DID (2001-2008)
(Georgie the second or the double Bush-whacking of America)

911 The Attack
(09.11.01)

On September 11, 2001, I was on a flight from Seattle to Houston when word reached us about the World Trade Center and the Pentagon. Less than thirty minutes out, the captain made an announcement saying a plane had hit one of the World Trade Center towers. At first people laughed—including me—as we all wondered how a small plane might have hit one of the towers. Then, a few minutes later the captain made another announcement.

"We have terrible news," the pilot said. "Another commercial airliner has hit the other Twin Tower in New York. We're sorry but when we land in Houston this flight will not continue and you will need to reschedule your flight."

I can still remember the shock, horror and terror on the faces of many of the passengers on that flight. Speculation ran rampant on the plane as to who had done this terrible thing. We still knew nothing. One of the passengers thought China had attacked us, another thought it might be Russia, while a few guessed it to be drug dealers from Colombia since we had just arrested the leader from one of their major cartels.

I assured them it wasn't Russia or China since they depended on our business to help their countries. There was also no way it could have been Colombia because whoever had done such a thing committed suicide and no drug dealer was willing to sacrifice his life.

"Then who could have done this?" someone asked me.

I responded with my own thoughts. "Whoever did this was someone who was willing to die for what he wanted. I'm probably wrong because the last time something like this happened it was Oklahoma City and many thought it was someone from the Middle East when it actually turned out to be an American. But I think I know who might have been involved. I've been reading and writing about a man, Osama bin Laden. His dream has been to destroy the World Trade Center. It is said he was associated with the Twin Towers bombing a few years ago. I'm probably wrong, but if I were to pick someone who was responsible for what has happened, Osama bin Laden would be my first choice."

Most of those listening looked at me like I was crazy.

Again the captain made an announcement that sent fear and chills through everyone. "Ladies and Gentlemen, another airliner has crashed into the Pentagon. President Bush has ordered all aircraft to return to their points of origin. We are to return to Seattle immediately. You will need to make arrangements for your connecting flights."

Everyone was talking, all were scared, and each time the plane hit a bump in the sky, some of the passengers would scream.

To me it was obvious there would be no more flights. I spoke loudly to those around me, "Think about this. The president has ordered us to return. Whatever has happened, it's very serious. Before there can be any more flights they must first figure out who did it, how they did it and how do we stop it? There won't be any flights today, tomorrow or for days. When I get back to Seattle I'm driving back to Houston. Who wants to go with me?"

Again they looked at me like I was some kind of nut, but many were lost in their own chaotic thoughts and fears. Something tragic and terrible had happened and we only knew what we had heard from the captain.

I added, "And when the flights do start again do you really want to be the first to test the airways? I don't. I'm driving back to Houston."

The flight returned to Seattle and when we disembarked it looked like the people were running from a fire. Fear and terror showed in all their faces. Everyone was deserting the airport. I went to the closest phone and started dialing. Two people, Rich and Maggie Pyle, approached me and asked if I was really driving back to Houston. I assured them I was. They also started calling for a car. In less than thirty minutes we were getting into one of the last rentals. It was so strange to see the rental garage void of all but two cars. It was empty. Never in my life have I ever seen an airport so deserted. We started our journey to Houston.

Upon arriving in Houston I contacted the FBI and told them what I had written and that I believed there were plans to do even more hideous things to America. They never returned my call. The reason I contacted them was simple. For more than fourteen years I had been putting together my novel *Moon Shadow*, studying the minds of terrorists and what they might do. In my book I had detailed numerous terrorist acts against our country.

There are things described in *Moon Shadow* that have not yet occurred. Will some of these events be like Desert Storm, the *Aurora Project* and the September 11, 2001, attacks? Will they too come to pass?

Our American military marches to victory not much differently than did the British troops in their bright red uniforms more than two hundred years ago. At that time the British were unbeatable, but they lost. Now America is unbeatable but has exposed its Achilles' heel. There is still time to correct it before it's too late. Not unlike the British Empire, George W. Bush and his American Empire are headed for the same fate.

You say, "Impossible! You are wrong!" I hope so. After all, *Moon Shadow* is only a work of fiction, but it is said truth is stranger than fiction. And don't forget what we were taught when we were in school: History repeats itself.

The Problem
(06.27.02)

It seems to me that America is losing its "Honor and Integrity." With a President that wants to blow up any country of his choice and also wants to shove democracy down which every country he decides unless they sell us oil and now CEO's that are more dangerous than Osama Bin Laden our future may be in serious trouble. We also contend with accountants that do creative accounting. They remind me of an accountant that said since he worked from six to six and gets 12 hours a day he was going to start working from seven to seven because that was 14 hours. I call that real creative accounting, not much different than that used by ENRON and WorldCom. There just seems to be no more honor or integrity in politicians, CEO's or accountants. These three groups are beginning to give attorneys good names.

AND NOW we have to deal with someone who is offended with the word God, so not to offend that one individual we have decided to ban the Pledge of Allegiance. I guess he calls himself an American. You know the dollar will be next. I'm beginning not to trust judges either. Well I just want to tell those judges that I'm offended by their decision. What are they going to do for me? When I went to Russia and they saluted their flag at an event I stood with them and also saluted their flag. Not out of disrespect for America but out of courtesy and respect for the friends and the country I was visiting. I was in Saudi and my Muslim friends prayed to Mecca. I got down with them out of respect for their beliefs even though I am Christian. This man that is offended should be honored to be able to say the Pledge of Allegiance and he should do it for honor and respect of the country that is his. He simply has no honor or respect for America and is just another selfish American. I'm sure he enjoys the money he has and would not be offended if you gave him more even though it says "In God we Trust." And one comment about the Judge. In my opinion he is un-American and he has taken my "God" given rights away. If Washington and Jefferson were alive they would be ashamed of what the country they created has now become. They would not stand for it.

Here is the real problem. Politicians, judges and attorneys have been so busy protecting each individual's rights that they have taken all of our rights away.

I DON'T UNDERSTAND
(04.03.02)

From the dawn of time, since man's creation or humble beginnings, whatever they might be, man has been able to reason, which has put him above all other creatures. I can still see the first man when he stuck his finger into fire and it burned him. Immediately he explained to all of his companions the danger and consequences of fire. He did not say because. And for that reason I do not understand. Since that time in history man's common sense has become clouded and jaded. Reasoning and common sense has been replaced by greed, selfishness and blind compliance. Never have I seen this more present than in America.

Common sense was still present when our forefathers wrote the Declaration of Independence, Bill of Rights and the Constitution of the United States of America. But those that profess to defend those very documents that are the very core of our freedom actually tear it to shreds. It's like an unknown disease has taken over and taken away all common sense. Sadly this applies to most Americans. Americans follow their leaders with only "blind faith." Blind faith is good when it is applied to something like God because his rules are common sense; don't steal, cheat, kill or murder. But the leaders ask you to follow them and charge to your potential death. If you look behind you and remember their words, "follow us" the very first question I would ask is why are they not leading and why are they staying behind in such fine conditions while I charge ahead to serve and protect while the possibility of death loom over my head. Now you are saying yeah sure, uh huh. Like the caveman that burned his finger let me give you examples. The one I enjoy the most is when I hear Americans scream with anger, "This is the best country in the world." The first thing I have always asked them is, "What other countries have you visited?" Strangely the answers have almost been identical when they snap, "I haven't been to any country but this is the best one in the world." I think those words fall in the category of, "just because." Words spoken without reason or understanding. As an example I think Costa Rica, Belize and the Caymans are far better places. Think for a moment about what I said in the last sentence. If you are an American who does not think, then you had a reaction to the sentence where I mentioned other countries. The reaction is typical of Americans who don't think anymore. You thought, "If you don't like America then get out!" And your thoughts betrayed the anger you felt. So I ask of you, what other countries have you visited?

Channel your anger in the right directions and one day you might be able to save your country.

Abortion is a tough issue and I don't want to go there. The pros and cons could be discussed all day long and we will never reach an answer. My problem is when I heard an anti-abortionist say that to kill a doctor who would perform an abortion is okay. I don't want to sound biased one way or another but isn't murder just that—murder? In doing so those that murder the doctors undermine the very foundation this country stands on.

Drugs. Now there is an issue. We demand every country in this hemisphere stop the flow of drugs. We literally give away billions to stop drugs from coming to the United States. Yet we pamper drug users as though they were a newborn child. Second chances given to actors and athletes are equal to the times they are caught. Common sense says punish them. Funny thing, my wife is from Colombia and she told me they hated drugs in Colombia and then she asked me something I will never forget. "Why do Americans keep buying drugs?"

Guns have always been a right given to us through the Bill of Rights. It's a guarantee, just like speech and religion. If you studied history and understand why it was put in the Bill of Rights then you know there is a reason it exists. When the right to bear arms is taken away, then the Bill of Rights will no longer exist and the foundation of freedom will crumble away. When the first stone is pulled away the others will soon crumble and fall away. If we let them take this freedom away the others will also be taken away. The Bill of Rights should never be tampered with or changed. Only men without commonsense will want to take your rights away.

The people of our country are no longer represented by those they have elected because their representation is purchased through the lobbyist while our freedoms are taken away through the donations to your favorite candidate.

Intelligence didn't Find Saddam
(12.14.03)

Intelligence didn't find Saddam Hussein, it was an accident, but he was caught nonetheless.

I want you to get a vivid picture, in your mind, of Saddam being captured. Got it? Did this look like a man who had been protected and living in luxury in Syria? I don't think so.

Two days ago President Bush's intelligence (the same ones that told us about

WMD's) said they have proof Syria is 1) helping terrorists 2) letting Saddam Hussein's men and money cross the "unprotected" border (Bush needs to look at the Rio Grande) 3) and was protecting Saddam Hussein. Because of these President Bush issued an order to sanction Syria for its inappropriate behavior.

Now I'm not a fan of terror or even the Mid-East for that matter, but I think people are important no matter whom they are. It seems a little harsh to sanction a country that has done nothing they have been accused.

I'm curious, who runs the intelligence that Bush always refers to? Shouldn't they be fired or dismantled?

What the President said yesterday really burns me!!
(12.12.03)
Before the attack on Iraq I tried to tell people in the engineering business the war was for oil. No one would listen. I'm in engineering and have worked for a variety of companies that do work for Halliburton.

Now we learn that Halliburton is overcharging for gas in Iraq. That's not the half of it. I was asked to go over there three days after the invasion to do estimates on the damage and cost of build back. I was offered $10,000 a week. I said no. But people went over there. Most of them are in Kuwait sitting in offices doing nothing. Think about it. The people sent over there are making from 6 to 10 thousand (or more) a week. Halliburton marks that up and charges double. How long will we let this continue? It must have been Halliburton that said, "The hardest part of doing nothing is knowing when you're finished."

Forget the gasoline that Halliburton charged double. And think about this, the Army Corp of Engineers has done most of the engineering done in Iraq. Where was Halliburton? There's more.

While our troops defended Halliburton, the same company was sending American jobs to India. Most of the people I know that worked for Halliburton were laid off and their jobs sent to India.

Yesterday, President Bush said France, Germany or countries that didn't help in the war would get none of the jobs to be done in Iraq. I don't have a problem with that but—if this is the case then Halliburton should not get any work either. Tell me how much help India sent us in Iraq?

Americans troops are giving up their lives to protect a company that at heart is worse than France or Germany could ever be made out to be.

President Bush has failed the American people. So to President Bush I say, "You're either with us or with them!"

His actions have already answered us.

Take a moment and think about it.
(6.09.03)
Some people were for the war with Iraq and some were against it. Regardless of your side or roll Americans should always back the troops. The troops fight for what they believe in.

But the leaders of our country, now that is another thing. The word was Iraq had weapons of mass destruction, including biological, chemical and nuclear. To make dirty bombs like President Bush told us about you need to have radioactive waste material. There was one site at Tuwaitha that held uranium ore. Let me remind you radioactive uranium ore is a primary ingredient to make bombs. And that's what bothers me. While we were being reminded every day of WMD's and the horror of radioactive dirty bombs, nothing was being done to seize the plant and radioactive material at Tuwaitha. We had no problem using American troops to secure the more than 1100 oil wells, but, and let me repeat, but we could not spare a few troops do secure an area ripe to construct and build WMD's. Why you ask? Oil probably, but obviously nobody cared about Tuwaitha. Now Halliburton did secure the Iraqi oil wells and did get paid almost a half billion dollars for the work that was mostly done by American troops. Granted Hussein was a tyrant but what about the WMD's? Obviously President Bush and Rumsfeld must have felt he had no WMD's. If they truly believed Hussein had WMD's they would surely have prevented Tuwaitha from being looted.

Of course we all know no weapons of mass destruction have been found. Before the war Rumsfeld and Bush always said they had proof of WMD's. All along I would ask, "What is that information? Show the American people." Without the proof President Bush said he had all along, then the whole war becomes a charade and it appears he knew all along there was nothing. Except of course oil.

They say what goes around comes around. Today President Bush asked for patience and wants the people to give him time to prove he was right. Funny that's the same thing the UN weapons inspectors asked President Bush to give them.

Rumsfeld and War
(4.11.03)

Rumsfeld saying, "Stuff happens," is proof we are only there for the oil and not the people like he originally said. Look at his face when he said it. He has no concern for any person what so ever. He says we are there for the people but order and control is one of those things vital for the survival and growth of a new democracy. If you don't care about the people then you don't care about freedom or democracy. A comment like his can only mean his agenda is black gold. If he was really concerned about the people and their freedom things would be done. Not things like giving Halliburton a large contract. You can rest assured the 1300 wells are safe from looters and under the protection of heavy military forces. Are our American troops fighting to conquer a people or free those people from an evil tyrant. If anarchy prevails then our valiant soldiers died for nothing but secret agendas of a group of people we never elected. If we can destroy a country in three weeks then we can help the people. If each Iraqi had an oil well in his back yard they would all be safe. If freedom of the Iraqi people is paramount on the agenda of Bush's people then I assume BP will not be moving into Iraq.

Letter to Mike Moore
(6.27.03)

Mike,

Please do not use my name because it will cost me my job, but so much is going on I just can't stand it. I work on the North Slope doing engineering for the oil industry. I have seen and learned things that I really don't even want to tell you. But that would also make me apathetic like most others. I voted for Bush but in all honesty I could never vote for him again.

Some people were for the war with Iraq and some were against it. Regardless of your side or roll Americans should always back the troops. The troops fight for what they believe in. But the leaders of our country, now that is another thing. The word was Iraq had weapons of mass destruction, including biological, chemical and nuclear. Of course we all know no weapons of mass destruction have been found. Before the war Rumsfeld and Bush always said they had proof of WMD's. All along I would ask, "What is that information? Show the American people." Without the proof President Bush said he had all along, then the whole war becomes a charade and it appears he knew all along there was nothing. Except of course oil. To make dirty bombs like President Bush told us about you need to have radioactive waste material. There was one site at Tuwaitha that held uranium ore. Let me remind you radioactive uranium ore is a primary ingredient to make bombs. And that's what bothers me. While we were being reminded every day of WMD's and the horror of radioactive dirty bombs, nothing was being done to seize the plant and radioactive material at Tuwaitha. We had no problem using American troops to secure the more than 1100 oil wells, but, and let me repeat, but we could not spare a few troops do secure an area ripe to construct and build WMD's. Why you ask? Oil probably, but obviously nobody cared about Tuwaitha. Halliburton, or actually the military for Halliburton, did secure the Iraqi oil wells and did get paid almost a half billion dollars for the work that was mostly done by American troops. I would like to see Halliburton's itemized bill. And what about our Army Corp of Engineers? Why didn't they do what they were trained for?

Granted Hussein was a tyrant but what about the WMD's? Obviously President Bush and Rumsfeld must have felt he had no WMD's. If they truly believed Hussein had WMD's they would surely have prevented Tuwaitha from being looted. The war was well planned. Two days after the invasion started I was called and asked to go to Iraq for Halliburton to survey structural damage and make estimates for re-construction.

This is the worse part. Here is a statement by a Halliburton spokesperson:

Halliburton's spokeswoman Wendy Hall said, "KBR is proud to assist with the restoration of Iraq's oil infrastructure, which is the fuel for the country's economic recovery."

Halliburton is laying off Americans in Houston and sending the jobs to India. They are friends of mine being laid off. I wonder how many of the people in India are Al-Qaeda? What about the infrastructure and economic recovery of the United States? Isn't our country important?

BP wants to pull off the Alaskan slope because they have been offered a big piece of the pie in Iraq. Do you know why it so lucrative over there? The word is that Halliburton and BP will get 35%(not sure) of the residuals of the Iraqi oil for the next 25 years and they are not required to conform to any EPA standards with their construction. To me it seems the air they breathe over there is just as important as the air over here. And so are their lives. Something Halliburton does not seem concerned with.

One more thing. Congress needs to take back the power to declare war and try to keep Bush and the wild ones in check.

If you know how to contact Toby Keith, let me know and I will send him this letter.

Sincerely,

Joe Barfield

President Bush Lies

(10.10.03)

Where is Osama Bin Laden?

Where is Saddam Hussein?

Why are we still in Afghanistan?

Who said, "We must attack them before they can harm us because they pose a danger to everyone in our country!"

Give up? Bush? No you're way off. Hitler said that to the German people before he invaded France. See any similarities?

Condoleezza Rice said, "We have proof Saddam Hussein did not get rid of his weapons!!" Duh, how stupid does she think we are? How can you get rid of something you didn't have? The citizens of Iraq have killed more Americans than all of the Iraq military. Where are the weapons? There were none.

Why are we giving more money to Iraq for schools than we do for our own American children?

President Bush says they have information that Iraq "tried" to buy 10 million dollars of rockets from Korea and that is good enough reason to invade. Let's see most of the rockets fired at Iraq by our military cost more than a million dollars each. One more thing think of the 10 million dollars to buy rockets and then remember that it takes us a billion dollars a day to keep our military over in Iraq. And that's not fighting that's just there. Remember what Saddam Hussein "tried" to spend, we spend more than a hundred times that amount each day in Iraq.

President Bush says they have information that Iraq "tried" to buy rockets from Korea and that is good enough reason to invade. Also, Iran had nuclear capabilities and that Qatar is harboring Al Qaeda. Also Israel has proof that Syria is giving haven to terrorists. BUT DID YOU KNOW, that this information is supplied by the same people that provided all the accurate information about Saddam Hussein's WEAPONS OF MASS DESTRUCTION! More food for thought. How can Bush have so much information about the world and attack counties around the world but he doesn't know who leaked information from his own office about a CIA agent? Makes you wonder doesn't it? If he can't protect one of the people supplying him information how will he ever protect us? There is one more even more terrifying thought. President Bush and his people did it on purpose and risked the life of an American trying to protect the United States. That thought is far more fiendish than anything Saddam Hussein has ever done because Bush is supposed to stand on the side of the righteous and dedicated to protecting "ALL" Americans.

There is nothing wrong with what Bush is doing. We did the same thing to the buffalo and the Indians. Now we need oil.

Did you know that Halliburton had received almost 1 billion dollars for the work they "haven't" done. Their employees sit in Kuwait waiting to do something.

All you will hear about are the things the Army Corp of Engineers have done. Also while American soldiers lose their lives protecting the interests of Halliburton, their subsidiaries are sending engineering jobs to India.

President Bush said that things are really good in Iraq and that 90 percent of the problems are happening in only 10 percent of the country of Iraq. He is absolutely correct but what he failed to tell everyone is that Iraq is mostly a desert and that 90 percent of the people live in 10 percent of the country. To make a comparison it is like saying there have been no murders in the Bonneville Salt Flats of Nevada. But then nobody lives in the Salt Flats.

President Bush's "Road Map to Peace in the Mideast" does not seem to apply to Israel. Actually as I watch the events that transpire in that part of the world I think the "Road Map to Peace in the Mideast" was written by Israel.

What about Valerie Palme the CIA agent whose cover was blown by insiders in the Bush administration? Who are they? You can't tell me Bush doesn't know.

Here are some quotes from the Bush Administration that that really make you wonder. If he doesn't know who leaked the information how does he hope to conduct a war half way around the world

On finding Osama Bin Laden in Central Asia:
"We're going to hunt them down one at a time. . . it doesn't matter where they hide, as we work with our friends we will find them and bring them to justice."
--President George W. Bush, 11/22/02

On finding Saddam Hussein in the Mideast:
"We are continuing the pursuit and it's a matter of time before [Saddam] is found and brought to justice."
--White House spokesman McClellan, 9/17/03

On finding the leaker in the close confines of the White House:
"I don't know if we're going to find out the senior administration official. I don't have any idea."
--President George W. Bush, 10/7/03

American Freedom
(01.23.04)
When you refuse to show the views of others you have done away with freedom of speech. But CBS has done something even worse. When you lobby and receive special advantages over others and then favor those passing laws to promote your own interest then you have become no better than companies like Enron. Part of your responsibility to all Americans is to show the news and the views of the people. CBS has failed to do this. You have now taken a giant step toward a government controlled media. The next thing we know you will only show the views represented by the President and not those of other parties. Our fore fathers would be ashamed to see how what CBS has become just for money and favors. It makes me think about the news you broadcast now and I wonder if it is the truth anymore. You are obligated to view both sides and show us that you truly are Americans and believe in truth and freedom of speech. If you view this information against the President as controversial you need to step back and look at all the obvious untruths told to us by the President of the United States. His actions tend to lean more in the direction of a dictator. I suppose you can't let the

democrats talk either since they are against the President. One more thing I voted for President Bush but what he has done in the last year has appalled me. I also want to let you know that thanks to what CBS has done there is no way I can morally vote for Bush in the next election. Remember while American soldiers sacrifice their lives to protect our basic freedoms, including yours, you deny those same freedoms to the American people.

Congress Let Bush Declare War
(01.29.04)

The actions of President Bush show the reasons Congress is endowed with the power to declare war. Ironically the people never elected the people running the country. What President Bush and his cabinet are doing is the same thing we did to the Indians and the Buffalo. What is most terrifying is the dangerous rhetoric President Bush throws about. Now Bush has information on Iran and Syria, yet that information is provided by the same people that had undeniable proof of Iraq's "Weapons of Mass Destruction." The same people we had trusted to give us accurate information are now leaking information about a CIA agent. If he can't protect his own people how does he expect to protect the American people? The fact is we are at war. There is something you must always accept when you go to war. You must be willing to die for what you believe in. Contrary to what most Americans seem to believe when they watch television is the enemy has the right to kill you back. There was no diplomacy and I can guarantee you they are angry. The enemy doesn't have rockets, or planes so think about what is coming. President Bush's lies will kill Americans.

A Diplomatic Withdrawal is Impossible.
(5.27.04)

War and aggression never has been and never will be a solution. This war was wrong before it started. I thought America defended not attacked. In the last twelve years there have only been two aggressors in the world and the United States is one of them.

Originally I thought this was a war on terror, not a mission to give democracy to a country that in incapable of handling it. After the botched job Rumsfeld has done we are not only trying to fight terrorists in the world but we can no longer protect our people or troops from the very people we went to save. The PEOPLE of Iraq, not terrorists are killing Americans.

Rumsfeld's cowboy tactics are now killing Americans. He let chaos destroy Iraq. The oil wells were his only concern.

We are trying to change something that has gone on for a thousand years. President Bush will neither win this war nor give a democracy to Iraq.

Do you believe in freedom of the press, freedom of speech, the right to bear arms and freedom of choice? Do you believe that the majority rules? If you say yes but add that the people of Iraq don't deserve it then all I can say is we have already lost the war.

The military under President Bush has shut down the presses, stopped freedom of speech and is taking all weapons. He has also told the Shiites that have no say so in the new government because they are too radical. Even if this is true it is not how you start a democracy filled with freedoms. The Shiites comprises 60 percent of the population. When we leave Iraq, who do you think will win the first election? I'd put my money on the Shiites. Who will be the new leaders? The leaders of Iraq will be future terrorists handpicked by Cheney, Rumsfeld and Bush. Sorry to list Bush third but I want them to be in the correct order of power and decision making that are running our country.

Already two of the handpicked leaders, Izzadine Saleem and Aquila al-Hashimi, have been assassinated. Ahmed Chalabi, another leader handpicked by the Bush administration was exiled from Iraq in 1989 for embezzlement. But he proved his greed was not much different than his American counterparts. The American military broke into his house because they had information he was corrupt and in contact with Iran giving vital information to Iran about U. S. movements.

If we demand freedom and democracy for the world, we must practice what we preach. To pick their leaders is to deny democracy and freedom.

I can still see President Bush strutting in his flying suit and walking beneath the sign "Mission Accomplished." His words still echo in my mind, "Because of our actions, Saddam Hussein's torture chambers are closed."

I'd like to ask Bush about the Abu Ghraib tortures, aren't we are supposed to be better than that? We are not bringing the Iraqi people up to our high standards of life and equality; we are pulling ourselves down to their despicable ways. One more note and I believe it to be the most important. President Bush said, "The world will see that we are rid of an evil dictator and the people of Iraq are better off. We have given them freedom. Because of our actions, Saddam Hussein's torture chambers are closed."

Sounds to me like the Abu Ghraib prison is not closed but under new management. Again I hope I'm wrong but you can rest assured that more happened in that prison than just a few photographs and underwear. Study your history; we are not above reproach. President Bush says this "abuse" is the work of a few. I doubt that plus Mr. Bush, WAR is abuse.

President Bush struts like he is an American cowboy and sadly we all remember what happened to the Indians.

As a little side note it is estimated that 10,000 men women and children were killed by American bombings. They were not terrorists. When asked about this, Rumsfeld made an interesting statement when he said, "Collateral damage. The Iraqi people will need to live with what we have given them."

What did we give them? Democracy? It's obvious they don't want it or know how to deal with it.

So, why are we giving democracy to a people that don't want it? The answer is simple. Oil. I know you scoff at the word but let me tell you what I heard from somebody on the inside at Halliburton. They want American troops to stay in Iraq until 2006 so they can be assured of amassing a small fortune. If I'm wrong American troops will be withdrawn from Iraq in June exactly like President Bush "promised." If I'm right then we will keep a large military contingency to secure the oil fortune for American oil companies. Are American lives worth the fortune a few companies want?

President Bush has not ridden the world of terror but rather he has spread the infection. President Bush's aggression has made the world unsafe. The world no longer looks to us as a defender and savior of the weak. Whatever grand image the world had of America, President Bush has managed to destroy over his determination to conquer Iraq.

We lost this war before it started. A pullout now will only save American lives.

Star Wars Presidency
(5.27.04)

I'm afraid America has lost its honor and integrity. Let's stop terror, not spread terror.

A pullout now will only save American lives. We lost this war before it started. While President Bush pounds on a country that had nothing to do with terror the real terrorist prepare and get stronger. The tax dollars should have been spent on finding terrorists not on a job of revenge to finish what his father started. The terrorist acts will probably continue this summer and we will be ill prepared because we are trying to control the world and not make America safe. Because of what the Bush's have done the terrorists are more organized and determined to bring their own revenge to our country. Thank you mister Bush for making this world, such a wonderful and safe place to live in.

There is one question I would like to ask you, Mr. President. Who is running this country, Cheney, Rumsfeld or Israel?

President Bush's regime reminds me of the old Movie Star Wars. Bush thinks he is Luke Skywalker in reality he is the Evil Emperor except that the Evil Emperor was intelligent and was not controlled by others. Rumsfeld is Darth Vadar with the only difference being Darth Vadar had redeeming qualities. And Cheney is "the dark side of the force" no one ever sees.

To the Editor:
(02.13.04)

First let me say I'm neither Democrat nor Republican as I choose the person and I voted for George Bush hoping he could bring good business to America. He did bring big business to the government but it looks more like a copy of ENRON, Global Crossing, WorldCom and Tyco. This was not the big business I had hoped for.

And there are other things he has done that trouble me. Because of the following I can only say that in my heart I'm compelled to vote against him before he does more damage to this country than all of the above companies and Osama Bin Laden but together. Where is Osama?

Maybe you could answer some questions for me? Why will it take President Bush more time to find out how he obtained inaccurate information about Iraq's WMD's then it took for him to decide the information was enough to attack Iraq? Don't you also think it is coincidental that he has already said they won't be able to figure out how or where the misinformation came form until after the election? It already sounds like he knows. Just more deceptions.

So far, the war in Iraq has cost US taxpayers more than $150 billion. It cost $14 billion between last September and last November alone.

Not only do we not know how much more American taxpayers will have to pay, but the Bush Administration won't even give us an estimate until after the election - the costs of military operations in Iraq are not included in the 2005 budget.

This isn't surprising, as President Bush has misled us from the beginning as to why it was so important that we launch a pre-emptive war, hiding the ambiguity of the intelligence from Congress and the American people. Now we know that Iraq was not an imminent threat to us, and that we could have used more time to work toward a peaceful solution, or at least to build more international support, which would have lowered the price we're now paying, in both dollars and American lives.

President Bush must be held accountable for his actions. I hope our Senators, Kay Bailey Hutchison and John Cornyn, will censure him for misleading the American people. I have already contacted them along with John Culberson, and voiced my opinion.

Just recently CIA Director George Tenet told us that the intelligence analysts "never said that there was an 'imminent' threat," and that there was disagreement over the status of Iraq's WMD programs. Now we know, of course, that Iraq didn't have any weapons of mass destruction.

From his first days in office, President Bush appears to have been planning for war with Iraq. That decision having been made, the president ran a campaign of misinformation, hype and hysteria that led America into an unnecessary war.

Before the war, Bush was repeatedly told there was no definitive evidence that Iraq possessed weapons of mass destruction. He knew Iraq was not a nuclear threat. He knew there was no Iraq connection to 9/11. Iraq posed no imminent danger to the United States. There was no case for a pre-emptive war.

Still, he relentlessly led us into a war that has cost hundreds of American lives, and wasted tens of billions of dollars.

I also believe the misinformation on Iraq is not much different than the deal presented to Americans on Halliburton. How much more will President Bush allow Halliburton to steal from American taxpayers before he stops them? I fervently believe Halliburton has committed a form of treason by stealing money during a time of "war." Why should a company that hides all of their assets offshore be given billion dollar contracts by America? My friends have lost their jobs so Halliburton executives can line their pockets at the expense of hard working Americans while Halliburton sends their jobs to India. I would like to see President Bush attack the CEO's who have stolen from America like he has attacked Iraq. But I'm sure he can't do that because most of his re-election war chest is from these very people.

To be "politically correct" I use the words "mislead" and "deceived" but they come nowhere near describing my feelings.

It makes me think of the great Kennedy quote that should now read:

"Ask not what your country can do for you, but why your country keeps doing it to you!"

To back up my points on President Bush here are actual quotes:

* President Bush overstated intelligence findings about WMD:

In the run-up to the war, President Bush said that the United States "must not ignore the treat gathering against us. Facing clear evidence of peril, we cannot wait for the final proof - the smoking gun - that could come in the form of a mushroom cloud. . . We have every reason to assume the worst, and we have an urgent duty to prevent the worst from occurring." [Washington Post, 1/28/2002]

That was not the message that he was getting from the intelligence community. Here's an excerpt from CIA Director George Tenet's remarks about the National Intelligence Estimate on Iraq, which summarized the pre-war views of the intelligence community: "Let me be clear: analysts differed on several important aspects of these programs, and those debates were spelled out in the Estimate. They never said there was an "imminent" threat." [Transcript of 2/5/04 speech at Georgetown University]

* Bush cited evidence that didn't exist or had been discredited: In a September 2002 news conference, President Bush cited an International Atomic Energy Agency report that purportedly said Iraq was six months away from obtaining a nuclear weapon, when in fact no such report ever existed. Bush said in his 2003 State of the Union address, "The British government has learned that Saddam Hussein recently sought significant quantities of uranium from Africa." [Official White House Transcript, 1/28/03] Yet Ambassador Joe Wilson, who was sent to Niger in February 2002 to determine whether Iraq was trying to purchase uranium materials there, concluded that "intelligence related to Iraq's nuclear weapons program was twisted to exaggerate the Iraqi threat." [Joseph Wilson, Op-Ed, New York Times, 7/6/03]

The Pentagon's year 2005 budget doesn't contain any money for military operations in Iraq or Afghanistan. The White House won't ask Congress for that money until January 2005 - after the November presidential election. [Drew Brown, Knight Ridder Newspapers, 2/11/04]

Jonathan Rauch wrote the following: The War in Iraq Was the Right Mistake to Make

The war in Iraq was premised on a mistake. Does that mean the war itself was a mistake? Yes. But it was a special kind of mistake: a justified mistake. A policeman shoots a robber who has killed in the past and who brandishes what seems to be a gun. The gun turns out to be a cell phone. The policeman expects a thorough investigation (and ought to cooperate). In the end, if he is exonerated, it is not because he made no mistake but because his mistake was justified. Reasonable people, facing uncertainty, would have thought they saw a gun.

George W. Bush and the CIA thought they saw a gun. So did French President Jacques Chirac, who last February warned of Iraq's "probable possession of weapons of mass destruction." So did Democratic presidential candidate Howard Dean, a former Vermont governor, who last February said, "My personal belief is that Saddam may well possess anthrax and chemical weapons. That being the case, he must be disarmed."

The above was Jonathan Rauch's justification of the war. For Jonathan Rauch I say of his article, "The War in Iraq was the Right Mistake to Make," the analogy of the policeman you used was very good but absolutely wrong. It should be more truthful and read like this:

A "gung ho" policeman, who never listens to anyone else and thinks he is always right, sees a known criminal and killer, who he knows in the past has killed many innocent people and has always carried a gun. The policeman assumes the criminal will use his gun so to save others the policeman guns down the criminal in a barrage of bullets that also kills innocent bystanders. After a thorough investigation they find the criminal had no weapon what so ever. Even though innocent people died the policemen feels justified because he knows he has prevented a great evil from killing in the future.

Vote for Bush No More
(7.03.04)

I want a President that will take care of America, not the world. I feel Bush has deserted America for his personal conquest of world domination.

I live in Houston and I voted for Bush. I won't vote for him again. I have watched thousands of engineering people lose their jobs as we watch them go to India. I am one of those who was forced to work in Alaska because Halliburton and all of its affiliates send the work to India. I have found a half dozen of my friend's jobs here in Alaska as the jobs continue to disappear and go to India.

President Bush said, "The jobs going to India makes America stronger and more competitive in the future."

If this is true then shouldn't Halliburton be forced to bid on the jobs they get? Wouldn't that make them stronger and more competitive?

I was offered a job in Iraq less than a week after the war started. Let me tell you the whole thing was already in motion. Those that I know who went over there had nothing to do but were making what I call "mega-bucks." Forget the $45 for a case of coke. Check the wages and back charges. Of course we all know Cheney had nothing do with Halliburton receiving all of the work.

Let's say everything is okay with all of this even the fact American's are dying while protecting the lives of Halliburton employees who are "stealing" tax dollars. Let's say it is okay. What I want to see if my tax dollars are going toward the 18 billion "no-bid" construction is a hundred percent of the labor, material, equipment and engineering to be all AMERICAN. If not then Halliburton should be required to bid on all of the jobs. After all BUSH said it best, "this will make them stronger and more competitive."

It sure makes you wonder why Cheney refuses to real what his earlier energy plans. I'm sure it wasn't anything illegal and most positively had nothing to do with Halliburton.

Another problem I have is with Bush being angry that Americans are not exempt from war crimes. As an example let's say a CEO of a large company promises to eliminate all embezzlement from the company but before he is hired the board must promise to make him exempt from embezzlement. Now why do you think he would ask that? Because he intends to embezzle the company blind.

If we want the world to have the freedoms and democracy we have then we must not be exempt from anything we demand the rest of the world adhere to.

And another thing makes me very curious. Let's say you work at a company where information is revealed that some employees are doing illegal activities, what would you do? Personally I would go home and wonder who had done it. If you knew that some of your fellow employees had sought advice from an attorney what would your first thoughts be? I would think they were guilty and obviously had something to hide. So why do you think Bush contacted a private attorney when it leaked out that somebody in Bushes organization authorized torture?

The final thing that concerns me about Bush is one of our most cherished rights is a trial by jury. To me this is just common sense. Mr. Bush why are you incarcerating hundreds that you say are terrorists and a danger to our country? If you have them in jail it most certainly is because you have proof so for your benefit hold a trial, reveal the evidence, prosecute them and put them in jail. If you have no proof then how can you face Americans and continue to hold foreigners with no proof. I want to believe in you but show me first you believe in the very same simple freedoms you demand the world use but you refuse to enforce on yourself.

Almost everybody I have talked to is tired of Bush but unless Kerry asserts himself or takes a stand then Kerry will not win.

I'm 55 years old, live in Houston and I voted for you but I won't vote for you again want a President that will take care of America, not the world. I feel you have deserted America for his personal conquest of world domination.

I have watched thousands of engineering people lose their jobs as we watch the jobs go to India. I am one of those who was forced to work in Alaska because Halliburton and all of its affiliates send the work to India. I have found a half dozen of my friend's jobs here in Alaska as the jobs continue to disappear and go to foreign countries.

You once said, "The jobs going to India makes America stronger and more competitive in the future."

If this is true then shouldn't Halliburton be forced to bid on the jobs they get? Wouldn't that make them stronger and more competitive? How can you give them 18 billion in work with no bids?

And look what Halliburton is doing. How can you not be angry that Halliburton is charging $45 for a case of coke? How can you stand idly by and watch Halliburton steal Tax Payers dollars while soldiers protect the interests of a company stealing America blind?

Of course we all know Cheney had nothing do with Halliburton receiving all of the work. Why do you not make Cheney reveal his energy policy? This is not a National Security item. It's obvious he will not reveal what he has done because he has something to hide. Just look at what Halliburton is doing to America. I feel Cheney is doing the same and you can't even control him. I've always felt you only hide things if you are guilty of something.

Let's say everything is okay with all of this even the fact American's are dying while protecting the lives of Halliburton employees who are "stealing" tax dollars. Let's say it is okay. If my tax dollars are going toward the 18 billion "no-bid" construction contract for Halliburton, then I want to see a hundred percent of the labor, material, equipment and engineering to be all AMERICAN. If not then Halliburton should be required to bid on all of the jobs. After all BUSH said it best, "this will make them stronger and more competitive."

Curious I thought stealing from America during war was an act of treason, including the kickbacks we already know Halliburton executives have received.

I have a few more questions that I hope you can answer. Why are you angry that Americans are not exempt from war crimes? As an example let's say a CEO of a large company promises to eliminate all embezzlement from the company but before he is hired he forces the board to promise that he will be exempt from embezzlement. Now why do you think he would ask that? Because he intends to embezzle the company blind. So why do you want Americans to be exempt from war crimes? The answer is embarrassingly and painfully obvious.

If we want the world to have the freedoms and democracy we have, then we must not be exempt from anything we demand the rest of the world adhere to. This is just common sense.

Mr. President why did you consult an attorney? For an example, let's say you work at a company where information is revealed that some employees are doing illegal activities, what would you do? Personally I would go home and wonder who had done it. If you knew that some of your fellow employees had sought advice from an attorney what would your first thoughts be? I would think they were guilty and obviously had something to hide. So why did you contacted a private attorney when it leaked out that somebody in your organization revealed the identity of an American CIA agent and authorized torture?

I hope you agree with me when I say one of our most cherished rights is a trial by jury. To me this is just common sense. Mr. Bush why are you incarcerating, for years, hundreds that you say are terrorists and a danger to our country? If you have them in jail it most certainly is because you have proof of their guilt, so for your benefit hold a trial, reveal the evidence, prosecute them and put them in jail. If you have no proof then how can you face Americans and continue to hold foreigners with no proof. I want to believe in you but show me first you believe in the very same simple freedoms you demand the world use but you refuse to enforce on yourself.

American Freedom
(1.23.04)

When you refuse to show the views of others you have done away with freedom of speech. But CBS has done something even worse. When you lobby and receive special advantages over others and then favor those passing laws to promote your own interest then you have become no better than companies like Enron. Part of your responsibility to all Americans is to show the news and the views of the people. CBS has failed to do this. You have now taken a giant step toward a government controlled media. The next thing we know you will only show the views represented by the President and not those of other parties. Our fore fathers would be ashamed to see how what CBS has become just for money and favors. It makes me think about the news you broadcast now and I wonder if it is the truth anymore. You are obligated to view both sides and show us that you truly are Americans and believe in truth and freedom of speech. If you view this information against the President as controversial you need to step back and look at all the obvious untruths told to us by the President of the United States. His actions tend to lean more in the direction of a dictator. I suppose you can't let the democrats talk either since they are against the President. One more thing I voted for President Bush but what he has done in the last year has appalled me. I also want to let you know that thanks to what CBS has done there is no way I can morally vote for Bush in the next election. Remember while American soldiers sacrifice their lives to protect our basic freedoms, including yours, you deny those same freedoms to the American people.

The Anti-Christ?
(8.17.04)

One more side note:

In the days following the attack on Iraq I was surprised at how polarized America was for war. Many times I tried to point out the necessity to wait and make sure. Most were angry at my words. Two days after Bush attacked Iraq, my minister wanted to pray for Bush and the war. I told him war was evil and I believed the war to be for greed and oil. He said a war for oil was wrong and the war could not be for oil. I told the Minister that as long as Halliburton didn't do all of the engineering then maybe it wasn't for money and oil.

Some will point to Bible verses ringing with truth and point to Armageddon. I do not consider myself a religious man but if you read Revelation carefully, the prophecy found in the words of the last book of the Bible could point to President Bush as being the Anti-Christ. I'm sure this will anger some and it does come as a surprise to me because I don't think he is capable of such a thing, but not true for those that guide President Bush and really appear to run the country. For those naysayers, I say read Revelation and decide for yourself.

Dan Rather
(9.11.04)

What Dan Rather did, is terrible journalism and reporting. To let false documents reach the public and lead us to incorrect convictions based on what he broadcast should actually be punished, don't you agree? He should lose his job and never be allowed to broadcast again after making false accusations to mislead the people against President Bush. False information can only lead to mistrust, dishonesty, deception and lies. Oops, isn't that the same thing Bush did to the people in regards to the war in Iraq? How many people died over what Dan Rather did?

My 911 Letter to the President
(9.28.04)

President George W. Bush: president@whitehouse. gov
Vice President Richard Cheney: vice. president@whitehouse. gov

Mr. President,

I can't believe it is so hard to get through. There is a way to save the hostage(s) that I'm surprised the military has not thought of.

I voted for you but I am rapidly losing confidence in your ability.

Right after 911 I contacted the FBI with thoughts about what the terrorists might do. You see I was in the air during 911. I wrote a novel in 1994 that described hijacking of American Airliners and crashing them into stadiums. Plus many other terrifying things that should be looked into. The FBI never responded.

Also Iraq might be too late to save. When Rumsfeld just let the infrastructure collapse it put not only the terrorists against us but also the people. So many common sense decisions lacking on Rumsfeld's part.

Again I'm sure it's too late to save the Americans but the terrorists have found a weak point and will continue to do this. I know a way you can save face and be a hero at the same time. I won't print it on the Internet.

Democracy and Terror
(10.13.04)

Why not release the women prisoners in Iraq? You can catch them again like Osama Bin Laden. Oops. Mr. President you say Clinton let an opportunity go when he could have killed Osama Bin Laden. At least Clinton had a chance. Now that you have declared war against Laden and terror you haven't even been able to find him. And Mr. President I know democracy is important to all countries including Iraq but didn't you declare war against terrorism? Why aren't you fighting terror anymore? You know Bin Laden is hiding in Pakistan, why don't you go get him? And think of the help you could give Pakistan or have you forgotten Pakistan is no longer a democracy? Shouldn't a democracy for Iraq be just as important as one for Iran, Pakistan, Cuba and…SAUDI ARABIA? Why are you letting Iran build nuclear bombs? Didn't you include them in the menu of countries on the Axis of Evil? A nuclear bomb is real terror, so why don't you stop it?

Humorous Thoughts
(11.15.04)

President Bush got support on his "leave no children behind" campaign. Michael Jackson says he is behind him one hundred percent.

And to the people out there quit complaining about Bush. He told the truth. He said he would "leave no children behind." He never promised the adults anything.

Bush said he intends to help all Americans and will immediately remove Rumsfeld from helping Iraq and put him in charge of the American infrastructure.

Bush agreed to debate now that they promised him three lifelines. Should he be unable to answer any questions he will be allowed to ask Cheney one question, let the audience decided which answer is better and he gets to call his mom at home for another. He is discussing making the moderator ask him if that is his final answer should he be unsure of what to do.

While discussing where the candidates will stand during the debate, Kerry chose to stand in front of the podium while Bush wants to stand behind Cheney

Honor and Integrity
(12.05.04)

I'm a conservative Republican who voted for Bush but I must say I get more honesty from you than all the Republicans I have listened to.

Sure Iraq needs a democracy but my concern is terror. The way I see it there is more terror in the world in one week than there was in the eight years before Bush was elected the first time.

Yes we need to punish those responsible for New York. And Oklahoma but you don't see us flying down Interstate 10 with F-14's taking out Ryder trucks. But we're doing the same thing in Afghanistan and Iraq.

If Bush is fighting "terror" then his intelligence should be able to help our allies. Sad thing our intelligence can't even protect our own agents so there is no Bush can save Americans from terror. This is obvious.

The one fatal mistake Bush has made was to make this a religious war. Who have we attacked? Muslims. They are uniting and we are in real trouble. No one has ever won a religious war. Bush is doing it the old "American way"; Indians--land, Iraq--oil. Bush is feeding American greed.

As long as Bush lies then they will be able to come here soon and do what they have done in England.

Only two things are lacking in the Bush administration; honor and integrity.

Waffling
(01.22.05)

Bush talks about Kerry waffling and changing his mind but look what President Bush did in regards to the female prisoners in Iraq. The administration said they had the female prisoners, then they didn't, then they said well we do have a few but they aren't in the prison that the terrorists said. If you have them does it really make any difference what prison they are in? And after a year why do you still have them? Why don't they get a trial? Isn't that what we get in this country? You are trying to give Iraq a democracy right? Isn't a quick and fair trial one of the guarantees in a democracy? Or is it a democracy based on the Bush plan? The waffling Bush did on the female Iraqi prisoners cost American lives. But most of all, the most important point, are those women worth the American lives you lost Mr. President?

We must invade North Korea
(2.11.05)

I never thought the invasion of Iraq was a wise decision, but let's say it is everything Bush told the American people. Let's also assume the WMD's was an intelligence mistake and Bush did what he believed was right. We don't want any country to have WMD's and we want to give the WORLD democracy, even if Bush doesn't believe in the people and what they want.

Already we have Rice virtually threatening Iran for WMD's and nuclear proliferation. Based on what these two say then with the current remarks of North Korea there is only one thing to do. We must attack based on all the logic Bush has thrown at us over the last three years.

Now there is no question as to the fact North Korea has WMD's, which I would guess is what a nuclear bomb is.

If Bush invades North Korea he not only will be able to save America from the weapons but he can also spread democracy.

Based on everything Bush has said an invasion is the only recourse. If he does not invade then everything he has been telling the American people is a lie.

This is your test President Bush.

There are only three reasons Mr. Bush will not invade.

Halliburton will not make enough money

There is not any oil, Or the President is a liar.

Can We Trust George Bush
(3.09.05)

I just want to say that I'm a conservative but with what Bush has done I find I believe more in what the liberals are doing. In reality Bush is neither a conservative nor a liberal but rather a radical. How can people continue to believe in what he is doing when everything he says turns into a lie. Still those I know that believe in Bush are behind him regardless of what he does. But then a whole country followed Hitler, even when he killed the Jews.

What do the following four points have in common?
Weapons of Mass Destruction (Iraq)
Mission Accomplished (aircraft carrier)
Bush says "Partnership and cooperation." (Bolton for the UN?)
Which brings us to --- Social Security is bankrupt.
All of the above are true.

If what Bush is saying is true, then assume the following statement is true:
Bush said Iraq was part of the "Axis of Evil" and needed to be invaded because of 1)WMD's, 2)Hussein was a tyrant and a bad leader, and that 3) Iraq needed a democracy.

If this is true then we already know North Korea is part of the Axis of Evil. Why? Because North Korea's leader Kim has WMD's (I consider a nuclear bomb a WMD), he is a tyrant and a bad leader, and North Korea needs a democracy.

Based on what Bush has said and promised there is only one logical solution. North Korea must be invaded. There are two reasons Bush will not invade North Korea: 1) There is no oil, 2) and Halliburton cannot make any money.

Can we trust Bush?

I've read a little about the bankruptcy bill but doesn't this protect the large companies? Doesn't it also force individuals who are out of work, because big companies have sent their jobs to India, to pay back even when they can't? And won't they have to pay the high interest?

Gee, who elected Bush, the people or big business?

Will Neal Bush still be able to get SBA loans for wildcat wells?

If Bush is coming down on bankruptcy so hard shouldn't he and his father be forced to pay half of the 8 trillion debt they incurred. Haven't he and his father mismanaged the United States worse than Lay and Ebbers of Enron and WorldCom?

What did Bush mean when he said, "partnership and cooperation with the world?"

Isn't making John Bolton the Ambassador to the UN a lot like making Alabama's Grand Wizard of the KKK the President of the NAACP?

The Lack of Response
(8.19.05)

Cindy Sheehan may not be a good person but her son died in war. Whether she agrees with the war or not that is not the point. Watching President Bush respond to Cindy Sheehan should make all Americans see the truth. Our President is ignoring all Americans just like he is this woman. While he vacations and plays on his property he refuses to address this woman. He can hold hands with a king and invite Ozzie Osborne to the White House but he can't take a minute of his time to talk to this woman. It's obvious she didn't contribute to his re-election or she would be on his ranch right now. Simply she does not qualify as one of the "haves and have mores."

I'm a conservative and a Republican but I feel grossly deceived by those that call themselves honest and conservative.

CNN QUESTIONS
(7.02.05)

I voted for President Bush but I have burning questions the news media is not allowed to ask or is afraid to ask. Can you ask him these questions for me?

Why is the news media afraid to ask these questions?

1. A democracy for Iraq is wonderful but why not Saudi Arabia (women have no rights and neither do Christians) and Pakistan?

2. It's great to defeat Iraq and give them a democracy but wasn't this a war on terror? I'm sorry but the terror is getting worse.

3. Mr. President you said you were putting sanctions against Syria for not protecting its borders against Saudi terrorists that infiltrate Iraq. Shouldn't Saudi be making sure terrorists don't go to Iraq?

4. Why must the new Iranian leader answer your questions but you don't answer our questions?

5. Why do you demand U. N. sanctions on other countries but refuse to let the U. N. check Guantanamo?

6. Part of the democracy you want to give to Iraq includes speedy trials, so why hasn't this been done to the prisoners in Guantanamo? If you have proof it should be easy. The only reason you won't have a trial is because you have no proof.

7. Do American laws only apply to others but not you?

8. How many days have you taken off to go to Crawford?

9. How can the CIA kidnap someone and take them to another country? Don't we owe Italy an apology? To me what was done was an act of terror to one of our allies?

10. Rumsfeld said it would be 12 years before we can stop the insurgency. Doesn't that mean you failed? You should have had a plan and not tried to dream one up now at the expense of American lives. Also if it will take 1 years then either they are incapable of having a democracy or it's a civil war we were unable to contain. At least Saddam Hussein did something you are incapable of doing. He managed to control Iraq.

What happened to the war on terror?
(7.03.05)

I think it's admirable that President Bush has promised nearly two billion dollars to Africa while not providing enough money for America's injured Veterans.

Please answer some questions that the media fails to pursue. Let's forget about the WMDs and the democracy for Iraq and concentrate on why we REALLY went to war and sacrificed near to 2,000 American lives.

America was united after 911. When President Bush declared war on terror everyone was behind him. So my question is what happened to the war on terror?

Why is the news media afraid to ask and report on the important questions? Fear? I want to know what is happening. I want the truth. Why is the Bush administration cloaked in such secrecy. The secrecy only proves they have things to hide. Why? What are they hiding?

Just like you would remove a tyrant like Hussein I expected more on terror. Look at the world and it is obvious terror is worse than it ever has been. If we declare war on terror shouldn't we be able to learn more about these terrorist acts? I think the war on terror is very much like the war in Iraq—out of control. It is obvious watching events as they transpire that the President has no plan to stop terror. His second term is like the war. It is not succeeding.

What happened to the war on terror?

Response to Iraq info by Debbie A. Corson XXX
(7.23.05)
(Debbie I find what you have written to be both interesting and troubling, so I've written my comments in parenthesis-Joe)

Debbie A. Corson
KBR - Government Operations
Camp Anaconda - Balad, Iraq
Logistics - Base Housing

I haven't verified these statistics yet, but I will look into them. All the tons of money being poured in here from around the world IS being used.
(By the CEO's or officials in Nigeria? Definition of CEO – Chief Embezzlement Officer. Can you explain the 8 billion dollars that was lost last year and still can't be accounted for?)
We don't hear all the stories about the GOOD things the soldiers do here, and the medals they win
(But almost two years ago Bush stood on the aircraft carrier with the sign overhead that read "Mission Accomplished" and said, "The war has over." The war had just started. About those medals, the same thing actually happens at work. You don't hear about the good things the employees do but you sure know when someone gets fired. Also don't get in a panic. You never hear of the good things over here either. Do you watch the news? Murder and mayhem sell the news whether you're Democrat or Republican.)
All the media tells us about is all the whining about the rights of few mass murders in Gitmo who slaughtered thousands of innocent civilians in an undeclared war to bring attention to what they wanted.
(WOW! Who are the mass murderers? If you know this to be a fact then you know who did it. Tell me their names. How did you know they killed thousands? I didn't know that. Do you believe we should give a democracy to Iraq? If so then part of that democracy is also a quick and speedy trial. If we know so much about "these murderers at Gitmo" being enemy combatants then we have proof which we will be able to use to prosecute them and keep them in jail. I say let's do it. I would think the only reason we don't take them to trial is because there is no proof of their crimes. Remember Bush says it is critical Iraq have a democracy. I agree everyone should, well maybe except for Pakistan and Saudi Arabia who are such staunch allies. Anyway democracy is a two way street not just one way. You agree? Part of a democracy is a quick trial. That applies to all democracies. And you must practice what you preach. If we demand quick trials we must

provide quick trials. If you have proof [which you seem to already have] then a trial only proves you correct and righteous. To deny a trial guaranteed in a democracy only proves you have something to hide, you have no proof, you are lying or you don't believe in the freedom of a democracy. Well which is it? This guy named Cheney says we have built new prisons in Guantanamo and that nothing is wrong. When my son tells me his car isn't working I don't go outside and then tell him the driveway is okay. That has nothing to do with the question which is exactly what Bush and Cheney have done. Avoided answering the question. Then again Bush hasn't answered very many questions. What I also find interesting is that Bush and Cheney demand the U. N. grant sanctions against countries we don't like but when the U. N. asks to check on the prisoners the United States of Freedom says no. Only one reason to say no, because they're hiding something.)

From the manipulations I have seen in the last few years of the U. S. media leading the citizens around exactly where they want them to go, like a flock of sheep, we are in dire need of cleaning our house in our media.

(Very interesting. Now remember in the above you said the "last few years." This means that the media led us around like a flock of sheep to do what they wanted and…oh, my God, we elected Bush. Are you telling me we shouldn't have done that since the media lied to us and led us around like sheep to pick Bush? Oh, my God what do we do?)

I have been wondering the last few weeks, while the media focuses on the Michael Jackson case, what is happening with the reforms going on here in the middle east, with the rebuilding of the Asian nations wiped out by the recent tsunami, with the civil wars in Africa and the efforts to stem the tide of Aids deaths there. What is the status of the negotiations with N. Korea, and the conflict between mainland China and Hong Kong. What are my representatives in DC doing to protect my rights as a Christian to pray in public or wear a cross, of put a painting of the Ten Commandments in a public courthouse. You know, important things.

(Ask Bush, if he'll answer you. He's too busy making a religious war in the world to worry about it here. For example, Syria you need to guard your borders or we'll sanction you but we don't guard our border to Mexico. And things like Syria don't meddle in Lebanon political business, but Bush spent close to 50 million American dollars to make sure the "right" candidate won in the Ukraine. He spent millions in Venezuela to make sure his choice beat Chavez. What does that say for democracy? If you want things done here find a candidate that believes in America and not conquering the world. Look I really do want to apologize for what I said about Bush. He has actually done a lot for us here. Look how much we are making for the oil companies paying over two dollars a gallon. What's oil now, almost $65 a barrel? And think of the money he has saved big business by doing away with the requirement for paying time and a half for overtime. And good news it's about time stupid individuals were forced to give up their homes to make way for corporate profits. You know, more business for the CEO's. But I must confess there were nearly 75,000 new jobs created last month [even though Bush has lost more than a million American jobs since he was president] but the bad news is that 65,000 of them went to India.)

(Tell me something Bush has done for the people? Not business but the people. He is wrong on Social Security so don't bring it up. But let's say he succeeds with Social Security. Just think, that's a trillion dollars or more in the hands of? You guessed it, big business. Commissions on your stock will be in the billions. Actually I would compare his ideas and programs to what he has done for NASA. Bush wants to go to Mars but he literally can't even get the program off the ground. What else is he doing that is faltering? Can't blame the Democrats because the

Republicans control Congress. I know they're too busy changing ethics rules to worry about helping the country.)

(Go to http://news. google. com/ if you want information on those things.)

Did you know, for example, that Kuwait elected a female government minister this week – a leading feminist in her country – where women have always been kept in the shadows of society?

(Hooray for Kuwait. Did you know our staunchest ally in the Mid-East , Saudi Arabia, still doesn't believe in women's rights or the above Christian items. In case you forgot, 15 of the 19 terrorists that destroyed the Twin Towers were from…Saudi Arabia.)

No, most of the world is unaware of these things

(It seems you are also unaware of many things. I'm telling you go to Google. Look I like car racing and I get very upset to see baseball and football on the front page but if you read the whole thing you will find what you want. You just need to do a little research and flip through a few pages.)

There was even a tsunami warning made in California this week after the earthquake in the Pacific, but the media failed to get the word out. But I doubt many people on the planet don't know that a mentally unbalanced pop star was released back into society to continue prey on children. But then again, the law cannot say, "Michael, you are a sick man. Get some help!"

(False the word was spread quickly around the Pacific Rim and people were evacuated. There ended up being no major waves from a Tsunami. You can check Google for the info. The media didn't need to notify New York, they needed to notify the Pacific Rim which they did. Funny I believe in trial by jury and innocent until proven guilty. If what you say about Michael Jackson is true, then the reason Michael Jackson is out of jail is because of you. That's right you. Your words exactly were, "a mentally unbalanced pop star was released back into society to continue to prey on children." If you have this information then it is your responsibility to give this it to the prosecution. They sure didn't have it at the trial. Since you know so much can you give me specific proof? I really am interested.)

Did you know that 47 countries have re-established their embassies in Iraq?

(Of course this is very critical for those countries—too much oil to let go. Why are you there?)

Did you know that the Iraqi government employs 1.2 million Iraqi people?

(You don't want to know how many the United States employees. And the important thing is not how many people are working for the government but rather how many people are working. I believe there are 24 million in Iraq? I'm more concerned about the 22.8 million)

Did you know that 3100 schools have been renovated, 364 schools are under rehabilitation, 263 schools are now under construction and 38 new schools have been built in Iraq? Did you know that Iraq's higher educational structure consists of 20 Universities, 46 Institutes or colleges and 4 research centers?

(So what is this all about? Did you know millions are being murdered in the Sudan? It's called genocide. Why don't we help them with the genocide and then the schools? Answer—no oil. I'm happy we're building things and giving a country a democracy but if we want to interfere don't you think we should stop genocide first?)

Did you know that 25 Iraq students departed for the United States in January 2004 for the re-established Fulbright program?

(Did you know that my wife is from South America and for seven years I have tried to get her sisters to visit but our government won't let them come even though I have signed an "Affidavit

of Support" guaranteeing they will go back. It's almost, well, racist on the part of our embassy. But you're right the Fulbright plan is good because the more Chalabi's we train the more security we will have in getting their oil. Where is that oil going?)

Did you know that the Iraqi Navy is operational? They have 5- 100-foot patrol craft, 34 smaller vessels and a naval infantry regiment.

Did you know that Iraq's Air Force consists of three operational squadrons, 9 reconnaissance and 3 US C-130 transport aircraft which operate day and night, and will soon add 16 UH-1 helicopters and 4 bell jet rangers? Did you know that Iraq has a counter-terrorist unit and a Commando Battalion?

(It's about time, after all we want our troops to come home. Don't we? That counter-terrorist unit and Commando Battalion don't seem to be doing a very good job. But if what you say is true about their military then why did Rumsfeld say we'd be there 12 more years?

http://www. kotv. com/main/home/storiesNL. asp?whichpage=1&id=85591

You know why? Oil. And if it's not Oil then it is poor planning or just plain stupidity on our part. Look South Vietnam was ready for a democracy and neither is Iraq. Iraqi people need to stop the insurrection. Now.)

Did you know that the Iraqi Police Service has over 55,000 fully trained and equipped police officers?

(I would like to have you send more information on this. I disagree. They are neither fully trained nor equipped. First of all if they were trained they would know how to defend themselves and make sure no one takes over their station and kills them.)

Did you know that there are 5 Police Academies in Iraq that produce over 3500 new officers each 8 weeks?

(One hell of a class with 700 at each class. Where are those Academies and what are their names?)

Did you know there are more than 1100 building projects going on in Iraq? They include 364 schools, 67 public clinics, 15 hospitals, 83 railroad stations, 22 oil facilities, 93 water facilities and 69 electrical facilities.

(Are these the ones we blew-up? No really I guess that's American tax dollars at work for us and of course the 7 billion no-bid contracts for Halliburton. Say you don't know where those 8 billion dollars went that the government can't find?

http://www. politinfo. com/articles/article_2005_06_21_1309. html

You can read about it here. You must admit that is one heck of an accounting mistake. Sure would buy a lot of $45 a case cokes. I bet even Author and Anderson couldn't lose that much. I wonder if Nour USA or Winston Partners got it. Those companies did get, I believe, 1.5 billion dollars in Iraq jobs. How about Chatterjee Group? Did you know Winston Partners is located in the Netherlands Antilles? Do you know who is involved with those companies? Marvin Bush and his brother Jeb. Of course if your brother will just hold hands with the King of Saudi Arabia you can get almost anything. What about China? Remember when President Bush suddenly told Taiwan to be quiet and literally cuddled up to the Communist Chinese regime? Well check out these companies doing business with China Grace Semiconductor, Electronic Engineering Times, and again Chatterjee and Winston Partners. Marvin and Neil on this one, even helping make computer chips for China. This information came out when Neil got divorced because of his adulterous action in China. Neil was getting paid something like $400,000 a year to help Chinese companies. Boy did they give him a good time. Click on the links below and read all about it.

http://pekingduck. org/archives/000761. php

http://www. corpwatch. org/article. php?id=9231
http://www. scoop. co. nz/stories/HL0501/S00274. htm
http://www. independent-media. tv/item.
cfm?fmedia_id=10173&fcategory_desc=Under%20Reported
http://www. independent-media. tv/gtheme. cfm?ftheme_id=37
Amazing and you are right about the media, this truth is not public knowledge.)

Did you know that 96% of Iraqi children under the age of 5 have received the first 2 series of polio vaccinations? Did you know that 4.3 million Iraqi children were enrolled in primary school by mid October?

(DID YOU KNOW that Bush gave more to each Iraq student than we get for American students?)

Did you know that there are 1,192,000 cell phone subscribers in Iraq and phone use has gone up 158%?

(I heard the Al-Qaeda is really thankful for those remote devices, I mean cell phones. We destroyed their economy and left them with nothing. And what we didn't do with bombs we did with a decade of sanctions. It's easy to increase numbers when nothing was left. Give me comparisons of before and after. Since you know about it then you can give accurate figures. Who paid for these things?)

Did you know that Iraq has an independent media that consist of 75 radio stations, 180 newspapers and 10 television stations?

(This is a terrible thing for Iraq. You already said the media manipulated Americans into electing Bush. My God what will happen to a backward country like Iraq with all of these manipulators in power?)

Did you know that the Baghdad Stock Exchange opened in June of 2004?

(And I assume you bought stock?)

Did you know that 2 candidates in the Iraqi presidential election had a recent televised debate? OF COURSE WE DIDN'T KNOW! WHY DIDN'T WE KNOW? OUR MEDIA WOULDN'T TELL US!

(I heard they shot each other afterward…just kidding. Did you know that Bush's administration paid Chalabi almost 3 million a year so he could take over Iraq after Bush defeated Saddam Hussein. In case you didn't know it Chalabi is the same man who later sold secrets to Iran. Oh, yeah and Chalabi was chosen the new Oil Minister to Iraq and immediately said America has been stealing Iraq's oil. Come to think of it where is that oil going? I'm sure you have information that will tell us the truth. Also Chalabi was a major source of information for the WMD's is that Weapons Might Disappear? Well they did. Did you know that there were political debates in Argentina, Venezuela, Spain and France, well heck almost every country but Pakistan, Saudi Arabia, China and North Korea, but they weren't televised either. Good news though, the Iraq people were able to learn about it through the 75 radio stations, 180 newspapers and 10 television stations in Iraq)

Because a Bush- hating media and Democratic Party would rather see the world blow up than lose their power.

(Let me get this straight. If we hate Bush and are Democrats then the world is going to blow up? Hey good news. As a true Christian you should be extremely happy very excited. This is called Armageddon or End of Days. Rejoice for the end is near. Actually I would like you to explain to me in detail how the world is going to blow up. I just don't understand.

Let's continue on the "blow up" item. Anybody out there worried about India and Pakistan? There is where we need to put nuclear proliferation. Why does Israel have 200 nuclear weapons? Even though no WMD's were found in Iraq and nuclear inspectors said there were none, we attacked Iraq. Let's just say all the false information given to Bush by exiled Iraqi's were true. You know this information is kind of like what you said about Michael Jackson, so should he be arrested based on the information you have? Get the picture? But for the sake of argument and to prove a point we'll say all the information Bush was given was absolutely 100 percent correct. Didn't we go there to stop terror? Later Bush said Saddam Hussein was a bad leader and killed people. Correct but was he worth 1700 American lives and remember that is 1600 after Bush said the war was over. Then Bush said Iraq needed a democracy. What did that have to do with terror? Hey, my eight year old son needs a car but I'm not going to give it to him. You know why? He's not ready for it. Now put them together, terror, WMD's, bad leader, killer, needs a democracy. That is why we invaded, correct? So let me ask you why haven't we done the same to North Korea? Hey we have those same things in North Korea, terror, WMD's [for sure], bad leader, killer, needs a democracy. So why haven't we invaded? Two words, NO OIL. In reality you can forget them, but keep an eye on Pakistan and India. We talk about stopping nuclear proliferation but Bush plans on making more atomic bombs. Look at this; http://www. truemajorityaction. org/bensbbs/

Not very good. Hope you don't live in Nevada because he wants to do the nuclear testing there. Do you know how many bombs we have? Think Hiroshima. Now it is estimated that 90 of those bombs would destroy Russia. We have 150,000 of them. You think we need more? Oh, yeah and Bush wants to start testing in Nevada. I think we should test in the deserts of Iraq.)

(**Now I want everyone to read carefully. The word "blow up" could be a metaphor for what is happening to our economy and it is a direct result of Bush's decisions. NOW THIS IS REALLY SCARY! You heard that Bush has promised to cut the deficit in half by the time he leaves office? How many of you know what that really means? The deficit is the amount the government overspends beyond what it collects each year. The last three years Bush has pushed the deficit to 600 billion dollars per year. IF he can cut that in half it will be a 300 billion dollar deficit per year. Now let me give you a quick comparison. Clinton's last year in office saw an increase to the debt of only 16 billion dollars and even that is not acceptable but it's a far cry from 600 billion. One side note, the last year that the government collected more money than it spent was in 1960. The DEFICIT has nothing to do with the NATIONAL DEBT. This does not reflect the NATIONAL DEBT which Bush has misled us horribly. Forget Social Security, worry about the National Debt. Currently the National Debt is almost 8 trillion dollars. At the rate Bush is going we will owe 10 trillion dollars when he leaves office. Now let's look at what the two Bush's have done. From 1776 to 1988 when Bush was elected our debt went from zero to 2.8 trillion. During Bush's four year term the debt went to 4.4 trillion. He almost doubled the debt. Eight years of Clinton saw it go to 5.6 trillion. Less than five years with Bush it has increased to 8 trillion. It has taken 228 years to make our debt 8 trillion dollars. But only nine years of two Bush Presidents added 4 trillion to our National Debt. And one of them isn't finished yet. The National Debt will probably reach 10 trillion dollars under Bush which will make the total debt for both Bush's about 6 trillion dollars. Currently the interest on the debt is about 250 billion per year because the interest is so low. Now other numbers. It takes about 2.3 trillion to run the government (taxes collected) but the government is spending 2.9 trillion per year. This cannot continue. If you know simple math figure this out. First suppose the National Debt is 10 trillion dollars, then let's say that interest rates go to 10 percent. The interest will be one trillion dollars. Suppose there is inflation and interest is 18 percent [it has been that high before under the other Bush]. Then the interest would be 1.8 trillion leaving only 500 billion to run a government that needs 2.9 trillion. So let me ask you, where is Bush taking us? How would you like to wake up

one morning and find out that the interest you owe each month exceeds what you make? Would this be a problem? It sure will. Sounds to me like we got Bushwhacked. **And one more thing, if Halliburton can make more money in another country they will leave and drop America like a hot potato. You know the Benedict Arnold of American business.**)

(Don't believe me? Then take a look at the National Debt by clicking on these
http://www.publicdebt.treas.gov/opd/opdpenny.htm
http://www.toptips.com/debtclock.html
Very interesting. Yes I have a problem with President Bush. And the Democrats are too far behind on my unhappy list.

Now something else. I'm all for getting the terrorists after what they've done but I have some perplexing questions that really bother me. I didn't know terrorism stopped in Iraq. If we've stopped it then why it there terror in Indonesia, Spain and other countries? So what about Syria, North Korea and Iran? I think there are more terrorists there. If we are going to save the world like George Bush wants then how do we intend to do it if we go bankrupt? Who is there that will help us? Think about it the world hates us now. Bush is a real diplomat. Even the sovereignty of our ally Italy was stepped on when we went there with CIA agents, kidnapped someone and took them to Egypt. Shouldn't we be working with our ally? By the way the CIA was staying in $450 a night hotels. http://www.washingtonpost.com/wp-dyn/content/article/2005/06/25/AR2005062501127.html
http://www.insidebayarea.com/argus/news/ci_2825336
The above makes for interesting reading. Ironically, we demand other countries do what we refuse to do ourselves. We demand information on terror but refuse to share. The U. N. must check them but the U. N. can't check us. Our enemies can't have nuclear weapons but our allies can. Do you know how many enemies we have that were once our allies? We demand fair treatment of Americans but will go to a foreign country, kidnap individuals and take them to countries that accept torture. The above five sentences are what dictatorships do. Has Bush become the dictator of the world? I know we're above reproach, but history repeats; the Indians had land, the Mid-East has oil.)

Instead of shouting these accomplishments from every rooftop, they would rather show photos of what a few perverted malcontent soldiers have done in prisons in many cases never disclosing the circumstances surrounding the events.

(Wow! How did you know our soldiers were perverted and malcontent? And you say "never disclosing the circumstances," does that mean if we knew the circumstances that the torture would be okay? Hey if the CIA can kidnap someone from Italy I bet they can torture people in one of our prisons. That means you would have to add, "perverted malcontent CIA Agents. Shades of Ruby ridge and Waco. As a country that promotes justice and freedom, we should be above things like torture. Soldiers risk their lives. That is part of their job description, they are not supposed to torture or kill prisoners. How about a little more on torture. Remember Abu Gharib? We didn't eliminate torture like Bush promised and boasted but rather our President but the prison under new management. If the United States of America tortured just one person then we lost. We did not elevate Iraq to our high ideals but rather they brought us down to their low moral standards. Now you have a taste of war. What do you think? Makes you want to spit out that bad taste doesn't it?)

Instead of showing our love for our country, we get photos of flag burning incidents at Abu Ghraib and people throwing snowballs at presidential motorcades.

(Another WOW! You said, "flag burning at Abu Ghraib." Did we give the prisoners the matches or shame, shame don't tell me it was the perverted malcontents. This is America. I'd take a snowball over bullets any day. So you are saying that those who showed photos of atrocities committed by our country don't love America?)

The lack of accentuating the positive in Iraq, serves only one purpose. It undermines the world's perception of the United States and our soldiers.

(I've got news for you, Bush, Rumsfeld and Cheney have undermined the world's perception of the United States all by themselves. Diplomacy is not a word found in the Bush administration vocabulary. What really made me mad was when the American soldier said their vehicles weren't safe and Rumsfeld said, "This is war you need to live with it." Not the right answer. If I had been Rumsfeld I would have said, "That is not acceptable. Our primary concern are our soldiers. One death is not acceptable. If there are other problems I want to hear about them now and the problems will be addressed immediately. America's top priority during war is the safety for all or our soldiers."

Something Cheney said really bothers me and makes me think. When a reporter asked him about the American Soldiers killed in Iraq. Cheney got angry and said, "A few deaths were to be expected it was war. [Angry] Why all the negative questions? Besides if you made Washington D. C. the size of Iraq there would be over 250 murders a month, so actually our soldiers are safer in Iraq." Sorry Cheney but Americans killed in action is unacceptable. We must protect them. Now let me ask you, is there anything about what Cheney said that bothers you? You know, "it's safer in Iraq than in Washington D. C. ? Is he saying our government can't control crime in our own capital but it's safer in another country at war? WOW! That sucks. Reminds me of a neighbor who used to criticize neighbors for the way they cut their hedges and lawns, but he never took care of his yard. If Cheney spoke the truth and I'm sure he does, then shouldn't our troops be in Washington D. C. protecting Americans?)

I AM ASHAMED OF MY FELLOW AMERICANS WHO WOULD RATHER SEE TERRORISM SUCCEED THAN A REPUBLICAN PRESIDENT.

(Now that's heavy. Let me get this straight, if I'm not for the Republican President then I'm for terrorism? You've left me no way out of this. Bush has an agenda but I don't understand it. Let's take Bolton. Bush should give the information about him to Congress and prove what he said about Bolton is true. If he doesn't give the information, then he is intentionally hiding something. Bolton is not an issue of National Security. What exactly is succeed? To disagree and want the truth and the information we need to make decisions is not terrorism and doesn't mean I don't want us to succeed. It is called a democracy. You say the press distorts the truth but Bush hides it. And to put it very simply, I don't feel Bush is doing the right thing and I don't think he is succeeding with a one-sided approach---but that in no way means I want terrorism to succeed. My disagreement is called a democracy and freedom of choice. I do hope you know what that means. Oh, and I voted for Bush the first time but I didn't like where he is taking us so I voted against him the second time. I was hoping he would bring big business fiscal responsibility to our government. What he brought was fiscal irresponsibility and a governing body that looks more like ENRON.)

This is verifiable on the Department of Defense website.

(I went to the Department of Defense website and couldn't find it. Please let me know where I can read these things.

Do you believe all men and women are created equal. Envision this scenario; a plant blows *up and 20 people are killed, including a janitor, workers and a few executives checking out the plant. The janitor had three kids and wife. The executives were also married but had only one child each. The insurance pays out 20 million dollars. Now the question is how much is a loved one worth. Does the family have any greater or lesser loss whether the lost loved one was a janitor or an executive? I would give each family a million dollars. What would you do? Some might give the family with three children more than the family with one child. Agree? I believe everybody is equal whether they are wealthy or poor, or black or white. Now let's back up to 911. Do you know how they divided the money to the families? Bush and other elite decided how to divide the money. First let me remind about a comment Bush made. Bush was at a thousand dollar a plate dinner and I know what he said was in jest or at least I hope it was, but he said, "It's good to see all of you here tonight. . ." He smirked and then finished with, ". . .the haves and have mores." Everybody laughed. Here is an example of how the money was divided between surviving families of 911. One person killed made only $20,000 a year and their family was given approximately $300,000. The family of a man who made nearly a million a year was given $7 million dollars. This is equality in the eyes of our leaders. This is not equality like Jefferson and Washington envisioned. If you agree with the way Bush divided the money then we have a caste system in the United States that is worse than racism and/or slavery. In Bush's eyes you're either a have or a have not. You're a "Rich Man or a poor man." Equality.)*

(Now I have a few things I would like to ask you. To aid the enemy is treason. Iran is part of the axis of evil. Halliburton does business with Iran but Cheney smugly said he didn't know that it was a subsidiary based in the Caymans, but when he found out he didn't stop the subsidiary. Still Halliburton continues business with Iran. If Halliburton believes in American it will cease business with Iran and will bring most of its business back to America. I just hope that the things Halliburton has helped in Iran don't come back to haunt us and kill American soldiers later. Here's a challenge. Halliburton, bring the work back to America. Either you're with us or you're with them. Now can you tell me who said that? And Darth Vader doesn't count.)

(Like you said the media doesn't seem to report the facts so I thought I would add a few I have found)

(Didn't Cheney cut $25 million in Halliburton retirement for the employees then when he retired he have himself a $20 million retirement package paid to him by Halliburton after only five years of employment. Does Halliburton still charge $45 for a case of cokes?)

(Dick Cheney appeared in a 1996 promotional video in which he praised the Arthur Andersen accounting firm for giving "good advice." A few years later, Andersen was convicted of obstruction of justice for shredding documents in the federal government's Enron investigation. See the video here!)

(The other convicted felon, Enron, which donated $113,800 to Bush/Cheney 2000, was the 12th-largest contributor to the campaign. So, in 2001, it was fitting that Mr. Cheney chose Enron's former CEO, Ken Lay, to handpick the new members of the Federal Energy Regulatory Commission (FERC). FERC is the federal agency in charge of ensuring fair and competitive energy prices, but Ken Lay's appointed members of FERC failed to stop skyrocketing and scandalous energy prices that ripped off California's utility rate payers in 2001.)

(Remember the $2.4 million in bribes Halliburton paid to Nigeria in 2003)

(More about Halliburton below:

Washington - The U. S. Army said on Tuesday it had awarded $72 million in bonuses (I think the bonuses should go to the dead American soldiers and challenge Halliburton to distribute that money to the families of the dead soldiers) to Halliburton Co. for logistics work in Iraq but had not decided whether to give the Texas company bonuses for disputed dining services to troops.

Army Field Support Command in Rock Island, Illinois, said in a statement it had given Halliburton unit Kellogg Brown & Root ratings from "excellent" to "very good" for six task orders for work supporting U. S. troops in Iraq.

The Army said its Award Fee Board in Iraq had met in March and had agreed to pay KBR bonuses for work it did in support of U. S. forces there.

But it said dining facility costs questioned by auditors from the Defense Contract Audit Agency had not yet been considered by the military's Award Fee Board.

The Army said it could not immediately provide more details on when the dining fee bonuses would be resolved.

Halliburton, which was run by Vice President Dick Cheney until he joined the 2000 race for the White House, has earned more than $7 billion under its 2001 logistics contract (NO BID) with the U. S. military.)

Show me the truth, a concerned American
Joe Barfield

(Now the trick phrase. I hate it when people do this but Debbie started it first. Remember, if you're not for Bush you're for terrorism so here it is)
For more information on Halliburton check this out:
http://www. halliburtonwatch. org/
and…. let's not end without a few laughs…
How many members of the Bush administration does it take to change a light bulb?
1. One to deny that a light bulb needs to be changed.
2. One to attack the patriotism of anyone who says the light bulb needs to be changed.
3. One to blame Clinton for burning out the light bulb.
4. One to tell the nations of the world that they are either: "For changing the light bulb or for darkness."
5. One to give a billion dollar no-bid contract to Halliburton for the new light bulb.
6. One to arrange a photograph of Bush, dressed as a janitor, standing on a stepladder under the banner "Light Bulb Change Accomplished."
7. One administration insider to resign and write a book documenting in detail how Bush was literally "in the dark."
8. One (Rove) to viciously smear #7.
9. One surrogate (Cheney) to campaign on TV and at rallies on how George Bush has a strong light bulb-changing policy all along.
10. And finally, one (Rumsfeld) to confuse Americans about the difference between screwing a light bulb and screwing the country.

New Rules Mr. President
(9.18.05)

New Rule, Halliburton cannot have a no bid contract to rebuild New Orleans.

New Rule, before we start rebuilding shouldn't we finish finding survivors? Why did you pull the troops out of New Orleans? Three weeks after the storm they were still finding survivors. If you can't find survivors for three weeks how do you expect to save Americans from terrorists?

New Rule, Mr. President when a disaster strikes is there any way you can take a few days off from your vacation? I know you must be exhausted from riding your bike and dodging the people across the street from your ranch, but please end your vacation and help America. You know your country.

New Rule, Mr. President please tell Condoleezza Rice that she can wait a few days to go shopping in New York. What is more important Mrs. Rice; Americans or shopping? What did you say? Oh, okay so you will still be a few days late. I'm sure America understands that you can't get a refund on those tickets you bought to the play.

New Rule, Jeb, Neil, and Marvin cannot have the job of rebuilding New Orleans. This also means that Winston Partners and Chatterjee Group cannot be involved in the reconstruction. You know them; they belong to your brothers Marvin and Neil. By the way Mr. President is it true that some of those companies are based in the Cayman Islands? Do they pay taxes?

New Rule, a case of cokes is not forty-five dollars.

New Rule, Mr. President, all companies doing work for the hurricane Katrina damage must be totally based in the United States.

New Rule, Mr. President don't forget Mississippi.

New Rule, Mr. Bush please get Colin Powell to come back. He was the only one we trusted.

New Rule, Mr. President are not Americans as important as Israeli's? If this is true shouldn't you give each person in New Orleans the same amount of money you gave each person who left the Gaza Strip? Wasn't that $244,000 per person? Is Halliburton handling the relocation?

New Rule, if Congress is correct and there isn't enough money to help New Orleans then shouldn't we quit spending money on Iraq? I know a democracy is important but come on Mr. President aren't Americans more important? Please Mr. President don't tell me we can't help because they are poor and black. I know you prefer the "Haves and have mores" but please don't forget the "have not's." There are many "have not's" that are Americans. Some of them even voted for you.

New Rule, Mr. President, don't cut project funding for New Orleans. Just a reminder but some of those funds you cut a few years ago for the war in Iraq just happens to be the levees in New Orleans. You cut those funds by almost 50%. I have an idea that will provide money and save American lives. Leave Iraq. After all how can you help a country that is still determined to kill themselves? They don't want Americans there.

New Rule, we need accountants. If three hundred thousand people are out of homes and you gave each of them $100,000 that would be 30 billion so where do you come up with 200 billion? Neil, Marvin and Halliburton?

New Rule, a friend of mine lost their husband when he was killed in a car crash on the way to the Twin Towers. Although he didn't make it in time shouldn't he still qualify for the millions you gave? The loss for that family was just as grievous.

New Rule, Mr. President you should know where you are. When you said you would help New Orleans you said it would help the world. Incorrect. It will help the United States. Did you forget where New Orleans is located?

New Rule, Mr. President you can only have one toy to play with. Your choice; Iraq or New Orleans. Which is more important?

New Rule, Mr. President, a policy we call, "No American left behind," and then we do it.

Questions for Bill Maher:
(9.25.05)

1. Outsourcing by an American Joe Sigelman, This is direct from an article on the Internet with my question below:

(Some economists say outsourcing is so pervasive that it helps explain why the U. S. economy is doing a poor job of creating employment. Analysts expected a net increase of 200,000 positions in July, but payroll growth totaled 32,000. The August employment report will be released Friday.)

(Sigelman said he was doing his best to keep American corporate hiring down.)

("We hope to be leading the move of white-collar jobs from the U. S. ," he told the Economic Times, an Indian paper, in December.)

("Once you've done it a couple of times, it's highly repetitive," says an Office Tiger client, an executive with a New York investment bank. "You can't be an idiot, but you don't have to be Albert Einstein.")

(The process is already moving beyond the associates.)

(Vinitha Venkat is an Office Tiger manager whose team assembles data for a Wall Street brokerage firm that declined to be named. She and a colleague are going to New York, where they will enroll in the broker's analyst training program.sd)

("I'm waiting for them to send everything to us," says Venkat, 27. "I don't think it will take that long.")

(Over the longer term, Celent Communications, a consulting firm, calculates that 2.3 million financial jobs are at risk. Researchers at UC Berkeley think that as many as 14 million jobs of all types are vulnerable.)

If investment bankers outsource the work and people lose their jobs then how do the bankers expect people to invest their money? And should we be required to train them to take our jobs like we trained al Qaida agents to fly?

Mr. Maher is there any way you could interview Joe Sigelman? Why would the companies not want to be named? What have they done wrong?

And one more question along the same line. Bill Gates has sent over more than a billion dollars of programming to India. Maybe that explains all the recent problems we are experiencing with Windows. Doesn't that make you feel comfortable? But the real question is; if Gates can get the work done for a tenth of the money it takes to pay an American employee, then shouldn't the price of Windows be eight dollars instead of eighty dollars?

Mr. Maher I was wondering if you could ask Mr. Bush a few questions for me:

Mr. Bush who runs this country, Cheney, Rumsfeld or Israel?

Mr. Bush when you were elected you said American jobs going to India was a good thing because we would become lean and mean. Shouldn't that apply to Halliburton? Wouldn't Halliburton become a better company if they were forced to bid like other companies?

Mr. President when you declared war against terrorism you asked the American people to sacrifice. Don't you think the Companies and CEO's, like Halliburton should also sacrifice? I mean like Cokes aren't forty dollars for a case.

It looks like the freeway to peace in the Middle East is only one lane and Israel is driving on it. At least that's the way I see it so maybe you could explain how the road map to peace in the Middle East works? Mr. Bush did you make that road map to peace or did Israel?

Mr. Bush you claim that America's enemies wish to destroy our freedoms. If we surrender freedom of speech in the hope that it will end terrorism, who then will have won the war?

Mr. Bush can you ever answer questions without Cheney?

2. Greenspan just said we won't be able to pay Social Security to the baby boomers. Mr. Bush what have you done to our Social Security? If we are all going to sacrifice don't you think it is right for Congress and you to retire on the same Social Security we will have? Mr. Bush you are one of us, aren't you? No fair asking Cheney.

Mr. Bush why does Iraq need freedom more than Cuba?

What has happened to Afghanistan?

Where is Osama Bin Laden?

Where are the Weapons of Mass Destruction?

Shouldn't you finish a job before you start another?

Why hasn't the terror stopped?

Are all the terrorists in Iraq?

Do Indonesia, Russia and Spain know the terrorists are all in Iraq?

If you have made the world safer and know so much how come you weren't able to warn Spain and Russia?

Why did we go to war?

Why does the world hate us?

Where is our overtime?

Forget the overtime, where are our jobs?

3. If you were proud of your father or yourself, wouldn't you tell people or brag about your accomplishments? Of course you would. Then why Mr. Bush, did you use your powers to seal all of your father's and your records and make them unavailable for public view?

It is said the truth will set you free. If that is correct then you would be bound as a prisoner for the words you have spoken to the American people.

Mr. Bush in case you didn't know a conservative is someone who is resistant to change, conforming to the standards of the middle class, opposes "big government," and supports low taxes and lower spending. A liberal, is someone who favors reforms and progress, and the protection of liberty, and tolerant of change, and will spend money to get this done. A radical is one with extreme political views and opinions, and only his views are right regardless of the outcome. Franklin Delanor Roosevelt said it best when he said, "A radical is a person with both feet planted firmly in the air." So Mr. Bush you aren't a conservative, but you also aren't a liberal, so what does that make you?

And Mr. President remember, no fair asking Cheney.

According to Section 3 of the Constitution, treason against the United States, shall consist in levying war against them, or in adhering to their enemies, giving them aid and comfort.

During this time of war, as Bush has declared whether it's a word or a country, Halliburton has given aid and comfort to the enemy by taking bribes, stealing tax dollars for their benefit and sending American jobs overseas. Shouldn't Halliburton be tried for treason?

4. Mr. Sigelman of Office Tiger sends tens of thousands of American jobs to India. This was from a newspaper article about his office in India:

(It can't be the ambience that is making them this way. Office Tiger's offices are high-tech, with rooms accessible only by electronic card swipes. The chairs would flunk any ergonomic test. There are three shifts, which means no one can personalize his desk, and no natural light. Not many clocks, either. Sigelman compares it approvingly to a casino: It's a place without distractions.)

If Mr. Sigelman is going to take American jobs away then Congress should act on the welfare of foreign workers doing American jobs. This is the child labor of adults. They should be given the same minimum conveniences that American workers have strived for.

Mr. Sigelman is the type of person that would buy slaves today to make a dollar. His company does work for American businessmen but he doesn't care anything about Americans.

I don't want to see American jobs go overseas but don't you think Indian workers deserve to be treated humanely and given minimum conveniences? Aren't you seeing American companies treating the people in India the same way they want to treat American workers? Now there is an atrocity.

Common Sense Mr. Businessman, if you send all of our jobs to other countries then how do you expect Americans, the largest buyers in the world, to buy your product?

Can you tell me what Congress thinks about the treatment of foreign workers?

Mr. Bush if you're honest and believe in the things you tell the American people there is no reason to fear a debate. Not agreeing to a debate where questions can be "freely" asked, instead of prearranged, is what a coward would do. There is another problem; when you debate, Cheney is not allowed to stand beside you and supply answers.

Greenspan just said we won't be able to pay Social Security to the baby boomers. Mr. Bush sent our retirement to Iraq. If you don't want your Social Security you should vote for Mr. Bush. Can you explain what has happened to our S. S. and where it has gone?

Mr. Bush why does Iraq need freedom more than Cuba? Oh, I'm sorry, I forgot Cuba doesn't have any oil.

If you were proud of your father or yourself, wouldn't you tell people or brag about your accomplishments? Of course you would. Then why did Mr. Bush, using his powers, seal all of his and his father's records and make them unavailable for public view? Must be to protect the national security. I'm sure there is nothing to hide.

Mr. Bush, don't use ads to attack your opponents. Just tell the truth. It is said the truth will set you free. If that is true then you would be bound as a prisoner for the words you have spoken to the American people.

Mr. Bush what has happened to Afghanistan?

Where is Osama Bin Laden?

Where are the Weapons of Mass Destruction?

Shouldn't you finish a job before you start another?

Why hasn't the terror stopped?

Mr. President, why did we go to war?

Why does the world hate us?

Where is our overtime?

Forget the overtime, where are our jobs?

Mr. Bush have you deserted the American people and waged a war to protect the vast interests of the wealthy that have stolen America blind by destroying the dreams and future of American's that trusted you?

Maybe you could explain Mr. Bush's road map to peace in the Middle East. I thought it was a two-way road for Palestine and Israel to find peace. Isn't it more like a one-way freeway for Israel and a gravel pit for Palestine? Could you explain how the road map to peace in the Middle East works?

Here is something I have always wanted to see, and you are one of the only ones who can do it.

Bring someone on your show like Eisner (Disney), or a CEO from one of the major oil companies that have made hundreds of millions on pay and/or bonuses. Find out who made the most and sent the most jobs overseas (Halliburton sent thousands to India laying off people from Kellogg and Brown & Root). Pick one of Bush's favorite companies that will make it even better.

Tell the CEO it will be an opportunity to explain why he has sent the jobs overseas. When you have found the American CEO that will come, find his exact counterpart in India and invite him over. The American CEO will say the same thing, they always do. He will tell you the bottom line for his company is the dollar and saving millions for the investors and making money for the company. He would do whatever it takes to make money for the company.

After you've hooked him you can introduce his counterpart and tell the audience the person from India has the same sterling qualifications as his American counterpart and is just as qualified but will work for one hundredth (or whatever) of his American counterpart.

Then I want to watch the craw fishing once HIS job is on the line.

Questions for Bush
(9.25.05)

They say you learn from your mistakes. If that is true then President Bush may be the smartest person in the world.

Clinton may not have had a large military force but Bush destroyed what there was of that force.

Only a person that is stupid and has no common sense would rebuild the futile wasteful levees of New Orleans. You say Bush is going to rebuild them?

Bush was a "golden spoon guppy" in his own bowl with his own people in an unreal world, oblivious to the pain and suffering of people in his own country.

I call on you to answer these questions whether your answers are lies or the truth I want you to face the people. Rove and Cheney cannot be with you.

Mr. Bush, where are the Weapons of Mass Destruction?

Mr. Bush, where is Osama Bin Laden?

Mr. Bush, where is the democracy the people of Iraq so badly wanted?

Mr. Bush, after two years shouldn't they be able to defend themselves?

Can we only train Iraq policemen that can are assassinated? Can't we train them properly?

Mr. Bush, how can you build a democracy with "freedom" when the foundation is based on Islam which is not even close to democracy.

Mr. Bush, if Iraq's constitution is based on Islam then didn't you lose the war and all of those American lives in vain?

Mr. Bush, who did the anthrax? How can we win the war on terror when we can't solve the crimes in our own country?

Mr. Bush, if you can't help Americans in a natural disaster how do you expect to accomplish it when there is a terrorist attack?

Mr. Bush, how is your war on terror going?

Mr. Bush, you promised to punish the person who leaked the identity of the CIA operative, so since you haven't done so I suppose that was just another claim of WMD's?

Mr. Bush, I think nuclear proliferation is a wonderful idea but shouldn't it also apply to Pakistan and India? Shouldn't we also quit making those bombs?

Mr. Bush, when there is a disaster or terrorist attack in the United States don't you think you could cut your five week vacation a few days short? Will Condoleezza Rice go shopping again?

Mr. Bush, shouldn't someone tell Cheney he doesn't need to hide in a bunker in Washington when Katrina attacked? You got the wrong information from Chalabi again, Katrina was not a Russian spy it was a storm.

Mr. Bush, where did the 8 billion go that disappeared when it was sent to Iraq? Halliburton or your personal account? Was Arthur-Anderson doing the accounting again?

Mr. Bush, do you know what a budget is? Do you know what a deficit is? If you do then you qualify as an Enron CEO (Chief Embezzlement Officer).

Mr. Bush don't you think that if you and Congress hadn't cut 44% of the New Orleans levee budget to fund your personal toy in Iraq that all of those that drowned would instead be alive today? I'm sorry only half of those died the other have died due to your failure to respond.

Mr. Bush, I'm glad to see you promised to stay out of the way during Hurricane Rita. I just wish you had done the same thing five years ago.

Mr. Bush are you going to help the world or America? Either you're with us or you're with them. Which is it?

Mr. Bush, I voted for you the first time but I just don't trust you anymore. At least we could read your father's lips.

Sadly President Bush reminded me of my own son when he appeared hopelessly lost trying to show how helpful he was during Hurricane Rita. I remember when my son had left his things outside (911 promise) and they were destroyed by other kids (hurricane Katrina), so in an effort to make things better, that following week, my son followed me around the yard promising to do anything but also promised he would stay out of my way. My son (Mr. Bush) didn't know what he was doing. It was cute for a kid. They learn from their mistakes. Mistakes haven't helped you much Mr. Bush. Your dad can't help you now. Even Rove can't help you now.

Bush
(11.12.2005)

Bush was a golden spoon guppy that swam in his own bowl protected and immune to responsibility, reality and actual war. Protected with his own people in an unreal world oblivious to other people's pain and suffering. Bush wants honesty but is not honest. He wants National Security but his own men can't keep secrets. He talks about surplus but gives us a deficit. He wants war but knows not about war. He demands countries protect their borders but he can't protect ours.

Corruption
(1.16.06)

I'm a Republican and I've been deceived by them. I'm conservative and believe in controlling the government. Conservatives have their agenda. King George is neither conservative nor liberal but rather radical. The closest word to describe him is dictator.

Corruption

Nana regional no bid contract for mobile homes Tom Ridge

Punishment 5 year band and triple for the overcharges

Accountants for all no bid contracts.

Serve their country not be a burden

CEO's pay scale is out of line.

Medical insurance

reasonable rates

good coverage

Social Security

wants to hire cronies

I want good retirement

all my social security should be in government stocks not with one of Bush's rich friend Stock Brokers.

Nuclear proliferation

Pakistan will be our enemy within the next five to ten years. They have nuclear weapons and probably a Muslim leader will take over.

Iraq There would be no talk of premature withdrawal if there hadn't been a premature war.

Our forefathers created a unique constitution with checks and balances to make sure no one had too much power but King George thinks he is above the law and the constitution. If Washington and Jefferson were alive today they would overthrow this King George.

And evidenced by the kidnapping in Italy, the places of torture and the bombing in Pakistan no country in the world is safe from his wrath even the children he has killed with his blatant attacks. If we know so much about what is happening in Iran then why can't Bush find you who leaked the information on Plume? A good Christian man would have avoided war.

I'm sick and tired of hearing what he has done for Iraq. Tell me just one thing he has done for the American people? New Orleans was a sign. It showed what the federal government would do for the American people. Nothing. If they had wanted to be saved they should have had an oil well in their backyard.

President Bush the Howdy Doody Politician
(4.20.06)

The Republicans are like Howdy Doody; someone is always pulling their stings and it's usually the lobbyists and wealthy, they don't have any brains, can't think for themselves, they can't speak for themselves and they have a stupid wooden smile. And they're like Clarabelle the Clown, always tooting their horn and thinking they're funny when all they do is trip over their own feet.

It's your choice
(9.19.06)

Chavez and Castro are similar in that they control their people, expose those disagree with them, torture those against them, give special contracts to family, friends and companies loyal to them without allowing other companies to compete and then tell their people they must obey because they know what is best. I'm sure we all agree that they should be removed from their positions.

With that in mind there is another ruler claiming a democracy but is doing the same thing to his people. This man claims to be a Christian but does all the above. This same man even swore on a bible to uphold the Constitution of his country. This man is George Bush. Do you believe in the Constitution of the United States of America or George Bush? If you believe torture is right, favoring special interest, wiretapping, and disregarding the Constitution of the United States then please read no farther because George Bush is your man. But if you believe in the honor of a Christian, truth, and integrity then you should read on.

Thirty years ago I read a "Pogo" cartoon that I have never forgotten. Pogo (a possum) and his alligator friend were trying to find an enemy when they came upon a lake and saw their reflection upon which they said, "We has seen the enemy and they are us." Those words are a reflection of our government today. President Abraham Lincoln was closer when he said, "America will never be destroyed from the outside. If we falter and lose our freedoms, it will be because we destroyed ourselves." This is happening as I write these very words.

Guess what the Senate is about to do now? Pardon Bush for breaking the law! Everyone should know that the Senate is moving now to Pardon Bush for breaking the law. Again let me warn you; if you do not believe in a democracy and freedom for all then you should read no further.

Ear Flap

(04.10.07)

This is how things get started and lies are passed around. I don't care whether it was a Democrat or a Republican the Veteran was mad at but he had his right to do so. It is obvious the information was created and passed around by a Republican and not somebody attuned to the truth.

Here is the truth:

The photo originally accompanied news accounts of a speech http://www. whitehouse. gov/news/releases/2005/08/20050822-1. html

Delivered by President George W. bush at the national convention of the Veterans of Foreign Wars in Salt Lake City on August 22, 2005 War veteran Bill Moyer (picture) chose the occasion to display his displeasure with President Bush's policies by wearing the "Bullshit Protector" over his ear during the President's speech.

You can find the truth here:

http://www. snopes. com/photos/politics/earflap. asp

I'm not much of a fan for most Democrats especially Kennedy. But there is something to remember that there are things worse than what a person does or believes in and that is lying. Those that create and try to perpetuate the lies are the people we must rid our government of because they cause us to believe such distortions and that is not a good thing. These people try to get us to argue and fight among ourselves so we will miss the main issues.

You're in Good Hands With…WHOOPS!

(4.13. .07)

President Bush has picked another winner.

Reminds me of being at the carnival where you shoot down the little metal men with your gun and win a prize. All the president's men could be lined up for this one. In fact they seem to be as smart as those little metal men. The only difference is you can trust the little metal men in the carnival.

So here we go again this week.

Paul Wolfowitz is to the honor and integrity of World Banking (our money),

As Haggard is to Morality,

As Rove is to National Security,

As Cheney is to open construction bids,

As Foley is to Family Values,

As Gonzales is to Human rights,

And President Bush is to winning a war.

How about a big round or applause for another one—-Paul Wolfowitz! And all the President's Men.

A note on the war. Terror is not in Afghanistan and Iraq but everywhere. Will the "Terror Peace Treaty" be in Afghanistan? And what about Drugs? That's becoming like terror. Aw, heck Mr. President we all know drugs are from Colombia. If you will stop it there then nobody will do drugs anymore—just like terror will end when we win in Iraq. WMD's, democracy, terror, OIL? Why the hell are we really there? When Halliburton bails out you know we're doomed. Didn't you tell Cheney to tell Halliburton not to leave Iraq? Aren't you paying them enough? If Halliburton is smart enough to get out why aren't you? Is Cheney headed to Dubai? Anyway let's get back on track. Every war is followed by negotiations, a treaty and then peace. If you have no plans to negotiate and stop the war then you are just as bad as them.

But you said it was Mission Accomplished. I saw it when you so gallantly landed on that aircraft carrier. I know you don't know defeat and that's okay. But read your history. Read about Waterloo. Oh yeah and remember you third grade teacher? She drove me nuts always repeating, "History repeats." Don't wear your swimsuit in the Arctic during winter and don't wear your Arctic gear in the Sahara.

In case you didn't notice we won the war; our soldiers showed proud. Now it's time for the Iraqi people to step to the plate. Either they will be like South Korea or South Vietnam. Right now it looks like that third grade teacher is pointing to South Vietnam.

Remember the song we used to sing, "London Bridge is falling down?" Check the newspaper because you can change the name to Baghdad. The "cradle of civilization" can now be called "the cradle of destruction." Mr. President do you have any plans for the destruction to stop? At least Saddam Hussein could do something you can't; control his country.

Wait, I've been two hard on Bush. He was right all those Democrats are liars and trying to deceive Americans.

BUT…remember the third grade teacher…one last question, Mr. President, is there anyone you have picked who has ever told the truth? Powell doesn't count he was smart enough to quit when you deceived him.

Here's Another One

(4.13.07)

President Bush has picked another one.

Reminds me of being at the carnival where you shoot down the little metal men with your gun and win a prize. All the president's men could be lined up for this one. In fact they seem to be as smart as those little metal men. The only difference is you can trust the little metal men in the carnival.

So here we go again this week.

Paul Wolfowitz is to the TRUST and integrity of World Banking (our money),

As Haggard is to Morality,

As Rove is to National Security,

As Cheney is to open construction bids,

As Foley is to Family Values,

As Gonzales is to Human rights,

And President Bush is to winning a war.

How about a big round or applause for another one—Paul Wolfowitz! And all the President's Men.

A note on the war. Terror is not in Afghanistan and Iraq but everywhere. Will the "Terror Peace Treaty" be in Afghanistan? And what about Drugs? That's becoming like terror. Aw, heck Mr. President we all know drugs are from Colombia. If you will stop it there then nobody will do drugs anymore--just like terror will end when we win in Iraq. WMD's, democracy, terror, OIL? Why the hell are we really there? When Halliburton bails out you know we're doomed. Didn't you tell Cheney to tell Halliburton not to leave Iraq? Aren't you paying them enough? If Halliburton is smart enough to get out why aren't you? Is Cheney headed to Dubai? Anyway let's get back on track. Every war is followed by negotiations, a treaty and then peace. If you have no plans to negotiate and stop the war then you are just as bad as them.

But you said it was Mission Accomplished. I saw it when you so gallantly landed on that aircraft carrier. I know you don't know defeat and that's okay. But read your history. Read about Waterloo. Oh yeah and remember you third grade teacher? She drove me nuts always repeating, "History repeats." Don't wear your swimsuit in the Arctic during winter and don't wear your Arctic gear in the Sahara.

In case you didn't notice we won the war; our soldiers showed proud. Now it's time for the Iraqi people to step to the plate. Either they will be like South Korea or South Vietnam. Right now it looks like that third grade teacher is pointing to South Vietnam.

Remember the song we used to sing, "London Bridge is falling down?" Check the newspaper because you can change the name to Baghdad. The "cradle of civilization" can now be called "the cradle of destruction." Mr. President do you have any plans for the destruction to stop? At least Saddam Hussein could do something you can't; control his country.

Wait, I've been two hard on Bush. He was right all those Democrats are liars and trying to deceive Americans.

BUT…remember the third grade teacher…one last question, Mr. President, is there anyone you have picked who has ever told the truth? Powell doesn't count he was smart enough to quit when you deceived him.

Apologize
((04.13.07)

I need to apologize to everybody. This is a poor time to admit it but I'm as bad as Imus. That's right I have said terrible things.

For my whole life I have been calling St. Nick a nappy haired, "Ho, Ho, Ho." I can only think of poor old Imus, who can no longer say, "Hi ho, hi ho, it's off to work I go!" But when he was seen leaving CBS they said they heard him saying, "Uh, oh. Oh, no, I have no work to go."

And I must apologize for the things I have said about President Bush. There has never been a leader that has done so much for Christianity as President Bush. He has brought ethics, honor, integrity, morality and family values to the forefront. Most importantly there is no longer a need to search for lost souls to save. You only need to look as far as all the President's men to see there are still a lot more souls to save.

What Would They All Say
(07.04.07)

Al Gore's son, Al Gore III, was arrested for possession of pot.
Al Gore noted that it looks like the third time is not the charm.
When Al Gore the third was seen being counseled by Bill Clinton, Al Gore changed his plea, "Yes, I did smoke the pot but I did not inhale."
Edward Kennedy was seen slipping Al Gore the third a Chappaquiddick get

109

out of jail free pass.

When George Bush was asked about Al Gore the third, he looked at Cheney and said, "I don't care if it is the fourth time, we is the President and this is an issue of National Security. The media needs to get off my back. You would beat a dead bush even if it was alive." A news reporter noted Gore's son is a hot issue, **whereas** Bush shook his head disgustedly, "I have faith in God and I know for a fact, that the sun is not Gore's. And, my God, do you think I'm a dumb ass? Everybody knows the sun is hot."

George Bush's daughter Barbara was overheard telling Al Gore the third, "Come to Texas and become a Republican and then you can do anything you want like my sister and I. Governor Perry will cover for you and if he won't you can count on the Texas Rangers." President Bush heard the last few words and screamed at his Secret Service, "I told you to tell me when the Texas Rangers were on." He was last seen running into his office with the television remote.

The news media asked Cheney if this could branch off into a bigger problem. Cheney screamed, "You are the problem and my branch is separate from the President and on my personal executive privilege I will not answer that question." Another Reporter asked Cheney what about the family values and Cheney was quick to respond, "Leave my daughter out of this. I'll tell you our family values when Halliburton finishes."

Again Gore the third was seen with Bill Clinton and Clinton, who was puffing on a cigar. Clinton caught sight of a shapely female Intern, smiled looked at Gore the third, looked at his cigar and said, "Did I ever show you how to use a cigar?"

When the senior Gore was confronted with the smoking marijuana by his son he said, "This is a ploy by the Republicans to take away from the real problem. The environment is the problem. Remember that. This is not really a problem. When the smoke clears you will find that my carbon credits will cover this whole problem because in two years we will plant a tree in Ecuador that will equalize the smoke from my son."

THE AMERICAN AMNESTY SEVEN POINT PLAN:

(Sent to the CNN News Media 5.30.07)

I'm a Republican and I feel I've been deceived by the Republican Party. Is anybody listening to the American People!!

To All Member of Congress:

One thing I'd like to know is why our borders aren't being protected? If there is a war against terror shouldn't we try to prevent them from just walking over?

The battle is in Iraq, the war is on our border, while the amnesty you are creating has shown the world we have lost the war!

Are we as safe here as the borders are in Iraq? What about the OTM's?

"Other Than Mexican" illegal immigrants pose a national security risk to the U.S.

The serious national security threat posed by "Other Than Mexicans" is not widely understood. Approximately 100,000 illegal immigrants entering the United States from Mexico each year are not Mexicans. The Border Patrol refers to these persons as "OTM's" - "Other Than Mexicans"

Within the last year, over 450 OTM's have been apprehended illegally entering the United States from such officially-designated "special interest" countries as:

Afganistán
Angola
Jordan
Qatar
Pakistan
Yemen
Are we safe?

If our military can't do the job over there how are you going to protect us in our own country? If you don't protect our borders now what is your plan to protect Americans? Must we wait for the terrorists to perform another Katrina to show us you have no plan? Protect the borders now and you won't need to come up with a plan when disaster strikes. And if all our military, including the National Guard and their equipment (Kansas), is everywhere in the world but here, how do you plan to protect your fellow Americans? Do you have a plan? I'm just a concerned citizen.

Now let's get to the problem of Amnesty.

There can be no real Amnesty until the United States of America secures the border. This is the most important war and we have lost it. Show Americans you intend to enforce the old laws. The reason you are trying to pass a new law filled with more problems and loop holes than the old laws because you are unable to enforce the old ones and are using a smoke screen to make us think you have a real solution. How do you intend to enforce these new laws when you have never enforced the old laws? Secure the border then makes rules for Amnesty.

THE AMERICAN AMNESTY SEVEN POINT PLAN:

1. The citizenship test will be offered only in English and you must pass it. If you don't have enough desire to learn English there is no reason to become a citizen. This is America learn English.

2. If you have lived in the United States for more than two years, speak English, can show proof you held a job and paid taxes, and have a child that was born within any of the 50 states or Puerto Rico you qualify to become an American citizen immediately and need only pass the test for citizenship.

3. If you have been in the United States but do not speak English you can apply for an extension to take the citizenship in 18 months after learning English. This will show your desire and determination to assimilate into the society of the United States of America.

4. You will automatically become an American citizen if you enlist in one of the military forces of the United States. Should you be a conscientious objector you will be assigned some working position. If you also speak English your rank will automatically be raised one position upon completion of your military training.

5. No illegal alien being granted citizenship will be eligible for welfare for a minimum of 10 years and no Social Security unless there is a death in the family.

6. All aliens that become citizens, and have worked in the United States, will be exempt from previous Income Tax so long as they list their "illegal" American

employer.

7. For this plan to go into effect everyone on welfare will be required to apply for all of those "unwanted American jobs." You will be required to work those jobs with the income you receive being deducted from your welfare check. You're an American show some initiative and determination. This is not a free ride. Any person on welfare refusing to take a job offered, except for physical disability, will be denied welfare PERMANENTLY. Show some pride and go to work.

A Word to Congress
(9.7.07)

War is not only victory but also compromise. Sometimes there is retreat but always towards the end there is negotiation, diplomacy and then a truce and treaty. Our President has led us astray. He feels unbeatable just like Napoleon did at Waterloo. Iraq is President Bush's Waterloo. A good General knows when to retreat. Apparently Bush does not understand that word. Remember for every Victory there is a defeat. We have a Congress that only knows how to spend money or stick their hand under the bathroom stall. They're too busy registering on a prostitutes list than to represent Americans protecting their health, homes and Social Security. The one thing they don't do is the one thing they were elected to do: Represent Americans. Not Corporate America but the working individuals that elected them. It seems to me the only danger to America and Americans are the Democrats and Republicans that have been elected to Congress. It is not too late to do what is right. There are no WMD's, the war is wrong and quit giving money to the Halliburton's of Dubai. I implore Congress to do something unusual. For once represent the Americans that elected you to office.

Letter to a Cowboy Friend
(He wants more war)
(9.24.07)

Is the civil war here or there?

Gosh, when you talk about your ex-**wife** it sounds like a Sunni talking about a Shiite. Divide and conquer? Already been done by **our** own Congress. Where did it ever say his goal was to control the strait? With his naval force or his army? What a joke. Or maybe even his WMD's. So who are the bad guys? Where are they? How do we defeat them?

The "bad guys" are not in Iraq…they are all over the world. Ask Indonesia, Spain and the UK. How do you fight them? It's easy but not with an army.

Liberal or conservative, Iraq has not stepped up. Korea did it in less than four years. Viet Nam never did. And Iraq never will.

When you talk about liberals you sound like the KKK going to a NAACP love reunion. Remember maybe half of the United States is liberal. Your words sound of a civil war. Forget Iraq. If we fight ourselves we **will** never survive. And by the way, being a cowboy and wanting war will solve nothing. Every war ends with a treaty and peace but if we continue to fight a war this will last forever. Including here in the United States.

There was a cartoon I read once. Pogo with a possum and an alligator. Pogo hit the nail on the head when he said, "We has seen the enemy and they is us!"

The Missing Billions
(3.142.07)
A few years ago Bush sent a C-130 with 20 billion in American dollars. CASH! He said it would spur the Iraq economy. Yeah. Well there was a little problem finding the "Yellow Brick Road." Seems that nine billon disappeared, and nobody bothered to find out where the money went. I'll bet they bought dinar since it's value was about 2000 to 1 in American dollars. Ask yourself why we're there working so hard to rebuild the economy. Before 1991 when the first Bush invaded the dinar was 3 to 1. Bush (father) did the same thing for Kuwait and had their money revalued. Okay here is my point, in the next few years the Bush's and his men will do the same thing for Iraq. That is why he wanted Chalabi but it didn't work out right. Let's go back to the value of 2000 to 1 and for the sake of easy math we'll say the dinar is revalued to 1 to 1. If you bought 2000 dinar for a dollar you now have 2000 dollars. Now where did the nine billion go? If they have nine billion American dollars in dinar it will be worth eighteen trillion American dollars when revalued.

Is the problem Illegals or Americans?
(6.12.07)
Sad thing is the real problem is not reflected in those statistics. Who funds the illegal immigrants in all of these? Who is supposed to enforce our laws? Who hasn't guarded the borders since 911? But more important is why? Don't know the answer? I'll give you a hint. They make the laws. I don't know why they do that, because they can't even enforce the old ones.

Now the real problem is not reflected in those statistics. Do we go after the drug user or the drug dealer? So who hires the illegal aliens? If you can't figure that out there is no reason to tell you.

Who promised to take care of Americans if there was another 911? What happened during Katrina? So tell me what will happen now? If you dig real deep you will find some politicians took contributions from major companies in south Texas to guarantee they could continue to hire illegal aliens. Those same people now say those against amnesty are un-American. I say those un-Americans are really patriots protecting America. Those who accuse us of being un-American are actually traitors. The same person who said we are un-American, just a few years ago said about the Al-Qaeda, "You're either with us or you're with them." I say it is obvious he is not with us.

We must tell congress that the battle is on the border of Iraq, but the war is on the borders of America. We have lost the war. Amnesty is surrender...defeat!

Tell congress it is easy to find the real problem. All they need to do is to look real close at what they see in their bathroom mirror.

President Chavez Atrocities Mount
(6.14.07)
Read closely what President Chavez has done.
Although democratically elected the atrocities of Chavez continue to mount. Chavez warned his people that his country is under threat of invasion from a

foreign country and that his country must prepare.

He tells his people they must be willing to sacrifice for their country.

He gives special government contracts to friends and allies.

Billions of dollars disappear from money collected by his government.

He blames the world for his problems.

Countries that violate human rights are given special concessions.

Friends and family have lucrative contracts with communist countries.

He condemns the news media and threatens them by telling his people the media is siding with the enemy.

He says the UN must sanction the enemies of his country and that the UN is incapable of governing the world.

He claims to be a Christian.

Even though it is illegal, he removes judges that oppose him and replaces them with people loyal to his cause.

He believes he is the best thing for the people and that only he knows what is right for the people even if they all disagree with him. He tells his own people if they are not with him they are with the enemy.

He tells his people that the opposition are all liars.

He tries to control the media.

Denying the rights of his country's constitution he puts those that are against him in jail and tells his people that those he put in jail are against their country and he has the right to do so.

He surrounds himself with **handpicked** people that are liars and hypocrites. A danger to any democratic society.

He denies trials to those he puts in jail by saying they are his countries enemy and that he has the power to keep them in jail indefinitely because they are enemies of his country and for that reason alone he has the power to keep them in jail without a trial even though his country's constitution guarantees otherwise.

He swore an oath to protect the constitution of his country but has failed on his promise.

What Chavez has done is terrible. Can you believe someone would have done any of those things to the citizens of his own country?

Well count your blessings that we have a President like Bush, who is honest, truthful, filled with integrity, and such a fine Christian man. Thank God for a man like President Bush who is leading us on such an honorable path. Our President is someone the world looks up to and trusts totally.

Republican National Convention Schedule
(1.09.07)
Invitation to RNC
2008 Republican National Convention Schedule
7:00 P. M. Opening flag waving of Saudi Arabia and Iraq with President Bush holding hands with the Saudi King7:15 P. M. Pledge of Allegiance to the New World Order 7:30 PM. Condoleezza Rice proposes a toast to her ability as a military commander 7:30 till 8:00 P. M. Family values led by Rep. Mark Foley and Rep. Dennis Hastert. Hastert finished up by stating, "I don't know anything."

7:45 Colin Powell makes a special appearance to present Dick Cheney with two awards, "Father of the Year," and "The Great American Hunter."

8:00 P. M. President Bush promises to never stop his fight against Terror. Looking confused he asks Cheney if Terror is close to North Korea or in Africa 8:05 P. M Ceremonial tree burning 8:15- 8:30 P. M. President Bush discusses the importance of bi-sexual marriages, where Rove quickly stops him and explains that bi is not two people of opposite sexes but people who have sex with both sexes but again Bush confuses this as Clinton with Monica and Hillary 8:30 P. M. Prayer and worship led by Shilling from a remote Federal Prison resort in the Bahamas8:35 P. M. Weapons of Mass Destruction and the Axis of Error by Rove, Cheney and Rumsfeld9:00 P. M. Keynote speech: "The Proper Etiquette for Surrender" by Tom Delay.

9:15 P. M. Lobbyist Jack Abramoff discusses the importance of gambling and pledging support to big business by giving all Republicans new Mercedes and a Caribbean cruise9:20 P. M. Collection to benefit Osama Bin Laden Kidney Transplant Fund to keep the war on terror going9:30 P. M. Unveiling of plan to free freedom fighters from Guantanamo Bay after the torture is completed: by Donald (Duck) Rumsfeld9:40 P. M. Mission Accomplished: Why I'm a Military hero: A short talk by President Bush9:45 P. M. "Why I'm a Christian and the sanctity of marriage," by President Bush9:50 P. M. Dick, Lin, George and Laura watch over the marriage of the Cheney's daughter to her girlfriend. The wedding is attended by Rep. Mark Foley and his 16 year old boyfriend.

9:55 P. M. Rove receives the "Honor and Integrity" award, presented by Cheney. Foley, Ney and DeLay receive honorable mentions.

10:00 P. M. Presentation: "How Bill Clinton brought down the World Trade Center Towers", by Rove10.15 P. M. Republicans receive pledges of continuing support from the CEO's of Exxon and BP. Profits for each company exceed 10 billion for the current quarter.

10:30 P. M. Nomination of Condoleezza Rice for President by Dictator Musharraf of Pakistan.

10:45 P. M. Million dollar pledges and new cars given to all present by Halliburton and personally presented by Cheney.

11:00 P. M. Rep. Mark Foley presents the "No child left behind" to his closest "pages."

11:15 Rep. Bob Ney gives a speech on ethics that makes Jack Abramoff all teary eyed.

11:30 P. M. "All Democrats are liars," discussed by Rove, Rumsfeld, Bush, Rep. Bob Ney, Tom DeLay and Rep. Mark Foley11:15 P. M. "The New 50-50 Fence along the border to Mexico", presented by Bush discussing half the border fenced the other half left unguarded stressing both the importance of stopping illegal aliens but also allowing enough to come in and mow our yards and make tacos. "Besides I need somebody to take care of my ranch in Crawford," says Bush.

12:30 P. M Coronation of Condoleezza Rice. She discusses the New World Order and the evils of drinking.

1:30 A. M. Clinton and Kennedy crash the party (security is weak) and after Kennedy and Rice are plastered Clinton convinces Rice to let Kennedy drive her home.

Shaky Terrorism
(4.10.07)

Shaky would have been great. Non-existent is more like it. Didn't we declare war on terror? Tell me where terror resides? Russia? Spain? England? France? The United States? Indonesia? Saudi Arabia? Somalia? Where is terror? Our President decided the base for terror was Afghanistan. They are not a base for anything but a spring board to attack Iraq. Weren't 15 of the 19 terrorists from Saudi Arabia? Just for terror's sack don't forget to toss in Timothy McVeigh. Negotiations kept Saddam at bay and would have until the day he died.

Based on your analogy we should have attacked Korea and Iran. Or previous leaders should have Nuked China and Russia. If you are right then we will attack Korea and Iran. If we don't then we know them. Error in the side of caution is not a bad thing, is it? I don't know maybe we should ask the Indians and buffalo. Hey, we needed meat and land, it's the American way.

Negotiations is the solution. Never war unless attacked and I've already told you who attacked us. We needed Afghanistan like we needed the buffalo. We wanted Iraq. Why? WMD's? Nukes? Democracy? Saddam was going to kill Bush's father? And how was he going to do that? The war was for one reason and one reason only. OIL!!!

Who said this? - "They are our enemy and will attack. We must attack before they have the chance to invade us." The words are close but not exact. Think about it and I will send you the answer in a minute.

If you are worried about nukes then let me tell you where it will come from. We aided China during WWII, Russia was our ally. Italy, Germany and Japan were our bitter enemies. Recently Noriega was an ally. The Shah of Iran was our friend. We put Castro in power. We gave Saddam everything he had so he could defeat Iran. Iran, Korea and Iraq were the axis of evil. We gave Afghanistan everything to defeat Russia. What happened to those people and those countries? Pakistan, Saudi Arabia and India are our allies. Do you see where I'm going? Do you know who helped us win independence and become a democratic country that could exercise free choice? France. But when France questioned our decision we didn't honor free choice. Instead we became arrogant and defiant. French fries became American fries. How childish. Do we still have free choice? Better to error.... You either agree with Bush or you're the enemy. Now back up to Pakistan and India. Our allies today our enemies tomorrow. Nuclear proliferation applies not only to our enemies but also to our allies. Here is what is going to happen. If Pakistan and India don't nuke each other then a fanatical group will assassinate Musharraf and then they will control the bomb and make sure our enemies have them. The bomb will come from within the United States.

And remember the error goes both ways. To do something wrong is bad but to do nothing is worse. Our Mexican border! The bombs will be driven across freely. You should ask why Bush attacks the world but doesn't protect our border?

If I remember right, almost all of our leaders were privy to the same intelligence and they all agreed to go to war. . . Funny how history has changed!

You proved my point about Democrats and Republicans. History repeats. You did read Moon Shadow?

I'd much rather have the fighting overseas then in my own neighborhood, wouldn't you?

Of course but you must remember when you declare a war the enemy has the right to kill us back. This is not a video game. Why does Bush not let us see the tragedy of the American dead in Iraq? Why is he keeping secrets? Americans are as safe and will have as much help during terror as they did in New Orleans during Katrina. Ask yourself why we've spent 120 billion on New Orleans. Run some numbers. Insurance covered most, so why did we spend so much? Over 200,000 were permanently displaced (I loved the $2000 charge card. Who the hell dreamed that up?) If you gave each of them $100,000 to build their own house somewhere else it would only have cost $20 billion. Why are we spending $120 billion tax dollars?

Democrats and Republicans--we has seen the enemy and they is us. . . Realistic?

If you think any politician is anything other than self-promoting you're mistaken.

You can't pick a party and call them hypocrites; both parties are full of them so watch what you say. We tried to impeach Clinton for lying about sex with an intern yet Bush lied and started a war. Is he being impeach for it? No way. So don't say party's leaders are all hypocrites. Or you'll be talking about yourself!

So to say one party is full of hypocrites and one is realistic and not self-promoting is just wrong.

Larry

On the other hand if you were them looking at us and realize you were called one of the axis of evil and we've already attacked one you would want to amass weapons for your own preservation so you don't become the France of WWII. And who made us the policeman of the world?

Remember we attacked Iraq because of how evil Saddam was to his own people but yet we do nothing in Somali where Muslims are slaughtering Christians. Do you know why we don't help? No OIL!

Attack Now Before They Attack Us
(5.23.07)

Hitler convinced his people to attack France before they attacked Germany. Similar to what Bush said about Iraq. I'd like to know where all the money from Iraq's oil is going.

Bombing and Terror
(5.23.07)

Actually France wasn't bombed in World War II. Hitler marched into Paris and took it with almost no resistance. Once Paris fell the French gave up. The destruction came when we fought the Germans there.

Too much paranoia. How are they going to get here? The best way is to walk across the border, get freebies and change the language. Defeat us from within. That's how it is done. Same way throughout history. But if Congress and Bush bankrupts the country how do you suppose we can defend ourselves? We won't be able to do it.

America Communicates only with Democratic Countries?
(5.23.07)

Also Bush has sworn not to communicate with countries that are not democratic. But he won't talk to Chavez (elected), but he will to Musharraf (dictator of Pakistan) and even holds hands with the king of Saudi. Allies today, enemies tomorrow.

Shocking Senate Vote
(5.23.07)

Not really shocking at all. This is an email set up to discredit the Democrats. Now I don't have much respect for Democrats, but tell me who you think would want to send around lies? Could it be…. ? No they wouldn't do that. Republicans would never do this. Down with Kennedy, Clinton and all those other scumbag, cheating, lying Democrats. Thank God for the Republicans and their honor and integrity. As long as we have honorable and trusting Republicans like Haggard (no gay marriages), Tobias(no prostitution), Foley(family values), Cheney(Halliburton), Rove(truth, top secret leaks), Wolfowitz(corruption), and Gonzalez(torture and enforcing the Constitution), and **Mr.** Bush (Mission Accomplished against WMD's, or bad ruler or democracy or Saddam was going to kill his father or—oh hell whatever!) this country is safe . Those Democrats are out to get the Republicans it's all politically motivated.

AMERICA LOVE IT OR LEAVE IT!!!! What did you say? I thought Halliburton said, "Goodbye!" You say they went to Dubai? Because they can't make any more money off of our government and they don't feel dying American troops are capable of protecting them? Cheney wouldn't let Halliburton do that because he gave them a no bid contract. Oh, my God what is happening!!

Those scumbag Democrats. It's their fault that 20 million illegal aliens are here. Thank God Mr. Bush protected our borders after 911. What did you say? More are coming across now then when the Democrats were in office. But isn't Bush protecting our borders? He's not? You say the illegal aliens are in Crawford working on Bush's ranch? It's because Americans won't do jobs like that? Oh, my God, you mean our borders really aren't protected? But what about those Al guys? The who? You say the, Al **Qaeda**? How can those Al guys be coming across the border? Bush promised we would be safe. I thought we were fighting a war against terror? Everyone knows, like Bush told us, that all terrorism is in Iraq. Once we defeat terror in Iraq there will be no more bombing **anywhere**. I guess they left Afghanistan and went to Iraq. But Bush says they're in Iran now. If we have the best military in the world how come we can't control Iraq? You say it's the Democrats fault. What do we do? How about we contract Saddam Hussein? At least he controlled his country. He's dead? But what about his appeal? Because he killed too many people, was a bad leader and a dictator? But aren't we killing a lot of them. Oh, it's for democracy. Well that's different. As long as we kill them so they can have a democracy well then let's do it. This is all Clinton's fault, 'cause I heard he had a chance to kill bin Laden three times. Bush will make it right. You say Bush has never been able to find bin Laden? How come you're so against Bush? He's doing this to free the world.

Okay. Now **let's** be serious for a moment. When I hear the Democrats talk about the Republicans and the Republicans talking about the Democrats I feel like I'm in a church meeting about "loving your neighbor" with a group from the KKK and the NAACP. But be careful it won't be long before we become like the Sunni and the **Shiites**. One day it might be Democrat killing Republican. I hope not.

In reality the problem rests with the people. The **ill-informed** people who don't want to listen or read the truth. There are only two problems with our government today and they are Democrats and Republicans.

Rebellion is my theme all day;
I only wish 'twould come
(As who knows but perhaps it may?)
A little nearer home.

You roaring boys, who rave and fight
On t'other side the Atlantic,
I always held them in the right,
But most so when most frantic.

When lawless mobs insult the court,
That man shall be my toast;
If breaking windows be the sport,
Who bravely breaks the most.
-- The Modern Patriot, **William Cowper**, *1779.*

The breaking windows that the English poet Cowper was celebrating were the windows of American Tories, broken by the Sons of Liberty in the run-up to the American Revolution. In Eighteenth Century America, windows were expensive and difficult to replace. It was said you could tell an American colonist's wealth by the size and number of the windows in his house. As most of the high-ranking Tories loyal to the King were rich, their windows became natural targets when the Sons of Liberty wanted to send a message. If the head of the local militia was a Tory, he would be persuaded to resign his commission by breaking his windows. If a Boston merchant refused to join the boycott of British goods, he would have to hire a glazier in the morning. Tax collectors and other crown functionaries shuttered their houses, only to have the shutters torn from their hinges by a mob and then have their windows broken. Sounds harsh? The rise of American independence was accompanied by the tune of breaking glass, and we wouldn't be free today without it.

Of course how free we are, and are going to be, is the question, isn't it? We have been too law-abiding. It's time to misbehave. But we must search out the truth. What you really want is the truth and here is where you can find it: http://www.snopes.com/politics/immigration/englishvote.asp

The Un-American
(5.30.07)

Yes, I used the Congressmen's email addresses and I was surprised to have only about six get rejected for incorrect email address and one sent back saying they no longer worked for them. Yesterday I sent a big email to Sessions about my seven point plan. But don't worry I don't think any of them really listen to us anymore.

I'm not against immigration and I think my idea of the seven point plan is good but through it all the border still needs to be guarded no matter what they decide. It's like they think if amnesty is passed the borders will be okay. That is not true. This is not a video game and I guarantee you that over the last six years terrorist cells have simply just walked across the border. We are in danger and it lies squarely on the heads of "all" of our politicians that have been in office since 911. That includes our Governor.

The sad thing is that freedom of speech and the right to dissent against polices is being shot down. For Bush to call those that disagree with him Un-American is well, simply Un-American. I think he is out of touch with reality and has his own personal agenda. I feel he is coming closer to being America's Chavez. He needs to look at what is good for America not what he perceives as what is good for the world. The world is not ready for George Bush and I don't think America is anymore either.

Don't Abandon Iraq
(5.30.07)

This is in response to your article: U. S Can't Abandon Iraq Amid Unrest.

First let me say I voted for Bush but I must say I'm disappointed now.

We abandoned the people within weeks after we invaded. Think about it. First it was a grudge, revenge war for Bush and a time to make a fortune for Cheney and Halliburton. Oil was the number one reason. Freeing a people from a dictator doesn't free the people. We took Iraq from the predator and gave them to the vultures and many of those vultures were our own people, Halliburton included.

You say no? A week after the war started Rumsfeld announced the military had secured over 150 wells. Wasn't the war over Weapons of Mass Destruction? Common sense says the first thing you would do with the "accurate information" Bush had would be to secure the sites you know had WMD's. Nuclear locations should be top priorities. At the same time Rumsfeld said he had secured the wells, CNN was showing pictures of Iraqi people looting a nuclear power plant. Wouldn't you think a nuclear plant would be a good place to store radioactive material for WMD's. So why weren't these critical positions secured? The answer is simple; because the war was for oil.

Immediately Halliburton started stealing tax payer's dollars. The same taxes the parents, wives and husbands were paying while their loved ones died to protect the greed of Halliburton.

Without being a military tactician, common sense says when you secure a country you try to maintain stability in the economy with the monetary system, electricity, water, employment, education and security for the people.

Within three weeks chaos reigned and American troops stood idly by while the country of Iraq imploded. That was when the U. S. ABANDONED THE IRAQI PEOPLE. The military left the people of Iraq to the "vultures."

I can still remember seeing the theft and chaos, banks being looted and nothing being done. Rumsfeld came on TV in his smug way and said Chaos was to be expected and the Iraqi people would need to deal with it. At that point the U. S. had already abandoned the Iraqi people.

This was a war for revenge, greed and oil. A war of stupidity by a group of run-a-muck "cowboys."

The president's men remind me more of the executives of Enron. Not only did they bring chaos to Iraq but also to the people of the United States.

Now they demand the Iraq people give up their weapons. They also demanded a Shiite newspaper shut down. Bush and his men also don't want the Shiite people to have a say in the government. It is a known fact that sixty percent of the people are Shiite. For example in the United States let's say sixty percent of the people were Catholic and our president said their views didn't agree with those of Americans so they would no longer have a say so in elections. Tell me what would happen?

The President demands a democracy for Iraq, a country that has not had one for a thousand years. Then he takes the foundation of freedoms the U. S. was based on and denies them to Iraq. You know what I mean. Freedom of speech, freedom of the press, freedom of choice (to pick the people you want) and the right to bear arms. What happened to these freedoms? You will find that through history the majority will rise up. The Shiites will take over! There is nothing Bush can do about it but loose more American lives. We will find out, and very soon, that the new leader of Iraq will be worse than Saddam Hussein.

Iraq was better off before the United States invaded. President Bush his men and the U. S. abandoned the people of Iraq a long time ago.

Treason – Bush Whacked
(5.30.07)

I agree. Lets focus. You've gotta try to laugh….otherwise you'll be depressed. Worried? I'm worried. You want some serious facts?

We have lost the war. In all wars you eventually win or lose. They end with negotiations and a treaty. I believe this is the first time in history a war was declared on a word. I believe we should fight terror and based on that fact due to the Oklahoma terrorist act we should be sending F-14's up and down Interstate 10 shooting down every suspicious Ryder Truck we see. Why I 10? Because just like Afghanistan and Iraq it is a main base for Ryder terrorists. We must catch them at their source and then there will be no more.

"Mission Accomplished" was four years ago. Remember the aircraft carrier? Lets back up in history to 1945. We did conquer the world. Four years later in 1949 we were being bombarded with good will, Toyota, VW, Porsche and Ferrari. Bush had no plan for Iraq except maybe oil and Halliburton. We succeeded, they have democracy and now they must step to the plate. But look at them. They hate each other and the only people they like to kill more than themselves are foreign people on their land. IT IS TIME TO LEAVE!

But first, I believe that Halliburton should be audited. I also believe that no company based outside of the United States should receive any job paid with our tax dollars. You know—AMERICA LOVE IT OR LEAVE IT!!! Well we all know what Halliburton did. They believe in the almighty dollar not America. So let's take their dollars away.

Did you know 73 foreign companies have contracts for military rockets, jets and weapons? Isn't this a national security problem? The enemy doesn't need to have spies; all they need are lobbyists to take people like Delay on golf trips so they can get secret military jobs. Hey we might as well have China and Russia make our weapons because India is making most of our computer products. You do know Microsoft invested 10 billion in India to do just that, right?

But the National Debt is the real problem. Financially our Congress and our President (chad) have done more to destroy this country than the Al-Qaeda. I estimate that in 2012 we should be bankrupt (government). Remember they have already spent all of our Social Security.

Now some serious numbers. We collect 2.5 trillion from taxes to run the government (up from 2.25 trillion). Congress sets a budget at 2.9 trillion. Let's say we spend 2.8 trillion. Common math says we owe .3 trillion more to the National Debt but no that's not the way the President or Congress sees it. The Budget was 2.9 so that means we have a 100 billion dollar surplus that they quickly spend. The last time we had a surplus (more collected than spent) was in 1960. Our National Debt on April 5th was 8,885,158,288,211.72. It should be close to 10 trillion when Bush leaves. At this time interest is low but just say that the U. S. pays 10 percent on the bonds to carry the debt. Figure that into the numbers above and it is very scary. Now I never did like Clinton very much but the National Debt went up only 18 billion his whole last year. On the third and the fifth of April the National Debt exceeded that amount on each of those days. The United States has been around a little more than 230 years. The National Debt is approximately 9 trillion. It went up 1.5 under the first Bush and 3.5 under the second Bush. So in a little less than 12 of those 230 years 5 of the 9 trillion is under the Bush's. Does that mean we just got Bushwhacked? He may be a cowboy but someone needs to tell ol' Toby Keith Bush doesn't wear a white hat.

The real "focus" should be on Congress and the President.

You can check out the National Debt here:

http://www. treasurydirect. gov/NP/BPDLogin?application=np

I consider myself a conservative and a Republican but I have been deceived by the Republicans for they are neither conservative nor liberal but rather a new type of radical that scares me a little. As far as I'm concerned Congress and the President are no better than the schemes and scams of ENRON. To me they have committed treason and we all know the punishment for treason.

Judicial System
(6.08.07)

Currently there are only two problems with the American judicial system. The courts are made up of Democrats or Republicans. Therein lies the problem. . Unlike most of our politicians today the courts should represent the people not their party demands. Sadly, this is where the courts are lacking. The judicial system should make laws not govern morality. The Constitution was clear on this issue; separation of church and state. The judicial system has been so busy regulating prayer and pledges that it no longer understands what it means. The church doesn't make laws, and the courts shouldn't regulate morality. Let the church govern morality, not the courts.

In public schools all who want to pray have that right, even if it offends someone else. The right to pray should never be denied in any public place including schools. Separation of church and state meant that the state will "never" interfere with religion at any location unless it supports the killing of others. To preach killing of others will not be tolerated. Remember that to deny prayer also offends the ones who want to pray. Those who do not want to pray should remember they have that right. One day the court may say you must pray. Don't let that happen.

Public schools should be able to teach evolution and about the various religions. This is called knowledge. The only ones who are offended with knowledge are those who are ignorant. Those who refuse to teach evolution or about God are one step removed from Hitler for they have already taken away free choice.

All schools need is to enforce discipline. For decades we have heard, "Spare the rod spoil the child." It doesn't work. Common sense says, "Use the rod, save the child." I guess those who don't agree must be lacking common sense. The former plan has never worked. Let's try hard discipline for a few decades and see what happens.

There are many religions and they all deserve respect as long as they don't preach the death of others regardless of their religious affiliation. Religions are like older people. Show them all respect because your day is coming.

When anger flares about the Muslims killing Americans in New York and we justify attacking other nations but remember it was a Christian that did Oklahoma City. With that in mind shouldn't be sending fighter planes up and down the interstates to attack and blow up any suspicious looking Ryder trucks?

To live by the Ten Commandments are good rules for everybody. All people, including atheists. To take away such a dynamic foundation of honor and integrity publicly displayed in any building is simply un-American. If the Ten Commandments offend you then you are in the wrong country.

Every American should be honored to say the pledge of allegiance. To deny the pledge is also un-American. If it offends you go back to your country. To say the American pledge is an honor all Americans should cherish.

If you are new to the United States and want to be a citizen then you should be required to speak English. English is not a hardship but rather an honor and showing respect for your adopted country. Election ballots will be only in one language—English. If you cannot read or speak simple English how to you expect to choose a politician that can best represent you? Show respect for your new country; learn English. Multiple languages will only accelerate the ethnic divisions in this country and only divide us more. Remember, "United we stand, divided we fall."

You have the right to be offended. Voice your opinion, it's called "freedom of speech" and the Constitution guarantees you that right. That same right is also guaranteed to the one who offended you. Learn to live with it.

No matter what is ever said or done, someone will be offended. This is part of life. The problem is the judicial system has spent so much time protecting each individual's rights that they have taken away all of our rights.

National Security
(4.23.07)

If national security is so critical that President Bush says those very words as reasons his men can not testify then isn't it ironic that most of our most critical weapons be made and supplied by foreign countries. Even those countries that we have questionable relations? In fact what countries are really our allies? Those that were our allies we kidnap people from their countries saying "national security" while at the same time denying those same allies their own sovereignty. We demand extradition of people from those countries while denying their request.

Shouldn't we step up a notch and do more than we demand? Just as Bush's religious counselor Haggard was for morality so too Bush has become the same for democracy, truth and NATIONAL SECURITY?

BUT NATIONAL SECURITY is critical and there I agree so I disagree when I learn that more than seventy foreign countries supply parts for some of our top secret weapons. I mean the next thing you know true dedicated honest American companies will be moving to places like Dubai. But don't worry I know our President will not let that happen and of course he, the Vice President and Rove will step to the plate and deny contracts to companies that would do something like that.

Foreign countries are not sending spies to steal our secrets. All they need to do is send lobbyists, give local politicians money for their re-elections and then wait to have those candidates give you lucrative contracts to build those weapons. You not only get the secrets but you make money at the same time. Weapons of National Security should be made here and if we are not capable of doing that then we should no longer feel required to give democracy to countries that are not ready for it.

How to transform a government
(02.12.07)

The guy that wrote the article below, Henry Lamb is just as nutty as the others and actually contradicts himself in the article. The Republicans, of which I am one, have gone too far. I don't believe Republicans represent the conservative side but rather the radical side of the wealthy. Profit is good but gouging us on gas and making more than 10 billion profit is ridiculous.

AND REMEMBER, he said we can vote out those we don't like. The people are angry and I believe in 2012, after the Democrats have screwed up, we will vote them out. The problem is we are only given two choices; Republican and Democrats. It's a two party dictatorship. We really have no choice. The Democrats will go the opposite direction just as badly as the Republicans.

And Lamb said the Democrats would give breaks to those that use alternate forms of energy. That's bad? King George said he wanted to cut fossil fuel consumption by 20% but offered no plan.

Henry Lamb accused the Democrats of something that has not been done yet.

I don't believe in socialism but I pay over $800 a month in insurance and just had an operation that cost $19,000. After all of the insurance company's deductions they only paid $4,000. I want socialized medicine that cuts out the Insurance (really they have become non-insurance) companies. Since the government pays for all government employees and illegal aliens insurance then shouldn't I have the same coverage? The government will actually come out ahead by charging a family $400 a month with a $2,000 deductible, then cover 100% after that. If that is socialism so be it but what we have now is legalized theft by the wealthy.

The Greedy and the Wealthy have pushed it to that point.

Comparing Hugo Chavez to the Democrats is a little silly. We still have a choice. When free choice is taken away then we have a dictator. For example if he had compared Chavez to Governor Perry (another lovely radical Republican) then I would have agreed. A dictator makes a choice for the people **without** discussion with anybody, like Perry on the forced vaccine. It might me good but we have no choice. That's a dictatorship.

Henry lamb sounds like the radical Republicans I have grown to hate. His assumptions are very much like the Weapons of Mass Destruction in Iraq—not real. If we have no freedom of choice then Henry Lamb is right in his article but do we really have a choice with only Republicans and Democrats?

Democracy Spread Inevitable
(6.05.07)

Your article about what Bush says on democracy doesn't really cover the actions of our President. His words ring with hollow truth. Without stability there is no peace or liberty. That is obvious by his operations in Iraq. Freedom has been denied and it will be denied and all you need to do is look as far as Guantanamo. Or, our allies in Italy. We don't respect their democracy or their sovereignty as shown by Bush blatantly going in and kidnapping one of their citizens. When we do away with freedom and at a single person's whim kidnap another person from another country, then freedom and democracy are dead. We must work with our allies and show we believe in honor and truth, democracy and freedom.

If the spread of Democracy is inevitable then why is Bush a hypocrite? He holds hands with the King of Saudi Arabia, bad mouths the elected President of Venezuela and Russia, but backs a dictator in Pakistan who has done the same thing as Chavez. Which side does he stand on? When America is against him he does what he wants not what is right or what the people want. They call that a dictatorship. Don't preach democracy until you're ready to practice it. He needs to try diplomacy and take down the European missile shields. Not a good or intelligent idea. And what does Bush want. He wanted to seal the borders and said the environment wasn't critical. Now he does a one-eighty on all the issues but the war. I heard Kerry say, "My it looks like Bush is flip-flopping on the issues. My personal opinion is that Bush wants the Iraqi oil for his buddies (Halliburton, Exxon, Mobil, BP) and that is why he continues to fight a war that has been lost. How much of the oil profits will those companies manage to steal? Fifty percent? Seventy-five percent? A good general knows when to retreat and before Waterloo looms in front. Blood for oil.

Poor Libby, he will need to serve at least 12 months before Bush can pardon him. Bush thinks he's a cowboy, but then he's probably right. Just look at the Indians and the Buffalo. If we act like the enemy we condemn, we will become the enemy.

Don't Pardon Libby
(06.05.07)

To me Libby is guilty of treason.

If Bush pardons his friend (who probably lied to protect Bush and Cheney) then Bush is guiltier than Libby.

Bush can prove me wrong by not pardoning Libby.

God Fearing Christian
(02.24.08)

It sure is a good thing Bush is a God fearing man and lives by faith and not by sight. Bush is the epitome of faith and not sight. But if he'd open his eyes and see what he's doing to America he'd be appalled.

Somebody needs to make an amnesty bill for Congress. A rebellion is coming and history proves that. Will Congress learn from history or make the same mistakes? It looks like they've learned nothing. They aren't even as smart as fifth graders.

Conflicts with Amnesty
(06.20.08)

Honorable Senator Hutchison;

Here is just one more flaw with the Immigration Bill.

Thousands of people are using 000-00-0000 and getting away with it......... . There are many other cases where the names and numbers do not match..... . Social Security Administration refuses to give the names and addresses of the companies and people to Department of Homeland Security.

The "true" Social Security Number holder is sometimes being taxed for all income reported on their number, whether they earned it or not. SSA will not confirm whether or not a person's number is being fraudulently used. I cannot visit a SSA office show proper identification and get any answers about who might be using my number.

Social Security Administration is not required to work with Department of Homeland Security. This must be fixed.

Americans need tamper-proof, biometric Social Security Card with my picture on it. Americans need a system which enables employers to quickly verify with SSA that the name and number match, and is being used for one person, and that weeds out illegal users.

Americans need SSA to work with DHS to find people and employers who are fraudulently using SS numbers and put them in jail, or deport them.

I've voted for you in the past and if you vote for this flawed immigration bill, will not vote for you again.

Definitions:
(06.21.07)

Politically correct – a term used to remove freedom of speech from a democratic society.

Politician – claims to be politically correct.

Untrustworthy – people who claim to be politically correct.

Good Christian – What a politician claims to be to win an election.

Treason – a Libby pardon.

Guilt – proportionate to the amount of money a person has.

Prison term – proportionate to the money you have.

Cry me a River – What a rich person like Paris Hilton does to get out of jail.

Field of Dreams – a wonderful Kevin Costner movie. Build it and they will come.

Field of Broken Dreams – true story starring George Bush, Karl Rove, and Dick Cheney. The Republican Party built it, but now nobody wants to come.

Scooter Libby – should have been tried for treason with Rove and Cheney for exposing an American Secret Agent during time of war. He will be pardoned by George Bush within the next year in order to cover the President's guilt. See Treason.

I love my country
It's the government I'm afraid of

God Bless America

Letter to Mr. Farah
(06.28.08)

Mr. Farah,

To me the whole war is about oil. I was offered a job with Halliburton the day after the war started in March. I can verify this for you.

I would like you to get a copy of the Halliburton invoice for the 400 plus million our government paid them.

What troubles me is, that as we pay hard earned tax dollars to line Halliburton's pockets (add Cheney to that) and lose American lives in Iraq, it is already known they intend to suck the oil out of Iraq.

Even that is not so bad, because as they do this they are also laying off Americans and sending the work to India. I guess their philosophy is lay off an American and feed 10 Al Qaeda. My friend's jobs are being taken away and given to India. The companies are Flour, Bechtel, Halliburton, Kellogg, Brown and Root, Texas Instruments, Microsoft, IBM and many others.

Pease publish a copy of the invoice Halliburton provided for the work done in Iraq. I'm in construction and I can tell you right now it is impossible to have done enough work to collect 400 million dollars. Why didn't we use the Army Corp of Engineers? Ask Cheney. I would also guess that whoever went over there for Halliburton, were sent by military vehicles, which is not an expense when it is free.

Joe Barfield

P. S. I will provide you information but please do not use my name. It could cost me my job.

I must apologize
(06.29.08)

I need to apologize to everybody. This is a poor time to admit it but I'm as bad as Imus. That's right I have said terrible things.

For my whole life I have been calling St. Nick a nappy haired, "Ho, Ho, Ho." I can only think of poor old Imus, who can no longer say, "Hi ho, hi ho, it's off to work I go!" But when he was seen leaving CBS they said they heard him saying, "Uh, oh. Oh, no, I have no work to go."

And I must apologize for the things I have said about President Bush. There has never been a leader that has done so much for Christianity as President Bush. He has brought ethics, honor, integrity, morality and family values to the forefront. Most importantly there is no longer a need to search for lost souls to save. You only need to look as far as all the President's men to see there are still a lot more souls to save.

A letter to Dobson
(07.03.08)

As a Christian, I must disagree with Dobson. Whoever is elected represents the people and should run the country. The most important thing to remember is that this country was based on freedom of religion. ALL RELIGIONS. When we as Christians demand that everything be done our way it really scares me. If we force our ideals on others, then the old saying of what goes around comes around really scares me. I expect and demand my rights to freedom of religion. This is something Dobson and our President have forgotten.

If the Republicans are so righteous then I want to see Halliburton audited. I want them to find the missing billions in Iraq and not make laws where it can't be investigated. Why did Bush send 20 billion in cash to Iraq and why is ten billion missing. Find it. A good Christian will find it. The only reason to hide the truth is if you are a liar or a thief. And since Bush is against abortion and stem cell research then I want to know if he has given his ten percent tithe like a good Christian. If Dobson can't find the answers to these questions then he is not a good Christian. Mr. Dobson to quote our great President, "You're either with us or you're with them." You can't be a weekend warrior. I also want and demand to find out how much Rove and Cheney tithed to their churches. Bush can't be a saint if he surrounds himself with demons. Although I'm a conservative Republican I will say Bush and all of his men have made me a believer in Revelation. They come closer to being false prophets, maybe even the Antichrist than they do being honorable Christians. In the end Mr. Dobson if you demand so much accountability from Obama, then do the same of the President. Do your Christian beliefs follow the lines of Haggard?

Let the new President run the country and let the churches run morality.

Do Republicans Tell the Truth
(07.29.08)

Obama wanting super high taxes is FALSE. Check it out:
http://www. snopes. com/politics/obama/taxes. asp

By heart I'm a Republican. I want lower taxes and less government. But there is something I hate even more. That is lies. Now I don't like lies but for some reason somebody is passing on lies about Obama. The only ones that will do that are Republicans.

Here is something to think about. If they will lie about Obama they have already lied to you. And if they lie about everything then I'm sure they are probably lying to you about what they propose about taxes.

Whoever wins as President will raise taxes. Actually I hope McClain wins so I can see how he crawfishes out of what I believe just might be the financial collapse of our country.

Ironically, both McCain and Obama tout a change to fiscal responsibility. As much as I hate Bush he only creates a budget. Congress passes that budget. Bush can do nothing without Congress's okay. McCain and Obama are members of that Congress they demand a change from. It's like the wolf asking if he can watch the sheep and protect them from wolves. It's just not going to happen....

WMD's or is the Problem Really DU?
(07.29.08)
I can't think how many lies are passed around by the President's cabinet (past and current) and we don't even elect them.

Not defending anybody but that can also be used to power nuclear power plants. Iraq had a few of those. The real problem is Pakistan. Think about our allies and our enemies over the last 200 years. Almost every country has been on both ends and many of those in the last hundred years. Pakistan will be our enemy and they HAVE nuclear weapons. If the Middle Eastern countries get nuclear weapons it will be from Pakistan.

As long as we're taking a look at uranium and their dangers I want to ask you a question; Is the safety of our military important?

Do a **Google** search for US military weapons using DU. There just might be a bigger problem than what Iraq had. Ever wonder why so many of our soldiers are getting sick?

He is the Candidate of My Choice
(07.29.08
Here is something that will blow you away. A lot of the blame goes on the shoulders of the people. Vote those jerks out. Here is my point; look at the two candidates for President. My question is, "is that the best they can give us?" It's been bothering me for a long time. I actually thought Romney and Huckabee were better than McCain. Same thing with the democrats. So why did the primaries give us who we have?

I think I know. A few weeks ago a friend of mine was all excited about Obama winning the nomination.

I asked him, "I thought you were a Republican?"

He said, "I am and that's the beauty of it. Some friends of mine and I got into the Democrat's primary and voted for him. That way they worst candidate will be running and McCain will win."

I thought about what the said and threw back, "I know. Some democrat friends of mine got into the Republican primary to make sure McCain won so they could beat the Republicans."

Man did he look shocked, then he got mad, "They can't do that. It's wrong."

Then I reminded him, "You did the same thing."

He looked sick but managed to say, "But what we did was different."

And that's the real problem. Both sides justify their actions but don't think it's right when others do it.

I can still remember my mother and father saying, "He's the candidate of my choice."

Now most of us say, "He is the lesser of two evils."

Wag the Dog Again
(7-4-08)

The night Obama was confirmed as the Democratic choice for President of the United States, McCain made a speech in New Orleans. He looked very bad. The next day President Bush declared an emergency against Iran. Could this be the return of "Wag the Dog"? I hope not, but take a look at what happens when America attacks another country.

Americans have rallied around the flag and backed the president in times when he declared an "emergency" or "dangerous times." What the president says doesn't even need to be true. A little more than seventy years ago, many Christians were behind their German leader. That's right, they believed everything Hitler said, and look at what he did. With that in mind it is not that far-fetched to believe that many Americans would rally behind their leader in desperate times, or what they are led to believe are desperate times. That is exactly what happened for Bush when he attacked Iraq in 2003.

But these are not desperate times, except maybe here in our own country. Sure the leader of Iran is a little whack-o, but we can't take care of all the nut cases in the world. Not even our own. Weapons of Mass Destruction? I would venture a guess they are about the same as those in Iraq. You decide.

Suppose the president bombs Iran a few months before the election. He will probably tell the people it is a national emergency. His public approval rating will go up as high as eighty percent. A majority of Americans will rally around our president. He will tell the people that in order to guarantee the security of all Americans, they will need to elect McCain as president.

If this happens don't be surprised at how fast people rally behind McCain.

In 1898 it was said the United States blew up the U. S. S. Maine to get national sympathy for the war against Spain. Some said President Johnson orchestrated the Gulf of Tonkin incident to gain favor for him in the re-election against Goldwater. Regardless of their true intentions, both incidents worked. I don't really think anything like that would happen now, but if it did, it would work. And remember, there are many Americans who don't care if it is true. Saddam Hussein was not a terrorist, did not back Al Qaeda, and did not have Weapons of Mass Destruction. President Bush said Hussein was all of these and a bad leader. Now he has started in on Iran and says they have a bad leader.

The smart thing for President Bush to do is to get Israel to take out a few plants in Iran, then claim they had nuclear capabilities like Iraq. You know WMDs. Those three nasty words that enable us to attack superior countries like Afghanistan.

Many Americans feel pressured to rally behind Israel. Anyone that doesn't is labeled anti-Semitic. I've been accused of that, but I'm just anti-war. BUT, if the president can get Israel to attack and instill fear in Americans, then he will be able to wag the dog and get McCain elected. Based on the past, and the things happening today, I feel that in the latter part of August or in September, Israel will make a bombing raid on Iran or even Syria to destroy any possible locations of what they will call nuclear potential to destroy Israel. The United States will rally their support behind Israel, or maybe will even be the attacking contingent instead of Israel. The president will tell how he saved Israel and the United States from a nuclear attack, thus ensuring the support of all Americans who believe him.

Will history repeat? I don't know. What do you think? Just remember my words if something like that happens in Iran before the presidential election. If it does happen, then it will be a sure victory for the Republicans.

Our Energy
(7-4-08)

The sad thing is that the statistics show more like a love meeting between the KKK and the NAACP. What both sides need to understand and will never do is that there needs to be compromise.

WE MUST DRILL for oil here---AND NOW! Any dumb ass knows that. We use our energy and find alternate forms to take us off oil. NEITHER side is willing to do it. The Republicans want to drill, drill, drill with no plan for the future, while the Democrats want to stop drilling and give us no future. Again both sides want their demands met but have no plans to solve the future.

They can go both go to hell.

A True Story About Jeremiah and Jesse
(07.30.08)

I'm going to sue Jesse Jackson for reparations. . I did a blood check and found out I also have ancestors and mine go way back too. But if it weren't for my great great great great great uncle Jeremiah, the great Jesse would not be here today. Reverend Jeremiah (that's right he was a reverend too) went to Africa and out of the kindness of his heart. And because the Good Book says, he deemed it more blessed to give than to receive. When he saw the primal sacrifice and the lack of God in these primitive tribes he saw only one recourse. Being the good Christian he was and a church leader, he "bought" children to keep them from sacrificial killings by their own tribes & families. He paid an American dollar for each child and like we know the money says "In God we Trust." One such child belonged to the lineage of Jesse Jackson.

Sadly when he was brought back to America he became a slave. But I ask which was worse; slavery or death by sacrifice?

For my great ancestor, Jeremiah, I ask the Reverend Jackson to return reparations in the form of the almighty dollar for, "In God we Trust." Based on past and current interest rates I would only ask what he owes, and that be in the amount of two and a half million dollars which will cover my menial retirement needs. Let me remind Jesse that God says it is more blessed to give than to receive. A true man of God, like I know Jesse Jackson to be, would fulfill my request and pay a lasting tribute to my ancestor, the great Jeremiah.

131

Weapons of Mass Destruction
(08.06.08)
To Korton and all his fabulous information.
This is a follow up article to "Silent Death" written by Fan Story member Korton. I found the article impossible to believe. America wouldn't do that! Korton was right and I was wrong. Here is what I learned.

Weapons of Mass Destruction
We all want to be safe from Weapons of Mass Destruction. Everyone fears the possibility of an attack. The dreaded WMDs. We attacked Afghanistan and Iraq to prevent such a possibility. Before the presidential election we will do the same thing to Iran. All to protect us and Israel. Makes you wonder why we never attacked North Korea when we knew they had and had already tested nuclear weapons or WMDs. But then they are not close to Israel and they don't have oil.

I believe, as I'm sure we all believe, that any leader of a country using nuclear weapons or any weapons containing radioactive material such as dirty bombs should be punished. To use such a thing would be a crime against humanity. President Bush said it best when he told Americans that Saddam Hussein was responsible for the atrocities committed against the Iraqi people by his men. I agree completely with President Bush on this issue. When people are attacked and killed by a government, their leaders are just as much to blame as the military that carries out such acts. This goes not only for the enemy killed but also to soldiers that are killed by their own leaders. Even more so on this issue. A leader who is capable of killing his own soldiers is guilty of a heinous crime. Not only the leader of the country but also those who lead their soldiers into battle knowing that they could be killed by their own weapons and not those of the enemy.

I am talking about American troops. Impossible? Our leaders could and would not do this to our American troops who fight so gallantly for freedom? I thought this too until recently. When we talk about the evils of Weapons of Mass Destruction, it does not only apply to the enemy but also to our own government. If we accuse another country of such atrocities and send thousands of American soldiers to die to prevent such crimes against mankind, then it is even more important that we abide by, and enforce, such laws. The American military has not done this.

Recently I have read articles and done research that makes me suspicious of the actions of our military leaders, including President Bush. We are guilty of the crimes we accuse other countries of having committed. We are guilty of war crimes against humanity and our own military.

Years ago I used to read a comic strip, *Pogo,* and the words he once said still echo in my thoughts. "We have seen the enemy and they are us." All we need to do is go back to Vietnam and Agent Orange to see what we are capable of doing to our own troops. So how are we doing it today? DU. And just what is DU?

Let me tell you how I discovered it. The first part of June, I read an article related to DU and laughed it off as impossible thinking it was more lies, because our military leaders would not use something as dangerous as this. Especially if it would hurt our own soldiers. A few days later I learned about something that shocked me.

Radioactive sand is being shipped from Kuwait to a disposal unit outside Boise, Idaho. American Ecology Corporation plans to dispose of 6,700 tons of sand contaminated with depleted uranium and lead from American weapons used during the Gulf War. The Nuclear Regulatory Commission said the radiation levels are not hazardous. Chad Hyslop, a spokesman for American Ecology, said, "We've received tens of thousands of tons from the U. S. military that have higher radioactive levels than this shipment."

For me this was like waving a red flag. We need to ask some questions. If the levels are not dangerous, then why didn't Kuwait keep the sand? Why is the U. S. military disposing of so much radioactive material?

I've asked those questions and tried to find the answers. I learned that in 2006 the same company disposed of Bradley tanks that had been contaminated with uranium. The BIG questions rose in my mind. How did the tanks become contaminated? And more importantly, what happened to the soldiers operating those tanks? Were they contaminated by weapons Iraq used against us? I wanted to know.

Here is what I learned. The tips of the shells fired from the tanks are loaded with DU or depleted uranium. The material is heavier than steel and can penetrate steel; hence we use it to attack the enemy. Common sense tells us that it contaminates the enemy vehicle and the surrounding air. Military officials say it is not dangerous. Then why destroy Bradley tanks? The military refuses to allow testing to see if there is contamination or if it is dangerous to our own soldiers. Why? Such a simple answer: because depleted uranium is dangerous.

Wherever or whenever an American soldier is at risk, there should be checks to guarantee the safety of our men and women. When the military leaders refuse to do this, it is for only one reason. There is a danger and they know it. Worse yet, the military leaders know it and refuse a simple check to assure the safety of America's fighting men and women. In a case like this, our military and political leaders become more dangerous than the enemy.

We dispose of Kuwait's sand and destroy our tanks, but our military leaders assure us it is safe at the same time refusing to check for dangerous levels of radiation that might be affecting our soldiers. What do you think?

A Good Christian Gives

(05.28.08)

During our church service on Sunday morning I kept thinking about the politicians running for President and also President Bush. Hillary, Obama, McCain and Bush all claimed to be Christians. Surely there was a way to test if they were telling the truth. A good test for a true Christian.

Our minister finished a "God loves you," sermon about no matter what the sin God will forgive you. As he walked away our other minister came to the podium and requested we tithe. Actually he demanded the tithe. He continued with a five minute lecture and finished with a hell-fire and damnation verbal attack, then finished up with, "If you don't tithe like the bible says you will go to hell."

Whoa! What happened to the love and forgiveness? That's when it hit me. Do they tithe? If everyone is a Christian and believes firmly, then they will give ten percent. Now I'm not a perfect Christian by any means, but since the President and all the candidates tout the fact they are I would really like to know how much each of them tithes.

I would get on television with a show like, "Citizens address the Nation." Kind of like the President does, but my show would make sense and mean something.

Before the nation I would offer the candidates a challenge. "To Hillary, Obama, McCain and George Bush I ask you to come on my show and answer some questions." Then I would finish with the killer, no way out, line, "If you are a Christian you will come on my show to respond to your fellow Americans." Not much of an option for them is it?

On the show I will ask each of them the same questions. First I will ask, "Are you a good Christian?"

This is a setup. Who would say no to that question?

With that done we will use Hillary as an example. The questions will go like this. "I'm sure America is pleased to know that you are a good Christian. Truly, God has blessed you for what you have done and shown this by rewarding your family financially." After her response I will ask, "You and Bill have made in excess of one-hundred million over the last eight year, and you must agree that is a real blessing." She will probably come back with a mushy response. Then I will finish with, "As a good Christian, and so the people of America know, I must ask you, have you tithed ten percent of what you made to your church?"

I can't wait to ask President Bush the same questions. First thing I'll do is confirm his Christian stand on adultery, abortion and gays in the Christian church. And after he has reconfirmed his devout stand as a Christian I'll ask how much he has tithed. Should be very interesting.

Aren't you curious? Don't you want to know how much each of them has tithed?

Angry
(7-4-08)

Actually, I'm **angry** at the Republicans. I thought they were conservative? They aren't even liberal. They're radical.

You have too much experience; they don't have enough. One side might as well be the KKK while the other is the NAACP. Anybody out there representing the people?

I got a can of tar and a rope for each candidate. No experience might be better. It's the experience that got us into trouble. The Republicans are a bunch of gung ho nuts. I want somebody that will try to be diplomatic and who knows when to retreat. The Christian right scares me too. Bush says he's a Christian, but what has he done to show it?

The new radical Republicans have deceived me. They're liars and hypocrites; they cater to the wealthy and will destroy America to save their wealthy friends on Wall Street. What they have done borders on treason. I believe there is more corruption and deceit in the American Republican party than there is in all the countries of the world. Republicans should be ashamed.

Anyway I'll just keep my bucket of tar and rope handy.

Joe

IN SUMMARY THIS PUTS THINGS INTO PERSPECTIVE

McCain vs Obama
(08.11.08)
A friend of mine sent me this. Read carefully – this makes sense!

John McCain
Congress - 26 Years
Military - 22 years

Barrack Obama
Congress - 143 days
Military - 0

I responded with:
Jim,
Good point. You made up my mind. We've been going through the same old stuff for fifty years and it's time to make a change. After all we do want a change and to go somewhere right? So who wants the same old corruption? Thanks for clearing up this whole issue for me.

I was going with McCain but you just proved to me that we need to go in a different direction. If McCain has 26 years in Congress and Congress has almost bankrupted the country then something does need to change. You're right about Obama and his no experience is critical to this country. Think about it. Almost everybody in Congress is experienced and look what they've done to America. Obama hasn't been corrupted for the last 26 years.

Thanks again for pointing that out this important information to me. I was going to vote for McCain but thanks to your editorial I've changed my mind.

Joe
P. S. Neither one will help us. Until we elect people that are not Democrats or Republicans our country is Doomed.

1975
(7-4-08)
In 1969 I became a Jehovah's Witness with my wife. I have never forgotten what they told us. The leaders of the church told the congregation to prepare for the rapture because it was coming and would arrive in 1975. Well the year came and went but nothing happened. The following are a series of e-mails between my friend Ruben and me. Both sides of an argument tend to intrigue me. I enjoy pushing the envelope. This conversation was no different for me than any other until I surprised myself in the end.

Ruben sent me the first e-mail. This is how it went:
Pass it on and pray for America…the Bible teaches us in the book of the Kings and Chronicles that as the king went, so went the nation. Very scary!

PLEASE READ TO THE END
This will make you re-think: A Trivia question in Sunday School: How long is the beast

allowed to have authority in Revelations?

Revelations Chapter 13 tells us it is 42 months, and you know what that is.

Almost a four-year term of a presidency. All I can say is "Lord, Have mercy on us!"

According to The Book of Revelations the anti-Christ will be a man, in his forties, of MUSLIM descent, who will deceive the nations with persuasive language, and have a MASSIVE Christ-like appeal. . . . the prophecy says that people will flock to him and he will promise false hope and world peace, And when he is in power, will destroy everything. Do we recognize this description??

I STRONGLY URGE each one of you to post this as many times as you can! Each opportunity that you have to send it to a friend or media outlet. . . Do it! I refuse to take a chance on this unknown candidate who came out of nowhere.

Ruben

MY RESPONSE:

So I was right all along. You're telling me Bush is really King George. Well as far as the king went, I can't wait for him to be gone before the country is bankrupt.

I hate to tell you this but whoever wins the election is going to lose. Bailing out all of these companies is going to destroy America. Just like I predicted in *Moon Shadow*. We don't have national health care, but we do now have national banking and soon we'll have national car making. It's all coming to a local bank or dealership near you.

We are not immune from what happened to other countries. If Obama is the anti-Christ then I was right about Bush being one of the false prophets.

Joe

RUBEN:

Hehehehe!! You're probably right Joe......According to the Good book Joe...the beginning of end times will be a time of anguish, strife, wars, famine , earthquakes, natural disasters and this is only the beginning! Glad my name is written in the Book of Life! Yea our country and the world is in economic chaos and turmoil. And no matter who wins it's a losing proposition! All we can do is pray that He whom is in power will be a man according to God's own heart as was King David.

JOE:

I didn't finish. If Bush is not the false prophet then Obama is not the antichrist because the false prophet comes first.

RUBEN:

I don't believe Obama is Antichrist either.... but a foreshadowing and precursor of one that is to come. The world stage is set and all pieces of the puzzle are in place...the only thing left is Jesus Christ and His coming which is imminent!

JOE:

When he does come I hope I'm not as dumb as those Jews 2000 years ago. I mean 1975 years ago.

RUBEN:

Just be ready amigo! What shall it profit a man to gain the whole world, but lose his own soul? Matthew 16:26

JOE:
A couple of ministers believe we are the blessed country and nothing will happen to us. We may be blessed but we sure aren't free of sinners. Look at the politicians, bankers and CEOs. All of them are taking the money to their permanent graves.

The end of times will not be easy. It will be a hard and difficult time. The US will not be immune.

RUBEN:
Only the Father knows in his omniscient time when He will begin the beginning of the end! Nobody knows for sure the exact time. But we can see the seasons and get a feel for the approximate terminal generation when that may be.

JOE:
Oh, my God! This is weird. It just hit me when I sent that number. In 1969 the leaders of the Jehovah's Witnesses said the end was coming in 1975. When it didn't, everything fell apart. The number I just sent you was the years since Jesus was executed---1975!

Golden Gate
(10.10.08)
Yesterday Golden Gate Bridge officials decided to put up a suicide net. How stupid. I sent an email and told them it would be a lot easier if you just didn't allow suicide jumpers on the bridge

Congress is like a Flood
(09.24.08)
I liked the comparison between the currency. Add this; like the banks of a river we need to control the currency within the banks. Let it overflow and you have a flood out of control. I guess Congress is the flood.

It's like the flooding of a river. Even the terms of the two systems are similar. A river flows between its banks. The movement of water is a current, we call money currency. The economy and a river both work well when there is not too much in the system. As long as it doesn't rain for a prolonged period, or lending institutions aren't flooded by too much money, both systems work very well.

Conservative or Liberal?
(09.24.08)
I would call myself a conservative. It's too bad we haven't elected any in the last 30 years. I feel deceived by the Republicans. I will vote for somebody who has an idea of what he wants to do for the people and the country. So far all the candidates talk about whom is bad.

I DON'T CARE! I can make that judgment for myself. I just want them to tell me what they will do for America and even more important is how.

Don't promise a Ferrari until you can describe exactly how it will be done.

AND no more bailing out wealthy CEO's (Chief Embezzlement Officers). I want them to serve America not make it a third world power.

Democrat or Republican
(09.24.08)

Are you a Democrat or Republican? Take a moment before you answer. Have you decided? Are you sure? In your mind you probably answered the question before you even read the next sentence. Why did you pick that party? Conservative? Liberal?

If you picked either one then our country is doomed. There is no hope. If you wanted neither party then we have a chance.

Democrats, Republicans, liberals or conservative there is really no difference. A Christian politician? They sell themselves on morality but they have lower morals than a prostitute. Actually they prostitute themselves.

The person you elect is picked by the people to represent America. All colors all religions. Not Democrat or Republican but the people. We will elect someone who promises no more abortion or stem cell research but will march off to war and bankrupt our country. Yeah Saddam Hussein was evil and all of that but there are other evil leaders. Where there is oil we will go to war. Why not save Somalia? Simple, no oil.

Why does Poland need a missile shield? Just to piss off Russia?

For once I want to see an elected official do something for America. Something for the people. Hey we have a good Christian running for President. Actually they both say they are Christian, but I don't care.

Ask them what they are going to do about my sky rocketing taxes. Why has my insurance gone from 500 a month to a thousand a month in only two years? What about work going to India?

Why is gas going up? One side promises to drill anywhere while the other side demands we drill nowhere.

Even the stupidest of stupid environmentalists should understand we must find alternate forms of energy. Al Gore should figure this one out on his own. His carbon credits are the dumbest idea I have ever heard. It's a scam.

Billions maybe even trillions for war and oil but not one penny for common sense and the future of America.

What about Fannie and Freddie Mae? What a corrupt family. Warning! Mae day Mae day. Why does our government bail them out but not prosecute them? The loans were fraudulent and they knew it. Before we give one penny to bail them out I want to see them all in jail.

Why worry about terrorists when we have the Mae family. I hope the Bush family of cowboys have finished with us. I think we've been Bush-whacked enough. Lets not forget the other terrorists; lawyers, lobbyists (especially lobbyists), Congress (but only Democrats and Republicans), the Supreme Court and the President and all his men (his cabinet; all the people we never elected). They have done more damage than all the terrorists in our history. At a time when our country is at war I call it treason.

He is the Candidate of My Choice
(09.24.08)

Here is something that will blow you away. A lot of the blame goes on the shoulders of the people. Vote those jerks out. Here is my point; look at the two candidates for President. My question is, "is that the best they can give us?" It's been bothering me for a long time. I actually thought Romney and Huckabee were better than McCain. Same thing with the democrats. So why did the primaries give us who we have?

I think I know. A few weeks ago a friend of mine was all excited about Obama winning the nomination.

I asked him, "I thought you were a Republican?"

He said, "I am and that's the beauty of it. Some friends of mine and I got into the Democrat's primary and voted for him. That way they worst candidate will be running and McCain will win."

I thought about what the said and threw back, "I know. Some democrat friends of mine got into the Republican primary to make sure McCain won so they could beat the Republicans."

Man did he look shocked, then he got mad, "They can't do that. It's wrong." Then I reminded him, "You did the same thing."

He looked sick but managed to say, "But what we did was different."

And that's the real problem. Both sides justify their actions but don't think it's right when others do it.

I can still remember my mother and father saying, "He's the candidate of my choice."

Now most of us say, "He is the lesser of two evils."

Muslim vs Christians
(09.24.08)

Recently, I was arguing with some Christians about Obama. They became almost violent. I saw in them many of the traits they hate in Muslims. When I pointed it out they got defensive. They couldn't even see it.

The next part is troubling to me. I was arguing the same points. I asked some fanatics what is the mission of Christians. They got that right about mission work to show the love of God and teach about Jesus Christ. That's when I popped the big one. "Then aren't all Muslims potential Christians if you show them love, kindness and faith.

Near my house a Muslim church (can't remember the name) was built. Graffiti is all over the building telling the non-believers to go home. Not really Christian love is it?

Another said they should all be punished for New York. That is when I told him that on his premise all Christians should be killed for what McVeigh did to Oklahoma City. McVeigh did it on warped Christian beliefs. No different than the few Muslims with the same warped beliefs.

Of course I got the same answer - That's different.

National Care?
(09.24.08)

We don't' have national health care, but we do now have national banking and soon we'll have national car making. It's all coming to a local bank or dealership near you.

I hate to tell you this but whoever wins the election is going to lose. Bailing out all of these companies is going to destroy America. Just like I predicted in my novel *Moon Shadow*. Hey, Congress and the President say, "Are you wealthy? Your business going under? Not enough bonuses for your management? Is your Golden Umbrella sagging? Need more than a 100 billion? Well come on down. Congress is giving away American's Social security at rock bottom prices. Name the amount you want today and we'll just put it on the American's tax payer's bill tomorrow. Time's ripe get the billions you need today before it runs out."

We must vote for a Christian
(09.25.08)

I consider myself Christian but I'm appalled at the way the Christian leaders are going. I was asked yesterday if I would vote for a Muslim. Insinuation is just as bad as calling someone Muslim. I want somebody to use common sense to run the country not a bible. If Bush was a Christian he would have given trials to Guantanamo. He would not have acted out of revenge for his father when attacking Iraq (but I forget the oil). This is just another time for the "New Crusades."

I had the same problems with my daughter as Palin did but I'm not sure she will be good.

I would like any of them to address the real problem; my hospital insurance in the last four years has gone from $390 a month to $1100 with double the deductible. Property taxes have gone up 50%. I don't want war we can't save the world. And if Iraq needs help what about the Christian in Somalia (no oil)?

And the big Christian question for the week I want them all asked is how much did you tithe? I bet none of them are near 10%. And remember God told Bush to be president. That is what he said. Oh, and how much did Cheney and Rove tithe. If you're going to vote Christian, then I demand you be surrounded by Christians.

I almost got attacked by some good old "Christian boys" in Alaska for saying Bush was crazy wrote Moon Shadow in 1995 and it shows how Bush destroyed the country---before he was elected! Also three hijacked airliners.

Nine months ago I called Bush the anti-Christ and was told to cool it or the IRS would audit me. Five months ago I was audited and the audit lasted for four months. The first thing they asked about was "Moon Shadow."

Our Energy
(09.24.08)

Our Congress, well the Democrats and Republicans has as good a chance of solving America's problems as oil and water have of mixing together. Both sides need to understand that there needs to be compromise. But that is also something they will never do. WE MUST DRILL for oil here---AND NOW! Any dumb ass knows that. We use our energy and find alternate forms to take us off oil. NEITHER side is willing to do it. The Republicans want to drill, drill, drill with no plan for the future, while the Democrats want to stop drilling and give us no future. Again both sides want their demands met but have no plans to solve the future. Both sides have demands from which they refuse to sway, but neither side has given any kind of logical solution. Gore's carbon credits don't count. His solution is like an adulterer paying into a fund where he is allowed so many affairs and then everything is okay. But if he does it too much he can still buy a few extra "adultery credits."

Both sides will be the downfall of America. Sad thing is it doesn't look like that is too far off.

Sent to America Solutions
(09.25.08)

No more taxes. No bailout. Before there is any help for any company lets realize that the sub-prime lending was criminal.

First we bring criminal prosecution against all the management. No CEO or management person receives a golden umbrella. They get fired and prosecuted.

Second no one in Congress can vote on any measure if they were given campaign contributions by any of the companies involved.

Now think about this. Congress keeps whining about how the Social Security can't be paid to those of us who contributed. BUT in less than 24 hours they are willing to give a trillion dollars to their wealthy friends. Not only do we not need to bail these companies out we need to adjust Congress.

If these companies are bailed out by Congress then we need look no farther than Washington D. C. to find terrorists bent on destroying America. Bush declared war against WMD's. Congress is about to pass "Financial Weapons of Mass Destruction."

Wars Are Different
(09.25.08)

Someone said we attacked Japan after Pearl Harbor and that makes the Twin Towers and Afghanistan justified. Not really.

When Japan attacked we attacked Japan. Attack Afghanistan? Doing that would be like attacking Mexico after the terrorists attacked New York. And remember fifteen of the nineteen were from Saudi Arabia. The same country milking us for $134 a barrel.

Wars have changed throughout history. This one is different and we're not even attacking the enemy. And never, never take a knife to a gun fight.

Congratulations to Colombia's President Uribe, who fought the FARC guerrillas the way a war is supposed to be fought. President Bush should take a lesson from this and fight the terrorists the same way.

Banking Fraud
(7-4-08)

This whole banking thing is criminal. These men who did the loans should go to jail. If they don't, it means they paid just enough to the re-election campaign of their supporting criminals—Congress! And the President of the United States.

Republicans and Democrats should both be ashamed. Most of the companies going under contributed to both sides. Some more, some less, but all the companies gave to both parties. Even if it is the Democrats' fault, the Republicans should stand up and say "enough." Both parties are giving to their wealthy friends on Wall Street.

Bush is the one recommending the $700 billion bailout. AIG is an insurance company. I'm not sure of the numbers, but they charge $2,000 a year to guarantee a million in loans. In other words if there is a default, they will pay off the loan. They are required to carry a percentage (say 10% in cash reserves in case there is a problem). They didn't do this. For the last six years, AIG made more than 40% profit on the insurance premiums; they made billions. Now they must pay, but what they did was illegal. AIG needs to go under, and all the wealthy stockholders lose what they have. Like a good enema, clean the shit out and let new come in. All sub-prime lenders should go to jail. Fanny, Freddie, they all need to just go under and we need to start over.

Our government is now talking about bailing out the foreign banks here in the US. I say NO!

Buffet was right. "Financial weapons of Mass Destruction." Get the terrorists; they are Wall Street.

We're setting a bad precedent. Ford and all other companies are going to be standing in line waiting for Congress to dole out billions of dollars.

And what is the truth anymore? The media fills us with lies. They can no longer be trusted. But you can add Democrats and Republicans to the group that can't be trusted.

A liberal spends all of our money. Correct? A conservative stops spending and has fiscal responsibility. Correct? The last year under Clinton, the deficit increased 16 billion for the year. The last four days the deficit has increased almost 100 billion. In Bush's eight years as president, our debt has gone up 4.5 trillion. Not really conservative. Now he wants to give 700 billion to AIG and other sub-prime lenders to bail them out. He also wants to guarantee the golden umbrella retirement worth hundreds of millions for the CEOs at those companies. That is neither conservative nor liberal—it's insane and out of control.

The terrorists are Congress and the President. They are using a weapon against Americans and have committed treason. It is financial "Weapons of Mass Destruction."

Here's what we do. First, CEOs will receive absolutely nothing. Second, we need to bring criminal charges against them. Third, let them go bankrupt.

A vote for a Democrat or a Republican is a vote against freedom. I sure wish we had a choice in this . . . and in the election only a fool would vote for a Democrat or a Republican. Who's more foolish, a fool or the fool who follows the fool? Now we are a country of fools.

Bailout
(09.25.08)

Taxpayers get the downside, management gets the upside. Paulson was CEO at Goldman and sold over $500 million in Goldman stock, tax-free, when he became Secretary of the Treasury.

It is time for Americans to think. It took more than a week for Congress and Bush to respond to Katrina. They said it would be better next time. I'm not saying the people needed to be rescued by the government but just think for a moment how they responded.

For the last seven years Bush and Congress have told us how Social Security needs to be fixed and that there is not enough money. Your money. The money YOU put into Social Security. The money they weren't supposed to touch but they have already spent. Money spent before this "crisis."

In less than 48 hours they have almost approved 700 billion to bail out their wealthy friends. One of those pushing to save Wall Street is Paulson. Our Secretary of the Treasury who made $500 million on a company that needs help. One of the President's men. And I guarantee you the management and CEO's will get their money. How? You will pay more in taxes to guarantee they get millions.

But the important question is how did Paulson get $500 million tax free?

I'm beginning to think there is more graft and corruption in Congress, Wall Street and American banking than there is in the whole world.

If any of them are really Good ol' Christian boys do you suppose they know they are going to hell?

Our stature, credibility, honesty and standing in the world are dropping like the stock market.

I'd complain to my local representative but they are the problem.

This is for Campbell Brown

(09.25.08)

You are right on. The bailout is criminal. Congress must prosecute those that have done wrong. They tell us there is no money for SS but they can bail their friends out in 48 hours

1) AIG failed on their own greed

2) Paulson should never have free reigns

3) Bush says this is a crisis. So were the WMD's--there were none

4) Bush declared war against WMD's. Well if that is true then attack Wall Street for using "Financial Weapons of Mass Destruction" against America

5) No one in Congress will be allowed to vote if they received any political contributions from any of these companies

6) If we bail them out they must pay the money back. Also all the companies bailed out will not be allowed to give any management especially the CEO'S (Chief Embezzlement Officers) any bonus or any stock options whatsoever until the money has been paid back. If they want stock they can buy it.

7) One more time—Paulson has no free reigns. How much in taxes did Paulson pay on the $500 million in Goldman stock he sold?

8) Does anyone in Congress represent the people?

9) Since this is a time of war all those involved should be tried for treason, not given billions of dollars.

The first Bush – savings and loan

The second Bush – Wall Street

Is this another Bushwhacking?

This country has been around over 230 years and the National Debt has gone up 10 trillion dollars. During our twelve years of Bush reign our debt has gone up 5.5 trillion.

I wrote a book, "Moon Shadow," that predicted most of this, including the financial collapse of America.

I'm a Republican and I ask, "Are there any conservatives out there?" And although I voted for Bush I say he is the worst president in US history.

Bloomberg Democrats Only a Half Story

(7-4-08)

To Kevin Hassett,

It seems that we can't trust the Democrats, based on what you have written. You stated that in 2005 the Democrats voted down a bill that would have controlled the financial institutions, and something like this would never have happened if not for the Democrats.

I'm a Republican and don't have any sympathy for the Democrats, but, if my memory serves me right, the Republicans won both houses in 2004. If the bill was introduced in 2005, then explain how the Democrats killed the bill when the majority were Republicans?

Tell me why both sides want to guarantee the "golden umbrellas" for the CEOs at AIG. Tell me why those that sold insurance and didn't have the monetary backing required by law are not going to jail?

Why are we looking for terrorists when we have 545 in Washington D. C. ? George Bush declared war against WMDs. Remember? If that is true, then he should attack Congress and the President for using "Financial Weapons of Mass Destruction."

We have two problems in this country: Democrats and Republicans.

Of course your article couldn't possibly be tainted, could it? Is it true you're an adviser to Republican Senator John McCain?

Wait. Add a third problem to that list: misleading journalists.

Have We Lost Our Common Sense?

(7-10-08)

For the last few days I've been trying to get a grasp on this $700 billion bailout for Wall Street. All the money goes to the companies that made what I consider fraudulent loans, which should be illegal. Now Congress wants to bail them out.

All the banks and insurance companies that need to be bailed out like AIG, Fannie Mae, and Freddie Mac, not only committed fraudulent loans and deceived their shareholders, but they also made huge contributions to both the Democrats and Republicans. And just about equally. Now our government wants to bail out the wealthy so the CEOs can still get their golden umbrella retirements of up to 100 million each. All this while our Social Security disappears.

Here is the unified reasoning from both parties: We need to maintain the value of the exorbitantly expensive property in places like Florida, New York, and California. Okay fine. Now ask yourself, why are the financial institutions in trouble? Because they loaned money on houses that were overpriced by as much as ten times the normal cost. Remember the loans were made because people couldn't afford them. I saw a house in California for 1.2 million. The same house in Houston would cost $150,000. These sub-prime crooks gave a million dollar loan for a payment of only $2,000 a month. Not good. Somebody makes $8,000 a month, it's not so bad except that in five years the interest increases and the payment goes to eight or ten thousand. Oops! See the problem? Now the payments are more than the mortgage holder makes. Common Sense tells you it won't work. The mortgage companies didn't care, because they were making mega bucks. So now we have a million houses on the market that have kept their value, but we still have no one who can afford to buy them. Seems a little stupid, doesn't it?

I say not one penny for any of those thieves and liars. I say they go to jail. Let the mortgage companies collapse and be replaced by honest companies. I don't want one single CEO to get his magic retirement for being a thief. To me this bailout would be like catching a person who just robbed a convenience store of a hundred dollars and then telling them it's no problem. And then telling them we'll give you an extra thousand to help you out and charge all the local convenience stores so you can have the money.

George Bush declared war against WMDs. A bailout of $700 billion is a WMD of a different kind but a WMD nonetheless. It's a "Financial Weapon of Mass Destruction." We need to stop our American financial terrorists. Performance based compensation practices on Wall Street pay off with big bonuses when the bankers bet right and ONLY impose losses on SHAREHOLDERS when they bet wrong. This time let Wall Street pay for their mistakes, not the everyday American.

Enough is enough. Call your local representative and tell them, "Don't give them money, give them jail time."

Letter to John McCain
(10.01.08)

Why is there such a big rush to save Wall Street but not Americans Social Security?

So Congress is going to vote until the bailout is passed. Not very democratic. More pork barrel needed?

So if you win the election can we have Congress keep voting on it until you lose?

Does anybody support a democracy in Congress?

Bush declared war against WMD's. If Congress okays the bailout then you will voted for Wall Street terrorism against all Americans, because they have attacked America with "Financial Weapons of Mass Destruction."

I'm a conservative Republican but I see none in Congress. If you vote for the bailout you will have lost my vote for the Presidency.

Washington and Jefferson would be ashamed.

Will the real George Bush please step forward
09.25.08

Well, by George he is a flip flopper. The following was written by Campbell Brown of CNN:

"Our policy in this administration - laws shouldn't bail out lenders, laws shouldn't help speculators."
-- **President Bush, May 19, 2008**
"Our economy has continued growing, consumers are spending, business are investing, exports continue increasing and American productivity remains strong. We can have confidence in the long-term foundation of our economy. . . . I think the system basically is sound. I truly do."
-- **President Bush, July 15, 2008**
Those were the words of President George W. Bush just a few months ago. Today, of course, they have been proven completely wrong. They are now telling us we are in a dire crisis, and that we must hand over hundreds of billions of dollars so they can lead us out of this mess. What's amazing to me is that the administration seems a little surprised that Congress and the American people are not marching in lockstep with them on this and not fully appreciating the urgency.

Based on his words **Bush** is a flip flopper or a complete dumb ass. You pick, after all you're paying the bill along with me. All CEO's are exempt from payment.

But this shouldn't be happening. Bush said he was sent by God. He said God told him the United States was his chosen country.

Hmmmph! All this time I thought it was Israel.

Well if we are chosen something bad happened. Tell God to come back! I say antichrist or false prophet. You pick.

Remember when it was the savings and loan? This time it's Wall Street. Damn, Bushwhacked again!

But Bush is a good Christian man. He surrounds himself with men that are good..... .

Now that is a good question. What are they? Hey, the Secretary of Treasury Paulson cashed in $500 million in stock and paid no taxes on it. That seems fair after all what the heck is 500 million on a 700 billion dollar day? Guess what Paulson told Congress two days ago? He demanded Congress give him all the money, he would make all the decisions and that his decisions "may not be reviewed by any court of law or administrative agency." Is he serious?

Again let me say that Bush is a good Christian. Actually he falls under the layman category of bible thumpers, pretending to be religious to get elected is like a wife having oral sex before the wedding. They do it out of convenience. The joke is that a little girl asked her mother if swallowing could get her pregnant. The mother replied, "No that is how you get a new diamond ring!"

Glenn Beck CNN
(09.27.08)
Attn: Glenn Beck

I liked your article and agree with it. Getting all the information from both sides and evaluating it is critical in coming close to the truth.

For that reason I would like to send you a novel I have written, "Moon Shadow." I did just like you and predicted many things that are happening today. In 2004 I stated in my novel that if Bush and Congress were allowed go unchecked our debt would be near ten trillion before he left office. But that is only one of the many things that have happened in my novel. Most are coming true but you should see what I predicted would happen in 2012. The total collapse of America. Please let me send you a copy.

Good News on the Financial Crisis
(09.28.08)
Once again George Bush has saved us.

President Bush has solved the financial problems for the United States. He has authorized low interest loans for lots on the Moon and authorized all the bankrupt institutions to sell lots owned by the American government.

Bush was quoted as telling Cheney that his father had always said, "In tough times you just shoot for the moon and hope you hit it." With that in mind and since the United States has already been there he added, "Why shoot for the moon when you can sell it."

Cheney was quick to respond and confidently said, "Good idea." He shoved some papers toward the President. "Sign this and we can start selling lots."

Bush started signing and as he did Cheney shoved another paper toward the President. "I've already written a no-bid contract for Halliburton to do the construction. Sign here."

Bush was excited and quipped, "Yeah, Halliburton would be perfect. They can do the same stuff on the moon like they did in Iraq. You know I know a lot about doing nothing and the hardest part of doing nothing, is knowing when you're finished."

"Halliburton can build nothing anywhere," said Cheney with a smile.

Bush agreed, "The bright side is that Halliburton probably won't get in trouble for hiring aliens on the moon this time."

Paulson jumped in and said, "I'll get a hundred billion dollars ready now."

"Will it be okay?" Bush asked.

"Of course. We'll take it out of the $700 billion that's going nowhere. Besides, no one is allowed to ask questions. Also, they are not allowed to know what I do with the money."

Cheney nodded, "It's the American way Georgie." He turned to Paulson and said, "We need a check tomorrow."

"Fine," said Paulson, "But I will take out my ten percent fee. And don't forget that I get an option of a million shares of super preferred stock with Halliburton."

"Oh, and don't forget to send it all to my Cayman account. I'll need to hold it until they can get on the moon."

With a smile Paulson said, "I understand fully. I also keep my fortune there."

Both men started rubbing their hands together and looked more like vultures than human beings.

Bush looked up in a daze, "Yeah, the American way. God bless, America. Now I know why God picked me to save our country."

Letter to Croyn and Kay Bailey Hutchinson
(10.01.08)
Why is there such a big rush to save Wall Street but not Americans Social Security?

So Congress is going to vote until the bailout is passed. Not very democratic. More pork barrel needed?

Does anybody support a democracy in Congress? The stock went up yesterday without a bailout. Why are we supporting the corrupt CEO's (Chief Embezzlement Officers)?

Bush declared war against WMD's. If Congress okays the bailout then you will voted for Wall Street terrorism against all Americans, because they have attacked America with "Financial Weapons of Mass Destruction."

I'm a conservative Republican but I see none in Congress. If you vote for the bailout you will have lost my vote for any Republican.

Washington and Jefferson would be ashamed.

Constituent Response From Senator Kay Bailey Hutchison
From: **Senator Kay Bailey Hutchison** <<u>senator@hutchison. senate. gov</u>>
Date: Tue, Oct 7, 2008 at 9:37 AM
Subject: Constituent Response From Senator Kay Bailey Hutchison
To: Joe Barfield

Dear Mr. Barfield:

Thank you for contacting me regarding the Emergency Economic Stabilization Act of 2008. I welcome your thoughts and comments on this issue. On September 19, 2008, Treasury Secretary Henry Paulson announced a plan by the Bush Administration to stabilize the financial services sector of the economy. This plan included broad authority for the Treasury Secretary to purchase troubled financial instruments with very limited oversight and few protections for taxpayers. In July, I voted against a similar proposed bailout of Fannie Mae and Freddie Mac because it did not provide taxpayer protection and limits on executive compensation for a government owned entity. For the same reasons, I was not willing to support the Administration's initial proposal, and I encouraged my colleagues to continue work on a plan that would protect taxpayers, provide strict oversight, and place limits on the benefits to executives who accept taxpayer assistance. In the days following the Treasury Secretary's announcement, concerns about the danger to the broader economy deepened. The high-profile failure of numerous financial institutions caused the commercial lending market to accumulate and hold cash. The credit markets effectively froze, making it difficult for consumers to obtain loans for purchases such as homes and automobiles. The lack of lending in these areas began to place further pressure on the troubled housing market and threatened to spread deeper into the economy. Similarly, many small and mid-sized businesses were finding it difficult to obtain financing to meet their payroll obligations and purchase inventory. Many cities were entering the bond market and getting no bids, even with AAA ratings. The current liquidity crisis still poses a real potential for significant job losses. After consulting with numerous financial experts, small businesses, and bankers in Texas, it became clear to me that normal commercial lending activity would not resume without action by Congress.

Despite this realization, I was still not inclined to support the Paulson plan. After weeks of negotiation, however, a bi-partisan compromise was reached. While there are provisions in the bill that I do not favor and would not have drafted, overall the need for action to stabilize the market and to protect the retirement savings of millions of Americans weighed heavily on my mind. Ultimately, I supported the Senate bill along with 73 of my colleagues. The bill we passed was a major improvement over the initial plan announced by Secretary Paulson.

We increased the deposit insurance cap from $100,000 to $250,000 so that families will have added protection for savings and retirement accounts. While the initial proposal authorized up to $700 billion to purchase distressed assets, the measure we passed takes a more cautious approach, initially authorizing $250 billion and requiring the approval from Congress and the President for additional funding. Importantly, the bill we passed includes restrictions on the benefits received by executives whose companies are selling some of their distressed assets to the government. In return for purchasing the assets, taxpayers will obtain an ownership stake in the companies. Many leading economists believe that the real estate market will turn around in the foreseeable future and government owned properties and assets will be sold at a profit. A provision in this bill that I supported requires any profits realized to be placed in the nation's treasury to reduce the deficit. If, however, after five years the government is facing a loss in the program, the President must submit a plan to Congress recommending how the money will be recouped from financial services companies. I believe that these protections are a dramatic improvement over the Administration's initial proposal.

The bill passed by the Senate included an important package of tax policy provisions. One of these provisions is an extension of the state and local sales tax deduction, which is a matter of fairness for states like Texas that do not have a state income tax. The average Texan will save $520 when they file their federal income tax forms next year. We also shielded low and middle-income taxpayers from higher taxes associated with the flawed alternative minimum tax (AMT) and included tax incentives to spur energy production and innovation including the wind energy production tax credit and the research and development tax credit.

As Texans, we have learned to take responsibility for our actions and being asked to pay for the mistakes of others is something many, including myself, find deeply troubling. However, after careful deliberation, I believe that the risks associated with doing nothing outweighed the risk of passing a less than perfect bill that nevertheless includes important protections for taxpayers. Economic evidence clearly suggested the problems were spreading into the broader economy. That is why I voted for the Emergency Economic Stabilization Act.

I appreciate hearing from you. Please do not hesitate to contact me on any issue of concern to you.
Sincerely,
Kay Bailey Hutchison
United States Senator
284 Russell Senate Office Building
Washington, DC 20510
202-224-5922 (tel)
202-224-0776 (fax)
http://hutchison. senate. gov

Racing with the Devil
(10.02.08)

The American Senators voted 74 for and 25 against the bailout. They added over 100 billion in more pork. Each yes vote is a person who has no common sense and should not serve this country or your state.

I fear this may be the downfall of America. We can continue to stay apathetic or we can act. But it may already be too late. Every state should recall and remove from office those Senators that voted yes.

ALL that voted yes are for the wealthy and big business. If Paulson gets free reign, without any checks and balances, to do with the money as he pleases, then America is doomed. I don't know yet but lets hope he doesn't have any control. As ignorant as the Senate appears to be I hope they maintain control.

Both Texas Senators voted for the wealthy. Let it be known that Obama and McCain voted yes. Neither one should serve as President of the United States of America. Biden also voted yes and in my opinion he should never serve in any capacity for our country.

It saddens me but I can tell you now that Americans will do nothing but pay the bill. The Senate and Wall Street are counting on that.

All claim to be Christians, but if you want to win the vote you must claim to be Christian. Although we joke and sometimes we hear in jest, "Kill 'em all. Let God sort 'em out," that day is fast approaching. All the "yes" votes are men racing with the devil.

Bright side of bailout
(10.02.08)

The bright side of the bailout is that we will now pull out of Afghanistan and Iraq. A new and more formidable terrorist have been found to be hiding in America. And lucky for our military forces they have all been found in Washington D. C.

After watching the recent bailout of Congress for their friends on Wall Street it makes more sense why Washington D. C. is the crime capital of America.

To Lee Rodriguez:
(10.03.08)

From: Rodriguez Lee

I have to live within my means also. I have a few toys – PAID FOR !!! Those that signed for the homes that they could not afford must have believed that the " government " would help them pay if they could not themselves. I have to pay my bills or I am OUT.

Just what this country needs now – Osama Obama increasing entitlements to those that don't want to work in the first place. There is your great " change " !!!! Palin did pretty good last night. She sure put Biden in his place when she quoted him from the Democratic debates when he said that Obama is not ready to be president – Biden's own words !!!!

Lee,

Everything you say is true but the people that didn't have the money were dumb. The ones that gave the money knew. They are the crooks. They are getting the 700 billion. And now those same crooks are going to help on the oversight committee. In other words we are having the wolves watch over the sheep.

The companies fed by greed should go broke. Not only are we going to give them 700 billion but our representatives have added 100 billion in pork barrel funds. Remember that was 100 billion in pork. The problem is we lost too much money and they want to lose more. Here are some of the things they are giving away. You know important things to bail out the economy.

But there is good news for Microsoft and NASCAR. The fund to bail out Wall Street is going to save NASCAR 109 billion.

Microsoft, Harley Davidson, General Electric and Citigroup are going to save $8.3 billion on their earnings each year.

And the one I really like…. a provision repealing a 39-cent excise tax on wooden arrows designed for children. We are also giving millions to American Samoa and Puerto Rico. Something else **bothers me. F**oreign banks jumped on the American Greed Band Wagon. We're also going to bail them out.

I SAY NO. Today the vote will pass after the dissenting votes get a little more pork. In a democracy you vote. There is a winner and a loser. When Congress votes we are the losers. A leader in the Senate said they will vote until it passes. One representative said they had almost a thousand constituents call in about the bailout. Only two were for it. **Looks like we're really getting represented by Congress, huh?**

We may be at a time in history where one of the greatest empires is on the verge of collapse. We may live to see it happen.

I know you say it can't happen, right? We didn't learn from the Savings and Loan debacle and it looks like history is repeating. Even in school we were taught that history repeats.

The funny thing is that Congress is like a magician. They want you to be a Democrat or a Republican. Root for you team while they do tricks behind your back. They want you to fight among each other as to religion, liberal and conservative while they simply steal your money and life away. I'm a conservative Republican. Now look at Congress and show me one. A conservative will not bail out the wealthy.

The Wall Street disaster is the same as Weapons of Mass Destruction. It doesn't exist. You could say that Congress just porked you. That's Democrats and Republicans.

But there is a bright side to all of this; we will now pull out of Afghanistan and Iraq.

Why **and how** can we do this? Because a new and more formidable terrorist have been found to be hiding in America. And lucky for our military forces they have all been found in Washington D. C.

After watching the recent bailout of Congress for their friends on Wall Street it makes more sense why Washington D. C. is the crime capital of America.

Throughout history every empire has collapsed. There have been no exceptions.

Letter to Oprah
(10.06.08)

Dear Oprah,

I want to know the truth and recently things have happened that really bother me. I believe you are the only one who can help. I consider myself a conservative Republican but feel I have been deceived. I think of myself as a Christian but the radical left bothers me. The lies being told about Obama should be revealed. Recently, I learned friends of mine, also Republicans, voted in the Democratic convention and voted for Obama saying they knew he couldn't win as President. They are Republicans like me, devout Christians and filled with hatred that is terrifying. I'm afraid the Republicans are stirring up hatred. I managed to get a recording of one of these conversations. Would you like to hear it?

You might say I'm a plain ol' Joe. I would like to ask McCain, Obama, Palin, Hillary and even Bush a few questions; one on one. These are simple questions all Americans want to know but none of the candidates are being asked. I believe the answers they give would surprise America.

You might find this very interesting. I write novels and I have one on Amazon, "Moon Shadow," that I finished writing in 1991. I rewrote it in 1994 to include bin Laden, and three hi-jacked airliners that crash into the White House. Coincidentally, I was on a Continental flight during the 911 attack. I updated "Moon Shadow" 2004 where I said the National Debt would be over ten trillion if Bush was able to continue unchecked. Last year some friends of mine said I would be audited for other things I have said about Bush. Six months ago I was audited. The first thing they asked me was about my book "Moon Shadow." The audit took four months and they found nothing.

Whoever is elected does not represent only Republicans. The President of the United States will represent all Americans; Democrat, Republican, Christian, Jew, Muslim, atheist, agnostic, black and white. I feel the Republicans are taking us down a path of destruction.

Letter to Dr. Phil
(10.07.08)

Dr. Phil

I consider myself a conservative Republican but feel I have been deceived. I think of myself as a Christian but the radical left bothers me. The lies being told about Obama should be revealed. Recently, I learned friends of mine, also Republicans, voted in the Democratic convention and voted for Obama saying they knew he couldn't win as President. They are Republicans like me, and devout Christians, but they are filled with hatred that is terrifying. I'm afraid the Republicans are stirring up hatred. I managed to get a recording of one of these conversations. Would you like to hear it?

You might say I'm a plain ol' Joe. I would like to ask McCain, Obama, Palin, Hillary and even Bush a few questions; one on one. These are simple questions all Americans want to know but none of the candidates are being asked. I believe the answers they give would surprise America.

You might find this very interesting. I write novels and I have one on Amazon, "Moon Shadow," that I finished writing in 1991. I rewrote it in 1994 to include bin Laden, and three hi-jacked airliners that crash into the White House. Coincidentally, I was on a Continental flight during the 911 attack. I updated "Moon Shadow" 2004 where I said the National Debt would be over ten trillion if Bush was able to continue unchecked. Last year some friends of mine said I would be audited for other things I have said about Bush. Six months ago I was audited. The first thing they asked me was about my book "Moon Shadow." The audit took four months and they found nothing.

Whoever is elected does not represent only Republicans or Democrats. The President of the United States will represent all Americans; Democrat, Republican, Christian, Jew, Muslim, atheist, agnostic, black and white. I feel the Republicans are taking us down a path of destruction.

Letter to Joseph Farrah
(10.08.08)

Joseph,

Sometimes I disagree with you and sometimes I like your thoughts. Your article, "Congress, the bailout and freedom," rings true in my mind.

What I hate most are the "golden parachutes" and the $400,000 party AIG had a few days ago. The 100 billion pork sure shows Congress doesn't care about America. Like I told someone, Bus declared war against WMD's so he should attack Wall Street and Congress for using "Financial Weapons of Mass Destruction" against America.

Anyway, I wrote a novel, "Moon Shadow," based on the demise of the United States. In one word it was greed. What is really weird is that things I wrote about are happening now. I wrote it in '89 base on what the other Bush had done. I revised it in '95. It was reprinted in 2004 and I made a statement in the back saying that if Congress and Bush were allowed to run out of control the National Debt would be over ten trillion. In my novel the collapse is final on the last day of 2012.

I know you're busy but I would like to send you a copy. Please let all your friends read it. It will make the hair on your neck stand up. In my book it does become a violent revolution.

For our sake I hope the pen is mightier than the sword.

New Name
(07.04.08)

Al Qaeda has taken a new name. They now call themselves Wall Street. Sometimes they may go under the alias Congress.

How to Save Our Country
(08.08.08)

"The only way to save this country is to never elect another Democrat or Republican. Get a bucket of Tar a box of feathers and lets get to work. We have our work cut out for us."

RINO'S
(09.07.08)

America has been destroyed by RINO's. That's Republicans In Name Only.

During this election remember if they are in office now---VOTE 'EM OUT!!!!

If Congress isn't careful they may become like the Indian and the buffalo.

Letter to Lisa
(10.01.08)

Lisa,

Is there a way I could bring you something and show it to you (let you listen)?

I consider myself a conservative Republican but I feel deceived by what the Republicans have done. I'm tired of the lies being passed around by "conservative Christians."

Also, how can you have a bailout that is so critical but Congress can add a hundred billion in pork? Right now Congress can't decide how much of a "golden umbrella" the CEO's (Chief Embezzlement Officer) are to get. To me it is simple. If we bail them out they get nothing. Is that too hard to understand?

Anyway I have some information that might help. I just want to read and hear the truth.

I know you get a lot of nut cases so I don't have a problem coming to the Chronicle.

The Difference?
(10.09.08)

Do you know what the difference between the debate last night and a group of old, senile, women having a tea party?

NOT MUCH!

Well, I'm sorry, I take that back. The old women are capable of thinking on their own and answering questions for themselves---even though they are senile

"I"
(10.10.08)

I was looking up the politicians that are running for re-election in November and found those currently in office had an "I" by their name. It made sense to me to have that "I" but I thought I would ask somebody that knew.

The first person I asked told me it stood for "Incumbent." He asked me why I wanted to know and I told him that I thought it meant something else.

"What?" he asked.

"After all the stupid things Congress had done in the last few weeks I was sure the "I" stood for idiot."

Is the Truth Out There?
(10.14.08)

Many people say Obama hired FRANKLIN RAINES (Chief Economic Advisor), TIM HOWARD (Chief Economic Advisor) and JIM JOHNSON (another advisor)? And they are crooks that quit and about 20 million with each of them. The Golden Umbrella thing.

Well then, you need to check out the information on HENRY PAULSON. He makes those three look like paupers. He has control of over 900 billion and nobody elected him. He took 500 million away from the company he worked for and it went broke. Being bailed out like Fannie Mae. Same crooked schemes. He knows how to take money.

McCain plans on keeping him. The stock market went up almost a thousand points because he put 300 billion in over the weekend including an additional 38 billion to AIG, the company that went on a 400 thousand dollar party the weekend after they got their first 82 billion.

Oh, the 300 billion over the weekend? You and I paid for it or we will be. Bailout a good idea? No. We can't keep giving hundreds of billions to Wall Street so the wealthy can even wealthier.

Watch the National Debt. It's like a cancer. That one trillion that Paulson is giving away will come back to haunt us in four years a hundred times worse than the bailout.

The assumption of the article is that Obama hired crooks (not proven yet, but I totally agree) then he is a crook. Now McCain associated and took money from Keating (remember the Keating Five) while Keating was stealing money. Cost the government two billion. Bush's brother Neil was involved. Does that make Bush a crook? BUT based on these theories then Bush is gay and pays for male prostitutes. His former Christian religious counselor was Haggard. Remember him? He lied but had an affair with a male prostitute and used a false name. Well you know. So what does that make Bush? If your father murdered someone does that make you a murderer? You decide.

Am I for Obama? No, I'm for America and the truth. Our congress men are not telling us the truth. Only two kinds of liars in Congress; Democrats and Republicans.

Greed brought down Wall Street. Greed will bring down America. Paulson is the beginning of the end.

I'm laughing and it's not funny

Congress just pulled a magic trick and Americans are happy. If it wasn't so ludicrous it would be funny. Reminds me of Abbot and Costello.

Like a magician waving his hand we don't take time to look at the other hand. President Bush, Paulson and Congress fabricated a false stock market that went up almost a thousand false points and Americans bought it, lock, stock and all laughing barrels. With the stock skyrocketing Americans are content again.

They might just as well have used monopoly money. When I buy on margin I have to pay it back. Our government is buying stock in banks, not helping the American people.

So Paulson took 300 billion of money that is not there to buy paper stock that is worthless. And worst of all Americans are blissfully happy.

Americans have their head in the sand.

2012 - Remember that number. It is the year that the interest on our debt will exceed the money taken in to run the government

Come Together Before It's Too Late
(11.02.08)

Don't believe what you read on the Internet. Well maybe, except for this. Most of the things being sent around are misleading and lies. Take time to research and find the truth. Listen to what Colin Powell said the other night. What he said is true; that is, if you're an American. America is made up of many people and backgrounds. All interesting and unique. I consider myself Christian, but I'm appalled at the attacks coming from Christian radicals. I feel I'm back in a time of the Crusades. The job of a Christian is to show love and kindness and convert a non-believer. Hatred and lies won't help to convert.

A friend of mine, who is a conservative, Christian, Republican voted for McCain because he is against abortion. How will that run the country? Ohh, I can already feel the heat and anger. Now wait a minute. We all know Bush is a Christian against abortion. Tell me what he did to stop abortion? If you're against it then shouldn't you have a plan to stop it? Tell you what; vote for me and I will give each and every one of you a Ferrari. Sounds great but how can I do it? In reality I can't, yet we believe. Think about it. I'm against abortion. Fine and dandy but how do I stop it? Isn't that the point?

Actually the point is who can run the country. As much as Christians hate this, we need somebody who can run the country and not make blind promises or stupid statements.

Remember Foley? He liked porno and making passes at young male interns. Along came Maloney saying he was a Christian and we should believe in family values. The Christian right voted him in. While he was condemning Foley he was having two affairs. The audacity of the man. Not only was he having an affair on his wife but he was even running around on his mistress. I mean the gall of that guy. Now I call that real family values. You know, three for the price of one, although he did need to pay one off with campaign funds. I would think that every time he goes to church on Sunday and harps on family values his butt would pucker up. Mr. Maloney should really be called "Phoney Baloney Maloney."

More than being Christian we need to vote for a man to run the country.

Now I went off on a tangent, but what I want you to really think about is the National Debt. I get tired of trying to explain but here goes again. If a politician says there was a budget surplus, well he's a damn liar. A surplus is when you take in more money than you spend in a fiscal year. That has not been done since the last year of President Eisenhower's administration in 1960. There has not been one dollar surplus since then. Those that said there was a surplus are LIARS. I can prove it and will actually give an Internet location where you can check it out daily. Oh, yeah, yesterday the National Debt went up 130 billion dollars in one day. The whole last year under Clinton it went up only 18 billion. The two worst spending presidents? Bush (Daddy) and (Son of a) Bush. They call that a double Bush-whacking. Anyway here is the webpage:
http://www. treasurydirect. gov/NP/BPDLogin?application=np

I will give you an example of how Congress and the president pass off a surplus to the American people. The president makes a budget for the year and Congress approves it. That makes 536 LIARS. Let's make the example simple. You make a budget with your spouse. You are paid 100 thousand dollars a year but you and your spouse add up the bills and realize your bills will probably be 125 thousand, so your budget is set at 125 thousand dollars. You immediately go out and borrow twenty-five thousand dollars to cover the budget shortage. At the end of the year you add it all up and find you only spent 120 thousand. You rejoice because you have a five thousand **dollar** surplus on your budget and immediately go on a five thousand dollar cruise to celebrate coming in under your budget. In reality you had a twenty thousand dollar deficit and you can add five more to that for the nice cruise. The following year you have the same budget but it will be 150 thousand to cover the twenty-five you went over the previous year.

HERE IS THE MAJOR PROBLEM. Say you make 100 thousand a year and spend 200 thousand. Each year you borrow a hundred thousand but only pay the interest. The bank loves it. You always pay the interest and they are making a fortune. Each year you borrow a hundred thousand dollars more than the previous year. Everything is going fine. Interest is low and nothing is happening. Ten years later you go in to the bank to borrow money but you need one million dollars. Interest has gone to ten percent and you will owe 100 thousand in interest. You only make 100 thousand. Everything you make goes on interest.

Now most of you are blaming the poor for getting loans that they couldn't pay off. You are electing politicians that are doing worse for this country than those people who borrowed money and couldn't pay. Our government is in worse condition than the companies they are buying stock in.

Here are some facts. Our government takes in a little over 2 trillion dollars a year. They set a budget of 2.6 trillion. This year they spent 3.1 trillion. Just a mere 1.1 trillion over budget. I predicted this in 2003 and it is in my novel *Moon Shadow*. Next year whoever is president, McCain (the Christian) or Obama (the Muslim terrorist) will probably go over the budget 1.5 trillion. You know we have important things to do like bail out the wealthy on Wall Street. Our government felt the best way to help America was to buy stock, not make loans to Americans. The government fiscal year ended on Sept 30th. From that day to October 23rd, only twenty-three days, the deficit has increased 500 billion. Not good.

I know what you are thinking. If you're a Republican it's a Democrats fault. You know like blame, say, Roosevelt. And of course if you're a Democrat a Republican is responsible like say, Abraham Lincoln. How long does it take to become responsible for your job? After eight years of Bush is it still Clinton's fault? Give me a break. Small minds think that way, but let me remind you that the problem is real.

The deficit will probably be over 1.5 trillion each and every year for the next four years. In the year 2012 we will probably have a deficit close to 20 trillion. Let's see, we take in two trillion, interest on the 20 trillion is say ten percent...uh, oh. Can you do the math?

I've been hearing the debt is the fault of the Democrats because they passed a law that would give loans to people who couldn't make payments. That is simply ludicrous and a bold-face lie even if you don't like Democrats. The Democrats might have held a majority most of the time but it was always close. Like in the Senate 52-48 or something of that nature. There were never a hundred Democratic Senators or 435 Democratic Representatives. The point is there were enough Republicans to do something. On the point of Democrats passing a law to loan poor people money that couldn't pay it back, it is absolutely wrong. It was passed under Clinton and it was to make low interest loans available to people who couldn't get them. For instance I had a glitch on my credit and I had to come up with twenty percent down on a house and pay twelve percent interest. A wealthy person could get no money down and six percent interest. Just what a poor person needed. Let's just say they did give loans to people who couldn't pay. That was more than eight years ago. Why are they repossessing the houses now? Because it was the sub-prime loans. Those sub-prime loans with low interest that skyrocketed after five years are what took us down and those loans started about six years ago. Opps, that was under Bush. Oh, that's right, it's Clinton's fault.

Let's just say it was the Democrats at fault and everybody knew it. McCain was elected by Republicans and he should have exposed it. McCain wants you to vote for him on experience. Twenty-six years ago when he was elected to office the National Debt was 1.5 trillion. Today it stands at 10.5 trillion. A nine trillion increase under McCain. One trillion for the bad loans today but eight trillion in overspending under McCain. He sees the budget every year and votes on it. He knows the budget was 500 billion more than the money taken in each and every year Bush was in office. He approved that budget. I don't need that type of fiscal irresponsibility anymore.

I'm also sick and tired of hearing, "those people are Godless." Whoever takes office does not represent just Christians. They will represent all Americans. The Republicans should look at the bright side. With all of those "Godless" Americans just think of all the souls they can save. But they will need to show a little more love. The hate is turning off America. This is coming from me and I'm a conservative, Christian, Republican. Oh, and if there is really a conservative Republican out there, could you tell me who it is?

Of all the things I've seen in this election it is the extreme hatred and anger expressed by fellow Americans. I was threatened by a few Christians when I discussed what was wrong with McCain. They told me nobody should be president unless they were Christian. One even told me this was God's country. I laughed at him and told him I thought that was Israel. This country was founded on freedom of religion, not freedom of Christianity. But right now we have bigger problems facing us. If we don't work together, we're in real trouble. The country is almost divided evenly between Democrats and Republicans. Right now we sound more like the Sunni and the Shiites.

When I'm around Democrats and Republicans in heated argument it's almost like I arrived at a picnic with the KKK and the NAACP. The love is lost. There must be sacrifice and we will need to work together, but I'm afraid that we won't be able to do it.

There is one way to end the hatred. Send a message when you vote, especially for your Congress representative, make sure they can do math. At least add and subtract. Now I know abortion is important but we probably need to elect somebody to run the country. Right now we have a president who will be out in a few months, and Paulson, a man we didn't elect, running a country and buying hundreds of billions of dollars of stock in their favorite friend's companies. I keep hearing that Obama wants to spread the wealth and take us into socialism. I don't think you're keeping up with current events. Bush and Paulson have taken us into socialism but the wealth continues to be pumped, literally flooded into the pockets of the wealthy. Hey, the first company Paulson bailed out was Goldman-Sachs, his old company. In fact I think he's still on the board. You would think that would be a conflict of interest. Thank God, Bush is a Christian or we would be in real trouble.

So when you go to the polls remember that the "I" next to a candidate's name stands for "Idiot." Vote for anybody but the idiot incumbent. Americans need to show all politicians that we want them out.

Next time I hear someone say, "You can take that to the bank," I think I'm going to start laughing. Take what to the bank? Dollars? Ameros? Maybe Pesos.

Oh boy, the next four years are going to be fun I can't wait to see what happens. What do you think?

My name is Joe Barfield and I approved this message.

Bailout – Even More
(11.15.08)

If I were President of the United States there would be many changes. As a fellow congressman from the state of Texas I have told you for years that we need to have more oversights into banking and Wall Street. No one has listened and it might now be too late. We don't need new laws; we just need to make sure everyone operates within current laws. They don't.

I believe it is truly time for a change. We need "Common Sense" solutions, something I think Congress has lost. Before Congress goes about business as usual and continues this bailout, I think it is time to address the real issues. We have an idea as to why it happened, but we need real solutions. The bailout is important but it needs to be just that. In less than two weeks it has become anything but a bailout.

Before we discuss the solutions, I would like to take a moment to tell you how the American people feel. I think Congress has lost touch with America. Recently, I have taken time to talk to the people in my district, other cities and here in Washington D. C. , and listen to their thoughts and concerns. Many have told me who they think is guilty of this whole financial fiasco. They have many suspects but the majority point to the same culprit. The people are more in touch with reality than Congress. Now take a moment and look at your fellow congressman next to you. The one on the other side and now the one behind you. What do you see? A man? A woman? A Democrat? A Republican? No they are none of these. The people of America say all of you are the ones who are guilty of America's problems. Congress, guilty as charged by the American people.

In 1864 Abraham Lincoln said, "I see in the near future a crisis approaching that unnerves me and causes me to tremble for the safety of my country. . . Corporations have been enthroned and an era of corruption in high places will follow, and the money power of the country will endeavor to prolong its reign by working upon the prejudices of people until all wealth is aggregated in a few hands and the Republic is destroyed." He also said, "America will never be destroyed from the outside. If we falter and lose our freedoms, it will be because we destroyed ourselves." Wise words written almost a hundred and fifty years ago. Every one of those words rings true today.

I'm holding up before you my personal agenda. I need Congress to give me four million dollars for my journal. Who will second my motion? No takers? We are giving hundreds of billions to the banking industry; surely my journal is worth a few million. No one? Okay, how about if each of you gives me seven thousand?

Still no one is interested? My journal talks about, "We the people," and things like the land of the free and the home of the brave. Any takers now? I need your help. Please. Who will give the money to me?

Interesting. Not one of you will pay me seven thousand for my personal journal, but all of you demand each and every American give the same amount to help the wealthy by purchasing stock in their companies. Actually, Congress feels the same way about my personal journal as Americans feel about the government buying stock in American companies.

Would you like to hear some of the comments your fellow Americans aimed at Congress?

One person asked me, *"Why do we fight terror in Iraq and Afghanistan when there is more damage being done to America by the 535 terrorists in Washington D. C. ?"*

"If this country collapses, Congress should be tried for treason."

"I'll tell you this, when I vote in November I'm gonna be looking for the letter "I" so I'll know who the incumbent is and then I'm gonna vote for the other guy."

I asked someone what they thought of Congress and he said, *"Congress? They're all crooks."*

"Bush declared war against WMDs right? Well tell him to attack Wall Street and Congress for attacking America with Financial Weapons of Mass Destruction."

When I asked someone who he planned to vote for he said, *"Not anyone who is in office now. It would be safer to vote for Benedict Arnold."*

"How can anyone be allowed to vote on the bailout when they were given campaign election funds by the same companies being bailed out?"

I thought this was one of the best questions, so I did a little research. Did you know that most of the members of Congress have taken campaign contributions from at least one of the companies that President Bush and Mr. Paulson are giving American's money to?

A woman told me she would never be able to retire and asked me, *"For eight years Congress has told America there are problems with Social Security and they won't be able to fund it, but in less than forty-eight hours you can come up with eight hundred billion to bail out the wealthy? What about my Social Security?"*

And finally one said, *"There are really only two problems with the Federal government; Democrats and Republicans. If you get rid of them, America will be fine."*

These are just a few of the things that I have heard from my constituents. Let's discuss the bailout. The first thing Paulson did was to bail out his old company with Americans' hard earned dollars. President Bush demands Americans have confidence and that it will take time. And how do we instill confidence? The guilty go free. We give billions to those who actually committed crimes and they want more. When we added billions in pork, even I lost confidence in those running our country. If we really need to bail out these financial institutions, then why did we give a tax break on wooden arrows? I like NASCAR but we gave them over one hundred million in tax breaks. Why? And we gave eight billion in foreign tax incentives to companies like Microsoft and Citicorp. Just one person tell me how these companies figure into the banking bailout? And foreign incentives at that. I thought America was in trouble? We should be ashamed of ourselves. First and foremost American's money should be used to help them get loans, not buy stocks in companies where CEOs get tens and even hundreds of millions of dollars each year. And for what? Bankrupting a company? When our government bought stock instead of helping Americans we became socialistic. We are being led by a president who is almost out of office and a man, Paulson, no one elected. Paulson is a man who stands for the worst of the wealthy in America. Actually worse than that. A socialist country uses the money to help the people. All of our money is going to the wealthy and we're asking the poor to pay for their folly.

Now, as we debate these issues and give banks billions of dollars to get the economy going, those same banks balk at loaning funds after they willingly took the money. Remember, Congress has taken every Americans' hard earned money that was put into Social Security and spent it. These are the same people we are now asking to bail out the criminally wealthy, while telling them there is not enough Social Security for them. This is wrong.

Of course you ask, "How could Americans say that after all we have done?" Actually, we've done nothing. Now let me tell you what should be done for Americans. We need to act swiftly to restore American's confidence in their government. Where do I start? The list is so long. But let's get started with the solutions.

Americans want criminal charges brought against these companies, and I agree. This is a long-standing crime of greed that has been perpetrated by these companies. A man will go to jail for stealing twenty dollars from a local store, so why shouldn't these corporate thieves do likewise for stealing billions, even trillions, and laughing in our faces?

The prime example is AIG. One of my workers calls them "All Illegal Gains." Probably not far from the truth. We bailed them out with eighty-seven billion dollars and the following weekend a hundred of their executives and salesmen went on a four hundred thousand dollar retreat to St. Regis. It included spa outings and golf banquets, and it was all paid for by the American taxpayers. It was a direct slap in the face. Not a real confidence builder like the president hoped for. And what happened to them? Nothing. But it gets worse. After the AIG jaunt and celebration they demanded more money. Thirty-eight billion more to be exact. And we gave it to them. Personally I believe every person who attended that weekend retreat should be fired.

By law AIG was required to keep cash reserves to cover ten percent of the loans they had insured. AIG failed to do so. They broke the law. Americans wants to know how they will be punished, but instead they see the executives celebrate with a half million dollar party. You need to understand that America is angry. Very angry.

First we will start with AIG. We will bring immediate charges against those who did not keep the ten percent reserves. All of those who attended the weekend jaunt will be relieved of their jobs. We will not buy stock in bad loans but we will take over those loans and give them to a company to manage at two percent over prime. This solution will keep the homeowner in his or her house and eliminate the necessity of enforcing a repossession. The loan will be able to be assumed by any American for three percent over prime, and there will be no closing costs. The people who received sub-prime loans were ignorant. The lenders were criminal. They must also be punished. As an example, I know of a person who was told they could borrow three hundred thousand with payments of eight hundred dollars a month for the first five years. Their total income was four thousand dollars a month. At the end of the five years their payment would be over three thousand dollars a month. Yes, stupid on the borrower's part but negligent and criminal for the lender. They also need to be punished, and now.

These will be the first steps in regaining America's confidence.

Many corporations mislead Americans. Cable television is a good example. Last year I signed up for a six-month special at ninety dollars a month for cable, telephone, and Internet service. I kept asking how much it would be after six months, but somehow they managed to avoid my questions. I never got a bill for ninety dollars in any of those months. It was closer to a hundred and fifty. After six months it was closer to two hundred and fifty a month. We all know about this, and that is how the sub-prime loans developed. Business is often misleading and that needs to change. Not later but now. Telephones, cable, electricity, and the Internet will no longer be able to force contracts. If their service is good, no one will switch. Whatever specials a company offers, they must print what the actual charges will be after their special. Both prices must be on the same page of the advertisement with the regular price no less than one-fourth of the special.

Yesterday, in the mail, I received an offer to obtain a charge card through one of the banks involved in receiving some of this bailout money. They set a low interest rate of twenty-nine percent. Any banks taking this bailout welfare will not be allowed to charge more than ten percent on their charge card offers. And I think that is too much. If the banks refuse the terms then they do not qualify for the bailout.

I want to put J. P Morgan, Citicorp and the likes, that received monies from the bailout, on notice. All home loans will not exceed two and half over the current one percent prime. The loan companies will not be allowed to charge points or prepayment penalties. All of these new loans will be assumable for the duration of the loan. Any company refusing to agree to these terms will be refused ANY assistance from the bail out.

We are going to have yearly audits of every company that receives money during the bailout. I want to see stock options and bonuses regulated. When I say regulated I mean the company must make money before the CEO's, or Chief Embezzlement Officers which is what I have heard some of my constituents call them, get any type of bonus or stock options. Really a very simple plan.

To this we will add companies like GM. Now I don't know how they figured into the home loan crisis, but for some reason an additional twenty-four billion was loaned to GM so they could update their manufacturing equipment to make them competitive with the likes of Ford and Toyota. If the other companies updated their equipment, why should GM be rewarded for not doing business as required? Add the GM executives to those whose pay and stock options are limited. It will only apply until the loan they received from the American people is paid off. Nothing harsh, just common sense. No rewards for stupidity.

Let's move to the next issue. Welfare was meant to help people in trouble. It is an honorable thing to do but welfare was not meant to be a way of life. I'll never forget seeing one welfare person on television. When asked why he didn't work, he responded that he made more money on welfare than he could make on a job. That is the problem. Those people on welfare need incentive as well as initiative, drive, and determination. They need to go to work. I offer a two-year program that will train them and make them useful assets to America instead of a burden.

The government will no longer give out special no-bid contracts to any company.

Another thing I learned recently really troubles me. President Bush authorized sending twenty billion dollars in cash on a flight to help get Iraq's economy going. That is American dollars. I don't questions his reasoning or authority, but nine billion of that money was misplaced. It's gone and nobody knows where it went. I want that money found. How would you like to make a hundred thousand dollars, but you tell your spouse you misplaced forty thousand and can't find it? Also, the companies over there are bilking Americans. This must stop. We need a complete expenditure audit of the war in Iraq. Ask yourself how many six hundred dollar toilets America paid for. Here is a simple plan. Whatever I can buy from the store retail, the federal government can be charged three times as much. I really think that is too much. So, when we run the audit the difference of the overcharge will be charged back triple to the company billing America.

From now on no civilian companies will be involved in helping with the war. If our military can't do it, then we have no business conducting war.

I also have information that more than seventy foreign companies supply parts for some of our top secret military projects. This needs to stop now. When it comes to the military I want every nut, bolt, and screw to be supplied and built with one hundred percent American parts and labor. Again, if a foreign company is needed to build our military we need to get out of the war business.

One of my relatives called the IRS for some information, and the company taking the calls was in India. Not anymore if I can help it.

The United States takes in two and a half trillion dollars. I want every penny taken in to be spent on American labor and American material. If American companies want to take work out of the country so be it, but our government will never do it again and we will no longer conduct business with those companies.

At this point in time our government is in trouble. I think we can learn from the Great Depression. Thank God, Roosevelt didn't buy stock in greedy banking companies. He did what this country needs to do now. Give America incentives. Create jobs; don't give money to the wealthy. Have a plan. Do that and you will instill confidence in the American people.

I also want, no I demand, an audit and the money used by Bush and Paulson to be tracked. I don't want half of eight hundred billion to go missing like the nine billion in Iraq. If money is lost then the last person touching it will go to jail. A few more whistle blowers will also help.

Elected officials serve their country. The people do not serve the elected officials. Elected officials will be paid a million a year. That will cover their expenses. Be frugal. There will be no trickery with the budget. The government will not spend more money than is taken in by taxes. If there is a deficit, then the elected officials forfeit their pay for the following year.

Everyone pays Social Security. That includes all government employees and politicians. Retirement will be based on Social Security. Sure, a government employee will receive more. I don't have a problem with that.

And here is the easy one. The one thing I have never heard mentioned. Cut spending. That's right, cut spending. If you demand the taxpayers carry more of the burden then it makes common sense we should cut our yearly spending. Cut the graft, cut the waste and abolish the pork. No more bridges to nowhere.

Earlier I told you I talked to hundreds of people on the street. The people we are supposed to represent. What I didn't tell you was for every hundred I spoke to only two felt Congress was doing an adequate job. Not a good job just an adequate job. The other ninety-eight wanted their incumbent replaced. And most believe Congress is more criminally negligent than the big businesses being bailed out.

This is a unique time in history. We can change history or like our old third grade teacher said, "History always repeats." Will we change history or will we repeat it? Are we no different than any powerful empire before us? Throughout history every empire has collapsed, there have been no exceptions.

Do you know who said, ""The budget should be balanced, the Treasury should be refilled, public debt should be reduced, the arrogance of officialdom should be tempered and controlled, and the assistance to foreign lands should be curtailed lest we become bankrupt. People must again learn to work, instead of living on public assistance." It was Cicero in 55 BC. Seems like the Roman Empire had the same problems we have today. And where is the Roman Empire now?

Know this, revolutions have started for less. Our own revolution started for less than what we have done to America. Show America that Congress still has one shred of honor and integrity.

For once in your careers put aside your special interest, if only this time, and take a moment to do something you have never done since you were elected. I want each and every one of you, today, to represent the Americans that elected you and not the special interests or companies that gave money to get you elected. With the coming elections many of you will not return to office, and justifiably so. For most of you your career is about to end. You have a chance to change the course of America. You have a chance to save America. Can you do what is right for America? Or are the American people right when they point their finger at Congress and say "guilty."

13
Obama bin Lyin (2009 -)

Founder of the new Muslim nation - the demise of freedom and the creation of the USSA (United Socialist States of America)

Bailout
(2.24.09)
The right to bear arms was originally conceived with the concept that Americans could and should defend their country from their government should that same government become corrupt or dangerous to all Americans. That time has come.

It's time to (Lets) go to Congress with Smith and Wesson,

And teach those un-American traitors a lesson.

Soon all Americans may repeat to Congress the same words Caesar said with his last breath, "Et tu Brute?" The laws they make are no different than a knife in the back.

Disastrous Bailout
(2.24.09)
We have two people who can solve the problem. Smith and Wesson for Term limitation.

If something happened to a Congressperson (politically correct) what would it be called?

Assassination: important persons

Murder: regular people

Execution: for those that commit treason against their country.

You be the judge.

Pull out of Afghanistan. The enemy combatants are in Washington D. C. under the alias of Congressmen.

Food for thought. The Jerk (can't remember his name) that works for Obama, says we need two trillion to bail out the banks that won't lend us money but give themselves millions each in bonuses. It means they are boning us.

How about this. In the last year four million Americans were laid off (no government workers). Give each one 30,000 dollars a year for the next year with the condition they get home loans and buy cars. NOW that will spur the economy

GUESS WHAT THE PRICE TAG WILL BE? only 250 billion. So why give the wealthy two trillion? Graft, corruption, lies and TREASON!!

It is time to end wealthy welfare. Audit all of them and Halliburton. Another thing. The government spends three trillion per year. I believe in free trade but the government is exempt. Every penny will be spent on American products and labor. No exceptions. None!

Save America, Nuke Washington D. C.

The biggest disaster? There's one bigger. The 789 billion dollar government stimulus plan.

Oh wait, THEY'RE DOING THAT ON PURPOSE!!!!!

Miraculous Healing

(2.24.09)

It has been noted that people have been miraculously healed when Obama has touched them. If so that would make him a false prophet, the Antichrist or the second coming.

NONE of these are true except maybe the first one.

Here is the truth. Hysterical lesion is a dementia where one thinks they are sick or debilitated and the right stimuli brings them out of their stupor and they think they have been miraculously healed when all that has happened is they have been awakened from a psychotic episode. In other words they are crazy and a shock bought them back to their senses. A good ass kicking used to be the stimulus, but today you can be sued for curing someone like that. Too bad, there are so many we could help, but litigation prevents it. Some people are alive only because it is illegal to kill them.

You decide.

More Lies

(3.14.09)

I just received this in an email:

Mr. Obama has indeed brought some change to Washington. At $192 billion in February, he has now presided over the largest increase in deficit spending a single month, ever.

I find the comments to be very interesting. The part about the 192 billion in February is correct. The EVER part is grossly wrong.

Between September 1st and October 1st of 2008, the deficit increased from 9.667 trillion to 10.148 trillion for an increase in deficit spending of 481 billion in one month. Between October 1st and November 1st the deficit went from 10.148 trillion to 10.556 for an increase in deficit spending of 408 billion in one month.

If I'm not mistaking I do believe 481 and 408 is not only more than 192 but more than double the 192 that and been passed along as the most EVER. Whoever wrote that article has been hanging out with Madoff, Wall Street and Congress too long. For them two plus two is anything but four.

If you want the truth Check it out:

http://www. treasurydirect. gov/NP/BPDLogin?application=np

Congress and whoever wrote the part about EVER are all liars. If you consider yourself a Democrat or Republican and are firm in your belief then have already lost.

The truth is out there somewhere; just not in Congress.

Cost of Al Qaeda

(3.25.09)

Terrorism is our main concern. The attack on New York or 9/11 was devastating to Americans and the economy.

Immediate and Short Term Direct Impacts of 9/11

The September 11 attacks inflicted casualties and material damages on a far greater scale than any other terrorist aggression in recent history. Lower Manhattan lost approximately 30 percent of its office space and a number of businesses ceased to exist. Close to 200,000 jobs were destroyed or relocated out of New York City, at least temporarily. The destruction of physical assets was estimated in the national accounts to amount to $14 billion for private businesses, $1.5 billion for state and local government enterprises and $0.7 billion for federal enterprises. Rescue, cleanup and related costs have been estimated to amount to at least $11 billion for a total direct cost of $27.2 billion. **Immediate and Short Term Direct Impacts on Toxic Loans**

AIG was GIVEN almost $200 billion OR eight times the cost of 9/11. In less than a year more than 4 million Americans have been laid off. This does not take into account the unemployment that if taken for a year could be up to 67 billion or nearly three times the cost of 9/11. Bush and Obama have claimed that the rescue, cleanup and related cost could be up to 2 trillion. Congress said they passed a law that will not allow them to get back the bonuses from AIG executives. Why not pass a new law? Eight out of ten Americans were against the bailout but Congress did it anyway. Almost 100% of Americans were against AIG bonuses.

Who does Congress represent?

Over four thousand Americans died in Iraq to protect freedom and America. Who's protecting America now? Don't look to Congress, they no longer represent the people.

So I ask you who are the real terrorists against America? Who is really destroying America?

Response to MoveOn. org

(4.01.09)

I'm sick and tired of Democrats and Republicans.

1. The bailout should never have happened. Eight out of ten Americans were against it. Congress voted for it anyway.

2. Nearly ALL Americans were against the bonus but they got it anyway.

Here it is. Congress should pass no more laws they are incompetent. Someone put in the bonuses for AIG. Who was it? They need to be removed. Remember that the last eight years the deficit has gone up more than five trillion. Do any of them know how to balance the budget?

No Congressman should be allowed to vote on the bailout if they received campaign funds from those companies.

Insurance companies are required by law to keep a certain amount of money in reserve, AIG didn't. Where are the criminal charges?

There should never be a bailout for an incompetent company.

The 911 terrorist act cost 40 billion and 200,000 lost jobs. AIG has cost over 200 billion directly with millions losing their jobs as a direct result.

So who are the enemy combatants? The Chief Embezzlement Officers of all the companies that were bailed out and Congress--Democrats and Republicans.

Bush and Paulson - Socialism

Obama and Pelosi - Communism

You are either a Democrat, Republican or an American Patriot. You can only be one.

The bonuses for AIG means that our soldiers in Iraq died for nothing. The enemy is in Washington DC.

Pogo said it best, "We has seen the enemy and they is us."

Government is Like Football

(4.03.09)

When you think about it our government is a lot like football--the field goal. Bush took the snap, fumbled it a little, placed it down and then Obama came through and kicked the s%#* out of the ball. The American people are the ball.

Baby Zoey

(4.03.09)

This is a thought for a friend who is about to have a baby.

Don't freak out if, "Tomorrow Zoey is getting out of high school." I know she hasn't even been born yet but time does fly when you're having fun. You will think the terrible two's will last forever, but they won't. This is just the beginning of the grandest of all adventures. Enjoy it to the fullest because things are going to speed up. The front teeth will go missing; the first day of school will be exciting, happy and sad for you. More school, then high school and then the much feared boyfriend. Graduation day will come with a speed never anticipated. Preparations for a wedding, the wedding and then she will be gone. Don't worry. One day she will return with a little bundle, another baby Zoey for you to watch and spoil. So enjoy every minute while you can.

A. I. G. Bonus

(4.15.09)

If you took the average American's pay (around 30,000) and divided into the 696 million dollar bonuses that AIG passed out to themselves, including the twenty or so that don't work there anymore and are responsible for the collapse of AIG, you could employ 23,200 Americans for a year.

So far Congress, Bush and Obama have given away three trillion dollars to the wealthy and they have not created a SINGLE new American job.

MoveOn. org

(4.15.09)

Dear MoveOn. org,

In response to the information below that you have sent me I have this to say:

If you don't respond to this it will prove that Obama's plan is no better than Social Security or Medicare. Both are bankrupt. I'm going to use this to prove Democrats don't' respond either. A plan with a bankrupt country is no good. This is no longer America and I consider any government giveaway to be simple communism. Wake up--government bureaucracy never works. So far we have given away three trillion jobs and not put a single American to work. Give me liberty or give me death but don't give me anymore Democrats or Republicans. The true

Americans are the 27 Congressmen who voted against all BAILOUT programs. The other 508 are no better than traitors and one day I hope they are punished as such. America as I knew it no longer exists and has been replaced by leaders that are socialistic--communistic traitors to America and the Constitution of the United States of America. Judgment day is coming and God is watching you.

It's Tea Party Time
(4.15.09)

Tea time anyone?

Let's make this perfectly clear. We are not protesting President Obama because he is black. We protest him because he is stupid.

Contrary to Congress' view; To protest is not Un-American. Live with it. It's the American way.

I have a dream! But the American Dream has become a nightmare!

Time for me to go. I haven't had my tea yet.

America—home of the free?
(04.15.09)

Congress represents Americans—or do they?

Over eighty percent of Americans were against the bailout. Congress and Bush did it anyway.

Bush and Paulson – socialism

All politicians polled said that basically 100 percent of Americans calling in were against the bonuses for A. I. G. Congress and Obama let them have it anyway.

Obama and Pelosi – communism

Now Obama says that states not doing what he demands will have criminal charges and denied tax revenue. What Obama is doing is un-constitutional and un-American. You reward failure. That is not and never has been the American way.

If he succeeds, then free America will be dead. If Obama and Congress continue as they please then the over 4000 Americans who died in Iraq to protect freedom will have died in vain. Of the 535 members of Congress only 27 voted against all bailout. Any state that does not help remove the other 508 puts another nail in the coffin of America. Those that believe in America and FREEDOM will remove their representatives in honor of all fallen American soldiers.

To President Obama:
(04.21.09)

I'm a little disappointed in you after backing you as President. You want to cut 100 million? Take away three of your 28 helicopters and you will save 120 million a year. Do you really need 28?

Are you really concerned about the environment? I can show you how I can develop and put into the market a car capable of traveling 600 miles on a charge with two years. This alone will create thousands of jobs and also clean the environment. Isn't that what you want?

Show America you will reward innovation and creativity. So far all you have rewarded are failures. Stop the bailout. None of the banks that have been bailed out are giving any loans. Take the money back. You have not created a single American job. Greed is the reason for the failure of America as shown by AIG (American Institute of Greed) and the car manufacturers. The CEO's (Chief Embezzlement Officers) have taken them down but the greed of the Unions have destroyed them.

Fix America don't destroy it. So far you have fulfilled the greed of the wealthy and the incompetent. You have rewarded failure. Your budget is worse than what Bush did and that is why I voted against him.

Your lack of response will be proof you don't represent the American people. Talk to the American people face to face. Let them ask you real questions and give them real answers. Let me be the first to ask you the questions that trouble me.

Show us you are a man of the people

MoveOn. org
(04.04.09)
QUESTION ASKED BY MOVEON. ORG:
Thanks for responding to the forum with Howard Dean. If you have a story to share or a question to ask about health care reform, please share it below.
MY QUESTION:
How is the Federal government going to make this work where Social Security and Medicare has been bankrupted? Isn't this just another government Ponzi scheme?
So far my insurance company has covered everything but claims.

Guns
(04.06.09)
Invest in precious metals; gold and silver. But remember the government has another precious metal. Lead. And lead can get you all the gold and silver you want. Even your land. Politicians are the reason guns were invented.

Party
(05.26.09)
Politicians of the two parties exist today to polarize the anger of Americans against each other. While politicians steal America blind and destroy freedom and democracy. Now they put a new radical form of communism. To be a Democrat or a Republican is no different than being a traitor or a communist.

The problems facing our country today were caused by the very people who say they can solve them.

The Twin Towers worked better than suspected. Single handedly Bush has almost destroyed America. Each year he over spent the budget by nearly 600 billion to fight war against a word—terrorism. Something he can never defeat. He has doubled his country's debt and added another trillion to the debt in his last year as he rewarded CEO's for failed companies and his wealthy friends on Wall Street, at the expense of hard working Americans.

He did just as I suspected he would. Americans are angry and that is good. Obama will be unable to slow the financial slide. He too will reward the wealthy while taxing middle America to death. I predict that in less than four years the United States will be bankrupt and nothing will save them.

Email to a friend
(04.21.09)

Ruben,

Based on these two paragraphs you just sent:

Have you ever tried going on a road trip without a map? Trying to plan your life without God is just as ineffective. We can head in the general direction of where we know we should be, but without God as our guide, we'll be just like the lost motorist, asking everyone else for directions. If we consult God in everything, asking Him to lead and guide us on life's journey, the Bible says His footsteps shall be our pathway and His plan will be to give us a future and a hope (Psalm 85:13, Jeremiah 29:11). Without Him, we will wander life's highways, not knowing where they lead. Then Congress and Obama are running the country without a road map. And they are definitely wandering life's highway with no idea where they are going.

Burma Shave

Oh, oh I almost forgot. The most important thing our money can teach us is "In God We Trust." Nowhere on our money does it say, "In Congress We Trust," or "In Obama We Trust." It's pretty clear the word is God.

Move On. Crazy
(07.21.09)

Are you crazy or just stupid. Don't you know there isn't enough money to fund this? You are fiscally irresponsible. This will be no better than Social Security or Medicare. Let all those in Congress submit to the same insurance and see how fast they change their minds. This is nothing less than Socialism and borders on Communism.

Just plain ol' Joe America

The Pullout is the point of war
(06.21.09)

Dick Cheney: Troop Pullout May Waste U. S. Sacrifices in Iraq

Tuesday, June 30, 2009 8:39 AM

By: Joseph Weber, The Washington Times

Former Vice President Dick Cheney on Monday expressed concern that the pending pullout of U. S. troops from Iraq's cities could reverse the military progress made by American and Iraqi forces there since the George W. Bush administration's 2007 surge. "I hope the Iraqis can deal with it," Mr. Cheney told The Washington Times' "America's Morning News" radio show. "At some point, they have to stand on their own, but I would not want to see the U. S. waste all the tremendous sacrifice that has gotten us to this point."

The article where Cheney says the pullout is a waste is from the point of a man who has no concept except to reward his wealthy friends.

A pullout proves our sacrifices were not a waste. There is a time to end the war and let them take over. If Cheney is right then he is actually saying we never won the war.

But if you don't like wars to end there is nothing to worry about because Obama will take it to Iran and/or Korea. It's just the American way and it really makes a President more popular.

Since Korea all of our other wars have been fought for money and to take Americans minds off the real problem.

The real questions are why has Halliburton not been audited and how much did Cheney get paid by Halliburton the last seven years. I wish I could get a no-bid contract. They made so much off war and death they managed to move to Dubai. Good American company.

A letter to President Obama
(08.13.09)

If the health care is so good then Congress should endorse it for themselves-- including President Obama.

I refuse to stand behind a program you personally don't use for yourselves. Also the government needs to stay out of business. You and all the others in Congress are already socialists with this and the other programs you have dreamed up. You are rapidly charging toward something even worse than socialism. How can you tell us that our Social Security is in trouble when you give trillions to the wealthy and their failures? Before you speak up for the medical field how about you fix our Social Security.

I challenge you to talk to me on public television to prove this is not a socialistic regime. Let's talk on Oprah or are you afraid to address a regular "Joe Citizen." I spoke up for you in the election but I can no longer do so with the programs you are forcing on America.

Your lack of response is a verification your program is a failure and I will not hesitate to pass this on to my friends.

Let's talk. Do you stand for Big Government and Big Business or for the Americans that voted for you?

You can also call or write to the President:
The White House
1600 Pennsylvania Avenue NW
Washington, DC 20500

Please include your e-mail address

Gifts & Items Sent to the White House

The President and the First Lady strongly encourage all Americans to consider sending contributions to their favorite charities in lieu of gifts to the First Family.

For security reasons, please do not send perishable gifts - such as food, liquids or flowers - to the White House. The White House is unable to accept cash, checks, bonds, gift certificates, foreign currency, or other monetary equivalents. Additionally, items sent to the White House are often significantly delayed and can be irreparably harmed during the security screening process. Therefore, please do not send items of personal importance, such as family photographs, because items may not be returned.

While President Obama, the First Lady, Vice President Biden, and Dr. Biden appreciate your thoughtfulness and generosity, they request that instead you look to your local community for opportunities to assist your neighbors in need.

So far this is the response I have received:

Thank you for contacting the White House.

President Obama is committed to creating the most open and accessible administration in American history. That begins with taking comments and questions from you, the public, through our website.

Our office receives tens of thousands of messages from Americans each day. We do our best to reply to as many as we can, but please be aware that you may find more information and answers to your questions online.

We encourage you to visit White House. gov regularly to follow news and updates, and to learn more about President Obama's agenda for change.

For an easy-to-navigate source of information on Federal government services, please visit: www. USA. gov

Thank you again for your message.

The Office of Presidential Correspondence

I hope all of you also respond:
http://www. whitehouse. gov/contact/?ec=11

Phone Numbers

Comments: 202-456-1111
Switchboard: 202-456-1414
FAX: 202-456-2461

TTY/TDD

Comments: 202-456-6213
Visitors Office: 202-456-2121

Obama Care

(09.02.09)

Actually it boils down to this. Congress says it's good and America is divided on the issue. Radically divided.

My solution is simple. What is good for America is good for all. Let Congress also take it. When Congress says it's exempt then the program is no good. When they say it's good enough for them then it's good enough for America.

First find out which ones believe in God and then remind them they are going to HELL!

Pelosi Care

(09.22.09)

I wish I had known that Pelosi was in Houston this last weekend. I wish I had known because I would have gone and given her my four cents worth. It used to be two cents worth but the dollar isn't worth a peso anymore.

Global Warming

(9-9-9)

I must apologize. President Obama and Congress are correct. Global warming is here. I will be the first to say we must act fast and we must act now to eliminate the source of this deadly problem. I do wonder how so many people (Congress and the President) have become so intelligent on a matter so serious that they know nothing about. But they surely know better.

But the cold spell in Texas proves the Congressional and Presidential theory of Global warming. As we know hot air rises. I, personally, have found the source and recommend, no demand, as Democrats and Republicans always do, that these gases be eliminated and it be done quickly. The bright side is that it will take no new taxes but sadly we not be able to lower taxes. To eliminate the hot air gases all you need to do is vote. Contrary to what Gore says you don't need to buy green gas credits. We all know from elementary school that hot air rises. This is evident from the cold air being sucked through the United States and toward the East Coast.

So how do we eliminate "Global Warming?" Vote. That's right vote. It will eliminate the "global hot air gases." You see the source is Washington D. C. All the hot air is there. It's really very simple: If you are an American you must vote out all Democrats and Republicans, thus eliminating the source of the problem. Global Warming? All the hot air is in Washington D. C.

The Truth About Healthcare
(09.24.09)

You're so right and I'm so wrong. Maybe Jack Nicholson was right when he said, "You can't handle the truth." The new way of the American people.

Here is the only truth about the Healthcare before us. (I made it up but it is true) Whatever is good for the people is good for Congress. If they demand to be exempt then the program is simply no good. It is "we the people" not "the people and then Congress.

When Congress takes the "Plan" for themselves then I can guarantee you will be good for Americans.

Michelle Obama spurring the America economy
(10.07.09)

Michelle Obama employees 23 people being paid a total of 1.4 million salaries annually. One employee is paid 40,000 a year to make sure she has all her trips set properly. Another is paid 60,000 to check her schedule every day. Many were involved in getting the Olympics to Chicago. This failed. It failed very much like her husband spending more than a trillion dollars and Americans losing more than 2 million jobs. But back to Michelle. She has a staff of 23, which I believe are the only new jobs in America. The average pay is 60,000 each. Who elected her? Who approved the staff hiring and more important how much do they actually make for the American people? What is there finished product? These jobs should definitely be sent to India.

Now let's take old "Joe Blow American and his companies for example. There are more than 5 million American companies that employ 20 or less Americans. They pay their employees about 600 million a year for an average of less than 6 thousand each. Remember these are working Americans that actually do something for other Americans. Almost all make a profit, although be it not much, yet still viable companies that produce useful services for fellow Americans.

What does Michelle's expensive entourage produce for Americans? A failed Olympics? And what about her $800,000 shopping trip in London. If this is what she is like to you really think Obama can save America?

Nobel Peace Prize
(10.14.09)

The rumor has it that Obama won the Nobel Peace Prize for given $529 million to bailout a Finland based auto company.

That's right.

http://www. latimes. com/business/la-fi-fisker23-2009sep23,0,6092445. story

OH, yesterday the value of the dollar dropped 10%. More than it has any time in history. Invest in something valuable. Buy pesos.

Al Qaeda is alive and well. They go by two names: Obama and Congress.

A. I. G. (American Institute of Greed)
(10.15.09)

Hey good news. AIG has done so well they are going to pass out nearly a billion in bonuses to their employees. Still they have not paid back the money they owe us since we are the ones who gave them the over 200 billion in bailouts.

I truly wish them the best and just to show that I have no hard feelings I'm sending them something for their victory celebration; a gallon each of some of the finest vintage "Jim Jones Grape Juice."

Trick or Treat
(10.31.09)

I can't wait for Halloween!

On Halloween I'm going to dress up as Obama. When the kids come to the door I'll greet them with, "Thanks for doing your part for America." Then I'm going to reach in their bag and take half of their candy.

Don't you just love America? Trick or Treat!?

Jason responded, "I love it!!! You should then ask them to take whatever candy they have left and give it to the kids with less candy because they're less fortunate and they deserve it!"

I answered, "Actually I'm going to do that but I'm really going to do like the government and keep it for myself."

America?
(11.05.09)

Viva la France!!! Viva Chavez!!

A movie is coming out in 2012 and the title is: "America—Does anyone speak English?"

Not funny but I wrote this is one of my fiction stories:

The year is 2050 and a teacher is talking to her elementary class about history. I've translated the following so that those so ill equipped as not to be able to speak English will understand:

The teacher addressed her students. "Class did you know that where we live today they used to Speak English."

All the little children laughed, unbelieving anyone even spoke such an obsolete language.

She admonished them, "It is true. They really spoke English."

"Who were they?" a little girl asked.

The teacher smiled and said, "They were from a country that was once called the United States of America."

Well this is not really funny but with an Obamanation it may come true before 2050.

Obamanation
(11.04.09)

Did you know last night that the movie "V" was a lot like the Democrats? Their leader also refused to talk to the Fox News Moderator. And they had a national health care plan that was full of lies and not real.

The reason Obama will not meet with the people at Fox news is because the people at Fox are white.

Last night I saw a movie that shows what is going to happen to the United States. Watch it and you will see. It's called "The Planet of the Apes." The original title was "Obamanation."

Obama's Enemy List
(12.02.09)

Fox News

Dissent

Capitalism

Freedom of Speech

Rush

Democracy

Bill of Rights

America

God

Christians

Constitution

A Citizens Guide
(12.02.09)

A citizen's guide to REVOLUTION of a corrupt government.

Starve the Beast. Keep your money.

Vote out incumbents.

If steps 1 and 2 fail?

PREPARE FOR WAR – LIVE FREE OR DIE

The time has come—TODAY!

He's pregnant
(11.06.09)

Looks like I may be getting laid off so I've been trying to sharpen my wit. The boss just came in and asked me if I was working tomorrow. I told him no but I'd be here. He did laugh.

Turns out they want me to do work for a guy that says he can't come in until Tuesday. I asked what he had and the boss told he didn't know but he couldn't come in until Tuesday. I laughed and said, "So he doesn't know what he has but it won't let him come back until Tuesday?" There were a bunch of people standing around and they laughed.

The Boss snapped, "He can't come back because he is pregnant."

I came back, "Was it because of him getting screwed around here every day?"

The bright side is I still have my job. Well I think it's the bright side.

Obama and jobs
(12.03.09)

Getting a job under Obama is a lot like winning the lottery – impossible! Keeping my job where I work is a lot like the lottery; everyone is a loser.

Obama the Expert on War and Finances
(12.04.09)

A Letter to my Friend John:

I think Bernanke is worthless. He should be out. BUT it could get worse. If Obama takes him out then Bernanke will be released by an Obama, thug, crook, Czar from Chicago. The replacement will probably be an expert on finances like Obama is on war.

Which do you want?

Congressional Vacation
(12.14.09)

If we could convince Congress to take a 365 day vacation every year we would need to worry only once every four years.

Dying for Freedom
(12.14.09)

When our soldiers died for freedom it gave people the right to do better for themselves. It was never intended to give things to people who didn't earn it. American soldiers did not die for welfare, or Congress to give hard earned money to those who failed. They died for freedom of opportunity, not for the survival of parasites. It is time to pull out of Afghanistan. If they can't stand on their own after seven years then they never will.

Freedom
(12.14.09)

Freedom is where all have the opportunity to WORK and make it in life. There were never any guarantees and there never will be. Welfare is rewarding failure and a secure way to destroy our country and everything our forefathers died for.

You Know a Marriage is in Trouble...
(12.14.09)

When a man and woman marry (sorry I still keep thinking traditional) they swear an oath to love each other forever; until the end of time.

You know the marriage is in trouble, when the man starts praying for the end of time..

Bad Economy
(12.14.09)

The economy is so bad that all I could afford were tears. Then the utilities increased and now I can't even afford the water for my tears.

Listen to my Mama
(12.14.09)

Tiger Woods should have listened to my Mama. She told me, "Be careful where you poke that thing. A stiff prick has no conscience."

America must respond
(12/15.09)

Americans are now left with only one response to Congress; A total violent overthrow of the existing government!!

Is Congress Fox Hunting
(12.15.09)

Congress thinks we're stupid. They act like a bunch of hunters going after the fox all the while laughing while they hunt. They treat the American people like the fox. Just a warning about pushing the fox in Texas. If they come here they need to be warned that the people in Texas aren't like the foxes everywhere else.

This is for Congress. In Texas they are no better than a rabbit.

The Texas Fox

Performance Increase for Welfare Recipients
(12/18/09)

Washington D. C. (CNN) - Yesterday Congress, led by Reid and Pelosi, approved a 12.5% performance increase for all people on welfare. At a cost of 150 billion, the increase will be retroactive from July 4th and the check will be rushed out with the hopes of arriving before December 21st to help improve the Holiday spirit of those so deserving in these difficult times.

Don't laugh the day may be coming.

Joe Barfield.

RESPONSES:

If Washington and Jefferson were alive today they would overthrow this government. Pelosi, Reid and Obama are like an incurable cancer - America is almost dead. What was that old saying? Kill 'em all; let God sort 'em out!
Joe

Gotta get um, out of office......Pelosi and Reid are idiots..... do not vote for Kay Bailey....... she is a turn coat..... she can't be trusted..... she claims she is a conservative, but she is NOT..... she is a liberal, like our former mayor, who's trying to run as well.... he's dangerous, just like her!!!!
Terry

They are doing everything they can to get the utopian vision of a government run society and there is little we can do until the 2010 elections. All the tea parties we have gone to have not helped very much. My motto is "Cram it down our throats now and will stick it up their A** in 2010." - Bill

I'm VERY tempted to vote against EVER incumbent. I wish everyone would just to send these guys a message that they need to LISTEN to the American people instead of shoving their policies down our throats. The good news is, they're going to tax the "rich" again to pay for all this which includes everyone but them. I don't know about you, but I ain't no millionaire, but somehow MY taxes keep going up. They're a bunch of thieves, and I'm about fed up with our president giving handouts and trying to take care of everyone. Here's an idea..... GET A JOB!! - Jason

Kay Bailey Hutchison joined Democrats and voted to prevent the filibuster on Friday--Guess she wants to go home for Christmas instead of continuing the fight against the Healthcare Bill debacle.
Please read this article for details and remember it when you vote for Governor.
Richard

The Assistant
(12/21/09)
For Pelosi and Reid: These two, along with Obama, will be remembered as the ones who destroyed America. They have taken us down a road to socialism. Reid has even been so bold as to call those who don't believe the way he does "slavers." I don't believe the way he does or any other radical liberal. But I have something for them and for Reid. Their day is coming and it won't be pleasant.
Liberals are assistants to Satan.

Warning to Congress...it's coming!
(01.05.10)
I've always said history repeats itself and predicted this. It's just the beginning
Las Vegas federal building shootout leaves 2 dead

Venezuela vs United States
(01.04.10)
Do you know what the main difference between the Venezuela government and the United States government is?

Venezuela has one dictator while the United States has 535.

RESPONSES:

Kim: Exactly!
Tony: Good point!
Dave: You got that right.
Robert: Pretty well hit that on the head.

American Nation
(01.05.10)
This is a song based on Lament of the Cherokee Nation and sung by Paul Revere and the Raiders

They took the whole American nation
Changed our laws for their satisfaction.
Took away our ways of life,
Our jobs and gave us strife
Took away our English tongue.
Forced their Spanish on our young.
And all things once made in our land,
Are now a day's made in Pakistan.

American people, American pride
Once so proud to live, now so bound to die.

They took the whole American nation,
Rocked us with their condemnation.
The Book that gave us faith in our land,
Are now taught from the Koran.
For our deep rooted belief,
The atheist and Muslims gave us grief.
Though they wear a shirt and tie
I'm still the American deep inside.

American people, American pride
So proud to live, so bound to die.

They say they work hard to strive,
They're to blame, the five-thirty-five.
And all things once made in our land,
Are now a day's made in Pakistan.
American laws passed by Congress,

Have destroyed American progress.

Their greed and corruption doomed to failure.
We can blame it all on American legislature.

Wealthy for the welfare has failed,
It is time for Congress to be jailed
Tax the poor give to the wealthy?
Not an idea that is very healthy.
When it came to America's need,
Congress succumbed instead to their greed.

American's what a sad sight,
We're no longer willing to fight.
If changes don't come soon,
Our American life is doomed.

Let's go to Congress with Smith and Wesson,
And teach those un-American traitors a lesson.

American people, American pride
Once so proud to live, now so bound to die.

But maybe someday if we learn
Our American nation will return,
Will return, will return, will return.

Transparency
(01.05.10)
Even Superman's X-ray vision can't see through the "transparency" of Obama's programs. We need a Czar of Transparency for the people.

"Bad decisions make great stories"
(01.06.10)
It is said that "bad decisions make great stories." If that is true then the book "Obama; America's President" will be the greatest story ever told.

To Air America
(01.21.10)
Don't you get it? I thought the Democrats were dumb. The majority don't want your socialistic views. The Democrats are done.

Try something like getting the working people jobs. You'd be better off working for Chavez. He believes in your views.

Think of the Era's we've been through
(01.12.10)
It is amazing whey you think of all the different eras we've been exposed to

or seen one way of the other.

Industrial era
Napoleonic Era (1799 - 1815)
Georgian Era (United Kingdom, 1714 - 1830)
Victorian Era (United Kingdom, 1837 - 1901); British hegemony, much of world, around the same time period.
Romantic Era (1850 - 1920)
Edwardian Era (United Kingdom, 1901 - 1910)
Meiji Era (Japan, 1868 - 1912)
Machine Era (1900 - 1945)
The Oil Era (after 1901)
World War I (Much of Earth, 1914 - 1918)
Interwar Era (Earth, 1918 - 1939 or 1937)
World War II (Earth, 1937 or 1939 - 1945)
Atomic Age Era (after 1945)
Cold War Era (Soviet Union and United States, and their allies, 1945 - 1989 or 1991)
Space Age Era (after 1957)
Modern Era (1958 – 1970)
Information Era (1971 – 2007)
The OBAMA ERROR (2009 to the end)

MoveOn. org
(01.22.10)
A note to Kat Barr at MoveOn. org.

Kat,
You just don't get it. The people voted. They don't want the socialistic health care. Are you a socialist or a communist? America is angry. Don't you get it yet?

State of Disillusion
(01.28.10)
After dissecting very carefully the spoken words of Obama as to the state of the union. I was actually able to come away with the true meaning. This is what his speech to the country really said in just one sentence.
"Ask now what your country can do for you but rather why does your country keep doing it to you!"
In 1864 Abraham Lincoln said, "If our country ever falters or fails it will not be from outside forces. We will be destroyed from within."

State of the Union Message
(01.28.10)
Same 'ol stuff last night. For Obama the hardest part of doing nothing is that he will never finish!!
Learn Spanish because in 2012 Americans will be swimming South across the

Rio Grande. At that time you might just find out that your dollar isn't worth a peso!!

And never forget; Politicians are the reason guns were invented.

FEMA
(02.19.10)
This was a series of emails about FEMA.

SAM: If any of you have never heard anything about this, it will be an eye opener for you. . . . . . Obama is about to assume the ultimate role of Ultimate Dictator. . .
http://www. mindfully. org/Reform/2004/FEMA-Concentration-Camps3sep04. htm

JOE: This was created in 1984 under Reagan and designed by Oliver North. The original scenario was to round up black militants should there be an uprising of riots. It was created 25 years ago by Republicans.

JERRY: These will be the new "death camps" of the millennium, for all those who resist the government, make trouble by protesting, and very soon if you believe in Jesus Christ, or attend ANY Christian services. . . . . . these camps are the final destruction attempt to destroy the family unit. . . . . .

JOE: Hooray for Smith & Wesson.

JERRY:
You'll need a truckload of them real soon. . . . . . only, don't wait for them to come up to your door, better start firing when they drive up, just as they're getting out of their vehicles. . . . . . and have someone watching on all four sides of your house!

JOE: You'll need a truckload of them real soon. . . . . . only, don't wait for them to come up to your door, better start firing when they drive up, just as they're getting out of their vehicles. . . . . . and have someone watching on all four sides of your house!

JERRY:
I know, so shoot at them before they get out of the vehicle. . .

Emails about the IRS in Austin
(02.18.10)
Look what the spin doctors have done over the last 10-15 years. Lot more damage than via knifes or guns.
SERIES OF EMAILS:
Subject: Guns kill people and so do. . . .
CNN Breaking News
A few minutes ago Obama came out and said, "Guns kill people and that is why people should not own any. And on that premise, after what happened in Austin, Texas, we are going to ground all private planes until the pilots go through an thorough mental examination. It is obvious that private weapons are less a threat to our lives than guns."

ROB: My endless comment is that over 39,000 deaths occur every year due to automobile accidents. That is 11 times as many deaths as the lives lost 9 years ago in the World Trade Center in New York.

Then, we say that over 500,000 deaths occur due to heart attacks caused poor diet, poor exercise habits, smoking and drinking

I would like to see Barack Obama say 'Cars kill people and that is why people should not own any'. The next thing would be for him to say "Beef, pork, sugar, alcohol and tobacco kill people and that is why people cannot have any of these"

Let's see how these two goes.

PS. What happened in Austin with a private plane?

JOE: What I have been predicting. People without hope will become like people in the Middle East. They won't care if they die. A plane crashed into an IRS building. Talk about people that give you no hope. The IRS took everything he had. He burned his house this morning then flew his plane into the building.

Sadly more are coming. With jobs and hope it goes away.

ROB: This story of the IRS reminds me of a long-ago friend of ours. Tom Linton of the Z Club but didn't pay his taxes for a couple of years. At some point, the IRS called/came by and said he owed all this money. So, he committed suicide. Then, his widow, Carol Linton got stuck with tens of thousands of $$ of past due taxes, fines and fees.

So, the IRS got him and really his widow too.

JOE: Like I said, I'm not going out alone…just kidding. As radical as I am verbally, I still say the pen is mightier than the sword.

Obama the Muslim
(02.31.10)

I don't like the President and I think he should be removed from office for treason and punished likewise for his crimes against America. BUT, I want the truth first. Look at the picture closely. The architecture in the background is not that of the White House. It looks more Middle Eastern. So I checked it out. The information is false.

http://www. snopes. com/politics/obama/photos/prayerday. asp

Even though this information about the President is false there is plenty of truth to still dislike him. For instance he is dishonest and a liar. He and his Czars will destroy this country. He has committed treason, and we all know the punishment for that.

Forced American insurance
(03.14.10)

It's clear and simple. If this insurance program were a good thing, Congress would be taking it. What Congress is doing to us is no different than what was being done to the black people in the 60's. Worse than racism is elitism. Congress thinks they are above us all. Congress is sending all Americans to the back of the bus.

Now, it's okay to be a conservative or a liberal. BUT watching Congress the last two years has made me realize that there are no Liberal Democrats or Conservative Republicans. Get away from thinking of those two parties. America was not formed on their ideals.

I've been saying this for years. I'm going to give you three choices. You can only pick one. You are a Democrat, or a Republican or you're an American. I'm an American and proud of my heritage. A side note. When I filled out my census they asked me what race I was. I marked "other" and then wrote in "AMERICAN." We should all do the same.

Joe Barfield.

RESPONSES:

That's what I'm going to do.

Article 31 of the Iraqi Constitution, drafted by the Bush administration in 2005 and ratified by the Iraqi people, includes state-guaranteed (single payer) healthcare for life for every Iraqi citizen.

Article 31 reads:

"First: Every citizen has the right to health care. The State shall maintain public health and provide the means of prevention and treatment by building different types of hospitals and health institutions.

Second: Individuals and entities have the right to build hospitals, clinics, or private health care centers under the supervision of the State, and this shall be regulated by law."

There are other health care guarantees, including special provisions for children, the elderly, and the handicapped elsewhere in the 43-page document.

Under force of arms, President Bush imposed his particular idea of democracy on a people not asking for it - perhaps a noble undertaking in one context and a criminal violation of international law in another. Bush's followers are proud of the Iraqi Constitution, a model for the world, they told us.

So, according to the Bush administration and the congress and senate members who supported the administration nearly all of the time, which includes many of the same republicans trying to stop president Obama's healthcare reform -guaranteed health care is good for Iraqis, but not good for us. Not good for you. They decry even a limited public option for you, but gleefully imposed upon the Iraqis what they label here as "socialism," with much Democratic Party member support.

Indeed, reading the Iraqi Constitution so near to the 8th anniversary of September 11, 2001 is instructive. It is the very definition of American right-wing hypocrisy.

AMEN !!!!! Lee

Joe:

Are we required to fill out the census and are we required to answer every question.

Amen…Borders closed…Language English only…Culture Constitution Bill of Rights the Bible…change we can believe in…Nov 2010 B. Cahill

Don't blame me…I didn't vote 4 UR MAMA!

(03.15.10)

Exactly. And yet our country continues to decline, no matter which party is in control.

who cares the president serving now has signed all the BS trillion dollar deficit things so he will get the blame from here on Bush is laughing at the American people for being so stupid to elect an idiot as him in the first place I bet if they knew then what they see know he would be back in Chicago with his terrorist gang members missing 60% of his votes.

Now the next time someone wants to send this just remember to not forward to everyone because most of us do not like the present situation.

God help America and our children for they are now deep in debt because of the idiotic people in Washington.

fill out you census so that we can get even more idiots to vote BS things for us that most of us could care about.

I agree.

The insurance issue is just there because the Insurance Industry and their lobbyists want to hold onto their power and money base.

Money, clear and simple.

DON'T YOU MEAN COMRADE OBAMA? It's amazing how stupid they believe we are

Hey, Joe,

I'm with you on this!

I think more people are getting involved in what's going on in the country these days, but they're still too busy with their personal lives to really delve into the details. And, too many people make their decisions on the gist of what they've heard on the topic, i. e. Canadian/socialized healthcare, than finding out all the details. (Greg and I can tell you some horror stories from of his family's care in Canada). And, can you believe the people who take what the politicians say at face value instead of *watching* what the politicians are doing?! i. e. just what you said, if it's not good enough for Congress, why are they trying to jam it down our throats.

I like how you said that elitism is worse than racism and comparing the two. That might get some of the racist people following the Big 0 only because of his race, to start opening their eyes…*some* of them.

Check out this YouTube video: http://www. youtube. com/watch?v=VebOTc-7shU It's long, but worth watching. I had to watch it in segments, but if you have a couple of hours to spare, like watching a movie. . .

If you are on FaceBook, look up a guy named William Iverson. He digs up a lot of stuff we need to know. Have a great day!

Carla

Not us…

(04.20.10)

I beg to differ with some people who say America no longer excels and/or produces anything anymore. They are wrong. This country excels at graft and corruption. I believe we produce more of these items than all the countries in the world combined. And don't forget transparency; it is so clear that even Superman's x-ray vision can't penetrate it. Our government only lacks two items; Honor and Integrity.

Viva Goldman Sachs!

P. S. Remember, as Americans, we need to keep Congress tied to the financial destruction of America.

Move ON
(04.01.10

If Congress is going to shove Healthcare down our throat, then all AMERICANS will be required to take it. Including Congress and all military and government employees. This bill is the most racist elitist program ever enacted. It's not socialist or communistic but rater feudalistic. The great King is taking from all the people and giving it to all his barons. Congress is destroying America and guilty or TREASON. Pick one, but only one. You are a Democrat, a Republican or an American. Which are you?

Also the last question is not a choice. That is what I despise most. Why is Obama lying? Where is the transparency he promised? Even Superman's X-ray vision can't see through Obama's presidential transparency.

They need to quit destroying America.

BP
(05.01.10)

Don't be surprised if Obama, Pelosi and Reid decide to Nationalize BP for the Gulf of Mexico incident. In other words the same thing Chavez did in Venezuela. Sounds farfetched, huh?? After all if they are going to protect our health shouldn't they protect us from those capitalistic oil companies?

President of Texas
(05.05.10)

When I become President of Texas, we're going to change the Internal Revenue Service. They won't do audits like before. All Texas will identify with them. They will become the Revenue Agents of Texas. For short they will be called Texas' own RATs.

Joe Barfield, running for President of Texas

Aw you won't like it. I believe in America but it no longer exists. It's just an Obamanation now.

No freebies and no welfare. This is a working state. No entitlement to government or industry. The country of Texas believes in capitalism. If you only make 10,000 a year you will pay 1000 in taxes. And quit you're whining. The guy that makes a million will pay 100,000. BUT he will not pay $500,000 like they want in the country of Obamanation. BUT he will have an extra 400,000 to invest, create jobs and possibly get you a job that pays 20,000. AND yes you will pay 2000 then.

What's good for God is good for our country of Texas. Ten percent income tax. No forms and no audits. Except for big companies.

There will be a five percent social security. FOR EVERYONE. The money will be used to make loans to the great citizens of Texas. The money will be in a fund never to be touched by any politicians. Companies don't have to match it. There will be plenty of money in the fund. The matching funds will be a raise instead. We will demand our Social Security that was stolen from us by Obamanation. We will demand they pay in gold. Blood will be okay too.

If you went to Harvard, Yale or Princeton or were ever an attorney you can't serve as a judge or hold any political office in Texas. If you don't like it the go to California.

People on welfare will be moved to military barracks and forced to work no matter how menial the task. If you don't like it get a job. And you will be trained for a job. If you don't like it call Arnold and move to California.

The government of Texas will give no money to any foreign entity. IF you want money they ask the grateful hearts of its citizens. The Texas government only helps it's people.

We will have a voluntary army. Everybody will volunteer. Our army will help our allies but our military operates on the PIA system. That's Paid In Advance. You need our Spartan military you will pay. And it will be in gold. Each soldier will be paid one million a year to participate in war. We value our soldiers. They won't go in harm's way unless it's worth it.

Our military will patrol the borders and make occasional forays into Mexico to relieve those drug runners of their truck loads of worthless American 100 dollar bills. They better not come into Texas. We're not evil, but it doesn't see anybody understands what the work "illegal" in illegal alien means. Illegal means against the law.

We will take care of the medical bills of all foreigners, no matter what the cost. Because we're going to bill their country double our costs. You will pay or we'll tax every truckload of products coming across our shores or our borders. But don't worry. If a Texan is taken care of in a foreign country we'll reciprocate and pay you back. But you'll find a Texan can take care of themselves. Why can't you all do the same?

We will drill for oil wherever we feel like it. And we're going to find alternate forms of energy instead of talking about it.

Every Texan will be asked to carry two weapons; a gun and a rifle of your choice. If you're a conscientious objector that will be okay but you will have a $500 registration fee you must pay each year. It's important that the patriots of Texas know who they can't count on when the going gets tough.

Everybody will vote. If you don't it will cost you a $200 fee each year you don't vote.

If you're a Democrat and want to give everything away then you're no better than a communist. Don't like it, then go to California. There's a lot Cali fornication going on there. Don't do it here.

We'll try to help the poor but no guarantee. Attorneys, Lawyers and Doctors will serve two weeks a year for the state of Texas. During those two weeks they will serve the indigent of Texas for free. If not, then their income tax will be 20 percent per year—no deductions. Your choice, your state.

English is the language. It's the principle of the thing. All tests for citizenship will be in English. If you don't care to learn that much you don't deserve to be a citizen of Texas.

I'm tired of the whining and I'm offended that everybody is offended. Politically incorrect in correct in Texas. If you're a citizen of Texas you are only one race: TEXAN. Make a choice but only one. You're a Democrat, a Republican, or a Texan. Which is it?

And that my friend are the rules I will run under as President of Texas.

Joe Barfield, running for President of Texas

America no Longer favored by God
(5.21.10)
Obama is living proof that God no longer favors America.
Islam is to Christianity as---
Democrats are to freedom.

Replacing CO2 gases
(5.23.10)
Sam,

Here's something the environmentalist haven't thought about. Say we do replace all the CO2 gases, what happens? Do you know? Let's go the other direction. Suppose Oxygen was bad for the atmosphere and we replaced it with CO2. What will happen to people? They will die. If we get rid of CO2 then all the plants die. What helps make Oxygen? Plants. Uh-oh....

Isn't it funny
(06.04.10)
Isn't it funny that we are so deeply engrossed with shoving freedom down Afghanistan's throat and turning them into a country like the United States while Osama bin Laden, I mean Broke Obama, is turning the United States into a country like Afghanistan.

Americans Love War
(06.05.10)
Americans Love War. No really. Most believe we're the saviors to the world when in reality it's no more than a popularity contest. That's right war is a popularity contest. In fact our personal "Nobel Peace Prize" winner will go to war soon. First you need to ask yourself why we're still in Afghanistan. When is that country going to be able to take over democracy for themselves? The answer is never. But, let's get back to the popularity contest. Check on the last few presidents and you will find that when their popularity wanes then war is in the wings. A war

will boost their popularity as much as thirty or forty percent and be the difference in winning or losing an election.

In the next few our "Peace Prize Winner," will probably attack Korea or Iran, for peace or freedom. Watch his popularity move up. This president can't even beat the Somali pirates.

Moratorium
(06.10.10)

If we have a six month moratorium on offshore drilling because of what BP did to the Gulf, then shouldn't we have a permanent moratorium on Congress for what they have done to America?

Do the Math
((06.10.10)

BP screwed up and it should take care of the problem. The cost of the cleanup will be in the BILLIONS. -----BUT, the president had the opportunity to deploy a safeguard of some kind to hold back the oil and talk to the head of PB to discuss a solution. He did neither. The cost to retain the oil with some kind of pontoons might have been a hundred million but Obama and Congress decided to fight with rhetoric instead of action. You know, "Sticks and stones will break my bones but words do nothing."

Only a hundred million.

By the way you should know that today, Obama made a quick and decisive decision when he approved 400 million in aid to Palestine. I think his motto is help the world--screw Americans!

Quicker than the Roman Empire
(06.14.10)

Obama is going to do in four years what it took the Roman Senate three hundred years: DESTROY THEIR COUNTRY!!

Where Are We Today?
(06.14.10)

Throughout history every great empire has collapsed; there have been no exceptions.

A great civilization is not conquered from without until it has destroyed itself from within. Where is the United States in history today?

Secede
(06.14.10)

Whelp, that's it. I'm running for governor. Texas is going to secede. Income tax will be ten percent. What is good for God is good for Texas. The person making 10 thousand will pay a thousand. The person making 10 million will pay one million. The money he keeps will be able to open new businesses that in time will pay the ten thousand person fifteen thousand. It will be good. No deductions.

Social Security will be five percent and it will go into a fund to give loans to Texans and small business. There will be no matching funds from business because it's not needed. Everyone will get four weeks' vacation. Two weeks will be spent working for the government in some capacity—that includes doctors, lawyers and CEO's. Anyone not wanting to participate in serving their new country will pay thirty percent income tax. If you have no specialty you will serve in the National Guard. EVERYONE will serve and be required to bear arms, including a pistol and a rifle. If you don't want to serve then leave Texas. Your choice.

Casinos will be open in designated areas. We will attract tourists. They will pay a ten percent fee on their chips. This will give a total tax exemption to every Texan on one piece of property (homestead)Persons running for office will not run on the Republican or Democratic ticket. We want no more trickery. The Party is over. Candidates running will be required to debate. They must offer logical plans that have no added taxes. At the debate there will be an audience of Texans. Any question can be asked about plans for the Texas government. Person questions are out. They have nothing to do with running the government. The candidates will be allowed to answer personal questions at their discretion.

Unlike the Bailout, when a bill is voted on, it cannot be voted on again for at least four years. To pass any new law the Texan Congress will be required to pass the new law with a three-quarters approval. New taxes will require a four-fifths approval of both houses and a vote by the people. If half of the qualified voters do not approve the bill it will be voided and not allowed for a revote for five years.

There will be no more bond votes. If there is not enough money to buy it then it can't be bought. Wealthy individuals are allowed to give their money in place of bonds. Elected officials serve their country. The people do not serve the elected officials. Elected officials will be paid a million a year. That will cover their expenses. Be frugal. There will be no trickery with the budget. The government will not spend more money than is taken in by taxes. If there is a deficit the elected officials forfeit their pay for the following year.

A toll fee on 59, 45 and I-10 except for the citizens of Texas. The US will be notified that they have not fulfilled their obligations as promised when we joined the union in 1845. It will be noted that it is with deep regret that this must be done. Should the United States get their act together we will consider rejoining. We demand payments for all the stolen Social Security.

Oil Spill? Listen to the mouth!
(06.16.10)

After listening to Obama and watching his mouth spill over I did some numbers and realized that he will add taxes to us that will amount to about 20 times more the cost of the BP oil spill.

Any bets the 20 billion BP promised goes back to the coiffures of Congressmen instead of the people actually effected?

BP Exec Assures the People
(06.15.10)

Just a while ago a BP executive tried to assure Americans by saying, "We're going to take care of the small people."

That sure is reassuring but aren't those the same words Jim Jones said at that grape juice party?

191

An American Hero
(06.22.10)

Gen. Stanley McChrystal has been relieved of command in the wake of his controversial comments, a source tells

General Stanley McChrystal will always be remembered as an "American Hero" who stood his ground against a dictator bent on destroying America. If all the military would stand their ground against this self-ordained dictator, America still has a chance to survive.

Freedom
(06.28.10)

As far as what I think, you have mirrored my own life.

In a way freedom is elusive. The older we get the less freedom we have as we are required to do things for others without regard to freedom. But we gain such joy from those things we do for others that are a sacrifice of our freedom.

I feel sorry for those that demand or depend on government to survive. They have given up freedom to experience nothing. You and I went out to Kress and others to experience the freedom of life.

We have lived the same freedom but only on different trails.

Worst Case Scenario for the Gulf Coast
(06.29.10)

Hey! Look at the bright side. If there is an official "dead zone" then there is no reason we need to stop drilling in that area because we can't hurt anything any longer. LETS DRILL!!!!!!

Why do we give?
(07.01.10)

Why do we give aid to foreign countries in the United Nations when they vote against us.

Think about this for a moment. America's representation in the United Nations is a direct reflection of our Congress and President. So I ask you; would you vote against our Congress and our President? I think the percentages below are less than the number of Americans that would vote against Congress and the President today. And as far as foreign aid, I'll bet you that none of that money goes to the people in any of those countries. The real question is why does our Congress and President give any money to any country?

I want to see every company that does work for the United States and every organization that receives handouts to have a complete audit. Next I want someone to go to Fort Knox go inside and see if there is any gold. I believe the gold is gone and that there will be no audits.

Remember, Kennedy actually said, "Ask not what your country can do for you but rather why does your country keep doing it to you.

Revelation
(07.02.10)

I was reading Revelation and the part about the Antichrist. Then I started thinking about Obama and I realized that we would be better off with the Antichrist as President. But then again maybe he already is.

News about Obama
(07.03.10)

There is bad news that death threats against Obama by Americans has increased by hundreds per month. Ironically the only good news is that the hundreds of thousands of Muslim threats per month have dropped to zero and there is already a movement by Al Qaeda to make sure Obama is re-elected to a second term.

An Al Qaeda was overheard saying, "Not all the agents we have sent to America have accomplished as much destruction as Obama has in just one year."

During the American Revolution
(July 4, 2010)

During the American Revolution there were more people in America that liked King George than there are people in America today who like Barack Obama (bin Lying).

The 2010 Obama Stimulus Pack
(07.05.10)

The new 2010 Obama Stimulus Pack arrived in the mail today. It contained:
Two watermelon seeds
A bag of cornbread mix
10 coupons to KFC
The instructions were in Spanish.
I verified this on factscheck. com and snopes. com
Your stimulus pack should be arriving in the mail soon.

Second American Revolution
(08.02.10)

If Washington's failures don't lead to a Second American Revolution, then America is dead. VOTE in November it is very important. Remember it's okay to a Conservative or even a Liberal but there is no such thing as either in Congress. When you vote in November always remember you have three choices but you can only have one; you can be a Republicant, a Democrap, or an American. Which are you?

If
(07.05.10)

I wrote:
If cavemen had been Democrats there would be no human race today.
My friends responded with:
Glenn: Yep there was too much intelligence for survival during their time. We had to wait until extreme stupidity evolved in mankind before democrats were born.

Robert: That is very true. And I can certainly see a number of reasons why that would be the case. . .

Marco: So easy a cave man can do it!

John: If cavemen had been Americans there wouldn't be any Democrats alive today.

Sam: But I promise you that Pelosi would have mutated thru the years somehow..... .

Souls

(07.10.10)

These are the times that try men's souls. If that is true then Congress is soulless.

Another word for soulless is Congress

Immigration or Invasion?

(08.12.10)

Here is the real deal. There is no illegal immigration problem. The United States of America is being INVADED by a foreign country. We must defeat the enemy. An invasion not necessarily with guns although the drug cartel has them and has offered a million dollar reward for an officer in Arizona.

Tell me why I MUST provide documents when I go to work but they don't have to provide anything? The invasion must stop or what remnants remain of America will be destroyed.

Obama makes a better Muslim terrorist than he does an American.

I think his words on election day were, "America is the greatest country in the world. I hope you join me in changing it."

God in America?

(11.25.10)

Obama is living proof that God no longer favors America.

Amazing Fantasy 15

(08.20.10)

Speaking of 1960's toys. All of you need to look up the value of this. Amazing Fantasy 15. It's a Marvel comic. I still remember buying it in 1962. My Mother gave me a quarter to go to a place called "Tri-Drive." It was like a Stop-n-Go. With the quarter I could buy two ten cent comic books and two pieces of gum for a penny (Dubble Bubble). And or a two cent Hershey bar. The gum and candy for the last five cents of my quarter. That was when I saw Amazing Fantasy 15. BUT it was 12 cents. What a dilemma. To buy that comic book I would need to sacrifice four pieces of gum or one Hershey bar. It was tough. But the story in the comic book. A kid that was bullied and a real dork had everything go wrong for him. He was everything I was. Then he was bitten by a spider. He gained super powers but even with that he still had problems with everything. Even though he could beat the bad guy he was usually beaten to a pulp. And then he had problems when he got home late. Peter Parker was me. Spiderman! I bought Amazing Fantasy 15 and gave up my Hershey bar.

So now go to the Internet and find out how much that comic book is worth.

A special note: In 1975 my Ex-wife threw away my Amazing Fantasy 15. She told me it was time to get rid of childish things. It made me think and I realized she was right. So I got rid of my childish thing—I DIVORCED HER! God I miss my comic book......

If

(08.25.10)

If illegal aliens are called "Undocumented Workers," then shouldn't drug dealers be called "Undocumented Pharmacists?"

And most importantly, don't forget we have an "Undocumented President."

Today I declare

(08.27.10)

Today I declare Americans have:

AN "UNDOCUMENTED ILLEGAL ALIEN, MUSLIM TERRORIST, PRESIDENT."

Calculator no Good

(08.29.10)

I was doing some figures in regards to the national debt on my calculator and realized that it doesn't work with numbers in the trillions. I had to go back to doing math with a pencil. Just goes to show that the more technologically advanced we become the farther behind we get.

With about 250,000,000 people paying taxes (I took out twenty million illegal aliens and the 40 million getting food stamps) and Obama spending about 4.5 trillion a year it means that each of those people pays about $20,000.00 each or about $60,000 per family.

Just thought you might want to know.

So where is this money coming from?

COMMENTS:

Jesse: Do think the illegal aliens...are smarter than us?

Terry: You have a faulty premise there are 300 million Americans only HALF are taxpayers that's 150 Million for $30k each or $120k per family of four.

Larry: YOU REALLY ARE MAKING ME FEEL GOOD. . . . . I AM SWIMMING THE BORDER NEXT WEEK.

Randy: What money? There is no money!!! Oh, you mean the toilet paper in my wallet.

If E=MC₂

(09.09.10)

If $E=MC_2$ ... then...

Working from 6:00AM to 7:00PM equals 13 hours so...

Working from 7:00AM to 6:00PM also equals 13 hours.

Democrat and Al Qaeda

(10.15.10)

Do you know what the differences are between a Democrat and a member of Al Qaeda?

There are none. Both want to destroy Democracy, Freedom and America. It's just that Al Qaeda is honest about it.

Looking

(09.02.10)

I saw an ad for kittens and here were the responses:

Looking for a home for my kittens.

The local Chinese restaurant is looking for some kittens.

Yeah, I saw a few hanging out around that restaurant. .

I hear they take all their cats for a wok.

What was that song by Jim Croce? "Cat's in the ladle, you need a silver spoon..."

The Truth

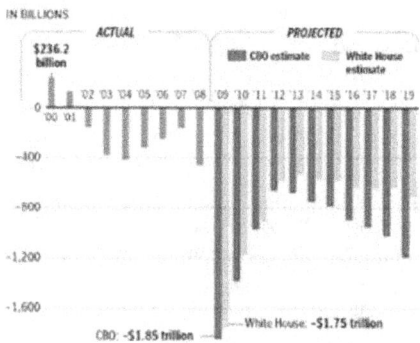

John,

You know I'm fair. I hate Democrats and Republicans. The chart at the bottom is grossly wrong. There has not been a surplus since 1960. All the numbers are wrong. Here are the years and the actual numbers the debt went up. Here is the webpage with the accurate information:

http://www. treasurydirect. gov/NP/NPGateway

Remember these are the amounts the National Debt increased. There was no surplus

2000 - 18 billion

2001 - 133 billion

2002 - 421 billion

2003 - 550 billion

2004 - 596 billion
2005 - 553 billion
2006 - 599 billion
2007 - 496 billion
2008 - 1.472 **trillion** (Bush's last year when Paulson gave away all the money)
2009 - 1.363 **trillion** (Obama's first year)

Now something to think about. There were years under Bush that the Republicans controlled Congress. I don't see much difference. Surely some, other than Ron Paul would have made a big deal about the debt. They didn't.

So here is the truth To save America you have three choices. BUT you can only choose one. You are a Democrap, a Republican or an American. Pick one.

War or Business
(09.05.10)
War is business. It has nothing to do about freedom. It's money. I guarantee you that our Nobel (that's not noble)Peace Prize winning President will make a lot of money off of war.

In September or October Obama will either attack or back Israel on an attack to Iran. Korea is a possibility but there is too much business with China to do Korea.

The attack for September or October will do two things; generate money and guarantee a Democrat victory in November. Sorry but Americans love war. Obama's popularity will go up 20 to 40 percent and guarantee Democrats facing defeat will see victory.

Lets hear it for our President! Victory or Death! Nope just business..... .

Did Kennedy really say that?
(09.08.10)
On November 23, 1963 John F. Kennedy said, "Ask not what your country can do for you but rather what can you do for your country!?

Black America heard:
"Ask not what you can do for your country but rather what can your country do for you!"

Working America heard:
"Ask now what your country can do for your but rather why does your country keep doing it to you!"

Today we all ask: "Where is our country?"

Democrat
(10.10.10)
Democrat is a synonym for Socialism and Communism.

Too Late
(10.20.10)
You can't fix an elevator on the way down.

Different Gods
(09.15.10)

Religions are amazing. Christian, Muslim, Hindu, etc. etc. Up in Idaho they are called Mormons. All kinds of Gods they worship. In Congress they are called the Morons and their God is Greed. And Greed's wife is Immorality.

How to fix Anger
(9.10.10)

Don't let Anger drag out and get the best of you....
Follow through quickly with Revenge and get it over with!

Anna
(09.20.10)

Anna,

When you wake up in the morning take a good look in the mirror. You are the extremist.

I know you won't listen but here it is. In December of 2012 our country will be bankrupt and it will be your fault. To call people extreme who want to balance the budget and save our country it just downright stupid. I joined MoveOn to save our country not destroy it.

On Wed, Sep 22, 2010 at 10:55 AM, Anna Galland, MoveOn. org Political Action <moveon-help@list. moveon. org> wrote:

Dear MoveOn member,

It's a terrifying combination: Tea party extremism and unprecedented amounts of corporate cash.

The far-right wing of the Republican Party is threatening to take control of Congress—and unseat some of our leading progressive heroes along the way. **We simply can't afford to stand by and let this takeover happen**. The Republicans may have hundreds of millions in corporate campaign cash, but we can still beat them if we recruit enough grassroots progressives to help get out the vote and turn the tide on Election Day.

So we're launching "Stop the Takeover" call parties on October 2nd and 3rd, as part of the huge "One Nation" mobilization happening across the country. While some of us are marching in Washington, D. C, thousands of us will get together locally to call other MoveOn members in key congressional districts to find badly needed volunteers for crucial get-out-the-vote efforts. **We need a place for folks to gather in Katy. It's easy to host a call party, and we'll give you everything you need—can you help out?** Click here:

http://pol. moveon. org/event/events/create. html?action_id=222&id=23584-6676765-fbqwM3x&t=3

Hosting is simple and straightforward—but the calls and community-building at these parties make a real difference. Last election, over 56,000 individual MoveOn members came to call parties that helped win it for Obama, and folks overwhelmingly reported that the calls to other MoveOn members were powerful, fun, and gratifying. This time, we're planning to make over 500,000 calls to help recruit volunteers for candidates in tight races—including progressive heroes like Barbara Boxer, Russ Feingold, Alan Grayson, Tom Perriello, and more. By calling fellow MoveOn members in these key campaign areas, we'll help make sure our candidates have the grassroots army they'll need to get out the vote.

And this particular weekend is really special. On October 2nd, hundreds of thousands of progressives will gather in Washington, D. C. for the massive "One Nation" rally—calling for bold action to create jobs and get America moving again. On the same weekend, thousands more of us will take action locally, including these Stop the Takeover call parties. As a party host, you'll be enabling other folks in Katy to get involved in the campaign. Here's what to expect:

You'll invite friends and family—and we'll invite nearby MoveOn members, if you'd like, to help fill up your party. We'll ask everyone to bring their cell phone and a delicious dessert to share. (Saving democracy can be tasty, too.)

We'll provide step-by-step materials to walk you through the event, including scripts and lists of names and numbers. We'll even have live volunteer support in case you have any questions during the party. It's simple, but hosting is a huge service to other progressives in your area. Can you host a party on October 2nd or 3rd in Katy? Click here to get started:

http://pol. moveon. org/event/events/create. html?action_id=222&id=23584-6676765-fbqwM3x&t=4

Thanks for all you do—Anna, Ilya, Amy, Lenore, and the rest of the team

Want to support our work? We're entirely funded by our 5 million members—no corporate contributions, no big checks from CEOs. And our tiny staff ensures that small contributions go a long way. Chip in here.

I Pledge
(10.15.10)
I'm proud to be an American.
But I'm not proud of America's government.
I pledge allegiance to America.
But I don't pledge allegiance to communism or Obamanation.

Is America Dead"
(11.22.10)
You no longer live in America. This is the Obamanation. Only two problems with our government: Democrats and Republicans.

The Family
(03.08.11)
Every time I hear a Politician say he's for "family values" I cringe.

Trust the Coin
(03.14.11)
The coin says, "In God We Trust," it said nothing about Congress.

Choices
(04.03.11)
You have three choices, but you can only pick one. You're a Democrat, or a Republican or an American. Which are you?

Truth or Fiction
(04.01.11)
There is more "truth" coming out of my fiction novel than there is coming out of the mouths of all the members of Congress. The words they speak are fiction.

Representation
(04.03.11)
Congress helps and represents everybody in America—except the people!

Failure
(04.022.11)
If you're a failure at everything you do, well. . . . you must be a Congressman.

Time for Action
(05.18.11)
No more words, enough said,
It's time for packing lead.

Electronic Meeting
(05.28.11)
Electronic meeting. Are all employees denied internet access? No, just the workers. Why? Who determines that? I guess since they get to position where they don't do anything they need something to do. Isn't their time more valuable?

Management Decides
(06.01.11)
Management decides what you can do.
Really? Suppose everybody uses the bathroom too much and the higher ups decide it is too much so everybody but the higher ups are denied use of the bathroom, wait a minute that makes sense that the executives need the bathrooms more after all they have proven with things like this they are full of s#*@

Gold
(06.18.11)
Do you really think the gold is still in Fort Knox?
What is Counterfeit?
(06.07.11)
What's the difference between a counterfeit 100 dollar bill and on printed by the Federal Government? Nothing, they're both worthless.

Audit
(06.20.11)
Audit the Federal Government expenditures for one year and you will find more crimes committed than crimes in all the states combined.

SS

(06.30.11)

Social Security? The original Ponzi scheme

Justice

(07.07.11)

The execution that happened in Texas today is called JUSTICE. The same thing that happens to politicians that commit treason to their country regardless of political affiliation. States have their laws while Congress commits treason.

True Majority. org

(07.07.11)

Daniel wanted, no demanded that Americans have Obamacare.

Daniel,

Were you born stupid or are you just normally that way. Look at the Middle-East and that is what is coming here if you expect a bankrupt government to keep giving you freebies. There is no more money. You are either a socialist or a communist.

Joe

Insurance

(07.09.11)

I went to my insurance man and told him after all these years I had a claim. He laughed and said, "We cover everything but claims."

More Insurance

(07.10.11)

I was watching an insurance commercial and I swear they said, "You're in good hands with—oops!"

Opps!

(07.10.11)

You ever notice that commercial that says, "You're in good hands with. . ," that their hands are empty?

Obamacare?

(07.18.11)

The truth, what word is lacking in Obamacare? It really should be Obama Doesn't Care.

The Plan

(07.20.11)

Obama's financial plan for America? Fiscal Irresponsibility.

America's Last Hope?

(08.26.11)

Obama is living proof God no longer favors America. . . .

The Boss
(07.24.11)
The boss said he was going to shoot the next dog (engineer and designers) that quit the company. I told him he would need a shotgun because they were more like birds in a bush as fast as they were quitting.

Nobel Peace Prize
(08.08.11)
Good thing Obama is a peaceful man and Nobel Peace Prize winner. If not just think how many countries we'd be attacking if he wasn't a peace loving man. Wag the Dog.

Lorena?
(08.15.11)
A woman at work heard about some man having an affair and said men who did that should beware of the Lorena Bobbitt syndrome. I laughed and said, "Wouldn't happen to me. Mine is allergic to knives and goes into hiding.

Texas Hunting Trip
(08.21.11)
I need some help putting some money together for a hunting trip. It should be really good. We're gonna have Cheney take Obama on a good old fashioned South Texas bird hunting trip. And Harry Whittington gets to go along and watch.

Politicians of Iraq
(08.22.11)
To the Iraqi people:
Yes. . . they sound like our Congress. What they have done is create a rift. The only thing I can see is the Kurds with Kirkuk breaking away to form a separate country and destroy Iraq.

They actually sound like America's Democrats. The need a severe case of lead poisoning. The sad thing is America will baby them, give the time and let them collapse. We need to come down hard on them and not guaranteed their money let it jump to 4000 dinar equals one dollar.

The Iraqi people need to execute some of their leaders to make them do something. I use the word execute because murder is killing somebody and that is against the law. Assassination is killing someone important and execution is killing someone that committed treason to your country.

The politicians of Iraq have a parasite that destroys common sense. It's called Obamacites and evidence of this disease is usually shown with the use of Teleprompters.

Kill 'em all let God (or Allah) sort them out.

Success?
(07.29.11)
I was in a group of people when a friend of mine told everyone that I had a print on demand book on Amazon. All were excited and I said, "Yes, I'm a

successfully unpublished author to which one person said, "Congratulations." A few laughed including my friend.

Two Reasons its Safer to Drive 110 Instead of 55
(08.26.11)

First you're on the freeway only half the time you would have been at 55. Second you'll be past the wreck you would have had when it happens.

Al Qaeda's Supercell
(08.29.11)

Al Qaeda's super cell is already in America and is going under the name of Congress to stop our Progress. To save America we must give Congress a 365 day a year vacation. That will leave only one day every four years they can do damage.

Healthy
(08.30.11)

My theory of healthy eating: If it tastes good then it's bad for you.

What's More Dangerous?
(09.02.11)

My sister told me she was getting a double-barrel sawed-off shotgun and said, "Can you think of anything more dangerous than a little old lady with a shotgun like that?"

I said, "Well yes. Obama with a pen and Federal Reserve checkbook."

The Real Problem
(09.04.11)

Members of Congress are problem makers not problem solvers.

It's Okay
(09.05.11)

It's okay to conservative or liberal but they don't' exist today. They are radicals bent on destroying freedom.

Show Me
(09.06.11)

Obama show us a solution.

The Real New Order for America
(09.07.11)

Congress will create a new category for would countries as the United States falls into a category knows at a fourth world power.

Days in the Old School Yard
(09.09.11)

When I was little I remember the KKK. They were evil and their ideas warped. I also remember seeing a cartoon of the KKK hanging a poor black worker. When I reflect on that cartoon it has a symbolism that resonates with truth today. The Blackman being hung stands for all Americans today and the KKK represents our Congress. Just like members hid behind their KKK masks while in real life they acted like benevolent business men so too does our Congress today, thinking only of themselves and finding a way to hang the next American.

The Platform
(09.08.11)
Obama's platform is "Fiscal Irresponsibility."

Congress Love Fest
(09.10.11)
Listening to the Republicans and Democrats talk to each other would be like going to a love fest put on by the NAACP and the KKK.

The First Step to Communism
(09.10.11)
Obamacare is really the first major step to communism. If Congress makes themselves exempt then we have lost our freedom. A democracy makes it good for each and every American. Obamacare, if passed will be the death of freedom and America.

Unions
(09.09.11)
In America the mob controls everything just like in Russia. The mob uses the name "Unions."

Donate?
(09.09.11)
I was in a group of Democrats trying to remain quiet and you know how tough that is for me, when one of them asked me, "Do you donate?"
I shook my head and said, "Yes." Then I shrugged and said, "I do it every week."
Surprised another said, "Really?"
"Yes, really." Then I smiled and added, "Every week I go to Shipley's and get two donates."

A Friend Said about Obama Care
(09.09.11)
WHAT COULD POSSIBLY GO WRONG? THIS CALCULATING, UNQUALIFIED IDIOT COULD BE ELECTED AGAIN BY THE IDIOTS THAT ELECTED HIM AND THE FIRST PLACE. And that my friend would be an absolute travesty for the United States of America.
Sadly, it is no longer USA. . . . . it has become USSA for the United Socialist States of America. By 2016 the United States will become divided. I see four countries; Alaska, Northern States of America (where they will give everything away and become a third world country demanding the world take care of them),

and the Southern States of America (where they will have jobs, low taxes and common sense). The northern part of California, Washington state, Utah, Idaho, Wyoming and Montana will become Western America.

China will be given a hundred year lease on San Diego and most of California will revert back to Mexico. Which means that pretty much nothing will change in Mexico, I mean California.

Congress
(09.09.11)
The Muslim super Jihad is in place in America and is called "Congress."

Obamacare
(09.09.11)
Congress cannot make laws specific to certain groups of people while exempting others. Obama Care(less) is illegal. The fact groups of people are exempt is illegal. A law passed by Congress shall apply to ALL Americans. Otherwise freedom and democracy are gone. Those groups exempt are simply Un-American. A vote for Obamacare brings the death of American freedoms.

Beware
(09.09.11)
Superman had Kryptonite. . .
The United States has Obama. . .
Obama is living proof God no longer favors America.

America
(09.11.11)
Watching Congress in action today, reminds me of one of Clint Eastwood's movies: Hang 'em High.

ADDITIONAL COMMENTS AFTER 911

Military Cross
(11.11.11)
North County Times
San Diego, California
ATTN: Mark Walker, Scott Radestki, Adam Housley, Colonel Nick Marano
About the cross, although I'm not a very good Christian, I believe they have the right to have the cross there. Who does the cross hurt? No one.

My suggestion is that you send this to General James F. Amos. Have a fenced in area away from the cross. Have nothing inside and tell the atheist it was erected for them and that inside the fence is a representation of what they believe in. . . nothing! And remind them that their belief in nothing will always be guarded by the Marines.

And while the Marines guard "nothing" for the atheist, they will also guard the "honor and integrity" of the Marines who protect our country.

Letter to WND
(04.04.12)
From: "Barfield, Joe"
Date: Wed, 04 Apr 2012 07:18:39 -0500
To: jcorsi@worldnetdaily. com>,
Subject: Fan of WND, BUT. . .
Jerome,
I count on information from WND to keep informed. I was excited about Joe Arpaio's information but in reality they are accusations. It would be like me accusing you of murder and saying I have information. I read "about" the proof you have but I have seen nothing.
Remember Tom Cruise when he said, "Show me the Money!"
Well, SHOW me the proof. I want to see the proof and who knows about it. Don't you want to see the proof and talk with those who have provided it?
Thanks,
Joe
From: Jerome Corsi [mailto:jrlc@optonline. net]
Sent: Wednesday, April 04, 2012 7:35 PM
To: Barfield, Joe
Subject: Re: Fan of WND, BUT. . .

Joe
Be patient. The proof is developing.
Best regards,
Jerry Corsi

Hitler
(04.04.12)
Obama is to white Americans and Christians, as what Hitler was to the Jews.

American Future
(04.04.12)
With Obama there is no American future. . . run Forrest run!

Tax the Wealthy to Help National Parks
(04.10.12)
To All:
Recently in a speech Obama made, I believe to "Occupy," Jeremiah Wright, Welfare recipients and Mr. Ayers, he said that if he was unable to collect taxes from the wealthy he would be forced to close "hundreds" of National Parks in America.
Not true unless he means all of North America and South America. The United States of America has a total of 58 National Parks. You can add that to the promise of New Jobs, No More War, Reducing the Deficit, and his Transparent Government. He said he would cut the deficit. So far he has added to the deficit an average of 1.5 trillion each year he has been in office. And he blames Bush. I'm not real fond of Bush and what he did but come on, Obama. How many years do you need to be in office before you begin to function?

Even Superman's X-Ray vision would be unable to see through Obama's Transparent Government.

Below is a list of America's Parks.

http://www. nationalpark-adventures. com/united-states-national-parks. html

Tax the Wealthy to Help National Parks
(04.12.12)

It's funny when your hear something but don't see it. Different meaning.

I was in the kitchen listening to one of my favorite television programs when I heard the announcer say, "Welcome to America's Biggest Losers. And tonight we have President Obama's wife, Michelle!"

Whole new picture when you can't see it. How ironic.

Good Christian
(04.12.12)

As a real conservative and good Christian, I stand behind abortions of any kind and Gay and Lesbian marriages.

So I ask you, who wants abortions? Democrats. Who wants Gay and Lesbian marriages? Democrats. If they get what they want where will they be in twenty years?

Reasons for the Secret Service Failure
(04.17.12)

I've found that many times a worker is a direct reflection of his boss. If he is late, then you are late. If he cusses, then you cuss. If he does his job only half way, then you will too. Almost always employees follow the lead of their boss.

For example when General Martin Dempsey, Chairman of the Joint Chiefs of Staff said, "We let the boss down." Now I don't like Obama and I KNOW his policies are a failure and that another term under his control will destroy America, but Mr. Dempsey didn't say, "We let the President down." A reflection of the employees following the lead of their "boss." They no longer respect him or call him President.

The Secret Service agents in Cartagena, Colombia were only following their bosses lead. Their Boss screws America so they thought they would do the same thing while they were working in Colombia.

They were a direct reflection of their "boss."

He is to America As. . .
(04.19.12)

I hope Barrack Obama leads a good full life, just like Judas Iscariot. Judas was to Jesus as Obama is to America.

God Has Plans for America
(04.19.12)

Be careful Obama. God has plans for America. . .

Just like he did for Sodom and Gomorrah.

CO2 Gases
(04.17.12)

Let's get rid of the deadly CO_2 gases. But what happens when we get rid of the gases? All that is left is Oxygen. Don't strike a match! BUT, why did we have CO_2 gases to begin with? What is important that needs CO_2? Plants!!!!! If we get rid of CO_2 what happens to the plants? They die. . . . . . Gore hasn't figured that out yet.

Gone to the Dogs
(04.19.12)

What does Obama call a dog riding on the roof of a car?
FAST FOOD!

Obama defends himself - Where's the beef? What's for breakfast?
(04.19.12)

The way Obama explained it was the way his father had told him as a child.

"When my father made my mother serve breakfast he would smile to me and say, 'This is what Americans have for breakfast all the time,' as we enjoyed our breakfast Beagles."

Obama the Writer
(04.19.12)

Shame on Dystel and Acton for agents continuing the fraud. I have had books published but not 19 pages like the Dystel short. Mine have been over 300 pages. BUT THE POINT is about the bio that said he was born in Kenya. THINK for a moment. Who does the bio? Not Dystel or Acton---it was Obama. The agents only know what he wrote about himself. That's right Obama wrote the bio. I wrote my bio. EVERY author writes his or her bio. AND the agents send it back numerous times to make you proofread the bio. It is very difficult, no it is impossible to write down the wrong city, much less the wrong country. IF Obama was really born in Hawaii then he lied about Kenya. More important his college information is locked and we can no longer access his records. Now this is just a rumor but before he was elected it was said he received a scholarship as a foreign student. Personally to seal your college records is just another trail of lies. If true that is fraud. You only seal records to hide something you are afraid of letting the people know. The truth is out there, just not in Congress or the Executive branch. Dystel and Acton have only continued the fraud.

History
(04.19.12)

Obama needs to pay attention to Charles Taylor and remember history repeats and that America is angry.

Faith
(04.19.12)

The good book says, "With Faith anything is possible!
So that must meant, "Without Faith, you have Obama."

Fast and Stupid
(04.19.12)

Mychal,

How can Obama seal the records to Brian Terry's murder? Great discussion with Katie.

Why not have Arizona file murder, and gun trafficking charges against Obama, Holder, and Napolitano. Add in the others that Katie mentioned.

Joe

Treason
(04.19.12)

Why worry about military defensive positions, security and strategy when you make secret agreements with Communist Russian leaders and GIVE THEM some of your countries most strategic land and oil reserves.

MY OPINION:

Many countries vary and some eat dog and a variety of animals they don't eat here. The fact he did it as a child is not important. What is relevant is that it was illegal where he lived.

YOU need to understand he probably hunted down a neighbors pet. Even if they drove away from their neighborhood, how many dogs run from you like a hunted deer? None. What troubles me is that the unconcerned pet probably walked up to the young Obama to be petted and have its ear scratched in a trusting manor and instead had its neck broken and served up as dinner in the Sotero frying pan. His father didn't say we are going to eat man's best friend, instead he probably said, "We're going to have our best illegal meal." I wonder what Michael Vick would say? I know, he would shrug and say, "It's a dog eat dog world."

The unsuspicious dog was much like Americans today. Hope and Change today and tomorrow secret agreements with Russia and giving a trillion dollars of Alaskan Island oil reserves to the enemy. Serving the American people up as a meal to the Russians.

Dogs in Indonesia, when Obama was a child, were much safer than Americans under his rule today. The important thing to remember is that eating a dog is and was a crime in Indonesia. He did to dogs, back then, what he does to the American Constitution today.

Ethanol to Gas
(04.19.12)

The bright side is that your guns don't need gas. BUT. . . . I wonder why Homeland Security bought 450 million rounds of high velocity, hollow point bullets? Is it to protect us against the drivers that don't use alcohol in their gas? Let's see 450 minus 33% for misses that would leave 300 million hits. . . OH, MY GOD, that's the almost the exact number of Americans in the United States. I heard we have to show them our I. D. 's before they can shoot. Birth Certificates aren't required. If you have too much alcohol in your cars gas system will they be able to haul it off because it's under the influence? That would be a DUI for your car wouldn't it?

Take Action
(04.19.12)
He's all you have left but sitting on our butts gets nothing done. You need to swing the hammer not look at it.

Ex-wives
(04.19.12)
Ex-wives and the IRS are very similar. They pretty much take everything.

Sherrod (The Truth?)
(04.19.12)
Sherrod,
Before I can help, and I would like to help, I need to know what "they" have said about you that is false or send me links to their accusations.

And for the truth what do you intend to do. Your email has no information and I have no idea what "they" have done and what you want to do.

Please respond.
Joe Barfield

Mychal,
Again thanks for your wonderful expose. Keep it coming.
This morning I read that Mr. Obama said only soldiers should have AK-47's. Does that mean the Mexican drug runners he and Holder armed are soldiers?
First of all what does he know about being a soldier?

Mr. Obama said only soldiers should have AK-47's
(07.25.12)
Thank you Mr. Obama for reminding us, all Americans, of our obligation to remain fast to the freedoms of mankind. Your words ring of truth and for that reason all Americans should have AK-47's for we are the soldiers of Freedom.

I must remind him you, Mr. Obama, that guns were invented because of politicians. Did Holder give 5000 automatic weapons to soldiers or drug runners? Was he enforcing freedom or just being a common criminal as he helped murder not only Mexicans but also Americans protecting our country. When men like Holder refuse to respond to questions of treason it becomes the responsibility of all Americans to arm themselves.

Did Holder and Obama give arms to the citizens of Syria to create a civil war? Someone needs to remind Holder that gun running is illegal, not buying guns. Think what would happen in America if they armed their friends. If Obama and Holder intend to enslave Americans then we must arm ourselves.

The leaders and people of America need to look at Greece, Spain, Islam, and especially the former leaders of Libya, Iraq, Egypt and Syria and know that Obama and Holder are bringing it to America.

Lest you forget, Mr. Obama, you were elected to enforce the Constitution, not to change it. Anything else could be construed as treason.

Thomas Jefferson said, "Sometimes a man must fight his government to save his country and freedom and to prevent enslavement from their leaders."

The Second Amendment gives us that freedom. Obama and Holder are the usurpers of freedom.

Mychal, keep the articles coming. We don't know how long you have before Obama declares freedom of speech to be the same as an AK-47.

Good news in Syria
(8.09.12)

The Rebels in Syria have split into two factions and are now fighting each other. If and when they defeat the Assad, there will be a civil war between radical Islamic fundamentalist and radical Islamic fundamentalist. Actually they look a lot like Democrats and Republicans when they are in session.

Whereas it was noted that the United States has been accused of supplying arms to the rebels, Holder was quick to respond but he finally commented, "We have not sold arms to the Syrian rebels. I understand that the Mexican cartels are selling automatic weapons bought from gun stores in America to supply the Rebels. This is the reason all citizens in America should not have guns of any kind."

Obama said it is important for all citizens in Libya to arm themselves, so they can take down their evil leaders.

Obama did quip, "This has nothing to do with "Fast and Furious." We're taking a cautious approach and call it "Slow and Stupid.""

To the Media: Do something before it's too late
(07.19.12)

Do any of you understand the debt? If you made a hundred thousand a year and you owed one million, and the interest was 10%, how much would you have remaining of the hundred thousand?

Now take a look at the debt and taxes collected. Do you see a problem yet?

Obama can pinpoint a doorknob in Pakistan but he can't stop the drugs and illegal aliens?

What is going on? It is time you told Americans the truth. It appears more like you are in bed with Congress instead of telling the truth to the American People.

I'd like to know the total debt of Europe vs. the United States.

If Congress can't take care of America then quit trying to protect the world.

When are we going to prosecute those that bankrupted Fannie Mae and the others.

I want to send the owners of Solyndra and the politicians who threw our money away on a bankrupt company.

Only two problems with the Federal Government Democrats and Republicans.

Since this is a time of war, as we seem to always be doing, then most of America's congressmen are guilty of treason.

Sadly, even the media has become the problem. Do something before it's too late.

Rahm Emanuel and Mr. Obama both appear to have similar beliefs and moral objectives. In face Obama surrounds himself with people like Rahm Emanuel. His people believe in same-sex marriage and are apparently extremely against traditional marriage. Obviously none of them believe in freedom of speech.

If it's okay to say you believe in same-sex marriage, shouldn't you also be allowed to say you believe in traditional marriage?

Based on Obama's hypothesis that only soldiers should have AK-47's, and since all Americans are the Soldiers of Freedom, then all Americans should be required to have AK-47's

Those on welfare need to fight for your rights to receive and not give. Obama is giving all your things (taken from working Americans) and giving them all to illegal aliens. I would help you protest this atrocity Obama has done to you, which might force you to work for something or actually earn it but I'm too busy working to make sure you get something for doing nothing.

When it comes to the president I "Hope for Change."

After four years of nothing what makes you think Obama knows anymore today then he did when he became president? I think someone said he heard Obama say, "The hardest part of doing nothing, is knowing when you're finished." That means he will never finish.

A Boy Scout Brownie
(07.19.12)

Well, Mitt Romney is for Gay Boy Scouts.

We need to think about for a moment. If a scout is gay and likes boys then it only seems reasonable that a gay Scout should be a brownie. Don't be dirty minded. I mean a Girl Scout Brownie. You see the girls will be safe because a gay Boy Scout only likes boys to they will be no danger to the girls except they will probably be chasing after the same boys.

Make sense?

Obamageddon
(07.19.12)

If you believe in God. . . and Bible prophesy, then you know—
OBAMAGEDDON is near!!!

Now You Know
(07.19.12)

My friend said:

The liberals don't have solutions. That is why they resort to gutter politics. The media has nothing to defend Obama on, so they have to go negative.

You and I know what the solutions are but do you think the lame brain independents or swing voters that could make or break this election have a clue? Do you think all of the illegals who began getting amnesty today by the way, care that they are part of the problem? Do the millions of people today on food stamps and welfare care about the right solutions? Conservatives have to realize that this is war, not politics, not bi-partisan agreements or anything liberal. You and I and allot of other good people stand a very high chance of losing the America and freedoms we grew up with. What are we going to do then, move out of the country?

I responded:

Financially it might be too late. I sent you the numbers on the "State of the

Economy" this morning, you saw the numbers. Maria Conchita Alonzo said be careful because Obama is bringing Venezuela to America. And remember 45 percent of Americans are getting some type of government assistance.

We have already lost most of our freedoms. Last week a law allowing Obama to arrest Americans as enemies of the state and be imprisoned indefinitely.

Leave America? Can't leave it if it doesn't exist.

Now look at Iraq and their former leader. Egypt and it's former leader. Libya and it's former leader. Syria and imagine what is about to happen to Assad. History repeats so close your eyes and imagine America and its current leader. Isn't it beautiful? Just like the Clint Eastwood movie "Hand 'Em High. You might say we'll see the heads roll, just ask Saddam and his sixteen virgins.

Did I miss anything?

Dogs and People
(07.19.12)

Dogs and People. . . . is that the same as Democrats and Republicans.

Sorry I digress and need to apologize to all dogs. At least dogs are faithful and loyal.

Help for Obama
(07.19.12)

Bill Clinton is helping Obama with his campaign so remember. . . .

. . . . Clinton is to Monica,
As Obama is to America!
Only we don't get a cigar and we'll need to clean up the mess. . .

If Obama is re-elected
(07.19.12)

If Obama is re-elected we may see. . . .

Within three years of Obama's re-election we will find that the drug cartels or Mexico will have discovered a business more lucrative than the drug crops and cocaine they now sell to American's. The new crop? Guns. Guns Americans will need to protect themselves from their government.

It's coming.

Obama's Muslim Freedom (Ha!)
(07.19.12)

The President said:

http://www. whitehouse. gov/the-press-office/2012/08/10/remarks-president-iftar-dinner

(PARTIAL) Now, every faith is unique. And yet, during Ramadan, we see the traditions that are shared by many faiths: Believers engaged in prayer and fasting, in humble devotion to God. Families gathering together with love for each other. Neighbors reaching out in compassion and charity, to serve the less fortunate. People of different faiths coming together, mindful of our obligations to one another - to peace, justice and dignity for all people - men and women. Indeed, you know that the Koran teaches, "Be it man or woman, each of you is equal to the other."

And by the way, we've seen this in recent days. In fact, the Olympics is being called "The Year of the Woman." (Laughter.) Here in America, we're incredibly proud of Team USA - all of them - but we should notice that a majority of the members are women. Also, for the very first time in Olympic history, every team now includes a woman athlete. And one of the reasons is that every team from a Muslim-majority country now includes women as well. And more broadly - that's worth applauding. (Applause.) Absolutely.

BUT THE MUSLIM COUNTRIES SAID:

http://www. whitehouse. gov/the-press-office/2012/08/10/remarks-president-iftar-dinner

The father of a 16-year-old on Saudi Arabia's Olympic team said his daughter has been called names by people in her home country for competing at the London Games.

Wojdan made history during the Olympics when she was selected by the kingdom to compete in judo at the Games, though the opportunity was almost derailed when the International Judo Federation said she could not compete wearing a head scarf.

The teen and her father signed an agreement with Saudi Olympics officials that she would be allowed to compete only if she wore "correct and approved" clothing that "sticks to Islamic principles," according to Saudi National Olympic Committee representative Razen Baker.

An agreement was eventually struck between Saudi Arabia, the International Olympic Committee and the Judo federation.

Opinion: Saudi women going to games is a sham

The duck stops here
(07.19.12)

Imagine a commercial, where that white duck from the commercial is strutting around and squawking, "AFFLAC, AFFLAC, AFFLAC."

He walks up to a man, Ben Affleck who looks down of the duck and says, "No I'm Affleck."

The duck continues to squawk, when suddenly a man bursts on the scene, arrogant and cocky.

It's President Obama who smugly says, "I'm Half-Black!"

LET FREEDOM REIGN, JUST NOT IN AMERICA WITH OBAMA
(07.19.12)

All of his statements carry the same accuracy as his dialog about how wonderful it is to be a Muslim.

I want Obama's college records.

Biden says Romney didn't pay taxes and I have accurate information that Obama's sealed records show that Sotero obtained foreign student status and loans. Criminal actions if he is an American citizen.

How about if Obama comes on Oprah and reveals the truth.

One more thing, I write books and the publisher requires the author to supply a biography. You must check it a dozen times. The same was required of Obama when he wrote his essays. It seems rather difficult to confuse Kenya with Hawaii. This means Obama is a liar or he can't read (stupid).

Hey Biden, what do you think about that.

Treason?

Can anybody out there think?

Next stop. . . .

Armageddon

Bullets for America or Americans?
(08.10.12)

Question: Why did Obama allow the purchase of 174 million hollow point bullets? To protect Americans or to kill them. They don't even allow hollow points in war.

Hope and Change
(08.19.12)

Been a lot of Hope but no change.

For the last four years Obama has fed us his secret drug. An illegal drug worse than marijuana or opium.

Obama has drugged us with Hope-ium!

The Truth is Out There. . . Somewhere. . . Just Not in Congress!!!!
(08.19.12)

With this election it seems hard to find somewhere you can count on getting the truth about the two candidates. As far as MSNBC is concerned I feel every other word is a lie.

They bragged about what a fine speech Michelle gave. BUT if you know about Obama's grandparents and his mother along with Dreams (the word should be Lies) of My Father, you will discover the two stories diametrically opposed. One is lying for sure. Mostly Michelle. And Obama should be a fiction writer, because none of his stories come with any truth.

But I may have found the truth. I was cruising through the internet new channels when I stopped. They were discussing the election and other items. I stopped flipping through the channels because from the brief broadcast I realized it was the truth as I knew and I feel the truth is the most important thing. I was amazed. The reporters were thorough and concise. They didn't lean left or right. And their words were unbiased. The first broadcast I had heard in over two months that didn't accuse some person of being racist and getting sidetracked from the issues. For the first time I didn't feel as though I was listening to two fifth graders bickering.

When the broadcast ended I clicked the remote to see what station it was so I could return to listen to more competent and precise news. The station? Al-Jazeera, believe it or not.

When I think of Congress only two words come to mind; Soylent Green.

The Arab Spring has become the Christian Winter

Obama quotes:
(accumulated from 2009)
"We're no longer a Christian nation." - President Barack Obama, June 2009
"America has been arrogant." - President Barack Obama
"After 9/11, America didn't always live up to her ideals."- President Barack Obama
"You might say that America is a Muslim nation."- President Barack Obama, Egypt 2009

America is a Muslim Nation says Obama
(08.19.12)
If immigration patterns and Muslims' comparatively higher birth rates continue: U. S. Muslims will go from a tiny minority now, less than 1% of the nation, to 1.7%. That's a jump from 2.6 million people in 2010 to 6.2 million. Muslim immigration to the USA and Muslims' share of all new legal permanent residents will continue to rise. (Many of those are walking safely across our southern border just as Obama planned. They are protected by Holder and Obama)
(If you know how to do math that means Obama let 3.6 million Muslims enter this country in less than 2 years. All under Obama. If they were only 1% of the total population how did they make such wonderful contributions to American society as declared by Obama?)
Though 64.5% of U. S. Muslims today were born abroad, that percentage will fall to 55% as the number of native-born Muslims rises.
Worldwide, Muslims will climb from 23.4% to 26.4% of the population, going from 1.6 billion people in 2010 to 2.2 billion in 2030, concentrated in Muslim-majority countries. (Remember, Obama said, "You might say that America is a Muslim nation." And they are only 1.7% of America? Oh, and those that claim to be American Christians? 76%. Jewish people comprise 2.2%)
Can't you see the evil coming to America.

Remember. .
(08.19.12)
Remember; Forty-five million welfare recipients can't all be wrong!!!!

Same Thing Happened Before
(08.20.12)
It is pretty obvious with a sure 45 million votes. But don't worry, the same thing has happened before, in Germany in 1938. Really the only difference is that Obama plans to substitute the Christians for the Jews. Why else would he have purchased 450 million, illegal, hollow point rounds of ammunition.

Hold on for the ride
I would say the stock market is going to drop.
Here is the National Debt in the last three days as of Tuesday. (Remember the weekend) 10.02.2012 - 16,171,037,3453,408.67
Check it out: http://www.treasurydirect.gov/NP/debt/current

The debt went up 156 billion in three days. That is almost one-tenth of the taxes collected for a year.

Elect Mitt Romney and you can keep your current calculator. Elect Obama and you need a new one with six additional zeroes for Mr. Zero.

A week ago Congress met at midnight and said it was okay to raise the debt over 16 trillion. They still haven't passed a budget.

How are. . . . ?

How are politics or Obama or corrupt similar? The same meaning only spelled differently.

To USA Today

I'd like you to write more on Amanda Marqotte's article about shameless race-baiting.

http://www. usatoday. com/story/opinion/2012/10/04/hannity-tucker-carlson-obama-video/1611601/

The 2007 video was not widely known. I saw nothing like this about Obama and that's why he came across so well. The race-baiting was by Obama and it was obvious. This doesn't address the fact that New Orleans was helped, he knew it and he LIED. He was with his black church the same way the KKK used to arouse whites against blacks. I thought and hoped we were past those days. Obama is trying to destroy everything Martin Luther King accomplished. Is this how he won the Nobel Peace Prize?

The sad thing is that I don't find the truth in the media. Will you tell the truth and show the people. I don't like Bush and didn't vote for him but when is Obama going to take responsibility for his lack of action, or are the over 300 million people in America just another bump in the road? If you don't tell the truth and bring it out then it makes you a worse liar than Obama's administration. The truth is out there somewhere, just not in Congress, and now it appears not in the media whose job it is to report the truth.

I'd like her to make a printed retraction and admit that Obama lied. Lies make you libel and you don't want writers running off with their pens with untruths. The thing is Amanda lied when she denies Obama lied. I'll be looking for the retraction. Do something MSNBC and the others don't do, and that is quality reporting and accuracy in the TRUTH. Opinions are fine put writing lies is wrong. Please send me a copy of her retraction.

Do you report the truth? If not I can go to Barnes and Noble to find all the fiction I want.

Muslims, bullets for Americans, and Obama's Cloudy Transparency

A while back Obama said something to the effect that, "America was becoming a Muslim nation and their love and what they have done for America is amazing." So I decided to do a little research.

Actually I could find no record of a Muslim with any real contributions to America. What I did learn; if immigration patterns and Muslims' comparatively higher birth rates continue: U. S. Muslims went from a tiny minority, less than 1% of the nation, to 1.7%. That's a jump from 3.2 million people in 2010 to 6.2 million in 2012. Muslim immigration to the USA and Muslims' share of all new legal permanent residents will continue to rise. Many of those are walking safely across our southern border just as Obama planned. They are protected by Holder and Obama. A rancher in the small town of Agua Pierta, Arizona, recently found a small notepad with hand writings in Arabic.

(If you know how to do math that means Obama let three million Muslims enter this country in less than 2 years. All under Obama. If they were only 1% of the total population how did they make such wonderful contributions to American society as declared by Obama?)

About 64.5% of U. S. Muslims today were born abroad, that percentage will fall to 55% as the number of native-born Muslims rises.

Worldwide, Muslims will climb from 23.4% to 26.4% of the population, going from 1.6 billion people in 2010 to 2.2 billion in 2030, concentrated in Muslim-majority countries.

(Remember, Obama said, "You might say that America is a Muslim nation." And they are only 1.7% of America? Oh, and those that claim to be American Christians? 76%. Jewish people comprise 2.2%)

While I researched this I read something to the effect that the Department of Homeland Security had purchased 450 million rounds of ammunition. About 7000% their normal purchase and the bullets were the type the Geneva Convention forbid use in war. Why was DHS purchasing so much ammo and who did they plan to kill? After all the DHS only serves in America. Hhhmm. . . that means the bullets must be for Americans but not as a gift you want to receive. While I was looking into this they purchased another 200 million rounds, including sniper bullets. And they purchased over 450 MRI's. That's like military meals in a bag. Or about 450 meals for a million man army that would last 250 days or almost nine months.

WHAT ON EARTH DOES DHS NEED OVER 650 MILLION ROUNDS OF AMMO? The DHS wouldn't use it against fellow Americans. . . would they? I checked and there are only 200,000 DHS employees. There are not enough to get the job done of controlling Americans. And what about weapons?

Then I read about Napolitano had hired two people in 2009 to run the DHS; Arif Alikhan and David Heyman. What was disturbing about the article it pointed out they were devout Muslims. Why make mention of the fact they are devout Muslims?

http://www. dhs. gov/news/2009/04/24/secretary-makes-personnel-announcements

Now it begins to add up. Three million Muslims walking across the border. Did they bring their own weapons? A million would be enough, even 500,000.

So ask yourself what are 650 million rounds of ammunition for? Why are the leaders of DHS "devout Muslims?" And how did three million Muslims enter this country?

Conspiracy? Paranoia? Not really. Just ask Obama or Holder or the heads of DHS what the bullets are for? Obama said he operated an open and transparent government, right? You should have no problem asking and receiving an answer. Well, it might be easier to obtain his sealed college records. The answer should be simple but if they refuse to say anything, well lets go back to conspiracy and paranoia

SMITH AND WESSON
Guard this house. Enter at your own risk

SEALED
When I was kid a friend had his records sealed because he had killed two girls. A year later when he turned eighteen his record was sealed. Another friend has his record sealed for stealing money. Two years later his record was sealed. They all had committed crimes.

Obama's records are sealed.

Trump offered Obama five million to open his sealed records. Obama waved it off. I guess that's called a transparent presidency

Obama's records are sealed. Why? He committed a crime.

Forget being a Christian. If you are an American you won't vote for Obama. He is un-American and judging conservatively by Obama's rhetoric he is radically racist. A vote for Obama is another nail in America's coffin.

Redistribution of wealth
http://www. wnd. com/2012/09/secret-retirement-plans-does-obama-expect-to-lose/

Where is Obama getting the $35 million to buy this house? Redistribution of wealth?

He believes my money should be taken so that the people below my standard can live like I do and still not be required to work. It that is true and since I live below Obama's standard of living than I demand to have a house like he will have in Hawaii.

That only seems fair that Obama redistribute his wealth so I can live like he does. Can I use Air Force 1 for my vacation? And why am I required to do my job within a few days of being hired? Discrimination? I should be like the President Obama and not be required to anything but golf and go on seventeen vacations that sometimes cost the tax payers up to one million dollars each.

Americans under Obama have about as much hope for the future and being saved by our President as Christopher Stevens had of being saved by the Marines with bullet less weapons. Remember never take an unloaded rifle against an angry crowd of Al-Qaeda determined to kill you. I believe one Marine or Seal can protect our Ambassadors against thousands, if they have bullets. But maybe they couldn't give those marines bullets because they need 650 million of those precious items to help the DHS defend us against. . . against what? Don't worry, those decisions for the DHS security is being made by President Barrack Hussein Obama are being made by the two czars (aren't czars communist?) he appointed: Canadian born, Hezbollah defender, Arif Alikhan, and Kareem Shora, who was born in Damascus, Syria. http://www. militantislammonitor. org/article/id/4108

I want that new law passed called "The right **not** to work law." But if it passes will I be required to join a union? And where would I go on protest to demand more for my lack of work?

Obama has said he needs four more years to finish what he was doing. Like they say, "The hardest part of doing nothing, is knowing when you're finished," which is a good job description for our President because we all know he isn't even near having finished nothing. Like his anger and defense of murdered Americans in Libya.

Final Meandering Scribbles
(End of Times)
Republican is an antonym for "Conservative." Example Romney
Democrat is an antonym for "freedom"
Obama is an antonym for "Christian"
Now that Obama Care is in the Supreme Court we need a little of Obama's "Hope and Change." I "Hope" the Court "changes" it.

I don't know why they used the Indian language as code during WWII. All they needed was for Congress to write it like a law. Nobody understands what they write.

Obama has done more for race relations than the KKK or the Black Panthers.

Listening to the Democrats and Republicans work together is like having a "Peace Fest" with the KKK and the NAACP

I've met dumber women at work than those that stay at home with their kids.

The Pulpits are Silent and Souls are Being Lost
(Christian End of Times)
It is sad. The churches I have attended preach the evils of Hollywood and demand we have family value movies. So when the students of Katy wanted to make a faith-based movie. We contacted 56 churches. Only one response and the pastor said we were not a member of their church. Actually, I thought I was a member of all churches. A church I went to, I send the email to the pastor, his wife and son. No response and they have a teen camp and could have made the movie very easily. The Pastor's son said they weren't interested. He could have delegated, but. . .

I contacted Joel Osteen and Ed Young. No response. I have found that Christian students making a Christian movie is of no interest to the pastors in Katy. There was one, Hispanic, bi-lingual church with 80 members that donated $2000. Other than that no response.

If you needed brain surgery or you would die in thirty days and then you contacted 50 brain surgeons but none responded in that month what would happen? You would die.

Pastors are the doctors of the soul. Today we find many souls that are dying.

So to all Christians; contact your pastor and if he doesn't respond in a week then you need another Pastor to doctor your soul.

40 Days of Prayer
When you called for 40 days or prayer did you remember to tell them to vote? I'm sure I'll get a standard reply. I asked for help once and not prayers but you sent prayers again. God didn't answer the prayer because it was for your help and you

didn't offer any. Do you read these emails.

Hey, you don't need to do work in South America anymore you can stay right here. The vote shows only 48% of Americans are Christians. It used to be 76%. You really need to work on your prayers.

Once more I want to thank you for your prayers but I need help with Christian kids that want to talk about their Christian movie.

If we could cash in the prayers we pay for the movie. Will you help this time? Remember, God is watching you!

Action time

One more thing, the time for prayer is done. You need to take action. Let's face it, this is no longer a country blessed by God. You want to do evangelical work but there are now about two-thirds of the Christians in America as there were eight years ago and there are about 20 million more in this country than there was then.

America is no longer in the line of Israel, but rather more like Sodom and Gomorrah.

Time to act, after all David didn't pray Goliath to death, he took action.

Definition of a Democrat

A Democrat is someone who believes only his ideas are correct. No one else. Example:

They can lie but you can't.

One who was known to have affairs accused a Republican candidate of having a extramarital affair. When he was called down on the fact he had multiple affairs he said it was okay for him to have an affair because he doesn't think there is anything wrong with affairs so he was okay but his opponent believed affairs were wrong, so since his opponent had an affair it made him guilty.

Better yet, a friend of mine the other night blurted out that he believed there should be gun control and I snapped back, "I also believe in gun control. I think American should have a gun and know how to control it. Then at the next Batman movie he would be gunned after a couple of shots." Then he said no one should have a gun. And here is the point. I said, "You mean you don't have a gun." That was when he said, "Oh, yeah I have a gun but that is different."

And that my friend is a Democrat. They believe the same thing about taxes. Everyone should pay taxes…except…

WMD's Against the People

Actually, Congress uses WMD's against the people. "When Many Deceive" is what congress uses against the American people every day.

God Told Him

Pat Robertson said God told him Mitt Romney would win the election. That was stupid and makes Christian's look dumb.

But wait.....God did tell Pat Robertson that Romney would win the election. And it is true Romney did win, but...

....God forgot to tell him who would steal and lie his way into office!!

THE TWO WORST PRESIDENTS IN AMERICAN HISTORY??

It's as simple as...

Black   and   White

Obama said...

When Obama was a small boy and learning things for his book, "Lies of my Father," his neighbors said, "When Barrack and his father were out in the neighborhood prowling around they knew it would be a 'Dog Gone' day.

Obama quote yesterday in Israel: Let me be perfectly clear, when I was a child my father taught me about America and their great meals. Let me say this we learned to eat wonderful Jewish dishes. Yes traditional Jewish dishes. Many times my father made breakfast where I became accustomed to that great Jewish meal, Beagles.

Congress and Vampires

Congress doesn't want the ten commandments anywhere near them. If you take time to ask yourself why, it is rather a simple answer. Do Congress men steal? Do they lie? Do they bear false witness? Do they commit murder? What did that Democrat say, oh yeah, "I did not have sex.....with that woman." If you were honest wouldn't you show your college grades for five million dollars?

Do they honor any of the ten commandments?

With that in mind think about this. The Ten Commandments are to Congress as sunshine is to Vampires. It burns them.

Response to MoveOn.org

The idea is stop government waste and spending not to tax us to pay for government folly. If you deny his freedom of speech one day your freedom of speech will also be denied.

Show proof not accusations.

Audit the Federal reserve and where the over spent 1.4 trillion each year the last four years has gone. How come we bailed out the banks and gave them loans for one or two percent and the save banks want 12% for a loan they gave me while my tax dollars bailed them out.

Our Country

Ask not what your country can do for you but rather why do they keep doing it to you.

Twice as Good as a Christian?

Obama, Reid and Pelosi came out yesterday to a let all Americans know that they are twice as good as Christians. Pelosi spoke for all three when she said, "As Americans we are two times better than Christians who believe in the cross because we stand firm in our belief of the double cross."

DOOMSDAY AMERICA 11.06.12

GOOD MORNING OBAMANATION!!!
Welcome to the United Socialist States of America.

Forty-five million Welfare recipients can't all be wrong.

God is with us......well maybe not. It seems like when we were told by American ministers to pray against Obama they forgot to tell us to vote.

The bright side is that now Obama can finish his destruction of America. This will come fast; two years max.

His government is as transparent as mud. We are at 16 trillion and mark my words it will 20 trillion in two years. That is the point of no return. I see a hundred year lease on San Diego to China.

If you think you're paying too much in taxes now, wait until next year.

I wonder who he will blame for the last four years?

And welcome to the Muslim Brotherhood. Allah Akbar. You could lose your head over it.

I understand the phones at companies are being changed to, "Para Ingles, presar dos." For those that don't know, you will need to press two.

From Congress let us say, "Tienes buen dia."

For free college education please say, "No hablo Ingles."

Next Stop.....

Death of a Close Friend
Would it be politically incorrect to say?:
It was a black day in America when Obama was elected for a second term. A close friend died that same day; America – 11.06.12

And the Difference Is?
What's the difference between Hitler and Democrats? The Democrats have managed to destroy America. AND they did it with your money.

OBAMA COOKBOOK OF MY FATHER

New book by Barrack Obama

It is called "Meals From My Father or "Cooking Your Dog." He was one smart puppy.

Excellent recipes from Indonesia.

For the quiet meal at home you can have "Hush Puppies."

Want soup, then don't miss out on "Noodles and Poodles."

And the wonderful casserole, "Puppy Chow," for when you really want to chow down.

A breakfast roll you will all enjoy; "Beagles." Really good with butter

The German specialty ground Schnauzer Schnitzel

How about the crusted pie for all those hearty appetites, "Shepherd Pie."

Got some hot sauce and try Obama's "Chihuahua Tacos."

Now I want to leave you with this final thought....

We all love somebody, but there is something special about a dog that brings joy, laughter, amusement and love. No matter how harsh you treat a dog it still loves you. Strangely, if you reverse the letters it spells God. Even when you make mistakes and become angry, a dog loves no less than God. For many, a dog is not only a person's best friend, but also their only friend.

If Obama is capable of eating his best friend, when it's against the law like it is in Indonesia, what will he do to our Constitution and our fellow Americans?

Lift Your Sword

Welcome to the new year 2013. Today America has officially been taken off Life Support. Hope is gone, the real Change is about to begin. Death is imminent, the lies will accelerate like never before. In the next two years, and before the end of 2014, you will witness the death of a nation.

Fiscal cliff? Nothing but more spending and lies. Congress is the "Fiscal Cliff."

Like the Bible when David faced Goliath, it not much different in America; where America is like David and Congress Goliath. Lift your sword. Prayer didn't kill Goliath—the sword did!

But what will America do? Nothing, as they will die the coward's death. You will not like it but you will also do nothing about it. Hate and racial strife will win.

Lift your sword before it too late.

OBAMA SAID...

When Obama was a small boy and learning things for his book, "Lies of my Father," his neighbors said, "When Barrack and his father were out in the neighborhood prowling around they knew it would be a 'Dog Gone' day.

Obama quote yesterday in Israel: Let me be perfectly clear, when I was a child my father taught we about America and their great meals. Let me say this we learned to eat wonderful Jewish dishes. Yes traditional Jewish dishes. Many times my father made breakfast where I became accustomed to that great Jewish meal, Beagles.

Obama the Author

Obama is still working on his greatest fiction novel ever, "Fiscal Cliff," a follow up to his other fiction novel "Dreams of my Father." He will soon write his autobiography, "Lies of My Father."

Harry Reid is at it Again

Harry Reid said the reason the Eight Marines were killed was because Americans have too many automatic weapons.

When someone told Reid that the Marines were killed in an accident he immediately said it was because of the "Republican Sequester."

The reason for 1.6 Billion Bullets

It's official. The bullets are to reinforce his re-election campaign in 2016. Plus a couple hundred thousand free cell phones.

Mr. President

I want you to know that Welfare is not a job description

Lawsuit Against the Executive and Legislative Branches of America

I want to file a lawsuit against the Democrats including but not limiting to Obama, Pelosi, Reid, Anti-Defamation leagues on grounds of racial, sexual orientation and religious freedom for discrimination against freedom of speech, bullying, racial profiling, religious preference to heterosexual, white Christians, denying freedom of speech, the pursuit of happiness, the right to bear arms and the right to my religious beliefs.

And also I want to file felony charges against Congress for forcing me to pay Social Security when they were supposed to invest those funds but turned it into a Ponzi scheme which defrauded Americans of their retirement. Also charges of criminal mischief if breaking the laws of SS which said Congress could borrow those funds not philander or spend (Biden vacation of $500,000 a night for two nights). I find Congress, Republicans and Democrats negligent in their fiduciary responsibility to America and guilty of misappropriation of those funds, extortion (Fiscal Cliff), fraud (Fiscal Cliff), embezzlement, political corruption with lobbyists, bankrupting America, falsifying documents, bankrupting American values, denying Christians of their Civil Rights voter fraud and buying votes, embezzling, Obama for dereliction of duty, conflict of interest to Americans, failure to defend the Constitution, Un-American agendas, falsifying documents, and hiding documents from public scrutiny, gun-running and murder (Obama and Holder). I move we revoke their pensions and traveling expenses and vacations, drug testing and identification will be required for all of Congress and their assistants, and defrauding all Americans. The lawsuit is against both parties; Republicans and Democrats.

And the Affordable Health Care Act or Obama Care(less). This is illegal for all the reasons above and more. Congress doesn't know what they passed, proved by Pelosi's own words, "We need to pass this so we can have time to read it and see what is in it." What really scares me is that I thought they did read it. Any law passed by Congress shall apply to all Americans—no exceptions. Yet certain groups are exempt. If the law is passed it shall apply to all, including all government employees and Congress. It they don't like it then they need to buy more insurance. If one person is exempt from the law then it is illegal.

To the two American Parties I would like to repeat the words of that late great quarterback for the Dallas Cowboys, Don Meredith; Turn out the lights the party's over."

I also accuse them of murder and treason. Also Holder and Obama are guilty of funding supplying terrorist with illegal American tax funds used to exploit and destroy America and her Christian values.

The Damage
The Damage Obama has done to America is of Biblical proportions. Even the two cities, he is from, Chicago and Washington DC remind me of Biblical prophecy; Sodom and Gomorrah.

North Korean Nukes
Yesterday someone was telling me about the dangers we face against North Korea and that they might devastate America with nuclear bomb. I scoffed at them and said, "Even if they nuked Washington DC and Los Angeles there would be less damage to America than what Obama has done the last four years. God only knows what he'll do the next four years.

Pierce Morgan Demands
He demands more gay Fairy Tales so Hollywood is coming out with Dildo Baggins.

If Only…?
It is said only the good die young. If that is true then Obama may be immortal!

Outlaw Magazines
I heard the government it going to outlaw magazines. Does that mean I can no longer purchase Sports Illustrated?

New Deadly Weapons to be Registered

Yesterday Obama came out and said, "Let me be perfectly clear and transparent. No one needs weapons like these and with Holder backing me we are going to eliminate these deadly weapons from all American homes. We have the backing of over five people in Connecticut. Legislation is being written by Pelosi, Reid, Weinstein and Boxer, with people's safety in mind. Critical times call for critical action and while I'm on vacation Pelosi will preside over this new helpful bill. But don't worry if this new bill doesn't pass I will just issue another executive order."

Reid quipped, "We hope all housewives will join in."

Pelosi urged, "We must pass this urgent safety bill now. We can read it later."

NEW WEAPONS TO BE REGISTERED

The Deadly Bowie Single-Action

The Bowie AK-46 Semi-Automatic

And of course the deadly KBA-999 Fully Automatic
(Note: KBA – Kitchen Butcher Automatic)
Good News for Liberals. This comes with a disposable clip.

The KBA-999 was the 666 but as usual the Liberals decided to turn everything upside down.

With a smile Obama glanced at the teleprompter and said, "We, the Liberals, with Americans freedoms and rights foremost in our thoughts, want to remind all Americans that the Democrats have a problem for every solution."

Obama's Democratic party stood firm behind him, "We believe in "Freedom of Choice," as long as your choice is ours."

After the knifing Democrats are already changing the laws and demanding more registration

Other Items Under Consideration for Legalized Registration

Congress has deemed these items as "Deadly, Dangerous and Divisive" or otherwise known as the "3D" dangers facing Americans.

Also items Liberals considered for Registration and deadly to Americans

Things REALLY most Deadly to Americans

Hitler did it why can't they?

SLAVERY

In 1865 Lincoln freed the slaves

In 2012 Obama made Americans slaves.

The only difference is that today the American slaves have guns.

Harry Reid is at it again

Harry Reid said the reason the Eight Marines were killed was because Americans have too many automatic weapons.

When someone told Reid that the Marines were killed in an accident he immediately said it was because of the "Republican Sequester."

What is the Difference?

What is the difference between a Christian and a Liberal? Christians believe in the Cross, while Liberals believe in the double cross.

When in Mexico…
I was wondering. When you're in Mexico do you dial "Uno" or "Dos" for English?

Physical Education
Man has physical education changed. When I was a kid we used to do jumping jacks. Now the kids jump Jack.

AMERICA
America = Benghazi Part 2
Obama = Manchurian Candidate from the Middle East
Napolitano = Danger

Obama the Good Muslim
Obama still follows the laws of Sharia. While in office he actually performed a be-heading and sent the head in a box back to the family. He took the gift of Winston Churchill's head and sent it back to England. How arrogant and ignorant. The gift of a hero sent back in a box. I'm sure Obama would also burn the American flag and step all over the image of Jesus while demanding American's respect Mohammad.

MSNBC said…
MSNBC came out this morning and said the bombings in Boston were because of the NRA. Now tell me how that is possible. After this bombing in Boston shouldn't we outlaw cooking pots? Oh, but then only people like the Wicked Witch of the North would have a cooking pot. She kinda reminds me of Michelle, but Pelosi could be a stand in double for the WW of the N.

Remember Kennedy was misquoted. What he really said was, "Ask not what your country can do for you; but rather why does your country keep doing it to you!"

Hey Mr. Obama
Social Security and Medicare are not entitlements. A tax was passed we were forced to pay and it was spent. Another Democrat, Johnson, said it was okay to borrow our Social Security not to waste it. Actually you've turned our SS into a Ponzi scheme. Now your vacations and retirement are entitlements. At least you can attend your security meetings. You are paid for that and don't even attend. As far as the 5% you are willing to sacrifice, how about instead you give up your vacations or at least pay for them. Could you try something different like make your government more transparent? Do you have any idea what transparency means. You are the worst President in history.

Real Insurance Adds
They also show a man holding fine China and says, "You're in good hands with---OPPS!" As he drops the China.

The one I like best is when you call in with a claim and they say, "Sorry we cover everything but claims."

A Country Divided

Sadly I saw the country divided in the election to a point of violence; voter fraud, threats and other un-American things reared their ugly head. When 50,000 people are given free phones to get their vote it is not only a travesty to America but also a crime, and yet nothing is done. There are those who are against Obama and his radical liberals; they are called Americans. And then there are those that perpetrated the fraud and those who voted for Obama and they are called the forever needy.

IF I HAD…

And God said, "If I had a son he would look just like…"

And Obama said, "If I had a son he would look just like…"

My Phobia

I'm Dumbassaphobic. In other words I'm afraid of the the Dumb Asses in Congress like Pelosi, Reid, Boxer and Feinstein. Oh and you can add Obama too.

The Boston Marathon

(04.15.13)

It's coming. BUT don't worry, Janet Napolitano promised the borders are safe. We know everything about North Korea and Iraq and Syria and Egypt and Libya, but the FBI and CIA had no clue about this. Before you complain about your neighbor's yard it would probably be better to take care of your own yard.

Our government is spending enough to take care of this country why didn't they have a clue? Because they are clueless. Good work Janet, you really know how to build confidence....and safety.

Oh, Ruben, all of these things were written in book Moon Shadow back in 1994. Did I ever give it to you? It was easy to predict because history repeats and remember no empire in history has ever survived. There have been no exceptions.

One more time I want to point out that Napolitano assured us our borders were safe. Are they? Our government has pulled the guards away and the politicians are going on weekend jaunts that cost taxpayers millions, but they can't really protect us. So I ask Napolitano, if you take the guards away from the prison and unlock the doors will they stay in prison? Check the Internet but a few years ago a person that lived on a ranch on the border of Mexico near a town called Agua Pierta showed a news person a tiny notebook. It was written in Arabic. Right now we are no safer than the people in Benghazi...and soon they will have our guns.

The Boston Marathon reminded me of another Marathon. I can still see Dustin Hoffman in Marathon Man as a hole is drilled through his teeth, and the question is asked, "Is it safe?"

Don't be surprised if the people behind the Boston Marathon walked across the Mexican border. You know Napolitano did say the border was safe and she is right. The terrorists and drug runners are safe; it's just not safe for Americans. Sad but true.

So now I ask, "Is it safe?"

And now for a big welcome to the Muslim Brotherhood
(04.16.13)
General Hayden say the bombing will be the new norm for America. BS

If they don't know about what is happening here how can they no so much about N Korea? Why are we antagonizing them? The helicopter crash shows we're pushing them too much.

I also head that Al Qaeda went to Mexico to teach the drug cartels to intimidate including beheadings. Now it makes more sense.

If our government can't protect us then they sure aren't going to take our guns.

How long until America looks like Mexico and Iraq?

We need a man in office not a pussy. Well it looks like Obama has brought the Muslim Brotherhood to America.

I guess they want to take our guns so it will be easier for the Brotherhood to kill us.

Could Saudi Arabia be Involved in the Boston Bombing?
There is only one thing worse than a President that seals his records and lies. To all of those that want to take away guns how about you tell everybody Obama might just be protecting a Saudi Muslim involved in Boston. Trying to get the truth from our President will be about as transparent as his college grades from Colombia.

He is feeding us a crock and I feel we should ban sales of all crock pots to prevent bombings. Oh, and don't forget those back packs.

I was told the bombers walked across the Mexican border. Don't know for sure because I think their records are sealed.

Why would Obama buy 1.6 billion Bullets for DHS?
DHS is buying the ammunition to kill Americans. 1.2 billion bullets are .223.

With that in mind the gun I recommend is the .223 If you use it in a defensive mode then it will probably be used against agents of DHS. They will have plenty of .223 ammunition

But I recommend running and hiding. Even if they come to take your guns let them take them. If you don't they might just take your life because that is why they are packing the .223 and other assorted deadly bullets. If you survive you can live to fight another day. The bullets are not for target practice and the sniper rounds are not for friendly persuasion when they come to your neighborhood.

Be safe, offer them food and poison it.

OBAMA IS TO AMERICA AS
Obama is to America as Hitler was to the Jews. Is it safe?

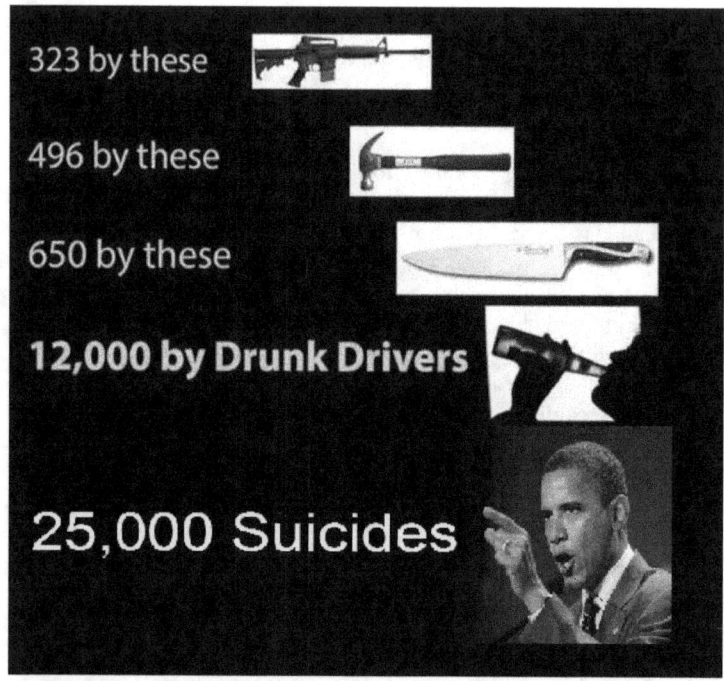

323 by these

496 by these

650 by these

12,000 by Drunk Drivers

25,000 Suicides

Obama taking executive action on guns after Senate vote - BUT WHAT ABOUT THE PEOPLE
Funny they don't talk about people and their guns in Boston after the Marathon bombing and the terrorist chase in neighborhoods.

I'll bet everyone who had a gun, had it loaded and ready, and those who didn't, wish they had one.

People in government are we are going to see more of what happened in Boston.

How do they expect us to protect ourselves????
THEY DON'T.

WISDOM
Wisdom is not knowing all the answers...it's knowing how to seek the truth. If that is true then Liberals have no wisdom.

EVERY TIME I THINK ABOUT IT...

Think about Benghazi for a moment. I'm sure the president knew the threats to the potential whistle blowers was coming from the Whitehouse and who was making the threats. With great confidence I would say Obama knew all about the cover up even though he doesn't go do security briefings. Now let's suppose he didn't know about it. Actually that is worse. We have a man that is attacking multiple countries with Iran, North Korea and now Syria on his top ten hit list. He says he knows Korea is going to nuke us and Syria has used chemical warfare. BUT he doesn't even know what is happening in the White House. IF that is true he needs to be removed from office.

So Obama wants to take our guns away from us, but he has armed Mexico Drug cartels with 5000 automatic weapons, if that is really the total. Now those same weapons are killing Americans. He has armed Al Qaeda in Libya, Egypt and Syria and that has also led to the death of Americans and Christians. He says God has blessed abortions. Now it is treason to be a Christian in the military. He is appointing a man to a position that has bankrupted another government agency and that same appointee says white people are racist and shouldn't serve in government.

I think we should keep our guns until we have an accounting for where all the weapons he has giving for all these wars. And I can save a lot of foreign aid. If we must accept same sex marriage and churches are forced to marry them (does anybody remember something called freedom of religion?), then I think it appropriate that Obama demand all foreign countries have their leaders endorse same sex marriage, women's equal rights, and give Christians the same rights as guaranteed by our constitution even though the denies those same rights to Christians in America. When leaders like Morsi come out in public to guarantee those rights then we will give them aid, otherwise not one penny.

He has united America like a love fest with the KKK and Black Panthers. The Civil War created lest unrest than Obama.

I laugh until I cry every time I think about how he won the Noble Peace Prize.

Did I miss anything?

New Symbol for Obama and his Liberal "gang"

WHAT IS REALLY KILLING AMERICANS
Is it this?

Or is it this

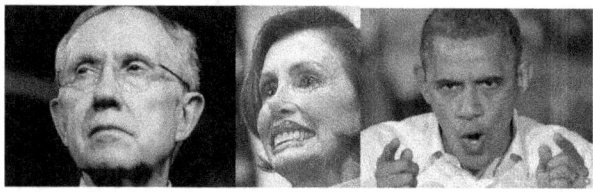

The same thing happening in the Middle-East has arrived in America and it's not the guns. It's the radical government elected by people without common sense or faith.

Without Faith there is no hope.

Without Hope there is no tomorrow.

For most Americans, under Obama, tomorrow is here.

Obama, Reid, Pelosi, Weinstein, Boxer, and Biden stand firmly behind this symbol.

They say to talk about Christianity in the military is TREASON.

WHITE'S SHOULD BE EXCLUDED FROM THE DEMOCRATIC PROCESS – MEL WATTS
Mychal Massie,

I hate to get into race but I'm white. What difference does it really make unless I get into hate or against faith. We must defend our faith. Mychal, if you or Cain ran for president I would vote for you. Cain had common sense solutions I still like and would vote for. I would like to see him come back.

And about the killing all over America; it has become an epidemic. The gun didn't kill those people our government did. Why? Faith. For example; treason for talking about faith? Don't we still have freedom of speech or is it another of our rights written away by Obama with his daily executive orders?

Without Faith, there is no hope.

Without Hope, there is no tomorrow.

Tomorrow is here and represented by the Liberals in our Government.

I'd have to say Mel Watt is definitely a racist. He sure has something against white people.

What if we said most blacks won't vote for a white person so they should be excluded from the democratic process. That is what Mel said.

Check it on Google: Obama housing nominee: Most white people won't vote for black candidate, should be excluded from 'democratic process'

RUN FOR PRESIDENT

Mychal,

You run for president you have my vote. BUT you probably won't win because you have too much common sense and people hate the truth. Suppose I have cancer and you lie to me. I die. Tell me the truth and I just might be cured. Maybe painful but I can recover. America needs the truth.

FROM MYCHAL:

Joe...I'll be writing on this very appointment early next week...

...I wouldn't run for dinner much less public office...

LAST NIGHT WAS...

(Explanation: May3rd in Texas is usually around 80 degrees, with lows in the 70's. Last night it was in the low 40's a record I think, so I sent this to my friends)

Last Night was brought to you by Global Warming.

Scientist have proven that once upon a time the Sahara Desert was a lush tropical jungle. So to the amazing, resourceful and intelligent Al Gore I ask, how many SUV's did it take to turn that lush tropical paradise into a desert?

And I would like someone to tell me; if the North Pole melted overnight how high would the seas rise around the world? I'm sure Big Al knows.

ENEMIES OF THE STATE?

Actually they are defending themselves from attack. Do they really look like they are enemies combatants? Do you really think a small boy, an old man and a pregnant woman are going to terrorize and overthrow the government.

Do you want to see the real enemy combatants?

Simpson, Boxer, Biden, Weinstein, Reid, Pelosi and the terrorist leader; Obama. And the other 530.

QUESTIONS AVOIDED
You will learn with wisdom that when people avoid questions or refuse to answer questions pointed at them, or give answers not related to the questions, are really already lying and guilty. Obama, Clinton and Holder refuse to answer the questions, so they are…. Remember, Americans died.

HEY, IT'S ADAM AND
Hey, it's Adam and Eve, not Adam and Steve.
Good news Jason Collins has just been selected to the "Gay Professional Hall of Fame." Many of his fellow players said, "I'll back him up but I just don't want to stand in front of him." Most denied Collins poked around in their business.

CHRISTIAN?
I've always considered blacks as truly Christian. Probably at least 80 percent follow Gods laws.
So it is strange that our president is for abortion, changing the Bible to concur with his demands today and for same sex marriage. Actually the president has no Christian values. In the end of days it is said the people and the leaders would do just that before the last days. Obama is that man and everybody knows it. So why did 97 percent of all blacks vote for Obama. Are only three percent of blacks Christian? After all Obama has proven he is not a man of God. So to all the Christian people who voted for Obama I want you to know that God is watching and I welcome you to the end of time.

WHAT SCARES ME
You know it is bad if Obama knows about the Gun Running, AP wiretapping, the IRS and Benghazi . Obama believes he is right and so did Nixon. BUT there is something worse than knowing what is being done and that is; if Obama knows nothing about what is being done around him. America needs a man who knows what is happening. Obama is not that man. The only differences between Obama and Nixon is the scale at which Obama is undermining American freedom and the fact Americans died over Obama's incompetence. Not only Benghazi but also Seal Team 6.

LATEST NEWS BROADCAST ABOUT OBAMA'S WORK ETHIC REPORT: OBAMA SPENT TWICE AS MUCH TIME ON VACATION/GOLF AS ECONOMY

By Wynton Hall, Breitbart.com

He played a thousand hours and worked 500. Look at the Brightside. Think how much damage he could have done if he had worked that other thousand hours.

LETTER TO MYCHAL MASSIE

First let me say I'm against Affirmative Actions, because I believe blacks are equal to whites. Those that believe in Affirmative Action make the statement which really says blacks are inferior and we must give them extra to be equal. I don't believe that is necessary

Obamacare is illegal and proven when certain groups are exempt while other will be given the burden of paying. Middle class America are the serfs deemed responsible for paying for Obamacare. Pelosi showed it discriminated when she said, "We must pass Obama Care so will have time to read it and see what is in it." The law should apply to all not just the serfs.

DO YOU BELIEVE IN GOD?

In the last week a man has said, "God Bless Planned Parenthood. I promise to keep the doors open for abortion." Did you know more black people percentage wise, have abortions that any other ethnic group? Could that be a movement toward genocide? And in the last few weeks to talk about Christianity in the military could bring a court martial for TREASON. From what I see happening to Obama it is obvious God is watching.

Why was a stand down order called in Benghazi? The only reason would be to protect the Muslim Brotherhood. American lives were obviously not important. Watergate? What about Holder and the AP? Nixon only did it in one building. And now the IRS. I'm curious. What was the percentage of Whites audited and how many auditors were white? I'm not racist I'm just curious. If I told you what the IRS did to me for what I wrote, it would curl the hair on your head even if you are bald.

Our country built on God has shoved him out. No different than when Moses tried to lead his people to the promised land. What did God do? He made them wander in the wilderness. Americans are in the wilderness now and running out of time.

Remember God is watching....

MEL WATTS NEEDS TO GO BACK TO SCHOOL

Mel it's time to go back to high school for Math 101.

You said, "Most white people won't vote for black candidates." Let's see, first of all I accuse you of making a blatant racist statement.

Numbers don't' lie. So who voted for Obama percentage wise?

97 to 3 Blacks voting for Obama

43 to 57 Whites voting against Obama

Now Mr. Watts who really votes along racist lines?

WISDOM

I was in an argument with a Liberal friend who reminds me of adults when I was a kid. Their response is just because. You know the AP, IRS, Benghazi, Obama Careless, etc. They are all just because. I was telling this friend of mine that government lacked "wisdom" and that was the problem with the country. They may be intelligent but they have no wisdom.

He had that "just because" look in his face when he retorted, "I have all my wisdom."

I continued on but in the back of my mind I kept thinking about what he had just said. It was like he would have lost "wisdom" like car keys or something. Finally I said, "What do you mean you have all your wisdom?"

He beamed when he touched both sides of his jaws and proudly said, "I'm the only one in my family that still has all four of his wisdom teeth.

OH, GOD, please help us…

WHAT ABOUT MURDER CHARGES FOR HOLDER?

What about murder charges for Holder and his gun running with Mexican Drug Cartels? I guess that has also been swept under the table. I wonder how much money he made? I guess Americans paid for it again, including death like Benghazi.

LANCE ARMSTRONG AND…

It is really sad what Lance Armstrong did for Tour de France. He can't really justify the drugs because everybody else took them. Even the rider that pointed the finger at Lance said, "Everybody did it." If that is true did Lance really cheat? But as long as we are on this issue why did America become so involved is prosecuting Lance. Shouldn't France take care of their business? Oh, yeah, they couldn't in WWII either; it was a gun control issue thing. So many years had passed they should have let the issue with Lance go. I swear those guys would play with a dead dog in the road if you'd let them. Really makes you lose interest in bike racing.

The American group that attacked Lance Armstrong so tenaciously was Travis Tygart and his staff at the USADA. I wish we could get them to go after Congress and Obama. Sorry I digress. If we go after Lance then we need to attack Barry Bonds, Mark McGuire, and Sammy Sosa for the same reasons. Of course professional baseball doesn't monitor. Why isn't Tygart chasing them down? Isn't it the same thing as Lance? We should mark their victory with the letters "DI" next to their name for Drug Induced. We're going to punish a French team but not American teams? We attack drugs in other countries, not here. Drugs are like the Iraq border and our American border, we want to make sure nobody crosses the Iraq border but "come on over" if you want to cross our border and we'll even feed you and give you medical care. Congress's answer is the same my parents gave me?…Just because! I want Travis Tygart and his staff at the USADA to take the homerun championship away from them.

Then I think of Pete Rose; Mr. Baseball. Why is he not in the "Hall of Fame?" He bet on his own team to win. Pete Rose didn't take drugs; he didn't cheat. He should be inducted into Baseball's Hall of Fame today, now!! Is that justice? It's ludicrous and to me illegal, but then again they don't' prosecute illegal aliens. I understand it is Politically Incorrect to call them illegal aliens but that is what they are. Actually we need politically incorrectness to return. More truth in being politically incorrect, than wanting to tongue-lash the person you're talking about but it is politically incorrect. Instead of telling him he is not very nice, you really need to say the truth and say, "You're an asshole."

Since we've settled that I want Tyler Tygart to check another group for drug use; the people who award the Pulitzer Prize for Peace. Whoever voted for Obama should never be allowed to serve in an intelligent decision making capacity for the rest of their life. When they voted they were obviously on drugs. They are the kind that would give Satan the "Number One Christian of the Year Award." Awards are earned. Obama didn't earn the Nobel Peace Prize and has shown he doesn't deserve it. He could win the award for *Liar of the Year, Number one American Assassin, Worst President in History, Mostly Likely to Help the KKK Return, Non-Transparent Government, Racial Civil War, Mr. War Monger, Muslim Brotherhood Award of the Year, and Mr. Incompetence*...BUT NEVER an award for Peace.

If Lance Armstrong's Tour de France awards are taken away, then the Pulitzer group should restore our confidence in their decision making and take away Obama's Peace Prize award.

NEW FORESTS TO FILL AMERICA IN THE NEXT YEAR

I can replenish all the forests in America in three years. Keep Obama, Holder and Clinton in office. Have all three make daily detailed televised reports to America. Then all we need to do is turn all three into Pinocchio.

SAVE THE ECONOMY

I believe in free trade but I think the government should be exempt. For example the American company that made our military's top secret helicopters sent the secret components to China to be made. Funny thing happened. Suddenly China has a helicopter just like us.

Free trade is okay except when it comes to the government. One hundred percent of every item our government purchases should be American made. Our government is exempt from free trade and for good reason. Let our politicians show a little wisdom and I don't mean their teeth.

OBAMA HAS CONFIDENCE

It's easy to have confidence when you don't know what you're doing. Obama says he has total confidence in Holder. The Muslim Brotherhood has the same thing to say about Obama.

Like America, Jesus had total confidence in Judas Iscariot. Look where that got Jesus. America is headed for the same destination.

EXPLAIN TO ME HOW WE KNOW

We know everything about what is happening in the world except what is happening in the United States of America. We know exactly what is happening in North Korea, Iran, Syria, Iraq, Egypt and Libya. Ironically we have no idea what is happening on our borders, or the gun running with drug cartel by our own government, or the truth about the Benghazi Massacre, AP wiretapping by Holder, and the IRS scandal. Are the Bill of Rights and Constitution safe with them? As safe as our borders. The question I want to ask is has anybody, including Obama told the truth?

Obama's been Lying

When Obama ordered a stand down
The military returned a frown.
His plan didn't work.
The man is a slimy jerk.
A "stand down" in Benghazi on one understood.
But Obama made a secret promise to his Muslim brotherhood.
"I'll protect you and let Americans die.
No problem, I'll just tell more lies."
Anyone who objects to my plan
I'll have the IRS enforce my stand.
When brave men in Benghazi died
Obama and his men continued spreading more lies.

I will make the IRS let my brother slide
They will audit Conservatives, as to who I'll decide.
So Lois Lerner approved the illegal application
For his brother's "Barack H Obama Foundation."
Obama said, "Now my brother is free
To go on a Liberal American Spending spree."
I'll tax the conservatives with much haste
So Liberals can continue to spend and waste.

Shades of Nixon and Watergate
Holder believes what he does is beyond debate.
I'm a gun runner, I'll pass the order
No one can protect the border
He decided to give arms to Mexican Cartels
Making everybody promise not to tell
I'll destroy the Constitution using reason.
Holder master of lies and crime, should be tried for treason.
He decided to give arms to Mexican Cartels
Making everybody promise not to tell

Obama is now America's dictator
But Americans will pay later.
Obama wants to be elected again,
But if you're Christian that would be a sin.
He said, "Third time is a charm."
It would bring America unmitigated harm.
Now God in the military is "Treason!"
And Obama is the reason.
Would you keep a man who lies?

When he cares nothing about Americans who die.
So when Obama is once again nothing but dust
America will return to "In God We Trust."

MUSLIM BROTHERHOOD SO HAPPY WITH OBAMA
The Muslim Brotherhood sent a thank you note to Obama for leaving the borders open and enabling them to insert super cells into America. They also thanked him for the stand down order he had promised them in Benghazi. The Muslim Brotherhood also gave him his official Muslim name: Obama bin Lyin'.

IRS THREATS
I'm a member of the Tea Party and I truly believe I was targeted because of my affiliation with them and because of what I wrote. Two books "Words That Don't Offend Liberals," and "Meandering Scribbles of an Old Fart." In an effort to make people aware of what our government was doing wrong the IRS went back and audited my 2006 and 2007. They disallowed my rental property for no reason and said I owed 1500, and when I found hospital bills I forgot to deduct and would have given me a refund they threatened me and said they would continue an audit over each item for another month. It was easier to pay and when I did they immediately told me I was going to be audited for 2007. Same thing. I consider that extortion and blackmail. I can't afford to fight them. Their threats put me in the hospital.
Each year they send me an additional bill for $1500 to $2000. When I turned in 2011 with a refund for $4000 using deductions for a Christian movie I was making they immediately said I owed $6000 for 2010. AND what was the difference? An additional $2000.
Instead of the approximately $10,000 they have made me pay I should really be getting back about six to eight thousand dollars. Between what I paid and what I should have gotten back from the IRS there is more than a $15000 difference.

PROPOSED AMENDMENTS TO THE CONSTITUTION
Proposed Amendments to the Constitution of the United States of America

1. Government expenses will not exceed taxes collected. If money is overspent the first cuts will be the payroll to Congress and all political workers.

2. No entitlements. All government retirements will be based on Social Security. Government retirement will be more than SS but not start until the same retirement age. The same applies for Congressmen with the added clause that for every dollar they earn it will be deducted from their monthly retirement.

3. There will be no foreign aid to any country and no studies or money wasted on any items such as the sex orientation of snails. All waste graft and corruption will be grounds for removal from office. No foreign student loans unless their country makes the same offer to Americans. Illegal alien laws here will be the same as those applied to illegal aliens in Mexico.

4. Identification is required for purchases and when obtaining a job so Voter Identification will be required. Voting will be done from home or business computers using purchasing ID as in stores. It will be required to have a password, SS and state driver's license. Voting from other locations with the same ID will be voided. If you do not vote in elections a $200 fee will be assessed on your Income Tax. Also, no applications will make reference to race. Everyone applying for a job is an American or an illegal alien which means they cannot apply for a job.

5. If we don't even know what is going on in the WH how do we know what is going on in other countries where we are fighting wars. With that in mind there is no need to fight wars because it seems like the terrorists and "enemy combatants" are all in Washington DC so all servicemen will be brought home. We only defend our allies.
EXPLANATION:
Think about it; why did we attack Iraq to "help," but not Somali? Because there was no oil. If we fight a war we will no longer be MIA but rather PIA. That is Paid in Advance. The country will pay all expenses and our soldiers will be paid one million per year. No assistance will be given to countries that kill Americans. We will take Syria for example: The freedom fighters, Sunni and Shiites are now fighting among themselves. And they are probably the same weapons (most likely Holder gave them) that killed our brave men in Libya. Before Obama took office American Christians could travel in Syria, Egypt and Libya without fear of being killed. Now with Obama's help the Muslim Brotherhood is in control and no one is safe as the freedom fighters are now killing themselves. And McCain should be ashamed. The picture of his standing next to the men who probably assisted in the murders of Americans in Benghazi is disgraceful. He has no business being their when America is in such turmoil. The picture of him standing next to him reminds me of Jane Fonda chortling with the North Vietnamese. It is obvious from his picture he has idea as to what is happening there than Jane Fonda did in North Vietnam.

6. Total welfare will not exceed minimum wages. No food stamps as those on welfare will go to military bases to obtain necessary food. Welfare will not last more than two years. After that if they are permanently incapacitated they will be required to stay on a military base where they will received proper aid. People on welfare will not be allowed to vote; as it is a conflict of interest. If you want the right to vote then find a job and work for it. Welfare was never meant to be a job description. We are now breeding people directly to welfare.

7. Lobbyists will be outlawed. Laws will be what are good for "the people." If the laws are good for the people then there is no need for lobbyists.

8. To pass a bill all members of Congress must be present. An outside auditor will read the bill make a simple 20 question true or false test. If any member of Congress cannot make 80 or higher the bill cannot be voted on. Member of Congress will be tested regularly and randomly for drugs and alcohol. Anyone who

is drunk or on drugs will be removed from office and their state will be required to send a new representative.

9. Tax increases must be ratified by two-thirds of Congress and the states. The IRS will audit all green companies that filed bankruptcy. Under Obama the government has spent 1.6 trillion more each year than taxes collected. The six trillion overspent will have a complete audit and any overcharges or theft found will be back charged three times the amount charged to our government. An overcharge for an item is when the charge exceeds three times the local retail price for said items.

10. Free trade is fine but every item purchased by our government will be 100% made in America (parts and Labor). Think about it; in WWII were we ordering parts from Germany and Japan? Any company that is found to do otherwise will obtain no more government contracts ever!!

Being a Christian in the military is not treason. The person who said that obviously has no concept of the Bill of Rights and freedom of speech. He will be demoted to a position where he will no longer make any decisions. I want charges of murder and gun-running filed against Holder and negligent homicide against Obama and Hilary for Benghazi. Every person involved with the IRS scandal will be terminated without any retirement.

I have been threatened, blackmailed and extorted by the IRS for two books I wrote.

I want the company that had China make parts for out top secret helicopters to be tried for treason and stupidity. They will never obtain a job from our government again.

Criminal actions will be taken against those that gave away cell phones. It was a cell phone for votes and illegal. Those that created the project and distributed the phones will refund the government for said expenses and all phones will be terminated. If people want a phone they need to purchase it. A job will usually take care of such items. America needs to create and provide jobs for people not welfare. The phones were in reality nothing more than buying votes which is illegal.

Also Bush, Rumsfeld and Chaney sent a C-130 with 20 billion in cash to spur the Iraq economy. They lost 9 billion. The money cannot be found. Not acceptable. I demand a full investigation and since it was a time of war the last person to touch the money goes to prison for treason and it will be for life with no chance of parole.

Obama needs to be tried for stupidity and not allowed to go on any more vacations.

Killing of Americans in foreign countries using drones is murder. They must be extradited and have charges brought against them in an American court of law. Using drones is simply murder and not justice. AND who decided they were guilty and killed them? What were the charges dictating assassination? I'm sure Holder and Obama know nothing about it. They were driving the car and as such are just as guilty.

Guantanamo? What ever happened to justice? Shouldn't we aspire to have foreigners enforce the same laws we so proudly represent? That includes a speedy trial. Now we hear the men in Guantanamo can be kept indefinitely. That is un-American and makes no sense. Show the world we believe in justice. It they are in Guantanamo then there is evidence. Have trials immediately. Show the evidence in court. There will be enough to find them guilty and put them in prison. It there is not enough evidence then they must be set free. Or are we treating them the same way the IRS, Holder and Obama treat Christians in America. Let's aspire to higher ideals or do we have them anymore?

What Price Liberty?

Your rights are one thing but what price are you willing to pay to save your liberty?

Benghazi? The IRS? The AP? Gun Running by our government on our borders that includes murder? To talk about Christianity in the Military can be construed to be treason. Today we learn they monitor Verizon.

They kill Americans with drones.

So I ask, "What price Liberty?" Before you answer be careful what you say about Obama. There just might be a drone coming to a neighborhood near you.

RATTLESNAKE LOGIC; AUTHOR UNKNOWN

The government controlled news media will spend months trying to determine why the Muslim men killed and maimed all of those Americans in Boston. They have been protecting the real reason why we let another bunch of Muslims kill our Ambassador and three other Americans in Libya for nearly eight months. They spend countless hours wondering exactly what Americans did to make these outstanding friends so angry with us. Most Americans really want to know why these obvious terrorists were not arrested before they killed these people. The media will spend months boring us with stories asking why these home grown radicals did what they did and wonder about how they could live among us and still hate us.

Well in Texas and especially west Texas where I was raised we have rattlesnakes. We have killed rattlesnakes on the front porch. We have killed rattlesnake on the back porch. We have killed rattlesnakes in the barn, in the shop and on the driveway. We kill every rattlesnake we encounter. We kill rattlesnakes because a rattlesnake will bite you and inflict you with poison. We don't stop to wonder why a rattlesnake will bite us. It will bite us because it is a rattlesnake and that is what rattlesnakes do. We don't try to reason with a rattlesnake…We just kill it.

We don't ever try to get to know the rattlesnake better so that we can find a way to live with the rattlesnakes and convince them not to bite us. We just kill them. We don't quiz a rattlesnake to see if I can find out where the other snakes are because (a) It won't tell you (b) We already know that they live on our place. We just kill the rattlesnake and move on to the next one. We don't look for ways that we might be able to change the rattlesnake to a non-poisonous rat snake. We just kill it. On occasion we kill a rat snake, because we thought it was a rattlesnake at the time. Also, we know that for every rattlesnake that we kill, two more lurk out there somewhere. We know that we will never be able to rid our place of rattlesnakes. Do we fear them? No! Do we respect what they can do to us? Yes! And because of that respect we give them their fair justice. We kill them. Maybe as a country we should give more credit to the Terrorists just being a rattlesnake! Hmmm…What is the difference between Terrorists and our Congress?

TIME FOR A CHANGE

Only One Hope For Change

Only one thing can beat Obama's Mickey Mouse organization. Another Mickey Mouse and it's ME! I have what it takes to run Congress another Mickey Mouse organization. Vote for me because if I do nothing for my first four years it will be more than Obama did in his first four years. And I can always blame him.

IT'S TIME FOR A CHANGE

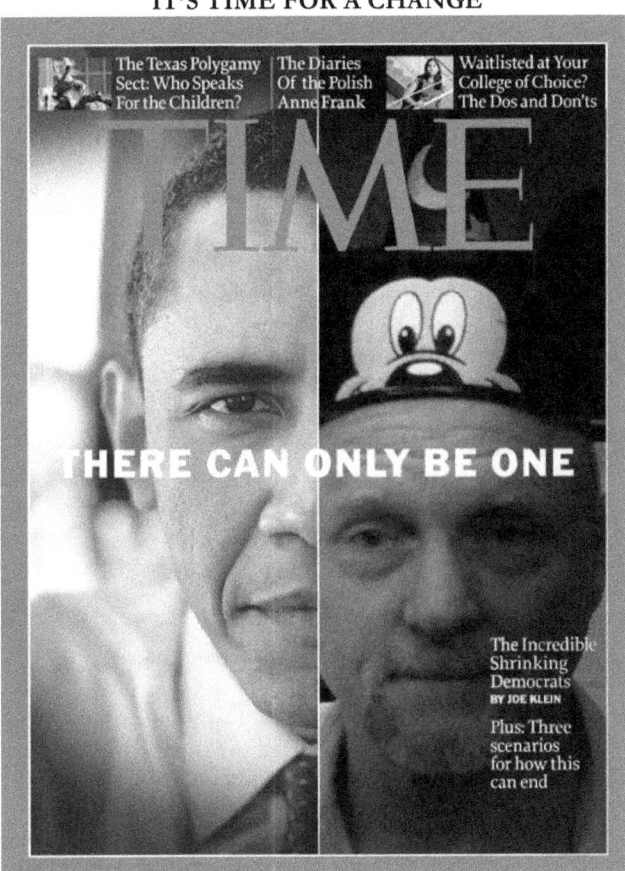

Let me bring you Hope and Change. I Hope you elect me so I can Change America back to the way it used to be.

Sherrod Brown Wants to Pay the Student Loans

Are you paying attention to what is really going on? I didn't get loans for my kids because I couldn't afford it. Those loans that are owed need to be paid back.

All you can think about is giving away more money. That is not the answer. They need good jobs for the education and the ability to pay them off. If there is more than 1.1 trillion in loans I want to know who approved the loans.

Make sure they have a job. That is common sense, something you seem to be sorely lacking. Your concept makes it where I will be paying the loan off. Not acceptable. I didn't borrow the money. Do you always give away others people's money?

Take away your house and money to pay the loans off. Or better yet why not all the family nepotism money earned from all the political figures and use that to pay the loans and interest off before you ask me to give away my hard earned money. Have the IRS audit the businesses you gave trillions and use that money to pay the loans off. Audit Liberals.

Speed Adjustor

I don't break the law when I speed, I'm just a speed adjustor for safety. You see there are two very good reasons to go 110 mph than 55mph. There are two reasons it is really a lot safer. Number one you will be on the road half the time. Second at that speed you will be past the accident you would have had.

It's funny listening to Liberals

It's funny listening to Liberals. Well not really. They don't want anybody to have guns but a Liberal Democrat Party leader said wants to shoot members of the NRA calling them terrorists. A supporter of Harry Reid, journalism professor Christopher Swindell argued that the National Rifle Association "advocates armed rebellion against the duly elected government of the United States of America." Then defiantly he added, "The NRA is guilty of "treason and worthy of the firing squad." I guess if he shot you , then you could always say you got "Swindelled" by a Liberal. Seriously, these are the people who want to take our guns away and also kill you. I am curious has anyone checked to see if any of these mass killers are Liberals? Or, God (Allah) forbid, maybe even Islamic fundamentalists? Of course that could never be.

What was that we said as kids? Takes one to know one. Maybe they want guns removed because they know what they would do with guns. A liberal friend of mine said all guns should be taken away but when I asked him if he had a gun he said with a touch of arrogance, "Well, yes but that is different." Liberals are out of control.

Recently it has been known if you talk about God in the military you are committing treason. To say anything about radical Islam it is offensive and you can be tried in court. To speak against same sex marriage makes you homophobic. Homosexuals have the right to demand you do what they say but you are denied freedom of speech to express your opinion against them. The DOJ demands you accept and even attend their functions but it is illegal for you to wear a cross. It seems being a Christian has become a crime.

The Senate voted not to approve the gun control demands issued by the United Nations but Kerry says he will sign it like he is some God or something. Kerry is a supporter of everything un-American, everything bad, and everything evil. Kerry, Holder, Obama, Pelosi, Boxer and Feinstein are living proof that the Bill of Rights is dead. The people mentioned are the death of freedom and America. If you are a Christian and you have a clear conscious then you can no longer vote for Liberals or Democrats and probably not any Republicans. A vote for them is a vote against God and morality. All of them are Un-American. Before you vote ask yourself, are you willing to sell your soul for a cell phone? Many people already have.

What will those politicians, including Kerry who we didn't elect, do for Americans? Think Benghazi. What will they do for Christians? Think Benghazi.

Prayer in schools was eliminated because one person was offended. Well I'm offended. It's time to put prayer, the Ten Commandments, the American Flag and the Pledge of Allegiance back in our schools and back in the public eye. It is time for Christians to be offended. As a Christian if you are not angry and not ready to fight back, and still want to vote Liberal, then you might as well stop going to church. It is time for Christians to rise up and fight. For once don't think Black, Brown or White; think Christian brothers, Christian values. UNITE! It's time to take America back.

If you're a Christian and you disagree with me I just want you to know that Obama and Holder want to invite you to the Coliseum for dinner and entertainment where you will be entertained by a group of lions.

God help us all before it is too late.

Obama Careless

Your new tax form for 2013 will include a line where you are to put your health insurance policy number. If you don't have a number the IRS will penalize you between 1000 and 2000 dollars for each month you didn't have insurance. What a surprise. Oh, Congress and certain groups are exempt.

I'm going to use the same code on my form the IRS uses; 666. Then when they call me in I'm going to take the fifth and it won't be a bottle of booze. If he IRS can lie and steal and take the fifth I should at least be able to take the fifth.

The Real Traitor

Mikey Weinstein want to make it treason for soldiers to talk about Christianity in the military. It's Weinstein who should be accused of treason and denying freedom of speech. Mickey is an attorney for the "Military Religious Freedom Foundation." He is what is called a hypocrite. He expects his demands be met that Christians not be able to talk freely. Ironically he wants you to give him the rights that he denies Christians. Christians think people should talk freely. What if I start the Military Religious Christian Foundation demanding that people who believe in nothing have no right to talk or demand thing of Christians and to do so is treason. It's the same thing Mickey Mouth is doing to Christians. Hitler would love Mikey. The only difference between him and Christians is that Christians believe in freedom of speech and God and Country. Mickey believes in none of that.

NSA I have a common sense question

Gen Keith Alexander and Obama defend snooping. Okay. They want security to prevent another 911. Okay. So let's say you have a security system at home. What happens when you leave the backdoor unlocked. They don't need to break in they just walk in. Hmmm, walk in. Common sense you would close the back door.

The only thing these tow lack is common sense. If security is so important and so critical, then why are the borders left unprotected? And why are mosques and Muslims exempt from snooping? Why? Because everything they say is a lie. All of them are lying or they are stupid. I'm sure it is both.

They aren't protecting us from them they are protecting them so they can take us. It's the only commons sense answer.

Obama while you sequester America why not do that to your wife and quit going on so many trips and three-thousand dollar a night hotels.

Do my comments qualify me for a drone?

The Problem with the Government

I figured out what is wrong with America. How can you run a country when all you have are Weiner-Holders and Boehners?

Is It Safe?

Let's say you have the best security system money can buy for your house. And the best lock systems on all of your doors and windows. Each night before you go to sleep you check the security; everything is locked. You are so safe you don't need to worry and you know it. You lock the doors and get ready for bed but your trusty dog, Liberal, whines and barks. He wants to be able to go in the back yard to do his business. So…you unlock the back door and turn off the security. Nothing can happen to you because you have locked all the windows and the front door. You aren't worried even though the local law has warned that gangs are breaking into houses almost every night and they like to come through the back of the house. But you have the best system not to mention the unloaded 45 next to your bed. Just to make Liberal happy you even crack the door so he can go through unhindered. A few hours later you are awakened to a noise and you see two men in the living room approaching your open bedroom door. They have guns. You grab yours but you remember the bullets in the bathroom. When you run to the bathroom you slip on something wet and fall on the floor and what is when you see Liberal who has just peed all over the floor. The dumb Liberal is whining and hiding and looking to you for help. It's too late; Liberals whining has just killed you. And after that gang kills like they did our border guards you might he unhappy to learn that old Liberal crawled over and licked your killer's hand.

That my friends is America today. For a moment I would like you to think. NSA is monitoring all Americans for safety and security. Why? Really ask yourself, "Why?" The border, our back door, is wide open. The only thing that could be worse is if you left weapons for the intruders. OH, MY GOD! That is what Holder did with the automatic weapons for the Mexican Drug cartels. And they have already killed Americans with the weapons Holder gave them. Now ask yourself this, "Why did Holder to such a thing?" Really why did he do it? I want him to tell us. And what kind of plan did he have to monitor it? He lost all the weapons and has no idea what happened. He gave criminals the type of weapons that killed fellow Americans in theaters and schools. His "Fast and Furious" distributed guns that kill our children and Americans trying to protect our borders. What is the solution? Take away the guns? No it is to arm yourself so you can protect your family from law breakers like Obama and Holder. Hooray for Katee Sackhoff, who thinks we should know how to control guns. If you haven't tweeted your support to her you should do so now.

So what is the real danger to America? Al Qaeda? The Taliban? No there are three immensely more dangers to America. The dog Liberal that comes in three varieties; the Executive, Legislative and Judicial branches of the United States of America government. NSA is proof our leaders are afraid of us, the true Americans.

Obama promotes people to their level of incompetence or he is recruiting people to take over the country. NONE of them care about our heritage, freedoms or the Constitution. I call it treason. But for a moment let's digress back to incompetence. How many remember Hanoi Jane? That is the Jane Fonda who went to North Vietnam and stabbed our soldiers in the back in an effort to stop the war. Guess who supported her (I have a picture) and I believe helped finance her. John Kerry. Yeah, that's right he was just as bad and could have been called Hanoi John, but you can just call him Syria John, or Egypt John now that I mention Egypt we'll just call Kerry "the Mummy." You know, dried up dead of no real use. So Obama promoted him to America's leader at the UN where he promptly signed a bill that would allow the UN to take our guns. What an American. Where is Benedict Arnold when you need him? Okay, back to the Mummy. A few days ago Egypt's leader Morsi talked about war and attacking Israel and America. I guess he generated some balls with the 200 million in jets Obama gave him. Last week the Mummy said Egypt was such a shining example of freedom that he gave Egypt 1.3 billion dollars. Hey it makes it easier to finance the war against America. The Mummy, what an American!

Now Obama wants to send surface to air missiles to Syria and arm the rebels who are busy killing each other over their personal Jihad. I bet he already sent them. To top it off John McCain went to Syria so he could promote himself by taking pictures with terrorists that probably killed our men in Benghazi. The picture reminded me of Hanoi Jane. Now we can call McCain; Syria John. A few days after McCain left Syria, those men and their leaders demanded that Christians leave Syria or they would be killed.

Why such a great concern for monitoring Americans? Or should I say really monitoring conservative Christians that believe in traditional marriage? Why no interest in guarding the borders? Why buy so many bullets. And if you are against weapons why give them to the drug cartels and the Islamic Brotherhood in all the Middle Eastern countries? Think about this; the previous are the things they have been caught in wrong doing. I understand most criminals commit dozens of crimes before they are caught. Just think what we don't know yet!

If Snowden is guilty of treason what does that make Obama and Holder and Clinton? For gun running Holder and Obama are guilty of murder. For the drones killing Americans they are also guilty of murder. Now Holder presides over the investigation of the DOJ.

If you put all this together and analyze it here is what I think will happen. In the military Obama is kicking out all of those that refuse to kill Americans, Christians are being singles out as traitors. Obama himself leaked information that got Seal Team 6 killed. We now have a military that will follow Obama and kill Americans with no remorse. The Middle East rebels are now armed well enough to attack Israel. Obama won't help and we have no military. Point of interest: I understand that hundreds of surface-to-air missiles have been given to the Syrian rebels but there is no air force to be shot down. So why do they have them? They are being sent across the Mexican border to be used at a future date to shoot down commercial airliners.

At first I thought Obama was going to issue an executive order so he could be re-elected for a third term. I know it's against the law but law doesn't slow him down. I realized he wants to control the world and after what Kerry signed, Obama wants to be elected to the top position in the UN. With no military in America the UN can go door to door and take our weapons just like Obama and Holder have always dreamed would happen. Sound farfetched? Take a look at what he and holder have been doing the last four years. They truly believe they are above the law. And what are we going to do? The same thing as the frog in the frying pan. You can take a frog and drop it in hot water and it will jump out immediately. Same thing in cold water. But put that frog in normal water and turn up the heat. The frog will stay there until the heat kills it. So what are we going to do? Nothing!

You think they do surveillance on Muslims and their Mosques?

Think about it tonight and make sure you lock the back door and load your gun. But be careful, that old dog Liberal might just bite you in the ass.

Is it safe….?

I have seen evil

And it has arrived in America. On November 6th, 2012 America's soul died and this once great Christian nation died a slow and painful death. It was not so much Obama as it was the people. I always considered black people to be more devout Christians than those white Christians claiming to God fearers, but when black ministers preach to their congregations things like, "Damn America!...," or "All whites are going to hell!...," then they have lost their souls. Obama and nearly all Republican and Democrat politicians have bought and sold your soul. It now belongs to the Father of Evil. The purchase price for you to follow them? The death of your soul. Hope and Change has brought the death of America. Ironically the devout black Christians have sold their souls into slavery. So many whine about slavery and never were, but are now. They talk about how the "honkey" or "white trash" have done evil to the black man but he has done it to himself.

In many ways the death of America is similar to the path of Jews that were slaves to the Pharaoh and how Moses led them to the promised land but like the Jews the blacks of today continue to whine about something that never happened to them and failed see or understand the freedoms and wonderful gift of life Moses and God had given them. Instead, like the blacks of today, the Jews whined cried, demanded more and worshipped golden idols, not much different than welfare today, and eventually lost the Promised Land and their lives.

Did you ever wonder why Congress is determined to remove the Ten Commandments from all public buildings? First let me say that the Ten Commandments are good for all people, especially Americans. When you think about I believe the Commandments are good rules for any free Christian society. Whether you are Muslim, Hindu, atheist, agnostic or any other religion, the Ten Commandments are good rules for all people, but I'm afraid America no longer believes. Much like the Jews when Moses led them from Egypt. They were never really happy. Now 52% of Americans, and 96% of blacks, no longer want to follow God. Woe unto them, for eternal death hounds their footsteps waiting to collect the soul promised to them.

And why do non-Christian politicians want to take us away from these rules? First they no longer follow God and our savior, his son, Jesus Christ. Also the Ten Commandment, given to Moses for us, are to Congress, as sunlight is to a vampire.

The Ten Commandments are wonderful rules led us to the promised land, and as we fall away from them the promised land is being taken away and leading us into slavery again; all Americans!

From the beginning of time all empires have failed. There have been no exceptions. America is dead and the Obama and Congress are throwing the last shovel full of dirt in our mouth as they laugh about their conquest of America and a return to slavery. Slavery for all; black and white.

The good news is that Obama has finally come up with an option to solve America's financial woes. He was quoted as saying, "There is a very easy way to end all this arguing over the financial cliff we face. We will solve America's woes by making money the "Old fashion way." WE are going to print it. So vote for me. You will no longer need to vote and I will give you whatever you want. Just go to Benefits.gov and we, America, will give you whatever you need. Whitey will pay you for what you need." Did Obama really say that? Oh, My God! This is not fair to the poor white slaves.

I'm not a good Christian although I try. To all my Christian brothers, and remember color is blind, I say stick firmly to God. It will not be easy and always remember God is watching you and walks in your footsteps to save your soul.

Following the 2012 presidential election, former Massachusetts Gov. Mitt Romney and talk radio host Rush Limbaugh were savaged by top GOP leaders for saying President Barack Obama won because he promised to give people "free" stuff.

Romney accused the president of promising "gifts" to minorities, young voters, and women, while Limbaugh dubbed the president "Barack Claus" (a play on "Santa Claus").

"In a nation of children," said Limbaugh, "Santa Claus wins."

"It's a proven political strategy, which is giving a bunch of money to a group and, guess what, they'll vote for you," said Romney.

Romney continued:

What the president did is he gave them two things. One, he gave them a big gift on immigration with the DREAM Act amnesty program, which was obviously very, very popular with Hispanic voters, and then number two was Obamacare … For a home earning — let's say $30,000 a year — free health care, which is worth about $10,000 a year, I mean it's massive, it's huge. So this — he did two very popular things for the Hispanic community.

Needs More Vacations
Isn't it funny how Obama says he knew nothing and won't say a word about Benghazi, the AP or the IRS.

YET, the guy in the NBA who came out of the closet, had Obama's endorsement and word almost immediately. If he had done the same thing for Benghazi those men would still be alive.

It's one thing when a President screws up but if all this happen without his knowledge or even knowing it was going on then he really needs to be removed from office. But to do that, you would need to find where he is vacationing, and bring him back on a leash. Form wherever he is, just not operating the country he will tell you to cut back and save. Did you know that Obama's vacations have cost? Over seventeen million. Is that conserving and cutting back? I think most of it was for campaigning. He should pay for that not poor Americans.

From Freedom to Slavery Under Obama
The reverse of what happened to black people before the civil war, has happened under Obama as the Middle class workers of today have been converted back to slavery.

Katie Couric Concerned
Katie Couric asked an interesting question of her viewers, "Why do women drink?"

Seems the problem really concerned her. A really thought provoking question I mulled around until I came up with the answer and responded, "Because they're thirsty."

You have three choices
In the United States we currently have three choices. But there is a conditions to the choices. You can only choose one. Just one choice so be careful. It is similar to choosing whether you are a communist, socialist or a person that believes in freedom. So here are your choices; you can be a Democrat or a Republican or an American. Remember you can only choose one. Which are you?

Separation of Church and State
I believe in separation of church and state. Today the government or state is interfering with the church and religion. The IRS audits Christians for Obama and our government. The government wants to punish Christian churches when they talk politics and about the candidates but Obama's wife demands her church vote for them. A person talking about Christianity in our military is deemed to have committed treason. Something is very wrong with our leaders today and I mean both Republicans and Democrats.

Moses leading the Israelites from bondage to freedom and the Promised Land is much like America today. Obama and the people on welfare are much like those Israelites that complained to Moses that they didn't have enough so they made idols and demanded more for doing nothing. Angered at the demands God punished them by letting them wander in the wilderness for forty years. None of them saw the Promised Land. Now we give away cell phones to assure those on welfare will never reach the Promised Land. We have spurned God for the promises of food, housing, and cell phones. We have sold our souls and it might be too late to change things.

Welfare should never be a job description and it is not an entitlement.

Children are raised to aspire to their parents high or low ideals. I raced cars and my son became the race director for the Indy 500. Now people on welfare grow up to be even better than their parents, for example my son and parents on welfare. It seems the kids of parents on welfare have time to get even more than their parents including free phones and housing we the workers' pay for. They are making a deal with the Satan for the apple and Congress is Satan giving the apple to them for their soul.

Are you a Christian? Answer these questions.

1. Do you believe the Bible is wrong and should be amended per the demands of Obama, Pelosi and Reid?

2. Should the church provide people with birth control?

3. Should girls of any age be able to buy "morning after pills" without the consent of their parents? (The pill is another word for abortion and government control)

4. Should churches be forced to have insurance to pay for abortions?

5. Do you believe prayer should be eliminated in schools?

If you said "Yes" to any of those questions then you are not a Christian. You are eating the apple.

Should we punish the wealthy? Obama and his faithful followers, including the media, believe and demand this should be done.

For example this is what Obama believes will make America a better country.

A wealthy man had $100,000 in gold, five houses 25 goats and twenty horses. There were also four people complaining about their plight but they also refused to work. They had nothing so our government would step in and say this is wrong. They would disperse the wealth like this. Each of the four people would be given from our government $20,000 in gold, one house, five goats and four horses. All five would have the same thing. What would happen after the wealth was redistributed you would find the wealthy man working hard while the other four would continue to do nothing. Soon the four would have nothing because they would spend the money and not take care of the things they had. The hard work of the wealthy man would pay off as he tripled his assets through hard work. And what would the results be? Soon the government would demand redistribution from the wealthy man again.

This is much how it works today as we give more and more to those on welfare who do nothing to earn it. This is similar to student loans. Our government wants to take from those who work and sacrifice and just pay off student loans. That is not the solution. Encourage business and give those with student loans a job. Give them the ability to pay off those loans through hard work. Wasn't that what they intended to do with the degree? If you pay off the student loans now, then they will be the ones demanding more later. It will never end. Don't throw away money. Get them a job.

As another example suppose I lost my job and a friend of mine says he will help by giving me $4000 a month to pay my bills until I find a job where I am able to pay my bills again. So I start looking for a job for a few months but find nothing. I begin spending more time at home until I finally quit looking for a job. Now I work on my house, watch cable television all the time and go fishing anytime I desire. Then one day a man offers me a job for $4000 a month. I laugh at him and tell him, "I'm making that now for doing nothing. Why should I go to work when I can get the same thing for doing nothing?"

That is the welfare state of mind and what is slowly becoming the concept of America. In other words we are wondering in the wilderness.

To the 99% that continually demand the one percent be punished I ask you one question; Who gives you your paycheck?

Now Obama and the leaders of the Liberal party demand a redistribution of wealth. Ironically you will find the leaders of this move have no intention of redistribution of their wealth; only the wealth of others.

I believe in separation of Religion and State but when the State interferes with religion then they must rise against the tyranny Obama and others have perpetrated on the American people.

There are no longer prayers in school because someone was offended. Well I'm offended prayers have been removed. Based on that shouldn't we have prayers put back in schools?

We have been so busy protecting each individual's rights that we no longer have any rights.

Now it's treason to be a Christian in America's military. Do they know that our country was founded on Christian Principles? I don't think same sex marriage is right. I wish them no ill will and I seek no judgment against them but don't I still have a right to voice my opinion. There is something sacred and beautiful about traditional marriage. I believe in traditional marriage. For that I'm called homophobic. Gays and Lesbians say I have no right to day that. They deny me the same freedom of speech they demand they must have and that I must agree. I don't agree. To those that deny my freedom of speech and want to take away my rights as guaranteed by the Constitution let me remind you of a saying I heard as a child; "what goes around comes around."

Today the church must take a stand against those in Congress. It they are not voted out then it shows America is no longer a Christian nation. If they remain in office then God forgive us.

Ironic Morality

Isn't it ironic that the people making laws about morality are the most immoral people in the world. An now it seems that also includes the Supreme Court.

Justice should come from the nine
But it seems they have also lost their mind.

C.A.I.R. DOES NOT CARE

CAIR plans to for Islam to take over America. CAIR's founder Omar Ahmad, while claiming to be a moderate and patriotic American, reportedly told a group of Muslims in Northern California in 1998 that they are in America not to assimilate, but to help assert Islam's rule over the country.

"Islam isn't in America to be equal to any other faith, but to become dominant," a local reporter paraphrased him as saying. "The Quran, the Muslim book of scripture, should be the highest authority in America, and Islam the only accepted religion on Earth."

Read more at http://www.wnd.com/2013/05/muslims-lawsuit-silliness-judge-asked-for-dismissal/#0QEFfFxXlCldTZ2E.99

They want to outlaw the book Muslim Mafia. The book describes CAIR and its efforts to have Islam take over America. It seems our President endorses it fully and he is completely against Christianity.

If I could go back in time...

(08.19.13)

I would like to meet Jesus. It would be wonderful to see dinosaurs. It would be neat to see the meteor that hit in the Yucatan. And I would like to go back and take more ammunition to the men at the Alamo.

But there is one thing I would need to do first and that is go back to October, 1960. I would want to be in Kenya, East Africa where I would find Barack Hussein Obama. I would work toward making a friendly relationship and build a trust with the young man. Once I had his trust I would give him a month supply of condoms and make sure he used them.

That would end today's problems in America.

As a Christian I don't believe in abortion but after listening to Obama more and more I realize this country fell one abortion short.

Obama said, "If you've got a business, you didn't build that. Somebody else made that happen."

He is one hundred percent right. That "Somebody else" is God. It could never have been done without God.

"We can go backward, or we can keep moving forward," he said during a speech at Carnegie Mellon University. "And I don't know about you, but I want to move forward."

Ask Jesse Jackson and Al Sharpton if they back Obama and the Muslim Brotherhood. Also ask what they think about these terrorists burning churches and killing Christians. It is obvious neither are Christians and backing Obama is like clapping for the lead act to the Anti-Christ.

Any person who approves of Obama and his backing of the Muslim Brotherhood is obviously not a Christian.

Obama isn't a clown…

He's a joker.

MSNBC host Melissa Harris-Perry says children are owned by the community and part of the collective. I agree with her but with a few differences. I see the collective as all liberals and lying conservatives. I envision a huge room with thick bars and a large lock. The collective of these miss-representatives present it that room. Now that is a collective I would enjoy seeing. Liberals are a collective…like the Borg.

LEAVE OUR CHILDREN ALONE

Rise and Shine

I've been trying to "rise and shine" all morning but it seems to be closer to "sink and rust."

I feel like retirement should be re-classified from "golden years" to "rust."

9/11 Muslim March

You going to the Muslim party in DC today? I finally know what DC means.Dumb Criminals.

Since the march is against God and Christ would the Muslim march be classified as the Anti-Christ march? Or pro-Satan?

Putin for the Nobel Peace Prize

You know if everybody in Congress and Obama ran for president again and then Putin entered the race I'm sorry to say I would vote for Putin. Probably because it seems he is the only one telling the truth. It's strange but I am able to relate to what Putin says more than any of the others. I also think he is right when he calls Kerry a liar.

The sad thing is that I would bet there are more than just a few people that agree with me.

To John McCain

Actually I'm ashamed of what you've become. You are what you were against. The picture of you with the Syrian rebels is no different than the one of Jane Fonda with the Vietcong. Have you seen the video of the Syrian rebel leader eating the heart and liver of a Syrian soldier? The Vietcong were more civilized. If you're for the rebels you need to start hanging out with Jane Fonda. You are supposed to become wiser with experience. What happened to you? You should be ashamed. Stop the war and guard the border. The first passenger airliner shot down with a missile will be on your head.

Wag the Dog (that's Republicans in Congress)

Here is a really sad state of affairs. The Syria thing is "wag the dog" or as transparent as Obama's administration. When it comes to the truth I find I'm listening to Putin to hear what is really happening at the G20. One thing for sure, Kerry is lying. I think all the other American's are also lying. When American's need to listen to Russian leaders for learn the truth we have real problems.

And the Republicans? McCain, please you are embarrassing the conservatives in office, that is if there are any more conservatives. McCain needs to retire— TODAY! So lets see…Republicans you can trust. There might be one or two you can trust but it looks like Obama must have given them a cell phone or something because now they are all voting for him and following him like puppies so excited they are peeing on the floor. This thing makes Revelation all the more intense. Wasn't there a part saying they will follow the Anti-Christ even though he is lying? If it's not happening then it sure is the lead in act.

Harry Reid's at it again

Harry Reid said the reason the Eight Marines were killed was because Americans have too many automatic weapons.

When someone told Reid that the Marines were killed in an accident he immediately said it was because of the "Republican Sequester."

KERRY

Watch this video and tell me you want to attack Syria. Is so then every Liberal and Conservative voting for the war should be removed from office. You are on the verge of destroying America. I understand the FBI could have stopped the Boston bomber if they could have monitored the Mosques.

This video will show you that both the Democrats and Republicans that want to help these rebels are sick and we should no longer help those in the Middle East. And it it time to monitor terrorists not Christians.

I want those who think they are Liberals and/or conservatives to watch this. If you do may never vote for any of those people in office again.

Your representatives have no concept of war, the Middle east or American values.

https://www.youtube.com/watch?v=GfHSPLW63Gg

No response means you condone cannibals.

Eye opening video for Liberals and Conservatives.

This video will show you that both the Democrats and Repulicans that want to help these rebels are sick and we should no longer help those in the Middle East. And it it time to monitor terrorists not Christians.

I want those who think they are Liberals and/or conservatives to watch this. If you do may never vote for any of those people in office again.

Your representatives have no concept of war, the Middle east or American values.

https://www.youtube.com/watch?v=GfHSPLW63Gg

For attorneys only

Obama wants to change it where an attorney only goes two years to get his degree instead of three. I say make it one, they don't learn anything anyway and they for sure don't pay their student loans. Just ask Obama, he and Michelle didn't pay theirs for about 20 years. I wonder if he paid the interest?

I hear he's trying to make a special concession to become an attorney. All you need to do is say you're a liberal and will vote for the democrats. They already have a long line but none of them speak English.

Wow just think about it. It will now be easier to become an attorney than it will to be a real estate agent

Here is the truth about the 600 trillion

The enemy are basically four banks about to implode:

The four banks in question: JPMorgan Chase & Co. (NYSE: JPM), Citigroup Inc. (NYSE: C), Bank of America Corp. (NYSE: BAC) and Goldman Sachs Group Inc. (NYSE: GS).

http://moneymorning.com/2011/10/12/derivatives-the-600-trillion-time-bomb-thats-set-to-explode/

A Sad Day in America

I know the whole thing with Trayvon Martin and Zimmerman is a tragic thing. A not-aggressive response on either side would have ended the confrontation. One surely pushed too much, probably the one most physically fit. I know because when I was in shape I felt invincible until a smaller guy pushed back but he did it with a gun. His hand shook as he pointed that gun at me. For some reason he took off and I'm still here to talk about it. I don't want to downplay the tragedy but I have a question; what about the genocide of black babies? Obama fully backs the genocide of 1300 black babies a day or about 500,000 a year. I know a woman has a right to control her own body but with all the forced birth control we are required to pay for them surely then can control the decision to abort before waiting 24 weeks. But I guess I have no right to voice my opinion. Van Jones says it is racism that Zimmerman is free. Actually it was stupidity on both parts and Van Jones accusations after the trial is really more racists. So a question for Van Jones;

what does he think about the 500,000 unborn black babies murdered each year. If Obama had stopped it there would have been 2.5 million black children alive today.

One more question, why did the New York Times call Zimmerman a white-Hispanic? The last six years has destroyed America. Fiscal Cliff not withstanding once you go over the cliff it really is too late.

The whole thing is sad, sad indeed.

Lois Lerner

To me Lois Lerner taking the fifth and Obama doing nothing is the same as Obama taking the fifth. The IRS has extorted money from me for the last five years. I look forward to Lerner and the others serving time.

The IRS was going to make me pay taxes on $50.00. I went nuts and they did drop that but still threatened and blackmailed me. If the IRS is looking for cheaters I would sure like to see them audit the 1.6 trillion Obama and Congress overspent each of the last five years. Not to mention that the 700 billion Bush gave away was supposedly paid back which would make it about 1.8 trillion or almost double what we take in for taxes.

Audit the government spending the last five years. Where did it go? I guess the same place as the 9 billion missing from the C-130 sent to Iraq. Where did it go?

Wag the Dog...again and again and again

Here is a really sad state of affairs. The Syria thing is "wag the dog" or as transparent as Obama's administration. When it comes to the truth I find I'm listening to Putin to hear what is really happening at the G20. One thing for sure, Kerry is lying. I think all the other American's are also lying. When American's need to listen to Russian leaders for learn the truth we have real problems.

And the Republicans? McCain, please you are embarrassing the conservatives in office, that is if there are any more conservatives. McCain needs to retire—TODAY! So lets see...Republicans you can trust. There might be one or two you can trust but it looks like Obama must have given them a cell phone or something because now they are all voting for him and following him like puppies so excited they are peeing on the floor. This thing makes Revelation all the more intense. Wasn't there a part saying they will follow the Anti-Christ even though he is lying? If it's not happening then it sure is the lead in act.

The Missouri Clown

The clown has shown us that the first amendment is dead. I guess that makes me bad because I see nothing wrong with it. I thought the clown was funny.

They say the clown needs sensitivity training. Shouldn't those who proposed that idea go to class in Stupidity 101? Sensitivity training for what?

I guess the maker of the clown is in real trouble. No bailout for them. That mask will probably be as dangerous as an AR-15 very soon.

How many of the Bill of Rights has Obama and Holder taken away?

They've really butchered Bill of Rights and the Ten Commandments. Oh, that's right freedom of religion no longer exists. Isn't Obama gonna have Reid and

Pelosi re-write the Bible? Of course they will need the help of the Muslim Brotherhood.

In Remembrance of 911
09.11.13
SOMETIMES YOU'RE A NUT; SOMETIMES YOU'RE NOT

The P–nut
The P stands for Propaganda

Sometimes you're the **NUT**

Sometimes you're not.

Sometimes you're the **nail**

Sometimes you're the HAMMER

Sometimes you just **WHINE!!!**

Every Time I Think About It

Think about Benghazi for a moment. I'm sure the president knew the threats to the potential whistle blowers was coming from the Whitehouse and who was making the threats. With great confidence I would say Obama knew all about the cover up even though he doesn't go do security briefings. Now let's suppose he didn't know about it. Actually that is worse. We have a man that is attacking multiple countries with Iran, North Korea and now Syria on his top ten hit list. He says he knows Korea is going to nuke us and Syria has used chemical warfare. BUT he doesn't even know what is happening in the White House. IF that is true he needs to be removed from office.

So Obama wants to take our guns away from us, but he has armed Mexico Drug cartels with 5000 automatic weapons, if that is really the total. Now those same weapons are killing Americans. He has armed Al Qaeda in Libya, Egypt and Syria and that has also led to the death of Americans and Christians. He says God

261

has blessed abortions. Now it is treason to be a Christian in the military. He is appointing a man to a position that has bankrupted another government agency and that same appointee says white people are racist and shouldn't serve in government.

I think we should keep our guns until we have an accounting for where all the weapons he has giving for all these wars. And I can save a lot of foreign aid. If we must accept same sex marriage and churches are forced to marry them (does anybody remember something called freedom of religion?), then I think it appropriate that Obama demand all foreign countries have their leaders endorse same sex marriage, women's equal rights, and give Christians the same rights as guaranteed by our constitution even though the denies those same rights to Christians in America. When leaders like Morsi come out in public to guarantee those rights then we will give them aid, otherwise not one penny.

He has united America like a love fest with the KKK and Black Panthers. The Civil War created lest unrest than Obama.

I laugh until I cry every time I think about how he won the Noble Peace Prize.

Did I miss anything?

Na, na, na na, na..It's your fault (remember fifth grade?)

Remember that line in fifth grade and he would yell at you, "I'm gonna tell the teacher." He would repeat it again and again until you did it to him?

Congress has proven they are not smarter than a fifth grader. They are still on the playground and not paying attention to current events.

I even read about a program in school set up by liberals that says if you can prove that 3x4 = 11 then you are right. We have big problems.

Now Obama and Kerry say the sarin gas is from Saddam. So Putin called Kerry a liar and Kerry immediately responded that Russia gave Assad the sarin gas. Wow! I'm back on the elementary playground in fifth grade again. Maybe Forrest Gump was right, "Stupid is as stupid does."

I know it's hard for Obama to break away from his permanent vacation but he did take a temporary work break to go to Russia to attend the G20 and discuss Syria. He immediately met with the Gay Lesbian leader to discuss the really critical issues and said he would force Putin to change and drop things like traditional marriage nonsense. One really critical issue was that Russia refuses to give information to minors about how wonderful being a lesbian or gay really is. Obama promised to confront Putin on the issue. Is there something inherently wrong with traditional marriage that I'm missing? Good thing Obama is addressing the important issues. Forget the Muslim Brotherhood is killing innocent people and Christians.

There is something I do that might be bad. I join organizations with contradictory views to mine to help write my fiction novels. In that way I'm able to bring them to life with beliefs they express through their own words. Makes the protagonist more believable. That's why I joined MoveOn.org. I don't like their views, but what I find interesting is that they took a poll for the liberals to vote on going to war. Seventy-three percent were against the war. I was shocked they would be so overwhelmingly against Obama. The country is opposed by 87 percent against the war. Are those guys in Congress listening? Sadly I don't think Kerry or Obama could pass a fifth grade test.

One last thing; I need more money. Then it came to me. The leader of the Syrian rebels is getting a billion American dollars right? It seems that Kerry and Obama have no problem with him eating a dead man's heart and liver so if I did that could I get a billion? Sorry. Actually watching that nut case eat another human I realized the Middle-East needs a few more dictators. You could go to Egypt as a tourist when the dictator was in power, now they literally eat your heart out. Hmmm, I keep thinking about that fifth grader. It would almost be funny if it wasn't so sad.

Oh, I forgot. Scientist just came out with information about the dinosaurs and why they are really extinct. Do you think Gore knows that the planet was actually a lot hotter then than it is now. They even had trees in Siberia. Hey Gore, how many SUV's did it take to get it that warm? Sorry I digress. Scientist have found the real reason dinosaurs are extinct. Same sex marriage.

DO YOU BELIEVE IN GOD?

In the last week a man has said, "God Bless Planned Parenthood. I promise to keep the doors open for abortion." Did you know more black people percentage wise, have abortions that any other ethnic group? Could that be a movement toward genocide? And in the last few weeks to talk about Christianity in the military could bring a court martial for TREASON. From what I see happening to Obama it is obvious God is watching.

Why was a stand down order called in Benghazi? The only reason would be to protect the Muslim Brotherhood. American lives were obviously not important. Watergate? What about Holder and the AP? Nixon only did it in one building. And now the IRS. I'm curious. What was the percentage of Whites audited and how many auditors were white? I'm not racist I'm just curious. If I told you what the IRS did to me for what I wrote, it would curl the hair on your head even if you are bald. Our country built on God has shoved him out. No different than when Moses tried to lead his people to the promised land. What did God do? He made them wander in the wilderness. Americans are in the wilderness now and running out of time. Remember God is watching....

TARGETED BY THE IRS

I was one of those targeted each of the last four years going back six years. It was because of what I wrote. The two books got me in real trouble (Words That Don't Offend Liberals and Meandering Scribbles of an Old Fart - both on Amazon). I sent two letters to Obama last month and a received a letter from the IRS within a week of each. The have threatened and extorted money from me. My accountant was there. You really need to worry about the debt. Obama has thrown away 6 trillion to help banks in the last four years. Ask for an audit. We really owe 17.5 trillion. Suppose interest was 10 percent. Do you know what that would be? 1.7 trillion Per year interest. We take in 2.5 trillion and our government spends 4 trillion per year. Ask Obama for an audit of where the money went. It should be easy with his transparent government. Ha! Even Superman's X-ray vision can't see through his transparent government. Look at Detroit. Guess what's coming to America.

Remember that line in fifth grade and he would yell at you, "I'm gonna tell the teacher." He would repeat it again and again until you did it to him? Congress has proven they are not smarter than a fifth grader. They are still on the playground and not paying attention to current events. I even read about a program in school set up by liberals that says if you can prove that 3x4 = 11 then you are right. We have big problems. Now Obama and Kerry say the sarin gas is from Saddam. So Putin called Kerry a liar and Kerry immediately responded that Russia gave Assad the sarin gas. Wow! I'm back on the elementary playground in fifth grade again. Maybe Forrest Gump was right, "Stupid is as stupid does." I know it's hard for Obama to break away from his permanent vacation but he did take a temporary work break to go to Russia to attend the G20 and discuss Syria. He immediately met with the Gay Lesbian leader to discuss the really critical issues and said he would force Putin to change and drop things like traditional marriage nonsense. One really critical issue was that Russia refuses to give information to minors about how wonderful being a lesbian or gay really is. Obama promised to confront Putin on the issue. Is there something inherently wrong with traditional marriage that I'm missing? Good thing Obama is addressing the important issues. Forget the Muslim Brotherhood is killing innocent people and Christians. There is something I do that might be bad. I join organizations with contradictory views to mine to help write my fiction novels. In that way I'm able to bring them to life with beliefs they express through their own words. Makes the protagonist more believable. That's why I joined MoveOn.org. I don't like their views, but what I find interesting is that they took a poll for the liberals to vote on going to war. Seventy-three percent were against the war. I was shocked they would be so overwhelmingly against Obama. The country is opposed by 87 percent against the war. Are those guys in Congress listening? Sadly I don't think Kerry or Obama could pass a fifth grade test. One last thing. I need more money. Then it came to me. The leader of the Syrian rebels is getting a billion American dollars right? It seems that Kerry and Obama have no problem with him eating a dead man's heart and liver so if I did that could I get a billion? Sorry. Actually watching that nut case eat another human I realized the Middle-East needs a few more dictators. You could go to Egypt as a tourist when the dictator was in power, now they literally eat your heart out. Hmmm, I keep thinking about that fifth grader. It would almost be funny if it wasn't so sad. Oh, I forgot. Scientist just came out with information about the dinosaurs and why they are really extinct. Do you think Gore knows that the planet was actually a lot hotter then than it is now? They even had trees in Siberia. Hey Gore, how many SUV's did it take to get it that warm? Sorry I digress. Scientist have found the real reason dinosaurs are extinct. Same sex marriage.

WMD? REALLY?

Here is something to think about. Kerry, Obama, Clinton and the other Liberal Democrats criticized Bush constantly saying, "Saddam Hussein never had WMD's and we should never have attacked Iraq.

Now the same people say Assad is using the Chemical Weapons he got from Hussein.

The logical question is how could Assad have used Chemical Weapons that the Liberal Democrats once said never existed? That is because they have no idea what they are saying or doing.

I suggest we elect Putin President of the United States. The birth certificate is no problem. I can obtain professional illegal birth certificate from our local flea market that is both cheaper and more realistic than those obtained from Hawaii. It has been working for Texas Professional Undocumented Workers (illegal aliens) for decades.

THE CROSS
Sold my House! Thank God for the Cross.

The real estate agent was really perturbed when she told me she had sold my house but the cross in the entry offended the buyer.

I asked why and she told me they were Muslim. I smiled and told her that was why I put the cross up. I didn't want any Muslim moving into my neighborhood. An hour later I had an offer for ten thousand more than I had been asking.

HILLARY ON SYRIA
I'd like to comment on something Hillary said about Syria:

If Syria's government immediately surrendered its chemical weapons stockpiles to international control, "that would be an important step," former U.S. Secretary of State Hillary Clinton said Monday during an event at the White House. "But this cannot be another excuse for delay or obstruction. And Russia has to support the international community's efforts sincerely or be held to account."

Let me get this straight she is accusing Syria of excuse and delay? I want no more excuses or fifth amendment for IRS employees. What about the NSA, IRS and Obama's transparent government. Oh, and Hillary, what about Benghazi. If Putin was listening to you he would call you a liar. Explain Benghazi before you attack Syria. NO more eating hearts and livers. Or do you just shoot off your mouth and not keep up with current events.

These are the men Obama supports. Holder's gun running is supporting them. Don't worry this won't happen in America--Obama uses drones. Now why do you think he wants to take your guns away? So let's wag the dog again. http://www.nytimes.com/2013/09/05/world/middleeast/brutality-of-syrian-rebels-pose-dilemma-in-west.html?hp&_r=0

WHY ARE WE HELPING THE MUSLIM BROTHERHOOD
How are you? Not sure if you remember but you interviewed me for a movie in Katy, "Live For Today." We are still looking for a copy of the interview but this email is not about that. I have grave concerns for our country. All people should.

I sent this to John Kerry and I hope you might show this on the news. It is controversial. In fact it is disgusting. Since I write books I get on web pages and blogs of conservatives and liberals. I consider myself conservative so I was shocked when about 75% of MoveON.org said they were against the war. It seems

Obama is intent on having the Muslim Brotherhood taking control of everything. Ask yourself, "Why aren't we protecting Christians in Egypt? Because they are against the Brotherhood. What is Obama's agenda?

I consider myself a Christian conservative that believes in traditional marriage. That does not make them an enemy of Lesbians and gays. I have gay friends. But ask them what will happen if the Muslim Brotherhood forces their beliefs and demands on America. It will be the same as Obama's transparent leadership, for example: NSA, Gun Running, IRS, etc. Why does Obama refuse surveillance on Muslims and Mosques when they are responsible for 97% of all terrorist acts? Obama now classifies "Christians" as terrorists. Why? I'm not a terrorist; in fact I invite the FBI to monitor our church--all Christian churches.

The man in the video that Glen Beck is showing is the leader of the Muslim Brotherhood that Obama and Democrats and Republicans want to give a billion dollars so he can defeat Assad. All Americans, especially Gays and Lesbians should look at this video. It's coming to America.

Oh, yeah that is not even Halal meat.

Really the media needs to get this out they are not reporting what is going on. If you can't do anything can you pass it on or let me know who I can send the video.

CHEMICAL WEAPONS?
The last time we attacked was for WMD's and they didn't exist. We need to make sure that Assad used chemical weapons. We couldn't help four Americans in Benghazi and now we plan to help the Muslim Brotherhood in Syria at the same time abandoning freedom and Christians in Egypt. Why the sudden push to make Africa and Asia Muslim Brotherhood? They are obviously not peace loving.

Wait and make sure. NO more WMD's.

I would think a man of peace and the Nobel Peace Prize winner would think of innocent lives and wait. Even our allies are hesitant.

LIBERALS OATH?
Doctors take the "Hippocratic Oath" while liberals take the "hypocritic oath."

Liberals do all but one thing while in office. That one thing they fail to do is represent the people.

NEGOTIATE
Isn't ironic that Obama will negotiate with Muslim Brotherhood terrorists in Iran but not elected officials in America.

OBAMACARE FOR EVERYONE BUT THOSE WHO MADE IT
How can they exempt themselves from Obamacare. He said it was good for all. They exempt the other terrorists called Congress from Obamacare....and other special interest groups but when the Catholics say they can't honor abortion and for that reason not Obamacare he says tough.

WE HELP MURDERERS WHO DON'T BELIEVE IN FREEDOM

What I'm concerned about is that he says America is a Muslim country, gives arms to radicals that eat the heart and liver of their enemy, and has stated that he would side with Muslims over Christianity. He also told the FBI and CIA that they could not do surveillance on Muslims or Mosques. He has granted immunity to millions of Muslims. In 2009 there were 3 million Muslims in America now there are six. There is proof they are walking across the border and one of the heads of DHS who claims to be a devout member of the Muslim Brotherhood has said they reason Christians are getting killed in Syria because they deserved it after what they said about Islam.

STRANGE TIMES

Two democrats and an actor said to kill Cruz and Palin but nothing was done. A rodeo clown wears an Obama mask and he is fired and sent to sensitivity training.

In the military Christians are considered treasonous.

I'm voting for Putin as our next president. He has balls and I can get him a great American birth certificate at the local Flea Market and guaranteed to be better than one you can get from Hawaii.

Did I miss anything? America is in real trouble.

Sorry to rant....

AMERICAN NEWS?

I've come upon a group in America more treacherous and dangerous to America and her freedoms than the onslaught of the jihadist and murderous Muslim Brotherhood. They are willing to to lie and decieve American to reach their goals at the sacrifice of honor and truth. They care nothiing about America. They are a group determined to mastermind the overthrow of America to reach their goals. No it is not liberals or the lying members of the Republcan Party who call themselves conservatives. Other than Cruz there are no convervatives in Congress. Congress is filled with self-satisfying, gluttonous, greedy theives and liars. Look at Detroit and you see Syria. What is happening in Detroit is coming to all once great American cites unless we change. Michigan, once know for manufacturing cars is now known better for manufacturing Muslim Jihadist that are killing Americans. You ask if Communist, Congress, or Muslim Brotherhood Jihadist are the dangers of what I speak? As much as I would concur, these are not the threats to American. This group is determined to undermine and destroy our once great American heritage. Forget the Liberals and Muslim Brotherhood for the most dangersou group lurking in freedoms shadows is the American News Media. There is nothing they say that is true. The news media will destroy America

It's Obvious Liberals Don't Read the Bible
2 Thessalonians 3:10-13

[10] For even when we were with you, we gave you this rule: "The one who is unwilling to work shall not eat."

[11] We hear that some among you are idle and disruptive. They are not busy; they are busybodies.

^{12} Such people we command and urge in the Lord Jesus Christ to settle down and earn the food they eat.

^{13} And as for you, brothers and sisters, never tire of doing what is good.

FORGET THE ARAB SPRING – MY FINAL COMMENTS

America had a heart attack in 2008. Hope and Change killed America in 2012. It seems Americans no longer want freedom or at least a majority of Americans what free things and on longer want to earn what they get. Our welfare country is a lot like a little kid that gets free cake every time he asks. But our economy like that cake on the plate is limited. In reality the plated is empty but they keep asking for more. When the entitlements and freebies come to an end America will be stunned. You can only write hot checks so long before it catches up to you and our liberal, radical government is on the eve of destruction. It is too late. There is no saving America. There is no feel good happy ending for America now.

I'd like Obama, Pelosi, Reid, Feinstein and others with their ignorant words and archaic ignorant rants. To look at what happened to Saddam Hussein in Iraq, Muammar al-Gaddafi in Libya, Mubarak in Egypt and what's coming to Assad in Syria. They should know that I get a warm feeling all over when I tell them History repeats and I can't wait until they get what they deserve. Forget the Arab Spring because what is coming is the American Winter. The sad thing is that violence is usually the only way to make change. Violence is coming prepare for it and accept it. History proves that. The American Winter is coming and it's coming soon. It is time to go back before "Hope and Change." I pray every day for a revolution.

I tried to warn people but nobody was really concerned. Now it's too late. There is nothing more to add except it's too late and we did it to ourselves. Prepare.

14
What is the greatest evil today?

A friend asked me a question and I thought it was very interesting. Here is what I was asked:

Serious question..... think about it and reply...

What do you feel is the greatest evil in the world today?

At first a variety of words thoughts raced through my mind. The question intrigued me. All I had to do was turn my mind to the problems today. Bush, the Congress, CEO's and bailing out the wealthy with hundreds of billions of dollars.

With those thoughts the answer came quickly. GREED!

So I did the same thing and asked by friends what they thought was the greatest evil.

Below I have listed them as they came back to me. I put my personal comments in parenthesis.

Frankie T. – greed

Rick – selfishness

Andres – the world itself

Nancy – apathy and ignorance

Forrest – women (Bear with my friend, Forrest, he thinks in an unreal parallel universe)

Ruben B. - Satan (he is very religious)

Gary – Janet Reno's underwear

Gary (again) – No really, tough question. I'll say Radical Islam

Wally – false religions with their false teachings. Influence is the greatest power someone can obtain, it can and will control the masses.

Dwight – mankind

Kim - Whether a Jew, Muslim, Christian, Communist, Agnostic or whatever. Wanting to kill anyone who doesn't believe in the same things you believe in and having the power and greed to want to conquer the world. . . .

Joe G. - ignorance

Terry – greed and sloth and religious fanaticism. Want more?

Beaux – religion

Ann – religion is the greatest evil, but it is also the greatest good.

Leonard – emails

Jene – ignorance

Ruben A. – Congress

Raymond – The incredible greed and sense of entitlement to the rich.

Rick – the money changers, liberated women, and bible thumpers.

Rhy – Religions, all of them, are the greatest evil on earth. Patriotism is a close second.

Nick – not to love themselves unconditionally.

Most of the responses I got went into detail. A few just used one word. I was one of those with, "greed."

Please bear with Forrest. He is a friend of mine and his relationships with women have not done too well. I would hate for him to hear this but a few of the women he dated would probably answer this question with, "men," after they broke up with him.

Ruben is sincere but religion is everything. God rewarded him or if it was bad it was God's will.

When Wally responded I knew what he meant. To him Bush can do no wrong although I wonder what he will say after the bailout. He has an intense hatred for Muslims. So I called him up, thanked him and told him his view was a hundred percent correct and very good and that I was surprised at the depth he could see into Christianity although I knew he meant Muslims. Well he went berserk and looked like a mad dog foaming at the mouth. It took a minute to tell him I was kidding. Well, kinda kidding.

I liked what Dwight said about mankind and told him I had a character in one of my war novels say the same thing but right after a main battle where almost all are killed in battle that same character says to his best friend, "As long as there are two men in the world there will be war."

Based on what I've read I've decided to make this a contest, with no word limit. Use a word or use a thousand.

Greed

(12.05.08)

What is the greatest evil today? I believe it to be greed. I wonder about religion at times but there is also great good in religion. There is no good to be found in greed.

When we think of greed, we see it in usually one form; money (or things). However, greed comes in three forms; money, power and religion. Greedy people will pursue these even if it denies the same thing or basic living essentials to others. Those who are possessed with an insatiable appetite for greed will do this even if it means costing lives or destroying lives. Greedy people don't care. To possess these ends greedy people will lie, steal, cheat, and even kill to reach their goals.

Never has this been more prevalent than what we have seen the last eight years in the United States of America. If the greed of Congress, Wall Street and the CEO's do not destroy America it will be a miracle.

Greed pushes politicians to do whatever it takes so that they can languish in the money and lavish gifts they desire only to want more. Already corrupt, the desire to have and possess will strip America's leaders and politicians of their last vestiges of morals and values. To maintain this exorbitant level of greed, they will make wars where they are not needed, they will waste money on lavish extravagances to please themselves, and the people. The infrastructure will begin to collapse and taxes will increase as the economy and employment drops to record levels. And the greedy will become immoral. All of these things are due to the greed of a few; our leaders and executives.

All of these things were some of the most important reasons for the collapse of the Roman Empire. Where do you think the American Empire stands today? Nowhere is this more evident than it is in our government today.

Greed has a strange side effect. Those infected with greed tend to believe only they know what is best for everyone else, and only they can make intelligent decisions regarding all others. They lose all vestiges of common sense. Prime examples are Paulson and Bush. They think only they know what to do in this financial crisis. Buying stock and helping other greedy people who have made extremely poor decisions is not the answer. If business men have bankrupted their company, they should no longer be in business. Soon you will see that our greedy leaders will bail out the automobile industry. This should not be done. They've made poor business decisions and should no longer be in business. But the greedy will keep them in business. Not a practical decision.

Those filled with greed will ask, even demand that all others be willing to sacrifice even though they refuse to part with any of their lavish lifestyles. This accurately describes Congress and the car manufacturers.

One way to tell when greed is taking over a country is when the contrast between rich and poor grows bigger. This is happening every year.

Today we see a much larger class that live in poverty, partly due to the uncontrolled greed of our politicians and business leaders.

Greed has destroyed every empire in history. At the rate we are going today, greed will destroy America. The greedy will need to sacrifice to save America. Even so, sacrifice is not a word found in the definition of greed.

The greedy will refuse to give up their lifestyle. AIG is a prime business example of how the wealthy demand and will continue to spend millions on their parties and weekend retreats while they laugh in America's face. In addition, they have the audacity to ask, even demand more. Why? Greed.

Another aspect of greed is that it is deceptive. Greedy people are scammers and they will do everything they can to deceive others so that they can take from people what is not theirs.

Of the seven deadly sins, I believe that greed can be directly attributed to the creation of the other six: lust, gluttony, sloth, wrath, envy and pride. Look at the collapse of so many of our national politicians. Greed started their downfall and soon the other six helped take them down. But they would never have faltered or failed if not for greed. Another thing is that of all the seven deadly sins greed is capable of bringing down empires.

Our original government and the people, remind me of a shepherd and his flock of sheep. The shepherd used his staff to protect the sheep, and he would guide them to green pastures. In turn the sheep give him their wool and together was good. But things have changed in the last thirty years. Like wolves, business began to prey on the people. Now as for the old shepherd, wolves came along and gave the shepherd meat. The shepherd loved meat. Soon he let the wolves go uncontrolled to watch the sheep. The shepherd wanted more meat and soon the wolves convinced the shepherd to follow them into the mountains, where he could have all the meat, he wanted. He did as they requested or more like demanded. There was more meat but there were no longer any green pastures. The sheep trusted the shepherd with their lives and gave up everything to follow their beloved shepherd. The sheep complained but the shepherd became irritated and told them the wolves would save them. Now the shepherd hated the sheep and let the wolves do as they wish. Once again, the wolves provided meat to the shepherd. The shepherd was happy but what he didn't know was that the red meat came from own sheep. So today we find the same thing as the president and congress let business lead the people, all in the name of greed.

For a final example of greed, I will use myself as an example. While I prepared this article I was laid off on Tuesday, November 19th, in the afternoon and told I had two days to clear out. They wouldn't even give me the week until Thanksgiving. If any of you do engineering you know how hard it is to find a job during the holidays. This came from a company where I had worked for three years. Ironically, they demanded employees give two week notice. My job consisted of engineering work for Conoco-Phillips on a refinery in Wyoming. The first plans for this site came up a few years ago. At that time oil was forty dollars a barrel. Conoco-Phillips was ecstatic because they would make a fortune. This week Conoco-Phillips canceled that job. And I was laid off. In the meeting Conoco-Phillips said they couldn't make money below sixty dollars a barrel. The reason the job was canceled? GREED. I reminded them that this job started when oil was forty dollars a barrel. They didn't respond. I also snipped that they should contact their "Buddy Bush" and ask for a bailout too. After all if you are going to bailout bankrupt companies why not dole out dollars for the viable ones?

Citicorp wants money from the bailout and to lay off 50,000 employees. What they are saying is that they don't care about the people or employees. All they care about is the money. Greed and a little selfishness.

Yesterday a friend of mine said stop complaining this is the best country in the world. I laughed and told him Mike Tyson had said something similar to that before one of his fights. Tyson had said, "I'm the best boxer in the world nobody can beat me!" A few minutes later he was knocked out for the first time. Is the knockout punch for America coming and is the glove called greed?

Throughout history greed has always had a lot to do with bringing down great empires. Today, in history, you may be in a unique position to see exactly what greed can do to a mighty nation. There is still time to reverse the process if our leaders can sacrifice their greed for the people. Now look at our leaders and watch their actions. What will it be common sense or greed?

The nice thing about today's world is that we don't need to go far to find examples of greed.

Two hundred years from now a teacher will be talking to her class and probably say, "Although we speak Spanish, just a little over two hundred years ago the country where we live spoke English." The children will laugh and the teacher will make them be quiet. "That empire was called the United States of America. Maybe it was the greatest empire in history. Today we try to learn from history and their mistakes. Hopefully, we will not repeat them. They were destroyed from within. Greed destroyed the United States of America."

The greatest evil today? You decide.

This brings an end to my scribbles and for your personal enjoyment I give you:

15
THINGS I SAID THAT GOT ME FIRED

Before reading on it should be noted that I've worked for a fair amount of engineering firms; seventy-seven to be exact. Of those I have I have quit forty-eight times. I've been laid off (or fired) twenty-nine times. But by far the most interesting ones are those from which I was fired. Sometimes there is not much difference between getting fired and being laid off. One is just a nicer term. And there were many times I quit before I was fired. AND one time I was actually locked out and told not to come back. Here are a few of those things that got me fired.

There was a time I was involved in racing but my boss thought it was a waste of time and quite often he told me so. A national championship was coming up and I told him two months before the race that I was taking off the first week of October for the race. He was smug when he said, "I won't allow you to take off for the race." I said, "Okay. Not a problem." Then I smiled and said, "Oh, one more thing. I just wanted you know now that I'm going to be sick the first week of October." (I was laid off a week later.)

Before cell phones we would have a single phone that all the workers used. At the time I was managing a softball team. One day was particularly bad. The boss called me to his office. He talked to me about the phone and I told him I understood and the season was almost over and it would stop. He wasn't satisfied and said, "What's more important your personal life or your job?" I actually laughed, then said, "No question about it. My personal life. I don't give a shit about the job." (Fired)

Turns out the VP of our company watched when we went to the bathroom and was keeping count of our time. He called a meeting for all the employees. There were about twenty of us in a room when he said, "I've noticed that too many people are spending time in the bathroom reading the newspaper." This seemed so ludicrous that I blurted out, "No wonder we don't have any new work here, if you spend all your time watching us go to the bathroom." I think too many of the people in the meeting laughed. (Fired)

The boss was angry that people were always coming in late. He called a meeting to discuss the issue and said, "I'm not stupid. I know that when I see someone coming in with a briefcase that they are late." I couldn't help myself, "And all this time I thought they forgot their briefcase and were going back to get it." Everyone laughed. (I managed to quit before I was fired.)

Still in the bullpen era (an open area with as many as twenty drafting tables) I was again on the wall phone when the boss came up and demanded I get off the telephone. I smiled and said, "If it's bothering you I'll quit right now." Turns out I was doing something critical no one else could do and I knew it. I kind of had him by the balls so I pushed a little more, "Well do you want me to quit right now?" He was flabbergasted. He knew I would quit so he said, "No, but hurry up with your call and get back to work." A week later I was finished with the critical part and he laid me off.

In Alaska I asked for a raise and told them I would quit if I didn't get the money. The boss snickered, "This is the best job you've ever had you'll never quit." I laughed, "You're talking to the wrong guy. I'm a professional quitter." And I quit. (Before he fired me)

This young engineer, with about a year of experience, was telling us how to design concrete but he was clueless. He had no concept. What he wanted to do was wrong. All of us had about thirty years' experience, but we were told to do whatever he said. We tried to show him how some of the things he wanted wouldn't work but he refused to listen. When he finished he acted like he had been doing engineering for forty years instead of only one. He asked, "Any comments?" I raised my hand like a kid and when he pointed to me I tried to sound like a kid, "Gosh, I hope one day when I grow up I will know as much as you do." (Fired)

I arrived at work late and the boss was standing there he glanced at his watch, touched it and looked back at me. I smiled, touched my watch like he did glanced back, grinned and then said, "I've got a nice watch too." Then I walked to my desk. I was laid off a week later.

I went into the office of my old friend and asked if I had gotten the raise. Basically he said that he didn't feel I could contribute to the job. It pissed me off. I knew his wife had left him and he was having an affair with a married woman but there was more to that and I knew what it was, so I said, "You shit head. Maybe if you'd quit sleeping with your employees wives you could accomplish something. No wonder your wife left you for another woman. I quit." He was shocked and I was out of the office ten minutes later. (Yeah, I quit)

This engineer had always been changing the way we draw things and it had really bothered me. Just before a meeting he decided to move things on a drawing for no reason. With a dozen people in the meeting, I said to that engineer, "I checked your calculations and the steel you designed in not correct." He turned red in the face and almost yelled, "You have no business doing engineering!" I smiled and said, "I know. And you have no business doing drafting." There was silence. (Fired)

The job had an impossible schedule. The pressure unbearable. The last few lead designers had already succumbed and quit. Now I was the lead. Still the boss was worried I would also collapse under the load. He came up and asked me, "Will you be okay with the schedule?" I nodded yes. He still looked worried, "Does the pressure bother you?" I acted like it didn't and said, "Naw, pressure never bothers me." The boss looked relieved until I added, "Pressure get too tough I quit."

We were about out of work and I knew I would be laid off in a few weeks when the job was done. The boss was worried we were going to slow down to preserve the work. Our boss came up to me and asked, "You're still going to work fast even though we need to lay you off when the work is done?" I shrugged, "Of course…after all the benefit here for doing a good job for you is getting laid off. What more incentive could I ask for?" (I did a good job early and as soon as I was finished I was laid off)

I went to work on a job that I knew was only three months. The boss was worried about production and came to check on me. First thing he said was, "You know when the job is over we need to lay you off?" I was calm and nonchalant when I said, "Yeah, I know. I don't have a problem with getting laid off." The boss was a little surprised and asked, "You're not afraid of us laying you off?" I chuckled a little and said, "No. My biggest fear is working here forever."

When I was hired they said no time-and-a-half for overtime. I swore I would never work overtime if it was straight time for my overtime. I made that clear to the project manager. One day they got in a pinch and the project manager begged me to work over the weekend. I looked at him and quickly said, "Okay." I can't tell you shocked he was and then he became suspicious. "I thought you said you would never work overtime unless it was time-and-a-half." I nodded and said, "That's right. I won't." He looked confused but this is straight time." Again I smiled, "I know. You see I'm going to work eight hours, and put twelve on my time sheet. You're going to think I was paid straight time but I'll know that I got time-and-a-half for what I worked and that way we'll both be happy." (Fired)

We had a critical job that had to be issued on Monday and most people were going to work on Saturday. My boss was really concerned because he would be unable to work and watch to make sure we did the work. He asked me, "Are you going to work Saturday?" I grinned and said, "No, but I'll be here."

We had an engineering meeting with all the employees. One of those pep talks about how bad we were doing and how there were a lot of people who could take our place if we didn't produce. It was already grinding me the wrong way when the boss said, "There are too many mistakes. Everyone needs to be more careful." He stuck out his neck with pride but looked more like a turkey when he added, "I don't make any mistakes." It just came out of nowhere when I blurted, "Hard to make mistakes when you don't do anything." Everybody laughed. (Fired after the meeting)

I was arguing with the lead designer when he said to me, "Don't be a smart ass!" So I responded with, "Better than being a dumb ass like you." (Terminated at a later date)

There was a new movie out and I wanted to see it so I called in sick one day and had goofed most of the day. Late in the afternoon I was coming out of the theater and bumped into a secretary from work. She had just gotten off from work so it was easy to see that I had skipped work. I guess she had said something. I had only been at work for a few hours when the boss called me in and was upset because they had a deadline and he knew I wasn't sick. I told him he was wrong really was work and was still suffering from the same thing today. He snickered and asked me what it was. With all sincerity I told him, "I'm sick of work and it still has me down today." Didn't' get fired but he wasn't very happy.

In a meeting an engineer was trying to explain something to us and it really appeared as though he had no idea as to what he was talking about. I blurted out to the engineer, "Have you ever done this before?" (Severely reprimanded but not Fired)

Another meeting this engineer was trying to let us know how much he knew when he said, "I know what I'm doing. I have 20 years' experience. . . I laughed and said, "Looks more like one years' experience twenty times." (Fired)

The engineering business always goes in cycles. The companies try to pay us nothing and we try to get everything. The cycle was in a downturn for the workers. Pay rates had almost been cut in half. There were very few jobs available. AND they want everybody to triple their output, hence the term "sweatshop." I managed to find a job at a sweatshop. Moral was low. Then the boss called a meeting. He demanded we double our output. I raised my hand and when he called on me I said, "If you double my pay, I'll double my output." Needless to say he was shocked and said, "Why aren't you doubling your production now?" I smiled and said, "Because you're only paying me half what I'm worth." Everybody laughed. The boss turned a little red. How sweet it was. A few hours later he called me into a private meeting. (Fired)

When I arrived at work I had a cup of coffee and then I went into my boss's office to tell him I had another job. The job I had really sucked and I wasn't very happy. The other boss would criticize you in front of all the workers and treated worse than people were treated in the '60's. There was a Cajun luncheon that afternoon that I really was excited about but I was more concerned about quitting and letting them know. When I entered his office I told him I had another job and I was quitting. He looked at me and squinted his eyes. That alone boded ill for me, as I had seen that look before.
    With an angry tone he asked, "How much notice are you giving me?"
    "Two weeks."
    He grunted, "We have a new policy around here. Pack your shit and get out now."
    I started laughing, and the laugh shocked my boss but before he said anything I said, "Sure no problem, but if I had known you were going to do that I would have told you after lunch so I could have had that Cajun lunch you're providing for us. But really thanks, now I can make a lot more money sooner." (remember I had already quit)

In progress meeting it really looked like we didn't have anything together and it was going nowhere fast. I shook my head and said to my friend, "Looks to me like Forrest Gump Engineering." The engineer heard and said, "What do you mean by that comment?" Too late I was already committed, "Stupid is as stupid does." (Fired)

We had a meeting about engineering changes. The worst thing about that was they would make changes multiple times per day and sometimes change it back to the way it was before the change. It was frustrating! Well they were in the meeting doing it again and I said, "This engineering reminds me of the movie Karate Kid." The engineer who had made all the changes looked confused and said, "What do you mean?" I smiled at him and then made circular motions with my right hand in the air, "Wax on engineering," then I did the same with my left hand, "Wax off engineering." Some of the guys laughed. I wish I hadn't seen "The Karate Kid." The next day they waxed me off the employment list.

I was going to take some drawings home to check when the head engineer warned me, "Don't lose those drawings are confidential. We don't want our secrets to get out." I laughed and said, "Only thing these drawings are good for are examples of how not to do things." (That was my last week)

In a meeting a boss said, "We are going to take samples of your best work to use as standards for the future." I snickered, "If you do that then you'd need to get my drawings from the last place I worked."

I was really frustrated with the company when they kept changing things for no reason and wasting valuable time. Then they asked how to save time in the weekly meeting. The responses were crazy and I mumbled out my thoughts a little too loud, "This Company won't win any Common Sense awards." (Fired for not being sensitive to other ideas)

An engineer came up behind me and pulled the pencil out of my hand. I was quick, caught his wrist and bent it back, and said, "Ever wonder what it's like to digest teeth?" (Almost fired but they kept me)

I didn't even start this job. The pay offer was so low I laughed at his offer and told him, "I don't work for welfare wages. I have a responsibility to pay taxes to support welfare recipients."

I'd been working at the company three years and thought I was safe. One day the structural engineer came in and said they had run out of work and I would be laid off. It was the week before Thanksgiving so I asked how many days I had and would be after Thanksgiving. He said, "No today." I said, "Two days?" He said, "No today, now." Well I just started laughing like crazy and he looked a little uneasy. I smiled at him and said, "Good thing I did a good job for you. How much notice do you give when somebody is bad?" Then I started laughing again.

The engineer was worried that I was angry and confronted me with his feelings. I told him, "No I'm not mad. In fact I'm going to take you to lunch and feed you a fist sandwich.

This engineer was always bragging about what a great paperboy he had been, but his engineering sucked. We were in a meeting and they were actually talking about the wrong way he was doing things. I laughed and said, "You would have been more successful if you had remained a paperboy." (Fired)

We had been working about sixty hours a week for almost a year. One engineer kept changing things daily and then changing them back. He just couldn't stick with a decision. One day there were five of us in his office and he was changing things again. He said, "I hope you guys aren't upset that it's changing again." We were upset but I laughed and said, "Hell no we're not mad. If it wasn't for you we'd be working forty hours a week." (Reprimand)

The Lead Designer blamed everybody when there were problems with the work. We were all tired of always being accused. One day he told us our group had screwed up. I told him that wasn't the problem. He said, "You're so damn smart tell me what the problem really is." Hhhmmmm. I did, "When you get up in the morning go in the bathroom, look in the mirror and you'll find the problem." Everybody laughed. The Lead Designer turned red in the face. (fired)

We were getting laid off in a group of twenty all at one time. After he finished laying us off he asked if we had any questions and I said, "I regret that I have but one job to give or my company.

The engineer asked me to work all weekend and change 25 drawings so they could be issued on Monday morning. I did and they were ready. When he arrived he came to my desk with a frantic look on his face. He asked if I had made the changes yet and I told him yes they were on his desk. He told me he wanted them the way they were and to print them. I explained that it no longer existed and would need to be changed back and it would take two more days. He looked sick, so I decided to make him feel worse when I said, "So let's get this straight. If I had come in this weekend and done absolutely nothing, we'd be finished now?" (Ass chewing)

We were having a meeting about the problems with the work coming from India. All the bosses and project managers were in attendance. One had spoken for a while and finished with, "It's difficult to get consistent work from India because there is so much turnover and there is a lot lost in translation because they speak over a thousand dialects." I acted serious and said, "That is a real problem we need them to be more like American and speak one dialect like we do," and as they all nodded in agreement I finished with, "Spanish." Some of the bosses were surprised. Most laughed and I kept my job.

The engineer was angry at me and I wasn't very happy with him either. Well he came up and threatened me, "You keep this up I'm going to fire you. You want to be fired?" I don't do well with threats so I said, "Being fired from here would be like a promotion." I got my promotion. (Fired.)

In a meeting the head engineer acted smug when he said, "We don't want to reinvent the wheel." I said, "You might want to rethink that. The wheel you're using is square. Even cavemen knew how to make a round wheel."

"You can't fix an elevator when it's dropping."

The engineer said, "What do they do at your new job?" I responded, "They do things the old fashioned way." He asked, "How is it different from us?" I smiled, "They do it the right way."

"The bright side of working here is that I don't pay much income tax."

The pay was low, very low. The Boss came in and told us we would probably have layoffs in a month." I said, "Pay me more so I can really be concerned."

I was working at a company and the boss was firing people so he could get his friends hired. I heard on the street that my boss was going to fire me so he could hire one of his friends. We'll call him Danny. I had done nothing this time and was shocked so I started looking for another job. Danny came in and asked if I wanted some time off and I told him no. He was serious when he told me that the company would lay off people on overhead and he had nothing for me at that time. I laughed and said, "Yeah, I think I would enjoy a few days off. He told me to come back on Monday.

The next day an engineer friend called me from the office and told me that during their daily meeting Danny had told them that I refused to do modeling and would only check and that I was going home until they had something to check. All lies, even my engineer friend knew I had taught modeling and would rather do that than checking drawings. Danny was stabbing me in the back. I found a job before I returned to work.

I went in to the Supervisor and told him what was happening and that I was leaving that afternoon and didn't want to talk to Danny. I was prepared for his argument but was really surprised when he responded.

"Well I understand and agree with you. Here is what I want you to do. Go to your office and send me an email that you are quitting in two weeks."

I interrupted, "No I'm leaving now."

"Yes, I know. I want them to know you gave two-weeks-notice which will look good for you." He nodded and grinned. "In the email I want you say how nice things were working here and the people you worked with."

"What?"

He held his hands up and said, "If you don't do that then when another company asks for a recommendation I won't be able to give it to you. And you will never be able to come back here again."

His words stunned me. Actually I was quitting because I had no intention of ever coming back and I already had another job. He was threatening me! Blackmail, intimidation. I smiled and said, "Yeah, I think I better go send that recommendation now."

Again he grinned and nodded confidently, "Good."

So I went to Human Resources and told them the whole story.

The next week the guy Danny wanted was hired. The week after that the Supervisor was fired. A little justice.

This was by far the worst job I've ever had. The day I walked in I knew it was over. Every engineering company allows you to plug in a hard drive so you can listen to music or download details for your work. You can also use the DVD player to listen to music. The morning I started to work I arranged my desk, sat down and plugged in my hard drive to download my standards and details for work. The USB ports didn't work and neither did the DVD drive. I told my boss Jerry and he said it was a work computer and not to be used for anything personal. I looked at their computer, turned to the boss, laughed and said, "Wow. That's the most expensive, worthless computer I've ever seen." He didn't like that. It really was the beginning of the end. He was like the Gestapo. Come to think of it the company was German. Well things went from bad to worse. There were a few guys doing texting. They didn't want us to make personal calls in the trailer. A few days later the engineer, Jerry, posted a note of the entrance to the Trailer. It read: No texting beyond this point. Later that afternoon when Jerry was walking across the parking lot to his truck I told the guys in the trailer, "Look there goes Jerry." They got up, saw him leaving and looked relieved. I got out my cell phone, smiled to them and said, "Get out your cell phones." A few did but one asked, "Why?" I smiled and said, "'Cause we're all going to send old Jerry a text message." They all laughed but one said, "You're crazy." I smiled at him and said, "Yeah, isn't it great!" Problem is there was a spy. They set up a meeting for a few days from that but I was in the hospital having tests on my stomach and missed the meeting. The day I got back Jerry confronted and threatened me. He told me he how great a company we worked for. That is always the kiss of death. He said there was too much texting so I got out my telephone and held it toward him and said, "I don't do text messages." He got angry and said, "This is a place of business. The computers are for work and not to be used for personal use. ONE personal email and we can fire you." I knew my time was up. Then he started on the spiel that people on the verge of going senile start, "Twenty years ago we had a phone on the wall for everybody." I interrupted, "Well you don't even have a phone on the wall here." He came to do verbal warfare and came unarmed. "This isn't a sweat shop." And of course I responded, "I don't know about that." He was incensed, "We're thinking on making everybody leave their cell phones in their cars when they come in." He left the office a little while later and I told my friends, "The little Hitler. Funny this is a German company, got the little Gestapo agent and he has just classified me as Jew." It really felt weird. They knew what I meant and I was sure he was going to lay me off and I told them so. Since I had a few emails I figured I might as well respond. Now it was a race to see if I could find a job before Jerry laid me off. One of my friends said not to worry because Jerry's bark was worse than his bite, and that Jerry never did anything. I told my friend that I had known people like Jerry and I knew he was going to get rid of me. The next day I had to go to my doctor's office to see what the tests revealed. On a scale of 1 to 10 my stomach was an eight. He gave me some medication and told me to watch my blood pressure, which was 165/95. When I got to the office one of my friends asked me what was wrong, I held my side and told him it was my stomach. He asked me what caused it and I said, "Lack of texting." My friend laughed but I forgot about his snitch, who I guess told Jerry. Two days later I went home. At seven that night my contract company called and told me Jerry had locked me out and I was not to return to the office. They sent someone to get my stuff. The little Gestapo agent had just gassed me. A few days later I called my friend and told him he was wrong about Jerry; he does bite. A week after I was laid off my blood pressure was 120/65. (Not fired, didn't quit, but achieved an all-time first—I was locked out)

16

The Last Empire
Final Thoughts by the Author

Throughout time every empire has collapsed; there have been no exceptions.

It is too late? America, well actually Congress, has destroyed the democratic and financial fiber of America. There was a chance until welfare voted for Obama so the people had a major part in destroying Americas. In reality they all have done something the Civil War and two World Wars were unable to do; destroy America. The enemy is not Al Qaeda, or Libya or Iraq, or Afghanistan or any other trumped up war. Iraq was just a personal and financial war for Bush that America was sucked into. Saddam Hussein had nothing to do with 911. The enemy is Congress for they are the real "enemy combatants." And they will continue to make wars as long as it suits their demands. Ask yourself why we don't help Somali? Because they have no oil.

It is too late to reverse the financial devastation Congress has reaped on America. Like Russia we will split apart into several countries and the one that offer work, freedom and opportunities will be the one to survive. Spending into oblivion has never worked, and that's one of the reasons for the Roman Empire's collapse.

There must be one language and we have failed. A hundred years from now a teacher may very well be teaching all of her students in Spanish only, on what was once called the United States of America. Soon taxes will approach sixty percent and there will still be nothing provided for the workers. Congress will become the elite and dictators of the world. The other enemy combatants are America's CEO's (Chief Embezzlement Officers), and America's Unions.

Barrack Obama. What a failure. We should use his true Muslim name because he acts like no American. It should be Obama Been Lyin'. Americans are very much like his cigarettes and he's sucking us dry. I'm sure his doctor has told him his cigarettes are killing him just like economists tell him his spending is killing America. Does he care? Is he still smoking? America is still dying along the malignant tumor called Congress.

President Obama wants to take our guns away while supplying Mexican drug cartels with unlimited weapons. He also supplies Al Qaeda and revolutionaries with unlimited weapons and deadly aircraft he gives to enemies of Israel.

Obama is a president that says he is going to correct the bible and make it right. I think the Anti-Christ is supposed to say that. He is determined to have churches provide abortions and birth control while making them accept same sex marriage and provide marriages for those couples. That, my friend, is not freedom of religion. He even had the audacity to say, "God Bless abortion." He has even gone so far as to have the military consider Christians who talk about God to have committed treason at the same time he hired two "devout" Muslims to run the Department of Homeland Security. Who calls anyone devout? And DHS have purchased more than a billion bullets. When the DHS gives you those bullets it won't be as the gifts you expect. There will be at least one for each American and they will be delivered "long distance."

As long as you can only think Democrat or Republican this county is doomed but I truly believe it is too late.

Now 47 million Americans rely on welfare or food stamps. Obama has shut down drilling and now plans to close coal mines. If he wins a second term we will be a third world country before his second term ends.

History shows only violence can save us now.

IF YOU STILL BELIEVE IN OBAMA
AND HIS SPENDING
LOOK AT THIS

It is very important that you closely inspect the 1934 cartoon below. Keep in mind there were Communist and Marxist operatives in the USA in 1934 when we were in the middle of the Great Depression. This cartoon was in the Chicago Tribune in 1934. Look carefully at the Communist's "Plan of Action" in the lower left corner.

Does this seem familiar? You can just as easily change the names to Obama, Pelosi and Reid. Remember the adage: "Those who forget history are doomed to repeat it."

AND THEN IT IS WINTER

(Author Unknown)

You know. . . Time has a way of moving quickly and catching you unaware of the passing years. It seems just yesterday that I was young, just married and embarking on my new life with my mate. Yet in a way, it seems like eons ago, and I wonder where all the years went. I know that I lived them all. I have glimpses of how it was back then and of all my hopes and dreams.

But, here it is... The winter of my life and it catches me by surprise... How did I get here so fast? Where did the years go and where did my youth go? I remember well seeing older people through the years and thinking that those older people were years away from me and that winter was so far off that I could not fathom it or imagine fully what it would be like.

But, here it is... My friends are retired and getting grey... They move slower and I see an older person now. Some are in better and some worse shape than me... But, I see the great change... Not like the ones that I remember who were young and vibrant... But, like me, their age is beginning to show and we are now those older folks that we used to see and never thought we'd be. Each day now, I find that just getting a shower is a real target for the day! And taking a nap is not a treat anymore... it's mandatory! Cause if I don't on my own free will... I just fall asleep where I sit!

And so... Now I enter into this new season of my life unprepared for all the aches and pains and the loss of strength and ability to go and do things that I wish I had done but never did!! But, at least I know, that though the winter has come, and I'm not sure how long it will last... This I know, that when it's over on this earth... It's over. A new adventure will begin!

Yes, I have regrets. There are things I wish I hadn't done... Things I should have done, but indeed, there are many things I'm happy to have done. It's all in a lifetime.

So, if you're not in your winter yet... Let me remind you, that it will be here faster than you think. So, whatever you would like to accomplish in your life please do it quickly! Don't put things off too long!! Life goes by quickly. So, do what you can today, as you can never be sure whether this is your winter or not! You have no promise that you will see all the seasons of your life... So, live for today and say all the things that you want your loved ones to remember... And hope that they appreciate and love you for all the things that you have done for them in all the years past!!

"Life" is a gift to you. The way you live it is your gift to those who come after. Make it a fantastic one.

Live it well, enjoy today, and do something fun! Be happy and have a great day.

Remember: "It is health that is real wealth and not pieces of gold and silver.

Look at the Arab Spring
Ironically the government wants to take our guns while supplying drug lords and revolutionaries with all the weapons they want.

The American Nightmare
My Dream, or Reality?

This article is about a dream but first I want to sidetrack to Obama and current events. I wrote about everything that is happening today. My novel "Moon Shadow" was written in 1996 and it describes a Democrat president that destroys the United States with a 20 trillion debt and speeches filled with promises that concealed lies. It was about Obama and I wrote it in 1996.

At first I thought Obama was stupid and ignorant. Christians are branded traitors; gays have more than equality as they relish their demands against Christians. Obama claims to be Christians while backing every program gay and lesbian and defending the Muslim Brotherhood while bashing Christian beliefs. It is against the law to prevent abortions while Christians are forced to pay for those abortions. He has the NSA seize and search Christians while make it discriminatory to monitor Muslims and Mosques in America. Think about it ninety-nine percent of the terror comes from two percent of the American population and we not allowed to question their actions. If Obama is really a Christian check what he tithes. I'll bet its closer to zero than it is to ten percent and I bet he donates money to militant groups or things that promote racial strife. And now ObamaCare. If he is truly a Christian then why did he call America a Muslim country? He also said if he had to choose between Christians and Muslims he would side with Muslims. Would a true Christian utter such preposterous words? Wouldn't he have stood up to defend Christians and say they were not traitors and had not committed treason? But he didn't. Instead he has willingly let Christian persecution continue unabated. I believe it was 2010 when he promised, "You will be able to keep your insurance policies-period! Your rates will not increase-period! You can keep your doctor-period!" His promises all have one thing in common- LIES!

There is more. I read an article "You Are a Terrorist Now" and there are 75 groups listed as potential terrorists. Christians are one group and anyone who speaks against the government (Obama) is considered a terrorist. To speak against the government has always been an American right called freedom of speech. Not anymore. If you speak against

Muslims you are now classified as a terrorist. Of the 75 groups neither Muslims nor Muslim Brotherhood are mentioned as a terrorist group. What is terrifying is that Obama is removing all Military leaders who are Christians or said they would not shoot Americans unless fired upon. Now the Pentagon has picked an anti-Christian extremist, Micky Weinstein to operate a religious tolerance policy for the Pentagon. Basically he says Christians are terrorists and Muslims are okay.

Think about this; the NSA has done all the monitoring for security of America. Really? Common Sense would make you ask these questions; why don't we guard the border? Why are we not allowed to question Muslim activities but we can question Christian activities? Why was the Department of Homeland Security ordered by Obama not to allow surveillance on Muslims or their mosques? Why the rush to give amnesty to 21 million illegal aliens? Let's start with the last question first. Obama says they deserve amnesty, even though they are Illegal Aliens. That's right; illegal. They were willing to break the law to do what they want. Obama loves them. The first two are almost one. The head of DHS is said to be a devout Muslim. Devout means all people must be Muslims or they will go to hell and a good Muslim is allowed to kill the blasphemer if they don't convert. It is obvious Obama, the NSA and the DHS allowed the Boston Marathon Bombing. It was orchestrated by Muslims in Mosques. What did you say? That's right we are not allowed to monitor those who commit 99 percent of the terrorist acts. Now ask yourself how many Muslims walked across the Mexican border unhindered thanks to Obama. Remember what Obama said? America is a Muslim nation. A true Christian would never have allowed this to happen.

We are on the verge of race wars all instigated by our President. It really started moving when he said, "If I had of had a son he would have looked just like…"

What about the likes of Lois Lerner, Kathleen Sebelius, and Marilyn Tavenner who refuse to answer questions? Sebelius even says those that went to fire her don't pay her. WRONG! She is paid by taxpayers and they all are required to answer the questions brought before them. Those that don't answer questions are fired and no retirement.

If you speak out against the government or Obama you are immediately branded "Terrorist" or "Racist" or both. And this man confesses to be a Christian. He is closer to the anti-Christ and if not he sure must be the lead in act.

Now I realize Obama is neither stupid nor ignorant but brilliant! He has accomplished what he set out to do; not change America but destroy her. He is the "Pied Piper" of words. Obama's flute of words is leading the rats and the children into hellfire and damn nation! The rats are the Pelosi and Reids, and the actors in Hollywood backing the destruction of America.

And the children that Obama leads to a fate worse than death? They are the blacks that follow their false prophet blindly but they are also the whites and Hispanics that want the working Americans to give them all they demand and it is clear in Obama's words. Working Americans are the new "slave class" expected to provide for half of America who demand something for nothing.

If you look closely you can see the end of America just a few steps ahead. I told people that what happened to Iraq and Iran would soon come to America if we didn't change. Change came to those countries and with it they lost hope. Soon they killed each other and with that came boredom and anger. They killed neighbors, friends and just those that passed. If they only had hope, even jobs.

What happened in those countries is not much different than those three boys killing the Australian jogger. For them the last few years had changed their lives and without jobs and a future they lost the "hope" Obama had promised. He has taken jobs but created none. Those boys were only bored but soon it will become much worse. If only they had faith, something bigger than the one they believed in; Obama with his deception and lies. Without faith there is no "hope" and without hope there is no tomorrow. Obama changed America and with it he has stolen our hope.

When Obama ends welfare, and that is his plan, there will be chaos, killing, race wars, and then he will bring the DHS into action with martial law. Now you understand what the billions of bullets were intended; death to Americans. With the death of America Obama may become America's Chavez. Members of the Muslim Brotherhood are already in control of the Department of Homeland Security and no telling what else. For the Gays and Lesbians I ask, "Do you know what Muslims do to people like you? Hideous deaths. Christians think you are wrong but they still love you. All Christians want to do is give you hope not death. When Obama brings it on remember you shunned and ridiculed the loving Christians because their beliefs did not coincide with your unwarranted beliefs. You denied Christians the same rights you demanded and received openly from America's Manchurian Candidate. Fret not; sadly it is too late for America, for she is terminally ill. No one heeded the warnings of the Pied Piper.

This was intended to be about a dream. I have strange dreams and this is only one of them.

I had a dream about Osama bin Laden in 1996 after reading about his bombing in the basement of the New York Twin Towers. In the dream Osama Bin Laden said he would use America's weapons against them. In my dream he hijacked three passenger airliners crashing them into; the White House, the Sugar Bowl and the Orange Bowl on New Year's Day. To me the dream didn't mean much but I incorporated parts of my dream into "*Moon Shadow*" (https://www.smashwords.com/books/view/29998), a novel I was writing about the invasion of the United States and had been reading and studying Osama Bin laden extensively. I was trying to come up with a logical concept on how the greatest county in the world could possibly be invaded.

There were other things in the dream that helped with the invasion concept of my novel *Moon Shadow*. Osama had a plan to destroy America from within. He would buy off Congress and Big Business. In my novel he buys off the politicians for his gain, taking American business to Pakistan and India. And he laid out a plan where he would bring the Muslim religion to America, slowly converting America to Sharia Law while making Christianity appear to be evil. At the same time he pushed for amnesty so his cells could work freely and gained political asylum for his Muslim Brotherhood. Political Asylum was perfect; no questions asked from the bleeding heart liberals and with it came instant citizenship. (This worked extremely well from 2010 to 2012 when American Muslims actually increased from just over three million to well over six million. Obama gave political asylum to hundreds of thousands of people from Libya, Egypt and Syria. Think about it; Muslims doubled in over two years.) The concept of asylum and amnesty was perfect for my novel. I added things like computers being made overseas thus they gained control over the software that operated computers and the Internet. I had a radical group of Militia called the "Minute Men" patrolling America's borders. Muslim's walked across the borders unhindered, bringing with them weapons and installing their cells. In the book, Greed and corruption destroyed America, leaving America bankrupt in 2014. Also language is an item that eventually destroys all great empires. Currently in Michigan you can get state files in Arabic. When you call the state you can get English, Arabic and Spanish. The best way to destroy an empire is to allow other languages. In America, English is almost a second language. Just a year ago I was told by a group of people that it was important to learn Spanish so I could better communicate with people in Texas.

In my novel *Moon Shadow*, I predicted a Democrat would become President in 2008 and the country would be bankrupt at the end of 2014 with a debt of twenty trillion. The invasion was simple because without money the troops weren't paid and they returned to their homes (furloughed just like Obama is doing now). There was no one to defend America. Gangs ran amuck killing people for no reason other than pleasure. Chaos reigned in America and the invading forces simply walked across the border. All of this in my fiction novel *Moon Shadow*, finished in 1998. There were two things I put in my novel that I later took out. In the novel terrorists went to schools and killed children and then they went to malls where they killed hundreds; actually blocking exits and killing Americans as the exited the malls. Both of these so upset me that I removed them from the novels, afraid somebody would copycat my story.

Moon Shadow "was" a fiction novel and I really didn't think much about it until September 11, 2001. Ironically I was on a plane from Seattle to Houston. It was dejavu when the pilot told us passenger airliners had crashed into the twin towers and the Pentagon. My first thoughts were my novel. The pilot turned the plane around and returned to Seattle. I told everyone there would be no flights for maybe a week or more and I was driving to Houston. Then I said, "I'm probably wrong but I think the person responsible is a man named Osama bin Laden." Two people went with me and I told them about my novel. When I arrived in Houston I called the FBI to tell them about the book and other things that might be coming but they never responded. There are many more things in my novel that have come to pass in the last four years. It's eerie and unnerving.

Actually, many things I have written about actually happened after the novel was finished. For example I wrote a novel, *Chem Storm* (https://www.smashwords.com/books/view/31482) about a chemical disaster on the Houston Ship Channel. A year after I finished an accident similar to the one in my novel, and almost exactly at the same location, actually happened but it was contained. In my novel *Formula 2000, the Dream* (https://www.smashwords.com/books/view/31512), which was about my son in professional racing, I wrote about the Formula Continental racing series. I hated the name so I changed the name of the series in my novel to Formula 2000 because the engine used in the series was two liters. I knew a racing reporter and used her for the racing series reporter. A few years after I finished the series was renamed to – Formula 2000. And yes they hired the reporter in my novel. A friend of mine who had read my novels asked me to put him in one of my novels. I agreed and then he asked me to make him a millionaire in the novel.

But I digress again. I'm writing a sequel to Moon Shadow and the reason I write this is because I had another more terrifying dream. Again I have been reading extensively and studying the Muslim Brotherhood ever since Obama's comments about America being a Muslim country but more disturbingly when he said, "If I had to take a side between Christians and Muslims I would side with the Muslims." A Christian wouldn't say that. What was more disturbing was when Mohammed Elibiary, who was appointed by Obama to be head of the Homeland Security Council, claimed to be a devout member of the Muslim Brotherhood and had said the reason Christians are getting killed in Syria is because they deserved it after what they said about Islam and their lack of respect for their religion. If a clown is fired for wearing an Obama mask, then surely a man appointed to a position of protecting America, and I mean all Americans, but relishes in the death of Christians should also be fired, unless he is really doing what he has been hired to do because of orders that come directly from Obama. I felt this disturbing and ironic when Christians are called traitors, and that was when I realized the Muslim Brotherhood is already in the White House. I fear this dream is an ominous premonition of what Obama wants and is bringing to America.

A few days after the government shutdown I had the dream. The following is that dream as well as I can recall.

Galleria Mall, Cambridge, Massachusetts

I do engineering work and my company had sent me on business where I had taken a break and was visiting the Galleria Mall in Cambridge, Massachusetts. A peaceful day of shopping, eating, fun and relaxation. The job wore on me and I needed this peaceful, safe and calm time in the mall. I continued browsing the store windows. There were a few security guards and I noticed some men in dark brown shirts and khaki colored pants with the DHS logo on their shirts. We continued deeper into the mall, where I noticed more DHS in mall and I also noticed many gay couples both men and women. It still feels strange to see men holding hands. I had friends that are gay and it really didn't bother me until they started kissing. Then I saw a few more DHS agents in the brown shirts. For a moment I thought how they reminded me of Germany's "brown shirts." I passed it off but saw a few more. Now I had seen about ten and thought it very strange. Maybe they were having a meeting or one of those expensive conventions the taxpayers seem to always be paying. I saw a few walk away with mall security and I looked around to see if there was a disturbance, but there was none. I saw a few more carrying duffle bags but didn't think anything of it. Then there were more. I looked at one. He also carried a duffle bag that touched the floor, his hands over the opening. The bag reminded me of when I played baseball because this man had what appeared to be a bat and the bag filled with balls or something like balls. Half of DHS men looked like guys I had played ball with in high school. The other half darker complected and serious looking but half of those appeared to be Middle Eastern and to me somewhat ominous, which was surprising because I liked everybody. I passed it off to an unwarranted paranoia of people from the Middle-East although I didn't really like women wearing veils out in public. I have always associated masks with criminals. I saw no masks but after all this was America where they had freedom. At that moment the man I had been watching turned and looked at me. I felt uneasy as his eyes pierced me like bullets. For some reason I looked around the mall and turned in a small circle, intent to see what the other DHS workers were doing and sub-consciously hunting for an escape. To my dismay the area was surrounded with the DHS agents and most of them had duffel bags like the first one I had seen. Something was wrong and I knew it. I didn't feel comfortable or safe with any of these DHS agents. But it was also too late.

On queue all the bags dropped open at once revealing automatic weapons; they looked like AK-47's, and wicked looking machetes. I had a permit to carry a concealed weapon, but I felt uneasy about bringing my thirty-eight into malls. Instantly, I regretted not bringing my gun but in reality what could I have done with my gun against more than twenty automatic weapons. For some reason I continued to stare at the bags in disbelief, but it was really happening. What I thought were probably balls were really dozens of preloaded clips, knives of varying lengths, rope, miscellaneous tools including numerous types of pliers, and what looked like giant fishhooks.

Everyone froze, disbelieving. There was no doubt they were terrorists and had come to kill. They continued to move quickly like a rehearsed play. It was surreal. Things changed quickly; a gun fired, women screamed, men yelled and everyone ran but the terrorists. More weapons fired, people fell to the mall's tile floors bleeding and screaming. I ran like a chicken with its head cut-off; no reason and no direction. We all ran and with each shot changed direction. One of the people I was with took a bullet in the side and fell. I continued to run and cover my head as though my fingers would protect me from the flying bullets that seemed to come from all directions. Then a brown shirt in front of me yelled for me stop and I did. Most of the people had stopped running and were being herded into a group like sheep to slaughter. Ten or more guarded us while the others moved to kill more and protect the entrances. We continued to hear gunshots. The wounded moaned and screamed. Many were already dead. Blood and glass littered the floor. My feet felt wet like I had walked through a puddle. When I glanced down I noticed my moccasins gone; I had literally run out of my shoes. My socks were dripping wet—with blood! It was not my blood and it was then that I realized blood from the dead and dying covered the floor.

The terrorists shouted a victory cry over and over, "Allah Akbar!"

A girl screamed, "Who are you?"

One of them sneered at her and shook his rifle in the air, "We are the Muslim Brotherhood and today is a good day to die."

The girl cried.

I'd seen it before on television, even read about the horror and cruelty in books, but I never thought it would happen to me; not here in America. But the signs were there all of America had seen it either at the Twin Towers or the Boston Marathon. Today would be another deadly sign from the Muslim Brotherhood. There would be no quarter from the Muslim Brotherhood. I was about to die. I thought about the mall in Kenya and realized it had come to America. I was helpless there was nothing I could do but watch the events as they transpired. I guessed there were a hundred or more of us clustered together. Dozens lay dead or dying on the blood spattered floor.

One man walked through the group and to people that appeared they might be Middle Eastern. He asked them questions. Many he nodded to and said, "Go." Some he asked questions and when they responded in what I guessed to be Arabic he motioned for them to leave. None hesitated and they all moved quickly to freedom. While he did this two others moved through the group separating them. One group I quickly noticed were probably gay and lesbian as they all tended to be clusters of two men together or two women together. All showed affection either clinging together or holding hands which was a dead giveaway. It was then I saw the two men I had noticed holding hands and obviously gay, were still clinging to each other. I had read enough from books to know what Muslims thought of gays and lesbians. None of them realized what was happening. For an instant I felt safe I was in the other group. Or was I safe?

A dozen of the terrorist surrounded the first group. They carried guns and nasty looking machetes. Suddenly, they attacked the first group hacking off hands and legs so they couldn't escape. Their plan was cold calculating and hideous; maim and dismember but keep them alive for the effect. With one swing a hand would fly through the air. They went for the legs to prevent them from escaping and while their prisoners lay helpless on the floor they hacked on the extremities. Others had their fingers pulled off with pliers. It was gruesome. All screamed hysterically. Blood flowed across the floors like it was coming from hoses. I could smell the blood; metallic like iron or rust. The smell boded ill for everyone. Why I don't know but I remembered going to the shooting range and the smell of gun powder. The smell was exhilarating and had given me a sense of control and power. Today the smell of gun powder hung in the air heavy and terrifying. The mixture of blood and gun powder in the air was ominous; the smell of death. The terrorists tortured all those in the first group them leaving them in painful agony. Some they hung with the rope from signs in front of the various store fronts using what I now realized were meat hooks. A once beautiful woman crying and moaning tried to crawl away on her elbows; she no longer had hands. A terrorist marched over and in one motion grabbed her foot pulled it up to waist height, took a mighty swing with his machete and threw the foot aside. The woman moaned and gasped for breath. Still she tried to crawl leaving a snail trail of blood where her foot had been. The terrorist laughed and walked back to us. Others tried to crawl away but it was obvious none capable of escape. Death would be soon in coming.

I thought about my wife. I felt a lump swell up in my throat. I would never see her again. I wanted to find someone so I could send her a message. I wanted to say, "I love you. And I'm sorry." God flashed through my mind and again I thought of my wife and wanted to ask her, "When the resurrection comes and if I make it to Heaven will you ask God if you can be the one to wake me? I'd like to see your face first." But there was no one to give the message. My thoughts soothed me and gave me comfort for a moment but they were rudely jerked back to reality. My thoughts would die with me. Where was God?

Then the terrorists came for those that remained; their evil work finished on the first group.

The obvious leader of the terrorists stood in front of us and told us to look at him. When he had our attention he said, "If any of you turn to look behind you we will shoot you."

The terrorist walked up to a man, pulled him out of the group and in front of us. He said, "Are you Christian?"

"Yes," he cried.

"Give up your God and swear allegiance to Allah," he demanded.

"Okay," he whined.

The terrorist looked at the quivering man and screamed, "Allah Akbar!" He screamed again.

The shopper, trembling confused and scared managed only a whimper, "What? I don't understand?"

"Repeat after me. I give up my God. Allah Akbar!"

His voice quivered, the horror surrounding him stifled his words, "I give up my God. Allah Akbar."

The terrorist smiled pointed behind us and said, "You are free to go. Run!"

The man never hesitated and ran. I could hear him running down the blood stained tile floor of the Galleria Mall. The terrorist picked the man next to me and started to go through the same ritual as he had with the first.

I realized there was hope, a way to live, and a way to save my life. I would see my wife again. I would live! The words would be easy. I considered myself a good Christian but I wasn't perfect. I would figure out things later. I was scared. I wanted to live. I was already mumbling, "Allah Akbar," as the second man began to run to freedom.

A pretty girl just in front of me and slightly to the right, probably not over seventeen with running mascara and cheeks still wet with tears from the fear and terror marking her face like tattoos turned her head slightly to watch the man run. An alert terrorist noticed and without hesitation, took two steps toward her reached over and shot her in the head. Her blood splattered all over me. As I looked down on her she blinked twice in horror, gurgled, then closed her eyes in death. I was suddenly jolted back to reality but with a plan where I would survive. I stared at the girl; how foolish, she could have lived. But I would live to tell about this hell hole. Tell about the girl at my feet and the others. Later I would ask God to forgive me. I would be able to hug my wife again and tell her how much I love her. As I stared at the woman who had been shot I noticed a slight movement from colorful glass panes decorating the store in front of me. It had a reflection that you could just barely discern the man running who had just been set free. I was excited to see he was only inches from freedom. Triumphantly he reached the mall door and passed through to safety and life. He shook his hands victoriously in the air, but as he passed through the doors to freedom, two terrorists charged him and started hacking his body with quiet but deadly machetes. When he fell I knew he was dead. We were all going to die! At that moment I realized I was a coward and had turned my back on God. I would forsake him so I could live. I had always considered myself brave even a hero, someone who could survive anything. I didn't want to die, I was afraid and with that realization, I knew that I was a coward.

A woman was now reciting the same words. As she began to run the lead terrorist grabbed me and pulled me forward. I slipped and almost fell in the blood.

He went through the same ritual with me. Terrified, afraid and a coward I wanted to cry but my response surprised even me, "Stick it up your ass." He hit me with the butt of his rifle, my knees buckled and I fell to the floor in all the blood. My nose bled profusely as I spit my front teeth to the floor. Then he gave me a second chance. I said, "Mohammed is a faggot." He roared his outrage and again he hit me and I crumbled to the floor, this time sure my jaw was broken. Again they pulled me to my feet. But before I was erect they took two of the wicked meat hooks and impaled me under each armpit. A rope attached to both hooks must have already been thrown over the sign and I screamed as they pulled me from my feet, leaving me dangling a few inches off the floor. The pain was unbelievable unbearable, nothing like I had ever felt in my life. Two men came toward me with evil looking butcher knives. I refused to let them gut me like a deer. I squirmed and shook, and momentarily the terror took away the pain as the hooks sunk deeper. Then a third terrorist came up behind me and I felt a bit of pain just below my neck. My legs and arms quit shaking and went limp at my sides, while my head slumped over on my chest. I couldn't move anything but my eyes. They had cut my spine. All I could do was watch the horrifying attack as they split me from my sternum to below my navel.. My intestines rolled to the floor. There was so much. I felt a tugging sensation but no pain. I could hear but I couldn't feel as my intestines. Thank God there was no pain. With my head hanging on my chest I could see part of my lungs and the bottom of my heart beating. Still I tried in my mind to struggle free but no movement came from my body. The veins in my neck pounded like drums. My breathing was labored; I was choking.

The lead terrorist put his face in mine reached for my heart and said, "Take this final memory with you. You are the first. Millions more will die when they drink the Boston water." He flashed a wicked grin, "Die Infidel!" He started to cut and everything turned black.

I shot erect in bed coughing, choking surrounded in darkness. I was dead! Mechanically I grabbed my chest; my heart was still there and still beating! The fear subsided as I became aware the choking came from the cold and sinus drainage in my head. I was alive, and breathing. I was also wet from sweating. My pillow was soaked. I turned and watched my wife's rhythmic breathing and signed in relief. I bent over kissed her on her cheek and mumbled, "I love you."

I rolled around and sat on the edge of the bed and tried to relax. I was afraid to go back to sleep. Afraid the dream might continue, I told myself it was just a bad dream. Just a bad dream. Or was it a sign of what was coming to Americas?

AUTHOR'S COMMENTS

This brings to an end over twenty-years of trying to make people aware. Inside I feel like I failed. Americans are too apathetic. I feel like I witnessed the death of American on November 6th 2012. People want to be led and not lead. They believe the lies being told to them. It is okay to be a conservative or a liberal but they don't exist in Congress. They are determined to destroy America and I think that day will come in 2014. Both sides are so radical in their beliefs I see only one solution and that is for America to be divided.

There is good news and that is my novel "Live For Today." It is being made into a movie.

Live For Today is based on a true story; mine. Most of the events and relationships in this novel essentially took place. I did in fact almost get suspended from school for raising our banner on the opposing school's side at halftime. I did meet a spectacular girl at the swing when I was twelve. My father died when I was ten and my mother told me to protect my younger brother. Although I wanted to beat my brother to a pulp many times, he did not die nor did he commit suicide. There really was a Jim Brown, but he never successfully beat me up. Jim attempted to pulverize me on the sandlot one day, and eventually we became friends. My nickname was "Tiger," and my close family still calls me that today. The story about the comic book, "Amazing Fantasy 15," happened exactly like it did in the story, but not at Concan. It actually happened in Corpus Christi in a store called Tri-Drive, and is a comic book I still own and cherish to this day. *Live For Today* is a combination of events that happened from my sophomore to senior year of high school. The Sandlot boys and I did have a confrontation with players from our school's football team in the front yard of Roy Hofheinz's Mansion on Sage Road. Following the altercation, they always let us play football with them. A student in charge of taking pictures for the yearbook came out after hearing about the story and took a picture of our unlikely group. Fifteen years after graduation we did form a flag football team; Yesterday's Heroes. I still have the jersey. I dated Marilyn in high school, what a beautiful, sweet girl. She had so much to offer, but she committed suicide. I never understood why. I hope this story helps those like her, and in a way it already has. Unlike the novel, I never did find that remarkable girl at the swing.

17

OTHER BOOKS BY JOE BARFIELD
AVAILABLE AS EBOOKS
AND IN PRINT AT
CREATESPACE.COM

MOON SHADOW – (action-adventure) by Joe Barfield

AVAILABLE IN PRINT

Set in 2015, Moon Shadow depicts the financial collapse and subsequent invasion of the United States. Completed in1996, this story is so close to current events that it seems more historical than a work of fiction. From a terrorist attack using three hijacked airliners to a top-secret space plane project dubbed "Aurora," and a Democrat elected in 2008 who bankrupts America with a twenty trillion debt, both the premise and content of my novel have become reality.

Moon Shadow, depicts America's leadership, greed, and corruption as the reasons for the collapse and invasion, will get people on both sides of the fence talking. It is an exciting edge-of-your-seat story about a handful of America's best jet pilots desperately trying to take America back after the invasion. Their reluctant leader, Beau Gex, is forced to lead them to safety. Trapped behind enemy lines, this small group of pilots fight against overwhelming odds. They are forced to fly one last deadly mission, where America's future depends on its best pilot, Beau Gex, defeating a technologically advanced F-14 fighter jet at night. But all he has on his side is an antiquated, World War II, P-51 Mustang and an old Indian Legend,

Moon Shadow.

For the not-faint-at-heart, Moon Shadow begins with one of the edgiest torture scenes since Marathon Man. And for those looking for love mixed in with their adventure, Moon Shadow satisfies as a tender romance between Beau and Krysti Socorro, an exquisite doctor. Will the betrayal of another tear them apart forever? Can a child save their love or is it too late?

Intended to be a work of fiction only to entertain, author Joe Barfield admits even he is surprised as events in his novel, Moon Shadow, are becoming more historical than fictional with each passing day. Barfield said, "Moon Shadow tells the story about the fall of the greatest country in the world—The United States of America. The collapse is not so much from outside forces, but rather from the greed within. I never dreamed how close Moon Shadow would describe events in America and the Mid-East today."

Begun in 1989 and completed in 1996, Moon Shadow was updated recently to better describe current events that are quickly changing the world. Reflecting on his novel, Barfield also said, "I originally based the collapse of the United States on the greed of American CEOs, the corruption of our Congressional leaders, and the collapse of the financial institutions during President George H. Bush's administration. Now it seems Moon Shadow is closer to depicting the events of President Barrack Obama's administration.

Abraham Lincoln said, "America will never be destroyed from the outside. If we falter and lose our freedoms, it will be because we destroyed ourselves."

Just a few disturbing things found in Moon Shadow are the use of three hijacked passenger airliners, with one crashing into a football game killing the president. Another war occurs in the Middle East that is very similar to Desert Storm but with a big difference—The United States is defeated. The novel predicted a Democrat would be elected in 2008 and he would destroy America financially with a National Debt near 20 trillion.

Where are we today? What if the President was an intentional traitor? See what happens when Obama destroys American in my novel Moon Shadow. While he blames a "Fiscal Cliff," it is in reality greed and corruption of America's leaders and a lightning move towards socialism and communism. In an effort to aid the Muslim Brotherhood, Obama removes over 200 military leaders, creates extreme racism, has the IRS audit those that oppose his views, puts members of the Muslim Brotherhood in positions to take over America, and uses the NSA to spy on those against him, creates extreme racism. Like the Pied Piper, Americans follow him to his ultimate goal to destroy America. Read how a group of American radicals calling themselves "The Minute Men" capture the president and execute him for treason in 2016.

The author was quoted saying: From the beginning of time every empire has collapsed. There have been no exceptions.

LIVE FOR TODAY – (YA coming of age – based on a true story)
by Joe Barfield

Available in **print** at CreateSpace.com: **https://createspace.com/4261312**

A broken promise, takes a gifted teenager down a path of self-destruction. Will the persistence of a coach and the love of a girl be enough to save him? When someone asks him about his future he says, "I live for today, there are no tomorrows for me." Will the love of a girl and the persistence of his coach be enough to save him?

"Live For Today" is based on my high school days. It sends a message to let everyone know suicide is not the answer. There is always hope for tomorrow. One of the characters is Marilyn. I dated her when I was eighteen. Beautiful girl. She committed suicide. There was no reason. Just this week, People magazine, had an article about three students who committed suicide after being teased and tormented by classmates. This story has a time and it's now. The message is hope.

A Note About *Live For Today*
The Movie

The story of *Live For Today* has been made into a heart tugging, anti-bullying, faith based movie.

It was filmed with Katy, Texas, locals and high school students using a $2,000 Cannon 7D camera. YouTube, Facebook, and our production company website are set up for viewing current news, trailers, movie posters, photos, cast members, author biographies, and fundraising information. Browse through our website and see how you can become part of this cause. The story is based in part on what happened to me in high school. The pictures in *Live For Today* are from the movie and accompanied by authentic photos from my 1967 Robert E. Lee yearbook. The production team still has more to do before we can completely finish the film and through financial help, such goals are achievable. For every book sold, a percentage will go towards efforts for finishing the movie. Help us prove that students can not only make a professional film, but that a big effort from a small town can make a huge impact on world-wide social media.

The Single Male Parent's Cookbook and Short Stories
by Joe Barfield

Available in **print** at CreateSpace.com: **https://createspace.com/4354201**

The Single Male Parents' Cookbook, is a delightful combination of food and humor, two subjects everyone will enjoy. As a single parent the author raised his children from the time they were four and six, and soon became an expert in the kitchen. As he said, "My cooking must have been good because both are adults now and still alive, which only attests to culinary skills . . . or luck!"

The Single Male Parents' Cookbook combines recipes with humorous anecdotes of things that did and didn't work in the kitchen (and in my life!). Joe includes lots of fun cooking ideas along with some that were not so good, and even a few you don't ever want to try at home! Everything from his Friday Night Special to his Motel Doggy (the electric hotdog). And let's not forget the ROC (Roaches on Chocolate). Each recipe is followed by a short story about his childhood antics or raising his children. Not everything always ran smoothly. There was that time his boiled eggs blew up all over the ceiling. Oh, and that grease fire. Don't ever pour water on a grease fire! But they say experience is the best teacher, and they are right. It wasn't always easy in those years, but he managed to retain his sense of humor. Joe said he once heard George Carlin say that although he's over sixty, he never stopped being ten. That describes the author perfectly. In fact, he said, "I've been ten six times over, and my life is as fun as ever." His final comments were, "Are you curious about my recipes for rattlesnake, rabbit, squirrel, and armadillo? I think you'd enjoy the rattlesnake. Can you picture me cooking the Roaches on Chocolate (ROC) on Rachel Ray's show?"

Don't let the cookbook confuse you. Joe is just a normal type of guy. Well, maybe except for the time he got married at midnight in a jail in Mexico. But that has nothing to do with cooking. Neither does the time he almost got kidnapped in the mountains of Colombia when he met his second wife. He's just a wild and crazy guy from Texas.

A Life in Time, My Story – non-fiction
by Joe Barfield

Available in **print** at CreateSpace.com: **https://createspace.com/4354226**

Remember lying on the grass in your front yard and watching the stars? Your best friend was beside you and neither one of you uttered a word. Then a meteor flashed across the sky and both of you got excited and pointed to the sky. Our lives are like a flashing meteorite. Often the moments go unnoticed, but we do manage to brighten and touch the lives of those around us. Although we are not all famous or well-known, our stories are important. Each of us has a life in time. These are a series of short stories about my life. In the past I have heard a comparison I'm sure you have heard before, so let me ask you again. Who won the Super Bowl last year? Who won the Indy 500? Who won the last game of the World Series? Who were the Best Actor and Actress at the last Academy Awards? You might remember one but you probably don't know the others. Now ask yourself these questions. Do you remember the names of some of your teachers? What teacher helped you in high school? What valuable lessons did your mother and father teach you? And who was your best friend? They may not be famous but they brightened your life the same as that flashing meteorite. I believe life has been an adventure and that we learn from all the things that have happened to us. The one thing I try to do is look at things in a humorous way. As a child I was called Tiger because I was always into things. I thought I was just curious. As a teenager the death of my father weighed heavy on me. We began to move around. I became angry; a "Rebel," as some of my close friends called me. I had conflicts with religion. When my children were four and six I became a single parent. I learned a lot from them. .Most of the stories, I hope, will keep you laughing. There are some that are sad, but that is life. And that is what *A Life in Time* is all about.

A Short Story Collection – fiction
by Joe Barfield

Available in **print** at CreateSpace.com: **https://createspace.com/4354238**

These short stories are based on actual events, and parts from some of my novels, and children's stories. *Sebring, the Rainman* is based on a race my son, Beaux, actually competed. What a race it was!

Some of the dialog from *Flight 223* actually occurred. You see I was on flight 223 from Seattle to Houston during the 911 attack. A very strange and chaotic event I will never forget.

I hope you enjoy these as much as I did bringing them to you.

URBAN KILL – (detective thriller)
by Joe Barfield

Available in **print** at CreateSpace.com: **https://createspace.com/4038605**

Ex-policemen are taking wealthy men on the hunt of their lives--human prey! The only two witnesses have already been murdered. To solve the case the lead detective must find a pimp called The Rat and the drug addict Pinky, because they have the answers. But the Rat and Pinky are trying to kill each other. The only ones that can help him are a gay bar owner, a hyper, absent-minded forensics expert from India, and his one-eyed, three-legged dog, Lucky.

THE CAJUN – (action-adventure)
by Joe Barfield

A little Crocodile Dundee and a little Rambo. With a million dollar reward on her head, Kelli Parsons hides in the treacherous Atchafalaya Swamp where living or dying depends on one man--the Cajun!

FORMULA 2000, *the DREAM* – (action – based on a true story)
by Joe Barfield

Hoosiers on Wheels.

Keeping a promise, a father enters his son, Shannon Kelly, in the Formula 2000 race series with only a dream and a prayer. When things go from bad to worse it takes a crusty old mechanic, Charlie Pepper, to show them how to win. They soon learn that with Pepper almost anything is possible.

CHEM STORM – (action – chemical disaster)
by Joe Barfield

Available in **print** at CreateSpace.com: **https://createspace.com/4325910**

A reporter and an engineer race to save Houston from a disaster worse than a nuclear explosion—a chemical storm!

Jean Alexander, a reporter for The Houston Post, is young and inquisitive and has gained unauthorized access to an area, where she finds five dead bodies. She wants to know why but a spectator alerts the guards to her presence and she is removed.

The following day a Civil/Chemical Engineer, Travis Selkirk, approaches Jean. She learns he is the spectator from the day before that alerted the guards. He points out the foolishness of her adventure and how the chemicals could have killed her. Jean baits Travis and gets him to agree to show her the dangers that exist on the Houston Ship Channel.

WORDS THAT DON'T OFFEND LIBERALS – (Satirical humor)

by Joe Barfield

Available in **print** at CreateSpace.com: **https://www.createspace.com/4221000**

A humorous look at words that don't offend Liberals. The book will probably offend Liberals. This is meant for the entertainment of open minded people. This is a book to keep notes. For a printed copy you can find the book here: https://www.createspace.com/4221000 Check it out before you purchase your printed copy. Fun gift for your Liberal friends. They may never forgive you.

PALABRAS QUE NO OFENDEN LIBERALES - (humor satírico)

Joe Barfield

Available in **print** at CreateSpace.com: **https://www.createspace.com/4287573**

Una mirada chistosa en palabras que no ofendan liberales. El libro probablemente ofender a los liberales. Esto es para el entretenimiento de personas de mente abierta. Este es un libro para guardar notas. Para obtener una copia, usted puede encontrar el libro aquí: https://www.createspace.com/4287573 Compruébelo usted mismo antes de comprar su copia impresa. Regalo de la diversión para sus amigos liberales. Es posible que nunca perdonará.

ABOUT THE AUTHOR

The author, Joe Barfield, has led an interesting life, scuba diving, racing cars with his son Beaux Barfield, lifting weights and playing a variety of sports. He met his wife Lucia in Cali, Colombia while on a trip. One time she took him on a trip in the mountains of Colombia and at one point they thought they had entered a guerrilla camp and he would be kidnapped. His first thoughts when he saw their 50 caliber machine guns, "Oh my God I'm going to be kidnapped." To reassure his thoughts, Lucia turned to him and said, "Don't say anything I don't want them to hear your accent." Do you know what he said his next thoughts were? "OH Boy! I'm going to become a bestseller!"

Turns out they were a group of the Colombian military looking for kidnappers. He spent a few days with them and even has a picture of him holding a 50 caliber machine gun with one of the Colombian soldiers. Showing his tenacity, once he was determined to win a Halloween contest and went as far as making an eight-foot monster with moving fingers. He won the contest. For him racing has always been an exciting endeavor, winning his very first race and two years later winning his first professional race at the 6-Hours of Sebring. His son went on to be Race Director for Indy Car. Barfield said there were as many adventures off the track as there were on. A quote from Jim Fitzgerald sums it all up, "When you do it and do it right it is the greatest turn on in the world.

I began writing racing articles and from there I have done movie reviews for magazines and newsletters. I have won a few short story contests.

My script "The Company" won best script in a Fan Story contest. My short script, "The Company," was one of the top six scripts reviewed by actress Dawn Olivieri from the series "Heroes."

I have completed nine novels and nine scripts in a variety of genres, including; action-adventure, family, teen, thriller, religious, drama, comedy, dark-comedy and science fiction. My best novel; *The Cajun*. My best script; *Live For Today*. My favorite novel is *Moon Shadow* because it started me writing.

Currently I'm working on some uplifting scripts and three novels. One of the novels is called *Secuestro*. I came up with the idea when I met Lucia in Cali, Colombia. It's a story of deception, intrigue, war and love. It shows the Colombian people in the true light I find them to be really, loving, caring and very friendly. Also I've working on a script called *El Norte*. This is based on a true story about two Colombians that walked from Colombia to the United States. It describes their adventures and miss-adventures and the love that develops between them.

I started writing twenty-four years ago and for me writing has solved all the problems I couldn't in real life.

Connect With Me Online

My Webpage - http://www.jbarfield.com

Also see Author page at:
http://www.smashwords.com/profile/view/thecajun

See the Live For Today Trailer
http://www.youtube.com/watch?v=M3KUyiXyYf0

www.facebook.com/groups/livefortoday/

www.k-tfilms.com

www.ingramcontent.com/pod-product-compliance
Lightning Source LLC
Chambersburg PA
CBHW070628290526
45790CB00001B/44